Panama Canal By Cruise Ship

DOCUMENTATION

Passenger Name________________________

Ship Name________________________

Date of Voyage________________________

Stateroom________________________

THE COMPLETE GUIDE TO CRUISING THE PANAMA CANAL

ANNE VIPOND

YOUR PORTHOLE COMPANION

OCEAN CRUISE GUIDES™

Vancouver, Canada Pt. Roberts, USA

Published by: Ocean Cruise Guides Ltd.
Canada:
325 English Bluff Road
Delta, B.C. V4M 2M9

USA:
PO Box 2041
Pt. Roberts, WA 98281-2041

Editors: Duart Snow, Richard Rogers, Mel-Lynda Andersen
Contributing Editors: William Kelly, Michael DeFreitas.
Addt'l Photography: Michael DeFreitas, Judi Lees, Martin Gerretsen
Artwork by Alan H. Nakano.
Cartography: Reid Jopson, Doug Quiring, Cartesia, OCG.
Design: Ocean Cruise Guides
Printed and bound in Canada.
Publisher: William Kelly
Phone: (604) 948-0594 Email: info@oceancruiseguides.com
Visit our Website: www.oceancruiseguides.com

Library and Archives Canada Cataloguing in Publication

Vipond, Anne, 1957-
Panama Canal by cruise ship : the complete guide to cruising the Panama Canal / Anne Vipond. -- 2nd ed.

Includes index.
ISBN 0-9688389-6-0

1. Cruise ships--Panama--Panama Canal--Guidebooks. 2. Cruise ships--Mexico--Guidebooks. 3. Panama Canal (Panama)--Guidebooks. 4. Mexico--Guidebooks. I. Title.

F1569.C2V56 2004 917.28704'54 C2004-905052-4

ACKNOWLEDGEMENTS

More than any other book we have done on cruise destinations, Panama Canal is a great story. During our research, we turned to many books published at the time of the Canal's completion in 1914 which provided insight into working conditions on the Canal and political concerns in the United States. For a more recent interpretation of events we can recommend one of our main reference sources for the history of the Panama Canal, the excellent book *The Path Between The Seas* by David McCullough, first published in 1977.

We'd like to thank various people and organizations for their help and encouragement throughout this project. Many cruise lines contributed valuable information of itineraries and port details as well as photographic material and field support. In particular, we'd like to thank Julie Benson, Denise Seomin and Morgan Kelley at Princess Cruises, as well as Irene Lui at Carnival Cruise Lines, Helen Burford at Celebrity Cruises and Courtney McKenzie at Holland America Line. We also thank Cruise Lines International Association and the many travel and cruise agencies for information and suggestions. We would specifically like to thank Harvey Strydhorst and Martin Gerretsen at Seacourses Custom Cruises for their kind assistance. We also appreciate the help and direction received from Dr. Alina Szmant, University of Miami, who specializes in marine life; and Frank Lepore of the National Hurricane Center in Miami.

These acknowledgements would of course not be complete without a special thank-you to the pilots and public relations department of Panama Canal Authority who answered questions, supplied material and made valuable suggestions. In addition, we thank the many tourism departments which were, without exception, generous with their time and resources. A special thank you to Nan Vipond, and to Captain Attilio Guerrini of Princess Cruises.

Contents

Part One

General Information

PART TWO

THE VOYAGE & THE PORTS

The Panama Canal changed the face of the earth. Upon its completion, the world's two great oceans were joined and a safe maritime route, sought after for centuries, was created. The story of how this passage was conceived, constructed and completed is not only one of mankind's greatest engineering feats, but a saga of human drama, infused with hope, despair, defeat and, ultimately, victory. Above all, the Panama Canal was a success story. Built by the United states, it was completed under budget, in both time and money, and has operated successfully ever since.

The Panama Canal has been compared to the Great Pyramids of Giza. Both were monumental projects, magnificent for their sheer size and triumph of engineering rather than their artistic merit, and both reflect the times in which they were built. The Pyramids are a testament to the supreme power of Ancient Egypt's almighty pharaohs, whereas the Panama Canal is a 20th-century icon to hard work, modern technology and democratic ideals. Built not for one supreme ruler of an empire, but for the benefit of the entire world, the Canal was constructed without slave labor by workers who were fiercely proud of the Herculean project they were part of. This monument for the world is not a passive structure symbolizing kingly power, but a massive machine that is constantly harnessing and releasing thousands of cubic tons of water as it lifts and lowers 10-storey-high ships in its locks. Operating night and day, the canal was cut through bedrock of the Continental Divide, enabling ocean liners to travel between the Atlantic and Pacific in a mere eight hours.

For cruise passengers, these are likely the most exciting eight hours ever spent on board a ship. From the moment the ship enters the first set of locks until its release into another ocean, the voyage is momentous – not only for what can be seen and enjoyed while underway but for the historic journey the canal represents. During its construction the canal was often called a battlefield, with thousands dying from disease and accidents. But those who sacrificed their lives to this courageous undertaking have given the world one of its proudest and most unifying accomplishments.

– Anne Vipond

A ship eases through the single lift lock at Pedro Miguel.

PART I

General Information

CHOOSING YOUR CRUISE

The highlight of a Panama Canal cruise is, of course, the Canal itself. Yet, there are a variety of itineraries covering the Panama Canal – from 10-day round-trip Caribbean cruises to three-week voyages which run between Florida or Puerto Rico and the west coast city of Vancouver.

It used to be that Canal cruises were offered only in spring and fall when cruise ships migrate between the Caribbean and Alaska. Called repositioning cruises, in reference to the ships positioning themselves in the Caribbean for the winter and in Alaskan waters for the summer, these itineraries remain the ideal Panama Canal cruise in terms of visiting numerous ports of call – the idyllic islands of the Caribbean, the tropical rainforests and Mayan ruins of Central America, the beach

resorts of the Mexican Riviera, and the exciting port cities of California. However, for people looking for a shorter mid-winter cruise, there are now regular Panama Canal transits available from November through March, including 15-day cruises between Fort Lauderdale and San Diego, and 10-day roundtrip cruises out of Fort Lauderdale which feature a partial transit of the Canal.

Partial transits of the Canal are made from the Caribbean side, providing passengers with the experience of being raised in the Gatun Locks, cruising around one of the largest man-made lakes in the world, then being lowered back into the Caribbean. Ships making a partial transit are likely to stop at the Panamanian port of Colon where there

An excellent view of the watertight miter gates of Pedro Miguel locks – one of the many engineering marvels of the Panama Canal.

are opportunities to take local shore excursions to the Gatun Locks or the old Spanish forts, whereas ships making the eight-hour daytime transit from one ocean to the other rarely stop in Panama. Occasionally ships stop at Balboa for refueling, which might present a chance for an evening visit to Panama City. On the Caribbean side of the Canal, base ports for Canal cruises are Florida's Fort Lauderdale and Miami, and Puerto Rico's San Juan. On the Pacific side, the cruise lines use Puerto Caldera, Acapulco, San Diego, Los Angeles, San Francisco and Vancouver as ports of embarkation and disembarkation.

The best time to take a Panama Canal cruise is during the dry season, which is from mid-December to mid-April. However, even during the wet season, the rainfall is not steady but comes in sporadic downpours. The temperature remains fairly constant throughout the year in the tropics, but the humidity climbs in the summer months, which is when the cruise ships are elsewhere in the world.

Most of the major lines send ships through the Panama Canal, which means a person can transit the "big ditch" on board a range of ships, from 10-storey-high megaships holding 2,000 passengers to small luxury ships carrying only 200 passengers. Many of the new ships have been built with an abundance of private balconies adjoining the outside staterooms and these are proving to be very popular with passengers, especially those taking a Panama Canal cruise when everyone wants to be out on deck during the Canal's transit to watch the shoreside activities as the ship is lifted and lowered in each set of locks.

Choosing a Cruise Line

Choosing a cruise line used to depend a great deal on your budget and, although that is still true, the competitiveness of the cruise business has

(Above) Celebrity's 91,000-ton Millennium offers a wide range of amenities for its 1,950 passengers and a generous space ratio of 46. (Below) Seabourn's 10,000-ton luxury Spirit carries 208 passengers.

resulted in a much narrower price band in the premium and mainstream lines. The quality of service and food will vary from one line to another, but this can also vary among the ships of a fleet, which goes to show the influence a good hotel manager or head chef can have on your cruise experience. Generally speaking, a ship is rated according to its level of accommodations, facilities, maintenance, cuisine and service. There are many other factors which come into play when cruise critics rate ships, right down to the ingredients used in the kitchen (fresh versus frozen, etc.). The ship's decor, quality of finishing materials, entertainment and shore excursions are also very important in gauging the sort of cruise experience to expect with a cruise line.

One important aspect of any ship is how crowded, or uncrowded, it might feel. Fortunately, a good indication of this exists with a measurement known as the passenger/space ratio (PSR). This measurement of overall spaciousness is determined by dividing the ship's tonnage by the ship's passenger capacity. The higher the ratio number, the more space there is per passenger. A ship carrying 2,000 passengers won't feel crowded if it has a high space ratio. A good ratio number is 35 (about 3500 cubic feet per passenger) and many of the ships built after 1990 are in that range or higher.

The Glossary of Cruise Lines at the back of this book provides a brief description of the various lines and ships (including their PSR) which are currently transiting the Canal.To obtain more information on

Relaxing days at sea are a welcome chance to enjoy the upper decks, swimming pools and deck chairs such as on the Dawn Princess.

picking a cruise line, peruse the Internet or book stores, and visit a cruise agent. In North America, look for an agency displaying the CLIA logo, indicating its agents have received training from the Cruise Lines International Association. Cruise agents are usually a very good source of information with personal knowledge of many ships. An agent can give you important detail including specific itineraries and cabin choices and, although it pays to shop around to determine what pricing is being offered, an experienced cruise agent will be able to get you the best deals available – both early bird specials and last minute promotions.

Buying a cruise through the Internet is an option, especially for experienced cruisers looking for last-minute bargains. However, for the average cruise customer, the results may not be wholly satisfactory. For example, cabins for a specific price category will be limited and those available may not be in desirable locations of the ship. At the very least, a travel agent can use their experience with a cruise line to try and find a cabin you want on the itinerary you want. Almost every cruise line strongly encourages their customers book through a travel agent.

CRUISE LINE CLASSIFICATIONS

Cruise lines that offer the ultimate in comfort, cuisine and attentive service are called luxury brands and their ships are the most expensive. These finely appointed ships are usually small but not always (Crystal Cruises has medium-sized ships) and carry relatively few passengers in spacious staterooms, often with private verandahs.

Next in rank are premium brands, which offer above-average cuisine, service and amenities, including a high number of outside cabins with verandahs. Most cater to all age groups, with facilities for children and a broad range of entertainment. Premium brands, like luxury lines, will have a high passenger/space ratio.

Ships of the mainstream brand lines have less space per passenger, and provide average food and service. Some, however, represent excellent value, with decor, entertainment and service that are comparable to premium lines but priced for a broader spectrum of the cruise market. Budget lines generally use medium-sized, older ships with fewer facilities than the new megaships. Food and service will vary widely but are often comparable to that provided on mainstream brands.

The size of cruise ships has increased dramatically over the past 15 years, from an average of 35,000 tons for newbuilds to over 70,000 tons. The *Titanic*, which held 1,300 passengers and was a huge ship for its time, was about 46,000 tons. Today there are many new ships over 100,000 tons carrying up to 3,000 passengers and although their massive size allows for such onboard amenities as ice rinks and shopping malls, they may not be the best vessels on which to enjoy the seagoing experience.

LAND TOURS

A cruise is a perfect opportunity to combine a vacation at sea with a land-based holiday. If time allows, fly to your port of embarkation at least a day before the cruise begins, thus avoiding the stress of making same-day travel connections. Better yet, stay two or three nights at the base port to get over jet lag, relax and have time to enjoy the local sights. Cities such as Fort Lauderdale, Miami, San Juan, Acapulco, San Diego, Los Angeles, San Francisco and Vancouver are all tourist destinations in themselves and warrant a brief stay either at the beginning or end of a Canal cruise. The major cruise lines offer hotel packages at their turn-around ports, and several offer extended land tours.

Some intriguing tours include a three-night road trip from Acapulco to the mountainside town of Taxco (known for its silver smithing and colonial architecture) and to the country's capital, Mexico City.

Fort Lauderdale, a popular base port for Panama Canal cruises, is known as the 'Venice of America' for its scenic canals.

Excursions by boat are popular at Cabo San Lucas and other Mexican ports of call.

Another popular tour is a rail journey through Mexico's Copper Canyon on the Chihuahua al Pacifico Railroad – a breathtaking stretch of tracks that weaves through the rugged mountains of the Sierra Madre, crossing deep gorges and passing through dozens of tunnels. Costa Rican land tours include an overnight stay in the capital of San Jose and a day or two spent visiting a rainforest or viewing an active volcano.

The walled city of Old San Juan is a delight to explore on foot, with enough colonial buildings, excellent restaurants, fine beaches and some of the best shopping in the Caribbean to justify a visit of several days. The mainland ports of Florida and California are all famous destinations where the tour options are limitless – whether walking, renting a car, hopping in taxis or joining a coach tour. Your travel agent will be able to sort through the hotel and tour options at these ports and arrange a complete cruise-tour package that suits your schedule and budget.

Shore Excursions

(See Part Two for specific shoreside options at each port of call.)

Most cruise lines offer organized shore excursions for the convenience of their passengers and these are usually described in a booklet enclosed with the cruise tickets. On-board presentations are also given during the cruise by the ship's shore excursion manager. Some cruise lines accept advance bookings of shore excursions, and all will accept bookings throughout the cruise. There is a charge for these excursions but they are usually fairly priced and the tour operators used are reliable and monitored by the cruise company to ensure they maintain the level of service promised to passengers, with the added advantage that the ship will wait for any of its overdue excursions.

Ship-organized shore excursions cover the whole range of possible activities and are attractive for their convenience. You are transported to and from the ship, any needed equipment is provided, and you know ahead of time the cost and length of the tour. They are especially useful for activities such as golf and scuba diving.

However, independent-minded passengers need not feel that pre-booked shore excursions are their only option when exploring various ports of call. If the ship docks right beside a town or city center, a person can simply set off on foot to do some sightseeing and shopping. Beaches are often within walking distance or a short taxi ride away and most are open to tourists, although it's not unusual for there to be a small admission charge. Beachfront hotels often rent lounge chairs, beach umbrellas and the use of lockers and change facilities, as well as watersports equipment, to the public. Many Caribbean and Mexican Riviera resorts let non-guests use their tennis courts for a fee, and the ship's shore excursion office can usually provide current resort information and recommendations for each port of call.

For independent sightseeing, renting a car is an option on most Caribbean islands. However, driving is often on the left, the roads can be narrow and winding, and a temporary driver's licence is usually required in addition to the rental fee, bringing the total cost above that of hiring a taxi for a few hours. However, it's fun to strike out on your own, and the roads are often quiet once you get away from the port area. Be sure to give yourself plenty of time to get back to the ship.

Hiring a taxi is another option. The cruise line will likely provide you with a port information sheet containing some sample fares, which are often set by the local taxi association and posted near the cruise ship pier. At some ports a taxi director is stationed at the cruise terminal to quote fares and direct passengers to qualified drivers. Other ports provide pier side information booths. Customized tours can be negotiated and don't hesitate to chat with a few drivers before striking a bargain. Always agree beforehand on the price of the tour and exactly which stops are included. Most drivers are a wealth of information and represent an opportunity to learn more about the local people while seeing the port of call's natural and historical sights.

Cartagena shore excursions include a visit to Fort San Felipe.

(Right) Mazatlan taxi driver provides custom tours of his hometown.

(Top) Dutch colonial architecture in Oranjestad, Aruba. (Middle) The Spanish colonial streets of Cartagena's Old City. (Bottom) A sunrise at Port Everglades, Fort Lauderdale's cruise port.

(Top) The magnificent Maya ruins of Tulum overlook the Caribbean Sea.
(Middle) Flowers that flourish in the tropics include the exquisite hibiscus.
(Bottom) St. Thomas is one of the most popular ports of call in the Caribbean, both for its natural beauty and its famous duty-free shopping.

Panama & Central America

(Above) The remains of the old French Canal near the Atlantic entrance.
(Left) Miraflores Locks, Ancon Hill in background.
(Below right) Embera children at Gatun Lake while children on a cruise ship watch their ship lift.

(Top) Mangroves line an estuary of the Tarcoles River, Costa Rica.
(Right) Enjoying the view of beautiful, island-dotted Lake Nicaragua.
(Bottom) The great Maya site of Tikal, situated in the jungles of Guatemala.

(Top) El Arco, Cabo San Lucas. (Middle) A dancer performs a festive folk number in Mazatlan. (Bottom) The tranquil fishing port of Zihuatenejo.

(Top) One of Acapulco's famous cliff divers. (Middle) The Arches at Puerto Vallarta were battered by Hurricane Kenna in 2002. (Bottom) The fishing village of Santa Cruz is now part of Huatulco, a growing eco-tourism resort.

DOCUMENTATION

Several weeks before your departure date, you will no doubt receive all pertinent documentation for your trip, including your cruise ticket, airline ticket (if applicable), luggage tags, a customs and immigration form, and information regarding your cruise. All of this documentation should be read carefully, the forms filled in, and a detailed itinerary left with a friend or family member in case someone needs to contact you while you're away. Be sure to include the name of your ship, its phone number and the applicable ocean code, as well as your stateroom number - all of which will be included in your cruise documents. With this information, a person can call the international telephone operator and place a satellite call to your ship in an emergency.

A valid passport is the best proof of citizenship a traveller can carry, and although Mexico and most countries of the Caribbean do not require American and Canadian citizens to carry a passport, this document is required for entering Costa Rica and other Central American countries. Citizens of countries other than the United States or Canada must have a valid passport for all ports on a Panama Canal cruise.

As a precaution, you should photocopy the identification page of your passport, your driver's licence and any credit cards you will be taking on your trip. Keep one copy of this photocopied information with you, separate from your passport and wallet, and leave another one at home.

With regard to travel insurance, a comprehensive policy can be bought when you book your cruise - one that covers trip cancellation, delayed departure, medical expenses, personal accident and liability, lost baggage and money, and legal expenses.

CURRENCY

Each country visited on a Canal cruise has its own legal tender, but American currency is accepted everywhere in the Caribbean, Central America and Mexico, as are major credit cards and travellers cheques. It's best to have several credit cards, and married couples should arrange for at least one set of separate cards (without joint signing privileges) in case one spouse loses his or her wallet and all of the couple's joint cards have to be cancelled.

Costa Rica's beautiful paper money.

Taxi fares are usually paid in cash, and it's prudent to carry enough to cover the fare back to your ship in the event you somehow miss your tour bus. It's also a good idea to carry a handful of small US bills for tips and minor purchases rather than receive large amounts of local currency in change. Travellers cheques should be cashed on board the ship unless you are planning a large purchase. Prices quoted in this book are in US dollars unless otherwise noted.

HEALTH PRECAUTIONS

No vaccinations are required for a Canal cruise but you may want to consult your doctor in this regard. Mosquito-transmitted diseases, such as dengue fever, do exist in the tropics and some precautions should be taken if embarking on a rainforest hike, such as wearing a long-sleeved cotton shirt and slacks, and applying insect repellent to exposed skin.

To avoid traveller's diarrhea, it's best to drink bottled water when ashore, avoid eating food from street vendors or open-air stands, and never eat a piece of unfamiliar fruit you see hanging from a tree. The poisonous manchineel tree, which grows near beaches in the Caribbean, bears fruit resembling small green apples. Contact with these or the tree's leaves, sap or bark will cause a chemical burning. Signs usually identify these trees but the best approach is to stay on designated paths to avoid hazardous vegetation.

All large ships have a fully equipped medical center with a doctor and nurses. Passengers needing medical attention are billed at private rates which are added to their shipboard account. This invoice can be submitted to your insurance company upon your return home. You may already have supplementary health insurance through a credit card, automobile club policy or employment health plan, but you should check these carefully. Whatever policy you choose for your trip, carry details of it with you and documents showing that you are covered by a plan. If you plan on doing any scuba diving, be sure to bring your diving certification.

Modern cruise ships use stabilizers to reduce any rolling motion when underway, so seasickness is not a widespread or prolonged problem with most passengers. However, there are a number of remedies for people susceptible to this affliction. One is to wear special wrist bands, the balls of which rest on an acupressure point. Another option is to chew meclizine tablets (often available at the ship's front office) or take Dramamine, an over-the-counter antihistamine. It's best to take these pills ahead of time, before you feel too nauseous, and they may make you feel drowsy. Fresh air is one of the best antidotes to motion sickness, so stepping out on deck is often all that's needed to counter any queasiness. Other simple remedies include sipping on ginger ale and nibbling on dry crackers and an apple. Should you become concerned about your condition, simply visit the medical center on board for professional attention.

WHAT TO PACK

Trunks of new clothes aren't a necessity for a cruise. Pack casual attire for daytime wear – both on board the ship and in port. Swimwear is unacceptable when you're away from the beach, so dress modestly when visiting the local towns of the Caribbean, Central America and Mexico, especially if you plan to enter any of the churches. Cool, loose cottons are best. Take a wide-brimmed straw or cotton hat and a comfortable pair of rubber-soled shoes for walking on cobblestone streets or trekking along forest trails. Also, take along a light, waterproof windbreaker for rain forest hikes. A light sweater or sweat top will come in handy when the air conditioning in restaurants, stores and museums is much cooler than the temperature outside. Sunscreen is also important, one with a protection factor of 15 or higher, to shield your skin from the sun's burning rays. Apply generously before going outside and reapply frequently if you are spending time at the beach, even when the sky is overcast.

Your evening wear should include something suitable for the formal nights held on board most ships. Women wear gowns or cocktail dresses and men favor suits. For informal evenings, the women wear dresses, skirts or slacks, and the men wear open-necked shirts and sports jackets. Most ships have coin-operated launderettes with an iron and ironing board, and hand washing can be done in your cabin, or you can pay to have your laundry done by the ship's staff, as well as steam pressing and dry cleaning.

Good walking shoes are imperative for getting around at the ports of call, where cobblestone walks are common.

Basic toiletries, such as soap and shampoo, are usually provided, and a hair dryer may or may not be installed in the bathroom, something you can determine at the time of booking. The on-board shops usually carry toiletries as well. Beach towels are supplied, upon request, for use on shore, and it's not necessary to pack snorkeling or diving gear, or golf clubs, because this equipment is included in ship-organized shore excursions or can be rented. For boat excursions, deck shoes or light-colored rubber-soled sneakers are needed. A pair of small, lightweight binoculars is especially useful for viewing wildlife in the rainforests.

Keep prescribed medication in original, labeled containers and carry a doctor's prescription for any controlled drug. If you wear prescription eyeglasses or contact lenses, consider packing a spare pair. And keep all valuables (travellers cheques, camera, expensive jewelry) in your carry-on luggage, as well as all prescription medicines and documentation (passport, tickets, insurance policy). It's also prudent to pack in your carry-on bag any other essentials you would need in the event your luggage is late arriving. Last but not least, be sure to leave room in one of your suitcases for souvenirs.

LIFE ABOARD

Cabins - also called staterooms - vary in size, ranging from standard inside cabins to suites complete with a verandah. Whatever the size of your cabin, it should be immaculately clean and comfortable and if not, let your cabin steward or the Front Desk know. Telephones and televisions are standard cabin features on most ships, and storage space includes closets and drawers ample enough to hold your other clothes and miscellaneous items for the length of a typical one or two week trip. Valuables can be left in your stateroom safe (standard on many ships) or placed in a safety deposit box at the Front Desk.

Breakfast and lunch on board a cruise ship are usually open seating, with meals served between set times. For dinner you will be asked, when booking your cruise, to indicate your preference for first or second sitting. Some people prefer first sitting as it leaves an entire evening afterwards to enjoy the stage shows and other venues. On the other hand, the second sitting allows plenty of time, after a full day in port, to freshen up and relax before dinner. Some ships now offer alternative restaurants for passengers who prefer a less structured approach to evening dining, and on most large ships the casual, buffet-style lido restaurant is open throughout most of the day, serving breakfast, lunch and dinner fare. Room service is almost always available for all meals, delivery of wines or beverages and for in-between snacks.

EXTRA EXPENSES

There are few additional expenses once you board a cruise ship. All meals (including room service) are paid for, as are any stage shows, lectures, movies, lounge acts, exercise classes and other activities held in the ship's public areas. Personal services and shore excursions, however, are not covered in the basic price of a cruise. Neither are any alcoholic drinks ordered in a lounge or with a meal. Most ships are cashless, which starts with an impression made of one's credit card and getting a shipboard card in return (which usually includes a picture of you and also acts as a security pass). Passengers can sign for incidental expenses which are itemized on a final statement and settled at the end of the voyage.

The good service on board a cruise ship is usually worth rewarding.

Tipping is a cruising tradition and most passengers do tip because the service is usually worth rewarding. Cruise lines normally provide guidelines on how much to tip various staff, but a general rule is to tip the cabin steward about US$3.50 per passenger per day, your waiter the same amount, and your assistant waiter half that amount. Tips are normally given at the end of a cruise although some cruise lines now add a daily service charge to your shipboard account.

PHONING HOME

Passengers can phone home from the ship, either through the ship's radio office or by placing a direct satellite telephone call. This is expensive, however, ($7 – $10 a minute) and unless the call is urgent, you can usually place it from a land-based phone using the easily available prepaid telephone calling card. If you prefer to use a personal calling card, you can determine the access codes you will need at various ports of call by calling your local telephone operator prior to your trip. Refer to

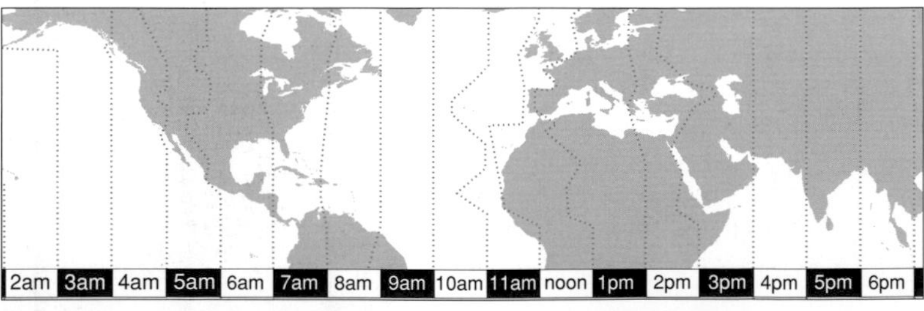

the map to determine the time difference before placing a call. Perhaps the easiest and cheapest way to contact friends and family is the Internet. Most ships have computers on board and offer a flat rate use (about $8 for 10 to 15 minutes). No matter where you are, at sea or in port, you can send an e-mail instantly.

VACATION PHOTOS

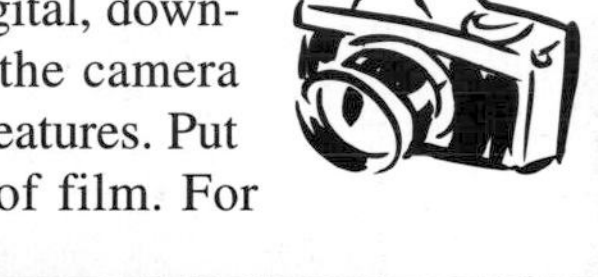

If you are taking a new camera on your trip, shoot and develop a roll of film at home beforehand or, if digital, download the images to your computer to make sure the camera works properly and that you understand all of its features. Put fresh batteries in your camera and pack plenty of film. For automatic cameras, 200-ASA print film is your best choice for all-around lighting conditions, and this speed of film is less likely to be damaged by the powerful X-ray machines now used at airports. Exposed but undeveloped film should not be put in checked luggage but placed in a carry-on bag where it can withstand about five X-rays at walk-through security checkpoints before being damaged. Another option is to place your rolls of film in a see-through plastic bag and ask for a hand inspection, or have your film developed on board the ship. If you're using a digital camera, take an extra battery pack and be sure to have a total of at least 128 mb of flash card memory storage. A laptop computer will of course give you lots of storage. Most onboard photo departments will now develop digital images into prints. If you're shooting underwater photos, be aware that water absorbs light, with red and orange colors reaching only a short distance below the surface, which is why the color blue dominates underwater photos unless special lighting is used (see top photo, this page).

(Below) A Guatemalan girl displays her merchandise.

SHOPPING

The Caribbean, Mexico and Central America are well-known for their

(Above) Street vendors in Mexico are open to bartering. (Below) Leading jewelers are located in the main shopping ports of the Caribbean.

excellent and colorful handicrafts, which include pottery, wood carvings and hand-woven textiles. Sold at open-air markets, where bartering is common, items to look for are covered in each destination's respective chapter. The Caribbean is also famous for its 'free ports' where the selection and savings on luxury goods are among the world's best. With few local manufacturing industries to protect, most Caribbean countries charge no duty on imports, nor is there sales tax, resulting in savings of up to 50%. These savings are passed on to visitors who, in turn, are allowed a duty-free allowance on goods they take home.

Before you embark on your cruise, you may want to visit your local customs office and register valuables you plan to take with you (i.e. cameras, jewelry) so that you have no problem re- importing them duty- and tax-free. Separate from goods bought at duty-free prices are those that are duty exempt. Any item purchased in its country of manufacture, such as locally made handicrafts, is duty exempt . Loose gems – emeralds, diamonds, rubies and sapphires – are also duty exempt.

Your ship's port lecturer will offer valuable advice on shopping at each port of call. Although recommended merchants often pay a promotional fee to the cruise line, they must guarantee products they are selling to the line's passengers. If you are considering an expensive purchase, it's prudent to shop at stores known or recommended by the cruise line. Good buys in the Caribbean include large single diamonds and tennis bracelets. The world's finest emeralds are mined in

(Above) A Mazatlan shop features Mexican hand-

Colombia and sold throughout the Caribbean at impressively low prices. Shops on board the large ships also carry leading brands of liquor, perfume, watches, jewelry, crystal and china at duty-free prices.

One word of caution concerns restrictions in the cross-border trade of endangered or threatened species of animals and plants. Special permits are required to bring home restricted animal products made from certain species, including sea turtles, most crocodiles, and all corals. To determine what you can and cannot legally bring back into your country, contact the federal department handling environmental matters.

Language: Spanish being the mother tongue of the Latin American countries visited on a Panama Canal cruise, here is a smattering of Spanish to help you communicate with your hosts:

Good morning	Buenos dias
Good afternoon	Buenos tardes
Good night	Buenos noches
Please	Por favor
Thank you	Gracias
How much does it cost?	Cuanto cuesta?

Spanish Place Words:
bahia – bay
lago – lake
rio – river
sierra or cordillera – mountains
malecon – sea wall or promenade
zocalo – central plaza
ciudad – city

A public lounge aboard Celebrity's Century (70,000 tons, 1995) - an excellent example of today's finely finished ship interiors.

The Panama Canal cruise is more than just a fascinating voyage through the "big ditch". It often includes cruising the coasts of Central America and Mexico, and it always includes a voyage among the intriguing islands of the Caribbean. Either way, there are many opportunities to ponder the complex workings of a modern cruise ship. Ships, however, have always been complex. Few people appreciate how difficult it was in the time of sail to beat against the wind from Portobelo to Florida. This voyage of about 1,500 miles could take months and required great knowledge of currents, changing winds and sail settings to take advantage of changing conditions. Today, a voyage across the Caribbean on a large ship takes only a matter of days.

The complexities of ships prompted mariners to develop their own colorful vocabulary adapted with lyrical precision to describe each task. As quoted in Smythe's Sailor's Word-Book, "How could the whereabouts of an aching tooth be better pointed out to an operative dentist than Jack's, 'Tis the aftermost grinder aloft, on the starboard quarter.'"

During the 15th century, when commerce with distant lands became increasingly profitable, trading countries began investing in improvements in ship design. This resulted in stronger, faster ships with better sailing characteristics but sea travel for passengers was usually a wretched affair until a huge wave of immigration to America in the late 19th century resulted in great profits and increased competition.

To attract passengers, ships became more elegant with opulent public areas and better cabin facilities. When grand transatlantic ocean lin-

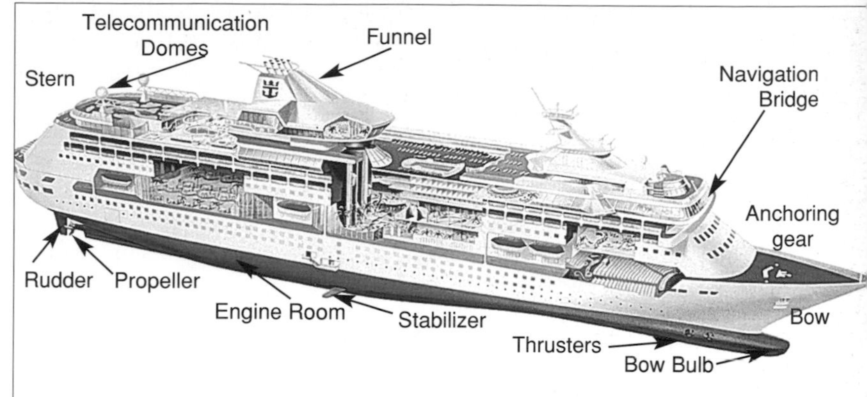

ers were introduced in the late 19th century, elegance, fine service and superb cuisine became part of the experience, at least in first class. Graceful and inspiring, these ships usually had an extended bow, rounded stern and raked funnels. Design aspects have changed since then of course, but today's cruise ships retain the ocean liner tradition of building ships with attractive lines and well-appointed interiors.

HOW SHIPS MOVE

Ships are pushed through the water with the turning of propellers, two of which are usually used on cruise ships. A propeller is like a screw threading its way through the sea, pushing water away from its pitched blades. Props can be 15 to 20 feet in diameter on large cruise ships and normally turn at 100 to 150 revolutions per minute. It takes a lot of horsepower – about 30,000 on a large ship – to make these propellers push a ship along and almost all cruise ships use diesel engines to do the work. The bridge crew can tap into any amount of engine power by moving small levers which adjust the angle (or pitch) of the propeller blades which determines the speed of the ship. In addition to propelling the ship, the engines generate hot water and electrical power. Cruise ships will normally travel about 16 to 20 knots between ports, depending on the time and distance from one to the next. San Juan, Puerto Rico and St. Thomas are so close that ships traveling between the two overnight are almost at idle speed.

The amount of soot smoke from today's ships is a fraction of that produced by earlier ships of the last century. Up to the end of the First World War, most ships used vast amounts of coal to heat large boilers along the length of the lower part of the ship. As a result, ocean liners of the past usually had two and sometimes three funnels to dispel the exhaust. Today, all ships use diesel engines to transmit the power by supplying electricity either to motors that smoothly turn the prop shafts or to motors mounted on pods hung from the stern of the ship, like huge outboard motors, which can swivel 360 degrees.

A modern ship's underwater appendages include stabilizers, which are small wings near the middle of the ship about 10 feet below the water's surface. The angle of the wings is constantly adjusted to minimize any rolling motion of the ship. Another innovation is the use of bow and stern thrusters, which have almost entirely replaced the need for tugboats when a ship is being docked. A symbol (which looks like an upside-down question mark with two small circles inside) on the hull near the bow indicates the location of bow thrusters in relation to the bow bulb. This bulb reduces the bow wave, allowing a ship's hull to move more efficiently through the water.

NAVIGATIONAL CHALLENGES OF A PANAMA CANAL CRUISE

The Caribbean poses a number of challenges for cruise ship officers, not the least of which are hurricanes from June to November. If necessary, cruise ships will take evasive action and alter course for less exposed ports. Ships are usually safer at sea than near land, where wind strengths can increase dramatically and there is the danger of a ship being blown onto a reef or suffering damage while moored to a dock.

For all junior officers, pinpoint navigation is lesson number one. Officers must always be aware of the ship's exact position and of any nearby hazards such as other ships, reefs or strong ocean currents. Currents are strong between Florida and Cuba where the Gulf Stream flows north at speeds up to five miles per hour. Old Bahama Channel and the Windward Passage (between Haiti and Cuba) also have strong north-flowing currents, as does Cozumel Channel. If undetected, a current can slowly push a ship off course and into danger. During the days of the Spanish Main in the Caribbean, many galleons came to ruin from currents pushing them onto sandbars or reefs.

A few Caribbean ports present special challenges during docking. The most difficult ports are: Cozumel for strong currents and afternoon wind, Ocho Rios for strong winds which start early in the evening, and

The Caribbean presents few problems in navigation but currents and hurricane season can present serious challenges for officers.

Pilots on a cruise ship in the Canal use computers and satellites to ensure the ship stays exactly on course through the transit.

Barbados for the port's twisting narrow entrance and strong afternoon winds. Grand Cayman also gets a mention by various captains for the swell which rolls into the bay where cruise ships anchor.

In the Panama Canal, the main hazard is the waterway itself. The pilot must instruct the helmsperson exactly when to turn and by how much. The Canal, in places, is less that 600 feet wide and for Canal authorities, there are few things worse than a grounded ship. Ships maintain a speed of about eight knots (about nine miles per hour) through the Canal to ensure maneuverability. While in the locks, a ship is held by six to eight electric locomotives (called mules) to hold it securely in place. Double gates in the locks ensure that even the largest ship can not breach the locks and cause a catastrophic breach in system.

Since the Panama Canal is a high-level lock system, with a dam controlling all rivers flowing into Gatun Lake, currents are minimal. Ships sometimes encounter strong wind across the lake, but not enough to affect navigation. Wind conditions can be a hazard at Pacific Ocean ports which are otherwise unencumbered.

Ship Size and Registry

A ship's size is called tonnage, which is actually an interior measurement once based on how many casks (or tuns) of wine a ship could stow in her holds. A tun is four hogsheads, 252 old wine gallons or about 100 cubic feet. Cruise ships used to be called large if they exceeded 30,000 tons and, while that's still a big ship, most ships built today are over 50,000 tons. The Panama Canal can handle ships up to about 90,000 tons.

At the stern of every ship, below its name, is the ship's country of registry. It may be surprising to note that your ship is registered in Monrovia, Liberia, Panama or the Bahamas. Certain countries grant registry to ships for a flat fee, without restrictions or onerous charges, and ships often fly these 'flags of convenience' for tax reasons.

Small ships (up to about 20,000 tons) will roll around a bit more in a bad sea, but are able to visit smaller remote ports. They also offer a more intimate onboard atmosphere, especially on the luxury ships which have the ability to cater to an individual's every need. This size of ship is not common on Panama Canal cruises as, generally, ships on this route are travelling longer distances requiring greater speed. Luxury ships in the small-size range include Seabourn Cruise Line's *Spirit* and *Pride.*

Medium-sized ships, up to 50,000 tons, are a good compromise for cruisers wanting some range of amenities and entertainment yet not wanting to feel they are lost in a hotel complex. Ships of this size are usually easy to find one's way around on and often have a small-ship, relaxed atmosphere. Good examples include the *Zenith* (Celebrity Cruises), *Royal Princess* (Princess Cruises), *Crystal Symphony* (Crystal Cruises) and *Statendam* (Holland America Line).

Large ships (above 60,000 tons) will generally have an easier motion at sea and will certainly have more public areas and an amazing array of facilities. Spacious and beautifully appointed, some of these new ships have been extremely well thought-out, conveying both grandeur and a sense of intimacy in small lounges and bistros. Good examples of this size of ship include the *Sun Princess* (Princess Cruises), *Splendour of the Seas* (Royal Caribbean International), *Galaxy* (Celebrity Cruises), and *Rotterdam* (Holland America Line).

THE SHIP'S OFFICERS AND CREW

The captain, the highest-ranking officer on a ship, is ultimately responsible for the overall running of the ship. He also acts as host to the passengers. Reporting directly to the captain are his officers (ranked 1st to 4th), with the chief officer overseeing the physical condition of the ship. In charge of all technical operations is the chief engineer.

The captain, chief engineer, and their officers and crew, make up only a small portion of total staff on board a ship. The majority of employees are engaged in transforming the ship into a floating resort. This extensive service staff is overseen by the Hotel Manager who is second in rank only to the ship's captain. Reporting to the hotel manager are various managers in charge of departments ranging from food service to housekeeping. Most

Pilot and captain navigate through the Panama Canal.

visible is the cruise director, who oversees the ship's entertainment and on-board passenger events. He or she usually has a background in show business.

Dining, of course, is a very important aspect of cruising, and the quality and preparation of meals receives a great deal of attention. Quality control begins on the dock as various food managers inspect shipments before they are delivered on board. Inspection continues on a daily basis to ensure kitchen staff prepare meals to the standard most passengers expect on a cruise. If a problem with a particular item occurs, a fresh supply will be purchased locally or flown to the ship.

CABINS ON SHIPS

In a bad sea, the cabins with the least motion will be those in the center of the ship. This means if you are booking an inside cabin, see if your agent can get you in the middle and, if motion sickness is a concern, the lower the better. If you like to sleep in, avoid cabins under dining rooms, promenade decks or pool areas. The sound of scraping chairs could be your wake-up call. If you like to go to bed early, stay away from cabins near the ship's discos.

If experiencing the sea is important to you, then an outside cabin is definitely worth the additional expense. Verandah cabins are especially enjoyable on a Panama cruise as most people want to be outside throughout the eight-hour transit of the Canal and soaking up the tropical atmosphere on your own balcony is a rare treat. Also, for those who like getting up early to explore ports, an outside cabin with the morning light coming in is a pleasant way to get started.

The size of cabins can vary greatly, especially on new ships, ranging from inside cabins of 150 square feet to penthouse suites of over a thousand square feet. Standard outside cabins will be around 200 square feet. Older ships generally have smaller cabins, some under 100 square feet which, surprisingly enough, can be quite cosy. The majority of new

An excellent standard inside cabin on Royal Caribbean's Legend of the Seas has all the comforts of an outside cabin except for a window.

An outside suite is the ultimate in cruise ship accommodations as shown here on Princess Cruises' Sun Princess.

ships have good amenities but be sure to ask your agent if one specific facility, such as a bathtub, is important to you.

SOME REALITIES ON A CRUISE SHIP

Ships depart, almost always, on time. If you are late arriving at your embarkation port from a flight arranged by the cruise line or delayed on a ship-organized shore excursion, the ship will wait for you. Otherwise, you will probably be out of luck. Ships will not wait for a passenger or group of passengers who have arranged for their own flights or those who may still be strolling about in a port. There is no roll call or tabulation at each port – it is your responsibility to get back to the ship on time. The all-aboard call is usually half an hour before departure and the gangway is lifted a few minutes before the mooring lines are let go. Make sure you check the ship's departure time at each port, as these will vary. Should you miss your ship, you will have to find your own way to the next port of call, so it's prudent to take a least one credit card when venturing ashore just in case you become stranded.

At some ports, the ship will anchor off a distance from the town and passengers are tendered ashore with the ship's launches. If you have booked a shore excursion, you will assemble with your group. Otherwise, wait an hour or so and the line ups will have lessened.

THINGS TO DO

There are so many things to do on a modern cruise ship, you would have to spend a few months on board to participate in every activity and enjoy all of the ship's facilities. A daily newsletter, slipped under your door, will keep you informed of all the ship's happenings. If exercise is a priority, you can swim in the pool, work out in the gym, jog around the promenade deck, join the aerobics and dance classes or the ping-pong and volleyball tournaments. Perhaps you just want to soak in the jacuzzi, relax in the sauna or treat yourself to a massage and facial.

Stop by the library if you're looking for a good book, a board game or an informal hand of bridge with your fellow passengers. Check your newsletter to see which films are scheduled for the movie theater or just settle into a lounge chair and gaze at the beautiful scenery gliding past the picture windows. Your days on the ship can be as busy or as unstructured as you want. You can play the slot machines in the casino or relax in a deck chair, breathing the fresh sea air. You can stay up late every night, enjoying the varied entertainment in the ship's lounges, or you can retire early and rise at dawn to watch the ship pull into port.

There are usually two sittings for dinner on the large ships. Early sitting is about 6:00 p.m., late sitting about 8:00 p.m. You should indicate your preference when you book your cruise. A recent trend on some ships (especially the luxury ships) is to offer open seating for passengers who prefer not to dine at a set time each evening. Complimentary room service is another option and dinner can be ordered off that night's dining room menu. Special dietary needs can usually be accommodated and low-calorie choices are included on each meal's menu.

Children are welcome on most large ships and special activities are often planned for them and for the teenagers on board. Not all ships will have extensive youth facilities and services, so check with your travel agent to get more detail.

A morning jog suits many active adults, while for kids there are playrooms, teen centers and organized activities.

PLATE TECTONICS

The islands of the Caribbean and the Pacific coastlines of Central America lie along the boundaries of the Caribbean plate – one of 20 or so crustal plates comprising the earth's surface. The boundaries of these plates are marked by fault lines (fractures in the earth's crust), and when the spreading ocean floors of the Atlantic and Pacific Plates are driven beneath an adjoining plate, such as the Caribbean Plate, a deepsea trench is created by a process called subduction.

A subduction zone lies at both ends of the Caribbean Plate, its eastern edge marked by an arc of volcanic islands (the Lesser Antilles) and underwater volcanoes (called sea mounts), its western boundary marked by another string of volcanic peaks lining the Pacific coastline of Central America. Here the deepsea Middle America Trench extends north along the coast of Mexico, terminating at a latitude parallel with Mexico City. From this point north, the boundaries of the oceanic Pacific Plate and the continental North American Plate come together. For several hundred miles between Los Angeles and San Francisco these two plates are moving horizontally past each other along a transform fault called the San Andreas Fault. Movement along this fault is slow and steady in some places, sporadic in others where friction prevents the plate edges from sliding smoothly.

The tectonic tug of war that created today's land masses began when the earth's newly formed crust first divided into plates. As the large plates rubbed against each other, pieces chipped off and became terranes. These fragments could move more freely than the large plates and the earth's crust became a sort of jigsaw puzzle as pieces slowly moved from one location to another. Over the last few hundred million years, terranes off the Pacific Plate have been pushed, as if on a conveyor belt, up the west side of the North American Plate. Baja California and the site of Los Angeles were once part of the North American Plate until they were snagged by the Pacific Plate and are now being carried north. If the terrane upon which Los Angeles sits continues moving north at an average rate of two inches per year, it will reach the northern Gulf of Alaska in 76 million years.

EARTHQUAKES

Earthquakes are generated by blocks of rock grinding past one another along fault lines. Their relative movements can be vertical, horizontal or oblique, and are usually measured in inches per year, except when a sudden release of stress along a fault triggers an earthquake. An earthquake begins with tremors, followed by more violent shocks which gradually diminish. The origin (focus of a quake) is underground or underwater, and the epicenter is a point on the surface directly above the focus. The magnitude and intensity of the seismic waves that travel in all directions outward from the epicenter are determined by scales, such as the Richter scale, which measures ground motion to determine

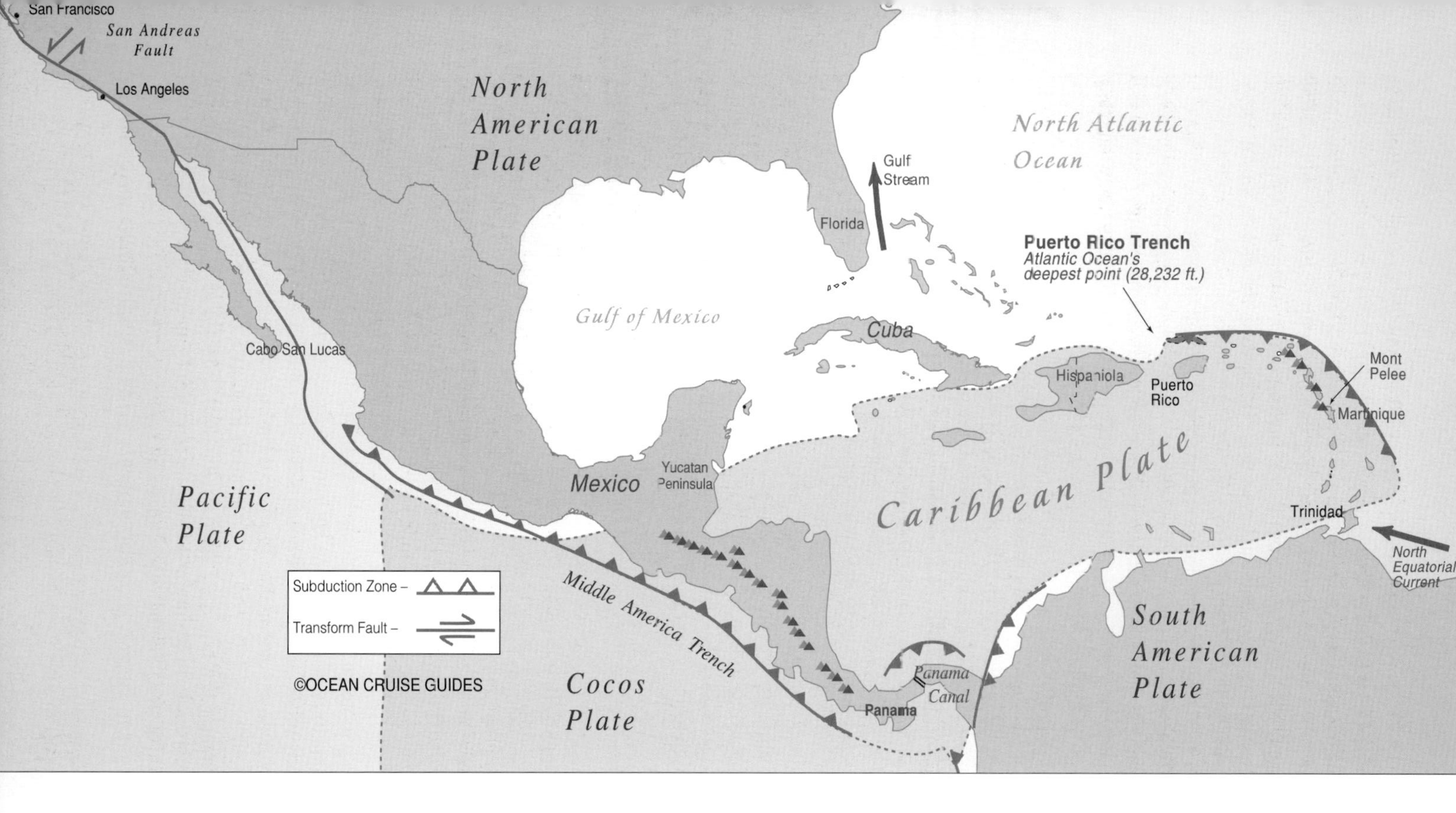
San Francisco
San Andreas Fault
Los Angeles
North American Plate
North Atlantic Ocean
Gulf Stream
Florida
Puerto Rico Trench
Atlantic Ocean's deepest point (28,232 ft.)
Gulf of Mexico
Cuba
Cabo San Lucas
Hispaniola
Puerto Rico
Mont Pelee
Martinique
Yucatan Peninsula
Mexico
Pacific Plate
Caribbean Plate
Trinidad
North Equatorial Current
Subduction Zone –
Transform Fault –
Middle America Trench
South American Plate
Panama Canal
©OCEAN CRUISE GUIDES
Cocos Plate
Panama

the amount of energy released at the quake's origin. A reading of less than 4.5 on the Richter scale indicates an earthquake causing light damage; a reading of more than 7 indicates a severe earthquake of devastating force. The nature of the epicenter's underlying rock and soil affects ground movements and the extent of damage.

The great San Francisco earthquake of 1906 registered 7.8 on the Richter scale, and was triggered by the sudden slippage of about six meters of rock along the San Andreas Fault. In 1971, movement of the San Fernando fault near Los Angeles rocked the ground for 10 seconds, thrusting parts of mountains upward 8 feet (2.4 m). Other California locations hit by severe earthquakes this past century include Santa Cruz in 1989 and two near Los Angeles, in 1992 and 1994. In 1972, the capital of Nicaragua, Managua, was almost totally destroyed by a severe earthquake, and in 1976 an earthquake registering a magnitude of 7.6 struck Guatemala and killed close to 23,000 people. Seismologists can predict where and how a potential earthquake will occur, but they cannot tell us when the next one will strike.

Tsunamis

A tsunami – meaning harbor wave in Japanese – is often referred to as a tidal wave. However, tsunamis are not caused by tidal action (although a high tide can increase their onshore damage) but by sea floor earthquakes or underwater landslides. Up to 100 miles in length but with heights of only a few feet, tsunamis can travel thousands of miles across the open ocean at speeds exceeding 500 miles per hour. Their movement is undetected by ships at sea, but when they approach a shelving coastline they build into a series of waves of disastrous proportion. Anywhere from 10 to 40 minutes can pass between crests and the highest wave may occur several hours after the first wave. The sudden withdrawal of water from a shoreline could be the trough of an approaching tsunami, so people who venture onto these newly exposed beaches risk being engulfed by the wave's huge crest. A tsunami warning system is in place for the Pacific Ocean, where almost two-thirds of all tsunamis occur. In Central America, a total of 49 tsunamis have been documented between 1539 and 1999. Nine of these were destructive, the worst striking the Nicaragua coast in 1992, when a massive wave several hundred meters wide and 9.5 meters high crashed onto shore and killed 170 people.

Tides, controlled by the moon, are usually minimal near the equator. However, the shape and orientation of the Gulf of Panama, facing due south, forms a large catch basin for north-flowing currents, thus creating large tidal variations at the Pacific end of the Canal. While the tidal range on the Atlantic side is measured in mere inches, the tide can rise over twenty feet on the Pacific side. To compensate for these large tides, the outermost locks at Miraflores can lift ships as little as 18 feet or as much as 38 feet, depending on the size of the tide.

VOLCANIC ERUPTIONS

Volcanoes form around an aperture in the earth's crust, through which gases, lava (molten rock) and solid fragments are ejected. A volcano's crater, its floor often covered with steam vents, is formed when the cone collapses during an eruption. A dormant volcano quickly loses its conical shape to erosion, so any mountain that is cone-shaped can be considered a potentially active volcano.

A line of active volcanoes will form above a subduction zone- where one crustal plate is slowly sliding beneath another – and this is the situation along the Pacific coast of Central America and southern Mexico, where recent eruptions of note include Guatemala's Santa Maria (1902), and Mexico's Paricutin (1943) and El Chichon (1982). In 2001, two more of Mexico's volcanoes erupted, namely Volcan de Fuego and Popocatepetl, the latter blanketing two cities southeast of Mexico City in ash. More active volcanoes are found further up the Pacific coast in the Cascade range of mountains which extends from northern California, where Lassen Peak erupted in 1914, into southern British Columbia, and includes Washington State's Mount St. Helens which erupted in 1980.

Numerous volcanoes in the Lesser Antilles are also active, including St. Vincent's La Soufriere (which last erupted in 1979) and Montserrat's Soufriere Hills volcano which, after standing dormant for nearly 400 years, roared back to life in 1995, eventually destroying the island's capital of Plymouth (which had been evacuated) and leaving the southern two-thirds of this once verdant island in ash-covered ruins.

The Caribbean's most violent eruption in recent times was that of Martinique's Mount Pelee on May 8, 1902. Gases within the volcano reached such a critical pressure that masses of solid and liquid rock erupted into the air and a superheated cloud of burning gas and fine ash swept down the mountainside, blanketing the nearby town of St. Pierre and destroying all life in its path. Torrential rain, caused by the condensation of steam, often accompanies such an explosion.

La Soufriere, volcano on the nearby island of St. Vincent, also erupted in 1902, shortly after Mount Pelee's cataclysmic explosion, as did Santa Maria volcano in Guatemala.

ROCK FORMATIONS

The earth's layers of rock have formed in a variety of ways, including the cooling and hardening of magmas and by metamorphism, in which the structure, texture or composition of solid rock is changed by heat, pressure and/or chemically active fluids acting upon it. During the formation of the earth's mountain ranges, metamorphism occurred on a grand scale as intense pressures and temperatures transformed the rock at great depths. The oldest of the earth's rocks have endured four billion years of tectonic activity, their changes recorded in the fossil sequence and disruptions of rock layers.

Minerals combine with one another to make up rocks, and these are called ore if they contain a concentrated source of a metal or gem which is extracted by various forms of mining. Mineral-rich hotsprings form along active plate ridge boundaries, where ground water seeps to great depths through faults in the earth's crust and is heated and recirculated back up to the surface.

During construction of the Panama Canal, especially in the cut across the Continental Divide, engineers had to deal with complex rock formations. Culebra Hill proved to be an ancient volcanic core of solid basalt (lava hardened into igneous rock) while the soil in the valley being dug for the canal was an unstable mix of granite, sedimentary rock, shales and many forms of clay which, when wet, would flow like a glacier down the newly exposed slopes and bury months of excavation work in just a few days.

As workers modified the area's existing soil mechanics, sections of the canal floor, newly relieved of pressure, would rise as much as ten feet within minutes. On one occasion the head engineer thought a steam shovel was sinking before his eyes, but it was actually the valley floor lifting him upward six feet, "so smoothly and so little jar as to make the movement scarcely appreciable." At one point, alarmed workers reported vents of smoke and boiling water escaping from the cracks in the earth along the valley floor. The fear was that they were digging into a volcano, but a hastily summoned geologist calmed the men with the explanation they were seeing the "oxidation of pyrite", a common mineral that is burned in making sulfuric acid. Geologists believe the entire Isthmus is slowly rising as the Cocos Plate is driven beneath the Caribbean Plate, presenting the possibility that some day the entire canal may have to be dug again!

TROPICAL WEATHER

The lands and waters lying between the Tropic of Cancer and the Tropic of Capricorn are referred to as the tropics, or the torrid zone. The sun's rays are more direct in the tropics than areas in higher latitudes, so the temperature remains high year round, although this is moderated by varying wind conditions and changes in elevation, with tropical highlands experiencing a more temperate climate than the lowlands. The seasons in the steamy tropics are defined by rainfall. During the wet season, from spring through fall, the trade winds draw moisture from the oceans and carry this to land where it falls in torrential downpours. The people of Central America rely on this weather pattern for their food production, and if the rains do not come and drought conditions persist for several months, the region's bean and corn crops soon die in the parched conditions, forcing residents to scavenge for mangoes and bananas. Prolonged droughts can also impair operations in the Canal, as they have in 1983 and 2001, by lowering its water level and forcing authorities to limit the draft of some cargo ships.

HURRICANES

When summer tropical storms collect over an ocean, they create a deepening low pressure center which can develop into a cyclone – referred to as a hurricane if it develops over the North Atlantic and a typhoon if it occurs over the West Pacific Ocean. Hurricanes occasionally form off the west coast of Mexico, but the majority of hurricanes develop over the North Atlantic from June to November when the northward shift of the sun increases the temperatures of the Atlantic Ocean and of the air mass lying between Africa and North America. In an average year, more than 100 disturbances (low-pressure systems) with hurricane potential are observed in the Atlantic Ocean; on average only 10 of these reach the tropical-storm stage and about six mature into hurricanes which sweep across the Caribbean Sea, Gulf of Mexico or eastern seaboard of the United States.

The wind speed, which exceeds 74 mph in a hurricane, is caused by heavy, cool air rushing to fill a low-pressure area where the warmer, lighter air is rising. If the low-pressure area is large and the pressure gradient (the rate of pressure change over distance) between it and adjacent pools of air is steep, it will attract larger amounts of cooler air. As the cooler air spins around the eye of the low-pressure system, it can begin to tighten the eye, making it smaller in diameter. This begins a cycle of increasing winds and an increase of air flowing upward. The warm, rising air loses heat and, as a result, water is condensed to form massive nimbostratus clouds. Heavy torrential rain is always a precursor of an approaching hurricane.

Although a hurricane's greatest wind strength (usually between 100 and 200 mph) is at the wall or edge of its eye, where the winds cause very heavy seas and spray that reduces visibility to almost nil, the eye itself is very calm with little wind and a warmer air temperature. A hurricane can have a diameter of 500 miles or more, but the strength or intensity of a hurricane is unrelated to its overall size and very strong hurricanes usually have relatively small eyes – less than 10 miles in diameter.

Hurricanes are assigned different categories depending on their storm surge, wind speed and other factors

Devastating hurricanes can occur in the Caribbean between June and early November.

that provide a measure of the storm's destructive power. The United States National Oceanic and Atmospheric Administration (NOAA) uses five categories, beginning with Category 1. A hurricane of this strength will produce winds of 75 to 95 mph that can damage unanchored mobile homes and vegetation. A Category 5 hurricane is potentially catastrophic, packing winds in excess of 155 mph. Such winds can rip roofs off buildings and create storm surges, prompting the evacuation of residential areas within 10 miles of the shoreline.

The last decade has been one of increased hurricane activity in the Atlantic. In 2004, an unprecedented four hurricanes hit Florida in a single season. The 2005 season was worse, with so many hurricanes making landfall that the World Meteorological Organization nearly ran out of names. An official list of alphabetical names (excluding Q, U, X, Y and Z) is drawn up annually for the naming of each tropical storm that forms in the Atlantic, even if it doesn't reach hurricane force. One of the deadliest hurricanes to hit Central America was Hurricane Mitch in 1998, its five-day rampage through the region claiming 9,000 lives and dumping several feet of rain which triggered huge floods and mudslides in Nicaragua, Honduras, El Salvador and Guatemala.

Prediction and surveillance of hurricanes has improved dramatically in the last 40 years. The National Hurricane Center in Miami provides accurate hurricane forecasts, and warning stations have been established throughout the West Indies. Weather systems in the Atlantic are monitored 24 hours a day with highly advanced radar and satellites to give hurricane forecasters the ability to detect and track storms long before they hit land, while reconnaisance planes measure the approaching storm's strength. Residents of the region are warned of an approaching hurricane up to three days in advance – time enough for islanders to nail plywood over windows and retreat to public shelters, built of solid concrete, to wait out the storm.

Cruise ships receive information from the National Hurricane Center and NOAA, and stay well away from the track of a hurricane.

This spectacular view of the eye of Hurricane Diana in 1984, shot by NASA, shows the intense center of the storm.

THE CREATION OF THE PANAMA CANAL

The seagoing movement of people and goods has determined human history since ancient times, and Panama has always been defined by its geography, namely the short distance across it from sea to sea. Viewed as a barrier to seagoing trade, the Isthmus nonetheless became a crossroads of commerce as people and goods travelled across this narrow neck of land, first on foot with pack mules, then by train. Spanish conquistadors, British buccaneers, American entrepreneurs – their legendary exploits in the jungles of Panama have given this part of the world an aura of adventure and adversity that endures to this day.

SPANISH AMERICA

When **Christopher Columbus**, the son of an Italian wool weaver, made his momentous voyage to the New World in 1492, the nation backing his audacious plan of reaching the Far East by sailing due west was Spain. Columbus did not reach the Far East, but his arrival in the West Indies marked the beginning of Spain's rise to world superpower. The 16th century would be Spain's Golden Century, with fleets on every sea and an empire encompassing nearly all of South America and Central America, as well as parts of North America and the Philippines. The Spanish conquistadors who landed on the shores of the New World proceeded to conquer vast regions in the name of crown, country and a Christian god. In an era of unscrupulous pilfering, these daring adventurers were known for their courage and cunning, as well as their ruthless ambition. Yet, the conquistador who first sighted the Pacific Ocean, on a late September day in 1513, was unlike the others.

Vasco Nunez de Balboa rarely displayed the rapacity that was characteristic of his fellow conquistadors, and his friendship with the local natives enabled him to successfully undertake an epic march across the Isthmus of Panama.

As long ago as 1524 King Charles V of Spain ordered a survey of the Isthmus of Panama to determine the feasibility of a faster and safer route for the Manila galleons crossing the Pacific.

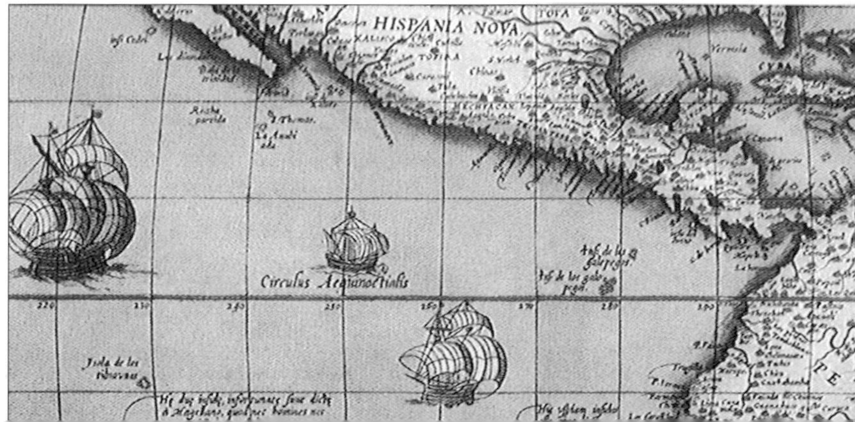

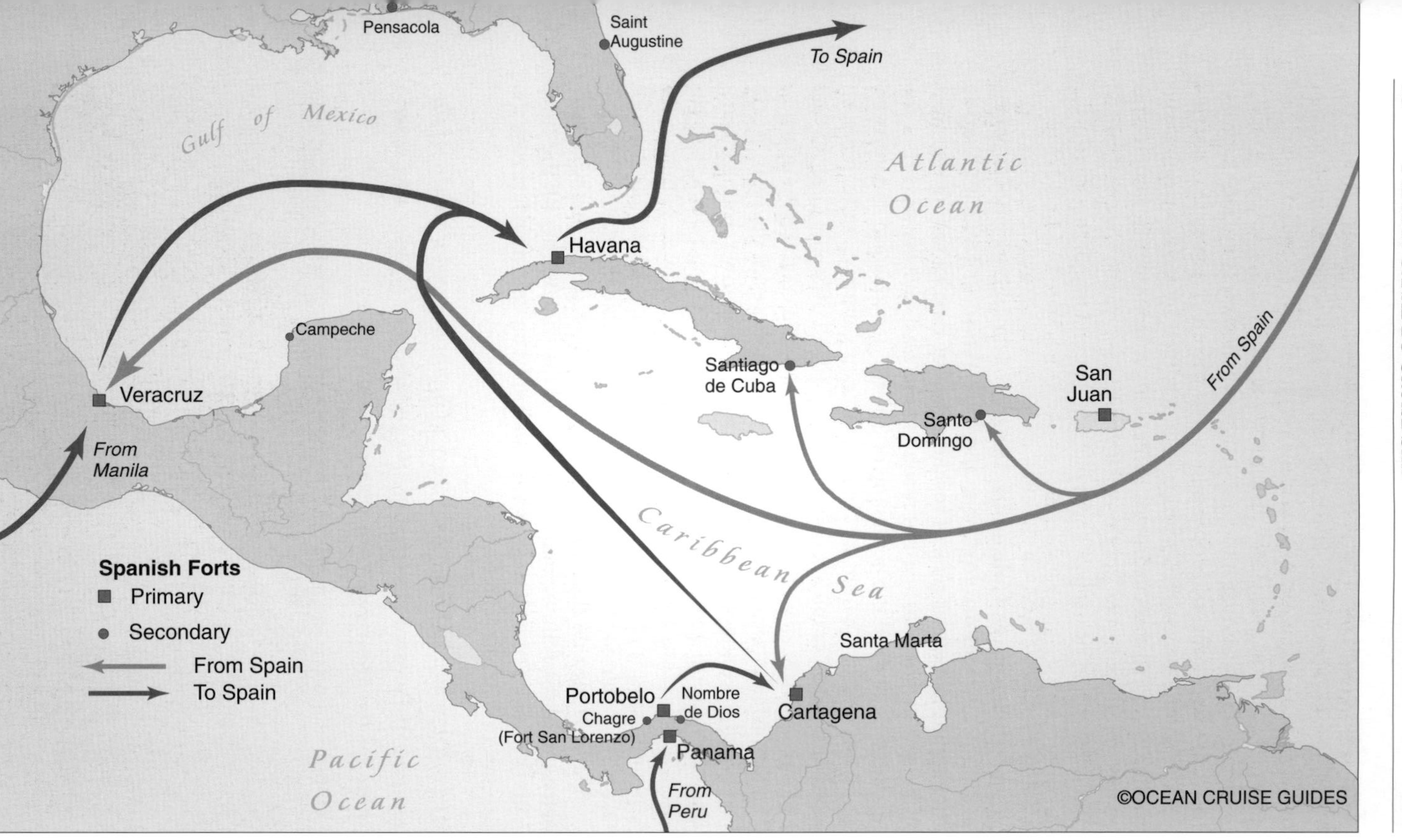
Pensacola
Saint Augustine
To Spain
Gulf of Mexico
Atlantic Ocean
Havana
Campeche
Veracruz
From Manila
Santiago de Cuba
San Juan
Santo Domingo
From Spain
Caribbean Sea
Spanish Forts
Primary
Secondary
From Spain
To Spain
Santa Marta
Portobelo
Nombre de Dios
Chagre
(Fort San Lorenzo)
Cartagena
Panama
Pacific Ocean
From Peru
©OCEAN CRUISE GUIDES

Accompanied by 1,000 natives and 190 Spaniards, including **Francisco Pizarro**, the future conqueror of Peru, Balboa led the expedition through a jungle wilderness that would, over time, claim thousands of lives. Although the Isthmus is only 40 miles (64 km) wide, anyone unfamiliar with the swampy terrain risked getting lost amid the twisting rivers and rain-soaked hills where the dense vegetation, the stifling heat and the clouds of mosquitoes could make the journey hellish. Balboa was fortunate. His guides knew the way and 24 days after departing Darien, the colony he had founded in 1510 on the Gulf of Uraba, Balboa reached the crest of the divide and saw before him the Pacific Ocean – the great sea his native guides had told him about. A few days later, after descending to the Pacific coast, Balboa stood at the ocean's edge and, in the name of King Ferdinand of Spain, claimed possession not only of the 'Great South Sea' but of all shores washed by it.

Balboa's historic discovery and triumphant return to Darien, replete with treasures he had gathered at the Pearl Islands in the Gulf of Panama, earned him the Spanish king's favor and title of Admiral of the South Sea. In 1524, King Charles V of Spain ordered a coastal survey of the region in search of a maritime passage from the Caribbean to the Pacific, but none existed. An overland route spanning the Isthmus of Panama was established along an existing trail where a road of sorts was constructed. Wide enough for two carts to pass, this road ran between Nombre de Dios on the Atlantic side and Panama (today called Old Panama) on the Pacific side. These Spanish-built towns contained royal storehouses and stone stables for the mules of the treasure trains.

Fort San Felipe was one of several forts the Spanish built to protect the walled city Cartagena, an important port for their treasure fleets.

Sir Francis Drake (above) and Sir Henry Morgan (below) were two of England's most celebrated privateers, famous for their exploits along the Spanish Main.

Near the end of the 16th century, Nombre de Dios was abandoned in favor of Portobelo as an Atlantic port. By this time, the volume of trade along the trans-isthmian route had made it the richest mule track in the world. Pizarro's conquest of the Incas had provided access to the gold mines of Peru and shipments would arrive at Panama for overland transport to Portobelo. From the mid-1500s to the mid-1700s, two armed convoys were sent annually from Spain to collect the precious cargo. The New Spain flotilla sailed in April for Veracruz to load silver from Central Mexico and treasures from the Orient. The Tierra Firme fleet would sail in August to Cartagena and wait for the gold and silver to arrive from Portobelo. The walled city of Cartagena was one of Spain's most prized New World ports, and when Spanish ships pulled into port loaded with goods from the home country, the townspeople would crowd the docks. Both fleets would rendezvous in Havana to reprovision for the long trip home through the Florida Straits and past the Bahamas. The majority of Spanish ships made the journey safely back to Seville, but some foundered on reefs or were caught in storms. Others fell prey to pirates.

The treasure fleets of the Spanish Main soon attracted the unwanted attention of pirates and privateers who hid out on abandoned Caribbean islands

The remains of Panama, which was abandoned after its sacking by Henry Morgan who left with 200 pack mules laden with riches.

deemed ‘useless’ by Spanish settlers for their lack of gold. Piracy was called privateering when it received tacit approval from the British, French or Dutch crowns in the form of licensing or commissions. This subtle distinction gave captains latitude to pursue innocuous activities, such as collecting livestock on Caribbean islands, when the real purpose was to pillage Spanish towns and ships. The captains would return home to divide their spoils with the crown while receiving the royal pardon. The exploits of **Francis Drake**, the greatest privateer of all time, fired the imagination of all of Europe when he captured an entire year’s production of Peruvian silver in 1572. With only two ships and 73 men he took Nombre de Dios and captured three mule trains transporting 30 tons of silver. This voyage brought Drake wealth and fame, and inspired generations of adventurers to seek their fortune in the Caribbean, among them the great Dutch naval hero Piet Heyn who, in 1628, captured the entire Mexican treasure fleet near Cuba, and **Henry Morgan**, whose great success in taking Portobelo in 1666 was followed by his spectacular capture and destruction of Panama in 1671.

Centuries of war with rival naval powers slowly weakened the once-powerful nation of Spain and by the early 1800s, the mighty Spanish Empire was crumbling. By 1825 most of Spain's colonies in Latin America had attained independence, including Panama which became part of Greater Colombia. The Mexican War of 1846-48 resulted in

Mexico ceding two-fifths of its territory (California, Arizona, New Mexico and Texas) to the United States in return for $15 million, followed by an additional $10 million in 1853 for a strip of land along the southern extremes of Arizona and New Mexico which contained the Mesilla Valley – the best southern route for a railroad to the Pacific. The last remnants of Spain's vast colonial empire were lost in 1898 during the Spanish American War, when Cuba, Puerto Rico, Guam and the Philippines all shed the Spanish yoke and entered America's growing sphere of international power.

THE CANAL QUESTION

In early 1848, gold was discovered near San Francisco, and over the next two years more than 40,000 prospectors rushed to California to strike it rich. There were three routes for getting there from the east coast – across the continent, around Cape Horn or over the Isthmus of Panama. The latter soon drew its first steamer full of Americans who landed at the marshy mouth of the Chagres River to set off through a wilderness the likes of which none had before experienced. They and others who followed would later write home of the heavy rains and stifling heat, the muck and the slime, the swarms of mosquitoes and sand flies, the poisonous snakes and scorpions.

The men who staggered, rain-soaked and hungry, into Panama City to board a steamer for California had ascended the Chagres by native canoe, then continued overland on mule or by foot where the jungle had reclaimed any trace of the Spanish wagon trails and the winding foot paths were overshadowed by a thick canopy of tropical trees that grew to 100 feet. Mind you, not all of the stampeders had a wretched time crossing the Isthmus. Those who traversed it in the dry season (mid-December to mid-April), when the rains abate, were often overwhelmed by the primeval beauty of the jungle. Monkeys chattered from tree tops and the hypnotic chant of cicadas became synonymous with the tropical rainforest's sultry atmosphere. The emerald green of the luxuriant foliage, the profusion of brilliant flowers and blue butterflies, the great gorges and broad mangrove swamps – all evoked a Garden of Eden atmosphere that could not fail to enchant an intrepid adventurer.

The Panama route was not the only option for crossing Central America. Many opted for the Nicaragua route, which entailed riding a boat up the San Juan River and a steamer across Lake Nicaragua before boarding a stagecoach for the final overland leg to the Pacific. This route, although longer than the one at Panama, was closer to the United States and became the popular choice for a future canal.

The 'canal question' was of increasing concern to the United States, where the American public's widespread belief in their country's inevitable expansion across the North American continent was referred to as 'manifest destiny'. In keeping with this expansionist sentiment was the Monroe Doctrine which, as enunciated by President James Monroe in his 1823 message to Congress, was a foreign policy based on the principle that European nations should refrain from any further colonization or intervention in the Americas. Rivalry between the United States and Great Britain was resolved by a treaty guaranteeing that neither country would have exclusive rights or threaten the neutrality of a potential interoceanic canal. Meanwhile, the countries of Latin America viewed the Monroe Doctrine with suspicion and dislike, seeing it as validation for American imperialism in the region.

In tandem with the tremendous growth of the United States was the Industrial Revolution, originating in England in the mid-1700s. The steam engine was its most important invention, and by 1814 the steam locomotive was being used to power early rail travel, followed by the first steamship crossing of the Atlantic in 1819. This rapid industrialization spread to the United States, and by 1869 the American frontier had disappeared as railways were built from coast to coast and people flocked in huge numbers to the growing cities.

A wealthy New York merchant named William Henry Aspinwall, owner of a steamship line, led an American venture to build a railroad across the Isthmus of Panama. This one-track, broad-gauge line, built between 1848 and 1855, was the world's first transcontinental railroad – and it was exactly 47 1/2 miles long. With Aspinwall's steamships operating on both coasts, the railway was the land link needed to transport passengers and mail between New York and California. The profits made by the Panama Railroad Company, with its monopoly on the Panama transit, were spectacular. Its success also accentuated the need for a maritime route connecting the east and west coasts of the United States, and in 1870 the first thorough survey of the region was carried out by the United States Navy, followed by six other expeditions.

The results of these surveys were presented at an international congress hosted by the Societe de Geographie in Paris in 1879, its purpose ostensibly being to determine the most feasible route for a Central American canal. A year earlier, a French syndicate had sent a young lieutenant, distantly related to Napoleon Bonaparte, on an expedition to Colombia to explore the Panama route. His survey was cursory, carried out by an assistant, while he spent most of his time travelling by horseback to Bogota to negotiate a concession from the government of Colombia. When he presented his plan in support of a Panama route to the congress in Paris, his lack of thoroughness was in contrast to the detailed surveys of the American delegation, which supported a Nicaragua route. Yet the congress voted in favor of a sea-level canal at Panama, mainly because of the persuasive powers of one man whose name was known throughout the world. He was Ferdinand de Lesseps.

The Panama Rail Road Barbacoas Bridge. Built of heavy wrought iron on massive stone piers, it was no match for the Chagres River and was destroyed just weeks before de Lesseps' first visit to Panama.

THE FRENCH EFFORT

The latter half of the 19th century, often referred to as the Victorian Age, was one of unbridled optimism and belief in modern science and engineering. And no man better epitomized this outlook than did **Vicomte Ferdinand de Lesseps**. Born in 1805 in Versailles to a distinguished family of diplomats and adventurers, de Lesseps exuded charm, charisma and an unwavering belief in his ability to succeed. Handsome, athletic, a natural leader and patron of the arts, de Lesseps began his career as a French diplomat. He became a national hero when he successfully planned and oversaw construction of the Suez Canal, which opened in 1869. Not only did this remarkable achievement restore glory to post-Napoleonic France, it made money for thousands of ordinary French citizens who had invested in the project.

De Lesseps, hailed as "The Great Engineer" was actually more of an *entrepreneur extraordinaire* with his vision, his unrelenting energy, his powers of persuasion, his suave diplomacy (some might call it duplicity), all of which contributed to his success at Suez. Basking in the public's adoration, de Lesseps maintained a high profile as president of the Suez Canal Company. He cut an elegant figure in Paris with his fashionable young wife and brood of children, and when he wasn't delivering speeches or granting interviews, his fertile mind was planning new and fantastic schemes – such as creating an inland sea in the Sahara – which seemed to belong in a novel by Jules Verne, who was a friend and fellow member of the prestigious Societe de Geographie.

France's Ferdinand de Lesseps was determined to build La Grande Tranchee (The Great Trench) across the Isthmus of Panama.

The self-confidence that had always propelled de Lesseps was now edging toward hubris as he cast his sights on Central America and the inevitable construction of an interoceanic canal. At an age when most men sought the comforts of a well-earned retirement, de Lesseps was still enjoying the drive and vigor of a man in his prime. In 1875, the year Great Britain bought the Egyptian ruler's shares in the Suez Canal Company and thereby gained financial control of the Suez Canal, de Lesseps first expressed publicly his interest in building a Central American canal. Opposed to this grandiose project was his 38-year-old son Charles, one of five children de Lesseps had with his first wife who died of scarlet fever in 1853. "You succeeded at Suez by a miracle," said Charles, who was his father's right-hand man. "Should not one be satisfied with accomplishing one miracle in a lifetime?"

Another who opposed the canal being proposed by de Lesseps was President Rutherford Hayes who declared in a message to Congress that America's policy concerning any isthmian canal was that it be under American control. The specter of French interests building a canal in Central America was, in the minds of many, in conflict with the Monroe Doctrine. The French government reassured the United States that it was in no way involved with the de Lesseps enterprise. It was de Lesseps, however, who most skillfully refuted this view when he barnstormed America by train in March 1880. Treated like a head of state and feted everywhere he went, de Lesseps won widespread public approval but could not interest a single New York capitalist in his scheme. The funds needed to finance a canal would come, as they had for Suez, from share offerings to the French public.

In retrospect it was clear that the French effort to build a canal at Panama was doomed from the start. There was no single reason, but several, including financial problems and a lack of medical knowledge concerning the mosquito-transmitted diseases of malaria and yellow fever. In addition, railway and hydraulic engineering had not yet made some of the advances necessary for the volume of excavating, dam building and lock construction required for such a massive project. The French success at Suez, ironically, contributed to failure at Panama. From the beginning, de Lesseps insisted on building a sea-level canal at Panama, as he had done so successfully at Suez. But Panama was not Suez, even though the comparisons were inevitable, beginning with de Lesseps' declaration that "Panama will be easier to make, easier to complete, and easier to keep than Suez."

It was not the similarities between the two projects that were noteworthy, but the differences. Suez was built in a hot, dry desert; Panama was a tropical jungle. The terrain at Suez was flat; at Panama it was rugged. At Suez the digging was through sand; at Panama it was through slippery clay lying atop rock stratum. Furthermore, there was no river to harness at Suez, unlike the mighty Chagres at Panama, which was fed by 17 tributaries and stood directly in the canal's path.

The French engineers who worked on the Panama project were of the highest calibre. In the late 1800s, France was considered to have the best-trained corps of civil and military engineers of any country. Their approach to their work was thoroughly scientific, based on sound mathematics and abstract computations, but these engineers had no training in improvisation – an approach they somewhat disparagingly applied to American engineering. Their inability to improvise, and to discard much of what they had learned in Suez, was the downfall of French engineering in Panama. With no prior experience in the tropics, these men of science waged a war with nature and lost. It was, however, a valiant effort, and their work paved the way for the Americans who followed.

In January 1881, the first shipload of French engineers arrived at Panama. Using a local force of laborers, they set about clearing the jungle along the canal line, and building barracks and hospitals. Survey parties mapped the canal route and made test borings. The canal company bought the Grand Hotel in Panama City and set up headquarters. It soon became apparent, however, that control of the Panama Railroad was vital for transporting people, supplies and equipment back and forth across the Isthmus, so the canal company bought the railroad at three times its market value. This purchase did not affect the 1846 treaty between Colombia and the United States, which guaranteed an American military presence to maintain both Colombian sovereignty on the Isthmus and uninterrupted traffic on the rail line.

The French canal company set up headquarters in Panama City's former Grand Hotel in 1881, and digging began a year later, marked by the blasting of dynamite and popping of champagne.

No sooner had the canal company set up operations when yellow fever struck. It arrived with the start of the rains, as it always did, which began in May and lasted until mid-December. By June, the first canal employee had died. Some 20,000 more would die before the French abandoned their efforts in Panama, earning the Isthmus its reputation of death trap. The region was feared long before the French arrived, its climate considered a killer by the early explorers and privateers. In 1698, a large group of Scottish settlers, attempting to establish a colony on Caledonia Bay, was decimated by disease. In more recent memory, scores of laborers who worked on the Panama Railroad were stricken with infectious diseases and died. Workers who recovered from malaria often suffered such severe melancholia that they would commit suicide.

Everyone knew that Panama was deadly. What they didn't know was why. There were many theories of course. One was that malaria was caused by a poisonous marsh gas released into the air by rotting vegetation. Yellow fever was also believed to be airborne, its source supposedly being human and animal waste, sewage and the carcasses of dead animals. It was treated as a plague and its victims were thought to be contagious. Of the two diseases, yellow fever was the most feared. Malaria could be treated with quinine, but there was little to be done for patients with yellow fever except pray it was a mild case from which the victim would recover and henceforth be immune. Those struck with

French housing and landscaped grounds in Cristobal brought civilization to the jungle but didn't eradicate the disease-transmitting mosquitoes that were killing workers by the hundreds.

a severe case of yellow fever suffered a horrific death. It began with fever, chills, headaches, back pains and extreme physical weakness. By the third day jaundice would appear, at which time the symptoms receded, only to return with a vengeance. Internal hemorrhaging is common in the final stage, with the vomitus now containing blood, before the patient lapses into delirium and coma, then death. Malaria was no picnic either. Bouts of chills caused uncontrollable shivering, and a fever was accompanied by an unquenchable thirst, these symptoms lasting several hours and reoccurring every three or four days. Survivors were left physically and mentally debilitated, and susceptible to recurrence of the disease.

Canal workers stricken with fever were reluctant to go the hospital, where the mortality rate was roughly 75% despite the efforts of trained French doctors and nurses working in modern facilities. The cruel irony of the situation was that the hospitals themselves and their manicured gardens were a perfect breeding ground for yellow fever. The Aedes mosquito, which transmits yellow fever, lays its eggs in still, fresh water, and they found plenty of this on the hospital grounds where no screens covered the windows, and the legs of patients' beds and pots of flowers were set in pottery dishes filled with water to protect them from ants. The Anopheles mosquito, which transmits malaria, thrives in the shaded streams and swamps of the jungle. Only by eliminating the breeding grounds of mosquitoes and segregating stricken patients, can malaria and yellow fever be eradicated.

As the death toll on the Isthmus mounted, moral decadence was blamed for the grim situation. As in any frontier town, the most popular pastimes were drinking, gambling and prostitution. Barroom brawls were commonplace and the empty wine bottles piling up in Colon were used (bottom-side up) to pave "Bottle Alley" behind Front Street. The three most profitable businesses on the Isthmus were said to be gambling houses, brothels and coffin makers. The clientele – technicians, tradesmen and laborers – hailed from a variety of countries, including Germany, Switzerland, Russia, Italy, Holland, Belgium, and England, as well as Jamaica, Cuba and Venezuela. Americans, who ran the Panama Railroad, also came to Panama to work for the French canal company as mechanics, contractors and laborers, the latter arriving from New Orleans and other Gulf ports.

The cosmopolitan nature of the local populace extended to the equipment, which arrived from various countries – often in parts – and were not always compatible. This lack of standardization made the chief engineer's job a daunting one. In 1882, the year digging began, the General Agent – the top official in Panama – resigned, citing "the disorder of details," as did his successor. Amid this confusion, an earthquake struck on September 7, in the early hours of the morning, the worst in recorded history for the Isthmus. The twin towers of the cathedral at Panama City toppled to the ground and much of the rail line was dam-

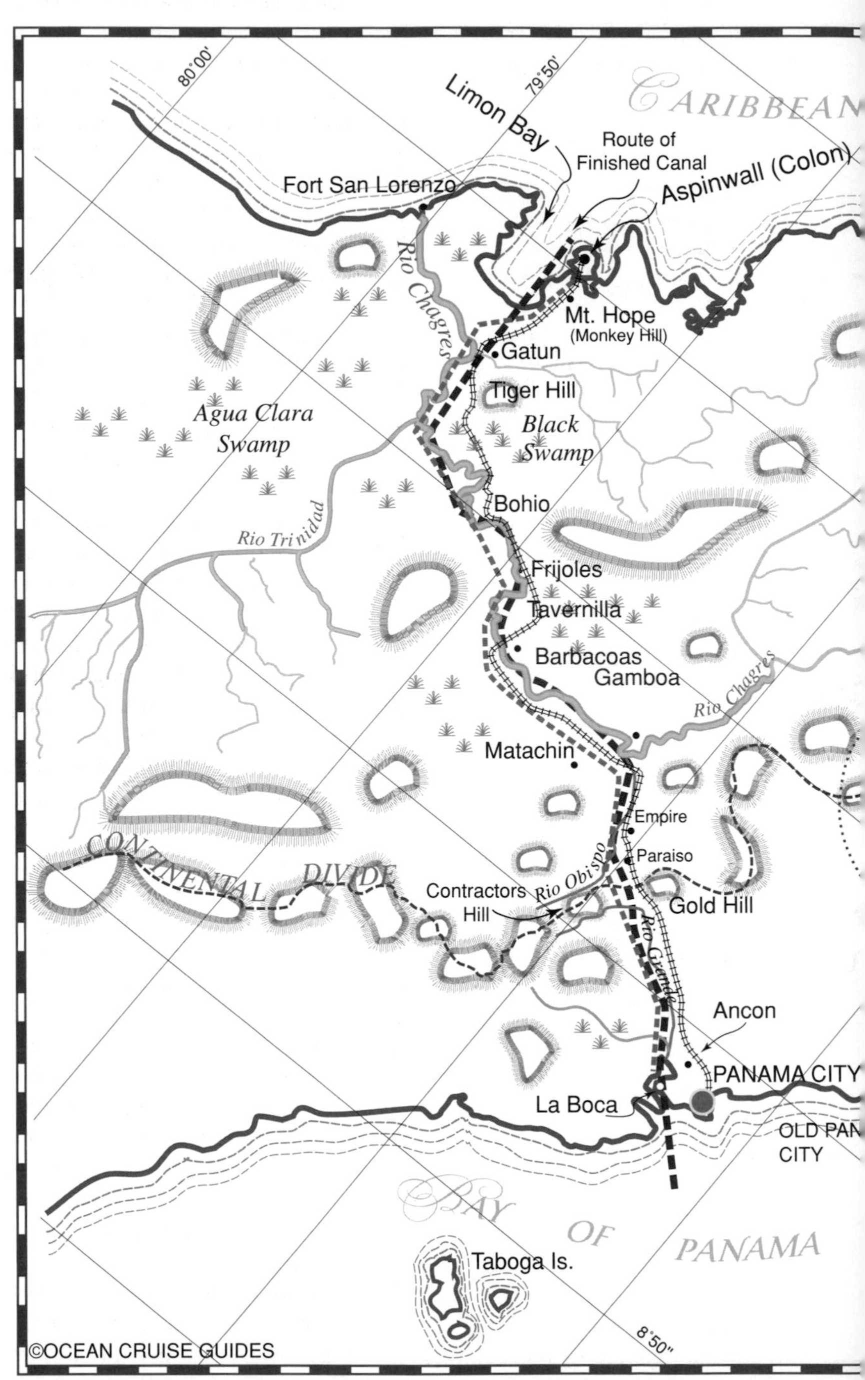
80°00'
79°50'
Limon Bay
CARIBBEAN
Route of Finished Canal
Aspinwall (Colon)
Fort San Lorenzo
Rio Chagres
Mt. Hope
(Monkey Hill)
Gatun
Tiger Hill
Agua Clara Swamp
Black Swamp
Bohio
Rio Trinidad
Frijoles
Tavernilla
Barbacoas
Gamboa
Rio Chagres
Matachin
Empire
Paraiso
CONTINENTAL DIVIDE
Contractors Hill
Rio Obispo
Gold Hill
Rio Grande
Ancon
PANAMA CITY
La Boca
OLD PAN
CITY
BAY OF PANAMA
Taboga Is.
8°50"
©OCEAN CRUISE GUIDES

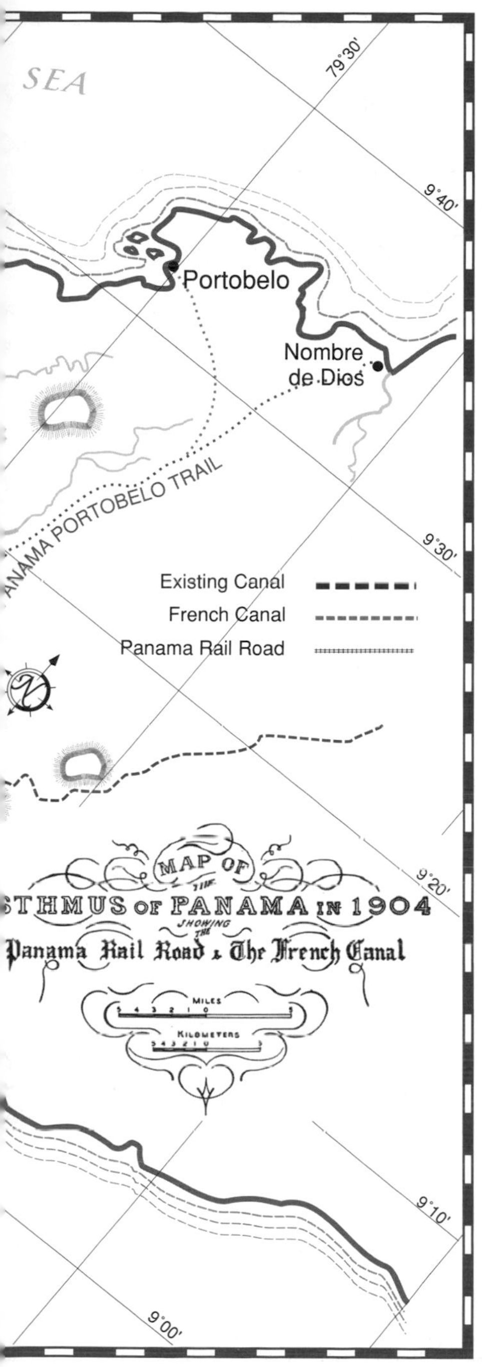

aged. Then, a few months later, the canal company's general contractor – a prestigious French firm – resigned, stating that work could proceed more efficiently using smaller, specialized contractors.

In early 1883, Charles de Lesseps and a new General Agent named **Jules Dingler** (pronounced Danglay) arrived from Paris to restore order and morale. Highly organized, Dingler prepared the first master plan for the canal and was soon issuing contracts for every conceivable piece of machinery needed – dredges, steam shovels, pick, shovels, wheelbarrows – as well as for hundred of laborers, mostly from the West Indies. The wages at Panama were good and the company had no trouble recruiting willing workers. The company's contracts were also lucrative and there were plenty of bidders in Europe, Great Britain and the United States who were eager to get a piece of the Panama pie.

In the fall of 1883, Dingler returned from a trip to France with his wife, son, daughter and her fiance. By the end of the following year, they had all died of yellow fever. Somehow Dingler managed to carry on his duties despite his grief, inspiring the young engineers in his employ with his dignity, courage and determination to succeed. The setbacks were, however, discouraging. The amount of excavation required was proving to be much more than originally anticipated, and the wet weather was blamed for the landslides that plagued the freshly exposed slopes of the Culebra Cut. The fill being removed itself became a source of slides. It was hauled by rail cars to adjacent valleys where pile upon pile formed an unstable, terraced slope of mud that would give way in a torrential downpour and bury the train track below. It was an inefficient system, in which time was continually wasted digging out from yet another slide, but it was indicative of how the contractors – seeking the quickest, most economical solution – operated.

To add to the growing list of problems the French canal company was facing in Panama, the region's politics were as unstable as the slide-plagued slopes of Culebra Cut, and in March 1885 two simultaneous uprisings, one led by a Haitian mulatto in Colon, the other by an ambitious Colombian politician in Panama City, resulted in the deaths of at least one hundred people (more than half of them executed by government troops). Colon was burned to the ground – which proved to be a quick way to rid the town of its filth and squalor.

By August, an exhausted and short-tempered Dingler resigned and returned to Paris, leaving forever the country that had claimed his entire family. His temporary replacement was a 26-year-old engineer named **Philippe Bunau-Varilla**. Small and slightly built, Bunau-Varilla was a man of high energy and pleasing personality who had risen rapidly in the ranks since arriving at Panama. Acutely aware of the health risks, he regarded Panama not so much as a death trap but a great adventure, a place where a man could prove his courage and competence.

Panama had become a battlefield on several fronts, and the stench of death and defeat could no longer be ignored. Back in Paris, the company's share prices were slipping and unpaid bills were mounting. To raise more funds and restore morale among canal workers, de Lesseps embarked, at the age of 80, on his second trip to Panama. His charismatic presence had the desired effect, and the French continued their advance at Panama. The next blow came from an influential report released in May 1886, in which abandoning the canal was not recommended, but government financial support in the form of a bond lottery was. The need for modifications of the canal plans was also stressed, which could mean only one thing – switching from a sea-level passage to one with locks, a concept de Lesseps had opposed from the start. France's great hero was starting to look like a stubborn old man as he steadfastly refused to alter his plans. Meanwhile, the company continued to borrow heavily.

A year passed, and digging continued. Then, amid ongoing rumors of pending collapse and bankruptcy, Bunau-Varilla, who had resigned from the canal company to work for one of its main contractors, came up with a incredible plan that would allow de Lesseps to save face. The contractors would build a lock canal adjacent to the sea-level canal route and use it instead of rail tracks to transport excavating equipment and carry away fill. In other words, build two canals.

The French had great expectations of the giant bucket excavators but these were far less efficient than the American 95-ton Bucyrus steam shovels which could handle three to five times more in a day.

Gustave Eiffel, designer of the Eiffel Tower which was then under construction, was hired to design and build the locks, but his high profile was not enough to stop the downward slide of the canal company's share prices. A government lottery was the company's only hope and in April 1888 the necessary bill was approved and share prices rebounded. This was a shortlived turn of fortune, however, for the lottery failed to sell enough bonds to keep the company solvent. De Lesseps, fighting to the end, tried to muster his followers with yet another battle cry to press on with construction of his canal, but the company's board of directors conceded defeat and the man who had seemed ageless now lapsed into a slow decline. To the shock of the company's investors, many of whom had invested their life savings, they had lost everything. The worst, however, was yet to come.

Nearly three years passed before the real scandal broke. An anti-Semitic journalist named Edouard Drumont began investigating and writing about the collapse of the canal company. Anxious to prove that Jewish financiers were the real culprits, he questioned the French government's failure to audit the company's books. As Drumont began turning over rocks, strange things began crawling out. An official investigation was launched into the possible misuse of funds and the willful deception of the public. Few realized how far it would go.

Members of government at the highest level came under suspicion of receiving pay-offs for voting in favor of the lottery bond bill, and two powerful financiers – Baron Jacques de Reinach and Cornelius Herz – were revealed as the major players. The de Lesseps, who had feared their company's financial lifelines would be severed if they refused to co-operate, had paid huge sums of money to de Reinach who was supposed to pay off the press but who was, as revealed in the criminal investigation, also paying off members of government as well as Herz, who was blackmailing de Reinach. The details of the intrigue were never revealed in a court of law for de Reinach committed suicide in the early days of the investigation and Herz fled to England where he died of kidney failure while under house arrest in a Bournemouth Hotel.

The scapegoats for the scandal, which deeply shocked the French public, were Ferdinand and Charles de Lesseps. The elder de Lesseps was not made to stand trial due to his age and failing health, but his son faced two sets of charges – one of fraud and maladministration, another of corruption (i.e. bribery) of public officials. Madame de Lesseps took her ailing husband to their country estate to protect him from the events unfolding in Paris, but when he eventually learned that his son had been arrested and was in prison awaiting trial, the elder de Lesseps was devastated.

All along, Ferdinand de Lesseps claimed that an Isthmian canal would benefit the world, and his motives reflected the motto of the Ecole Polytechnique: For country, science, and glory. Millions of francs had changed hands, but neither de Lesseps nor his son Charles had personally profited in spite of having ample opportunity to pad their own pockets. De Lesseps had in fact invested more than he made from the Company, losing a considerable sum which included part of his wife's savings. As for Charles, he was found guilty of both sets of charges but served only a light sentence. He maintained his dignity throughout the ordeal and for the remainder of his life never talked of Panama.

Philippe Bunau-Varilla, who first came to Panama as a 26-year-old engineer, played an important role in the creation of the Republic of Panama.

President Theodore Roosevelt believed in sea power and was determined to build a canal in Panama to join America's two coastlines and guarantee the country's security. He, perhaps more than anyone, made the Panama Canal happen.

AN AMERICAN CANAL

Three weeks after his 89th birthday, Ferdinand de Lesseps quietly died in bed at his country home. The year was 1894 and **Theodore Roosevelt**, still in his thirties, was on the ascent. Born into a prominent New York family, raised by nannies and educated by private tutors, Roosevelt travelled widely with his parents before graduating from Harvard and studying law at Columbia. He was an intellectual, an outdoorsman, a conservationist, a reformist, an expansionist and a fighter. A man of boundless vitality and enthusiasm, Roosevelt as President would capture the imagination of the American people with his pithy phrases and adamant defence of the rights of the "little man" versus the powerful industrialists. He stood 5' 8" but he was stocky and appeared to be much larger. And he exuded confidence, in his walk, in his talk. Suffering frail health as a child, he led a life of vigorous pursuits, returning home a hero from the Spanish-American war in Cuba where his famous Rough Riders regiment was victorious. Above all else, Roosevelt believed in military muscle and the importance of sea power if America was to achieve world supremacy, a point sharply illustrated during the Spanish-American war when it took an American battleship two months to reach Cuba, sailing from San Francisco via Cape Horn. It was obvious that a Central American canal must be built. And it must be American built and under American control. And the place to build it, most Americans agreed, was Nicaragua.

Nicaragua had a shining reputation. Not only was it closer than Panama to American shores, Nicaragua was viewed as politically stable and disease-free. The proposed inter-oceanic route would follow a navigable river and the sparkling waters of Lake Nicaragua before reverting to a man-made canal on its Pacific side. Volumes of data from American surveys supported the Nicaragua route, as did the Nicaragua Canal Commission, a presidential study of the best potential route for the canal. And, perhaps most important in the minds of the American public, Nicaragua would be a fresh start, far removed from the 'junk heap of Panama' – as veteran Senator John Tyler Morgan of Alabama liked to refer to the abandoned French canal.

In 1899 a second study was ordered by President William McKinley, called the Isthmian Canal Commission but widely referred to as the Walker Commission, for the name of the Admiral who headed its board of eminent engineers. When the Commission's report was released in November 1901, it contained some surprising recommendations. Based on two years of field work, including trips to Paris to view the French canal company's records and plans, and to Panama, the board maintained that Nicaragua was still the most feasible route. However, the deciding factor was not an engineering one, but the high price tag the French had put on their canal holdings. Within weeks of

There were, at one point, five possible routes across the Isthmus as shown below. Panama and Nicaragua were the popular choices.

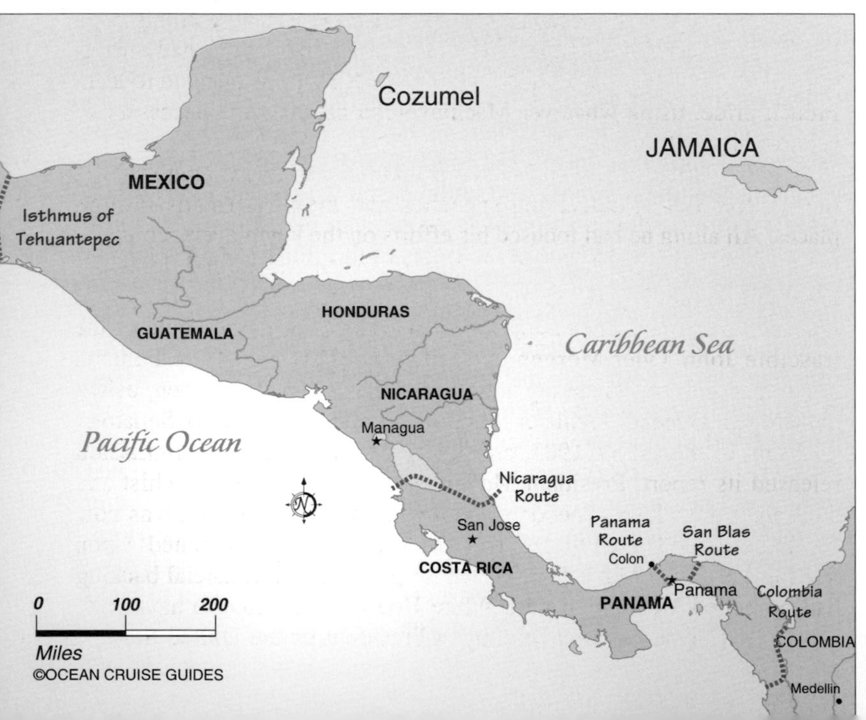

the study's release, the new canal company slashed its asking price from $109,000,000 to $40,000,000, and a month later the Walker Commission reversed its decision, unanimously supporting Panama as the best choice for an American canal.

How this remarkable about-face occurred was due in large part to the behind-the-scenes efforts of two highly effective lobbyists – Philippe Bunau-Varilla and William Nelson Cromwell. Bunau-Varilla, a chief engineer with the original canal company at Panama, was the organizer of the new company which had taken over the canal rights. He and others, including Gustave Eiffel, were penalty shareholders in the new company, which meant they would have faced fraud charges for the profits they had made from the original canal project had they refused to invest in the new venture. Cromwell, an American, was a high-powered corporate lawyer hired in 1894 by the new canal company to represent its interests, i.e. sell its canal holdings to the United States Government.

These two men, working independently and openly disdainful of each other, proceeded to unleash their powers of persuasion and logic on the key American officials who would play a role in deciding where an American canal would be built. Cromwell was simply earning his $80,000 commission, while Buneau-Varilla's motives were more complex. As a shareholder in the new canal company he certainly had a vested interest in selling its holdings to the United States government, yet he convincingly claimed he was on a mission to resurrect the Panama Canal and restore French glory. The impeccably polite little Frenchman struck Americans as being slightly eccentric with his huge black moustache waxed at the ends into sharp points, but he had a steel-trap mind, a riveting personality and was zealous in his quest to redeem French pride, using whatever Machiavellian means were necessary to achieve his goal.

In early 1901, Bunau-Varilla had embarked on a three-month tour of the United States, delivering speeches and making friends in high places. All along he had focused his efforts on the key players, convincing Ohio Senator Mark Hanna, a powerful industrialist and dominant force within the Republican party, that Panama was the superior canal route to Nicaragua. Bunau-Varilla even paid a visit to the home of the irascible John Tyler Morgan, a vociferous opponent of the Panama route, and their brief meeting almost ended in a punch-up when, baited by Morgan, Buneau-Varilla came close to striking the elderly Senator.

Then, in the fall of 1901, shortly before the Walker Commission released its report, President McKinley was shot by an anarchist and died eight days later. Theodore Roosevelt, at the age of 42, was now President of the United States. The response was far from muted. Upon hearing the news, **Mark Hanna**, whose political and financial backing had propelled McKinley to the White House, is reported to have said, "Now look! That damned cowboy is President of the United States."

Back in Paris, Bunau-Varilla was aghast, for he had not even bothered trying to meet Roosevelt when he was Vice-President. Bunau-Varilla now hurried back to the United States to try and meet with the new Commander in Chief.

The shift in presidential style was swift and spellbinding. The Harvard-educated New Yorker who enjoyed horseback riding on his ranch in Dakota Territory was now the center of the country's attention and he revelled in his new role. He was the first President to call his official residence the White House (instead of the Executive Mansion) into which he moved his large and boisterous family. While distinguished guests arriving for state dinners would gather in the mansion's public rooms, the President could be found upstairs in the nursery having pillow fights with his children.

Roosevelt's youthful vigor struck a responsive chord with the American people, yet he was a complex man, whose passion for physical pursuits and outdoor activities belied his scholarly mind. An avid reader and progressive thinker, Roosevelt harbored an intense interest in the 'canal question' and was painstakingly familiar with all aspects of the potential canal routes, right down to details on topography. And it would soon become apparent that Roosevelt had changed his mind about where the canal should be built. Like most Americans, he had long favored the Nicaragua route. However, the case for Panama now seemed the more logical when based on engineering considerations, namely that the Panama route had better harbors, was shorter, required fewer locks (five versus eight), and its potential problems had already been exposed by the failed French effort. Nicaragua on the other hand was an unknown.

In addition, there was the issue of volcanoes – with no fewer than a dozen located in Nicaragua – a point Bunau-Varilla kept making in his speeches but which no one seemed to take very seriously until May 8, 1902, when Mount Pelee on the Caribbean island of Martinique erupted with such force that a mass of solid and liquid rock exploded into the air and a superheated cloud of burning gas swept down the mountainside, blanketing the nearby town of St. Pierre and killing all 30,000 residents but one – a prisoner protected by the walls of his jail cell. Days later, Momotombo in Nicaragua erupted, followed by another explosion of Pelee and yet another volcanic eruption on the Caribbean island of St. Vincent.

While volcanoes were erupting, the Senate hearings got under way. Morgan delivered a vehement speech against Panama, warning that it was only a matter of time before the United States would be compelled to take Panama by force in order to protect the Canal, should it be built there. He did not address the engineering aspects of the two routes, only the political pitfalls of Panama. This was in contrast to the contents of Mark Hanna's speech, possibly the best of his career, in which he convincingly listed the reasons for favoring Panama. Backing his argument were statements by dozens of shipmasters and pilots who would be using the canal, all of whom agreed that the shorter the canal, the better, for the less time spent in a canal meant less risk of damage to their ships. Reiterating the points made by the Walker Commission, Hanna stated that a Panama Canal would have fewer curves, would cost less to run and, most importantly, it was the route the engineers studying the issue recommended, an argument Morgan had scoffed at earlier, declaring that the Walker Commission's preference for Panama had nothing to do with engineering arguments but with the cheap price the U.S. was being offered for the French company's holdings.

The pending vote in the Senate looked like it could go either way. The American press still supported the Nicaragua route and political cartoonists like to poke fun at the pro-Panama forces' "volcano scare". Throughout the hearings, the Nicaraguan embassy in Washington steadfastly denied that Momotombo had just erupted, even though it had. In a final pitch, Bunau-Varilla hit on an idea of sending to each Senator the one-centavo Nicaraguan stamp which depicted Momotombo in full eruption. Days later, when the Senate vote was held, Nicaragua received 34 votes, Panama 42. A week later the House passed the Spooner Bill, which authorized the President to build a Panama canal.

Revolution and Remuneration

When the Spooner Bill was passed by an overwhelming majority in the House on June 26, 1902, the Isthmus of Panama had been part of the republic of Colombia since 1819, the year Simon Bolivar was made president of Greater Colombia after leading his revolutionary forces across the flooded Apure valley and over the Andes mountains to defeat a surprised Spanish army in north-central Colombia. After three centuries of exploitation under Spanish colonialism, during which the Isthmus of Panama was ruled first by the viceroyalty of Peru, then by the viceroyalty of New Granada, this strategically located neck of land was for the first time part of an independent nation. In 1830, Venezuela and Ecuador broke away from Greater Colombia and the remaining country would eventually be called, after several name changes, the United States of Colombia. The Isthmus of Panama, although physically separated from the rest of Colombia by the dense Darien jungle, was highly prized by the Colombian government as a source of revenue. Its annual share in the earnings of the Panama Railroad was $250,000, and potential profits from a canal promised to be even more lucrative.

Although rich in natural resources, Colombia, like many a former Spanish colony, struggled with self-government. Social and political stability remained elusive, and a revolution in 1885 was followed by the outbreak of a bloody civil war in 1899, which raged until 1904 when internal order was restored. By then it was too late to save Panama. Colombia had lost its cherished province in an insurrection supported by the United States and orchestrated by Bunau-Varilla. It was one of the strangest revolutions the world has witnessed.

It began back in Washington, where negotiations were tediously slow between Secretary of State **John Hay** and three successive Colombian foreign ministers. The soft-spoken Hay was a man of letters, trained in law and journalism, who had served as President Lincoln's assistant private secretary and written several books. He had negotiated the Hay-Pauncefort treaty in which Britain relinquished to the U.S. the right to construct, control and fortify an isthmian canal in Central America, and his Colombian assignment seemed straightforward enough. But Hay, the experienced and erudite statesman, was dealing not only with Colombian diplomats whose Spanish sense of pride and decorum were at odds with the 'let's get on with it' American approach, but with a cryptic Colombian government which seemed to be continually shifting its position in its instructions from Bogota. The two main issues were Colombian sovereignty and money. Colombia's diplomats in Washington felt they were being bullied by the American administration, which threatened to enter negotiations with Nicaragua if Colombia persisted in delaying a treaty settlement. Dr. Tomas Herran, the multilingual and highly educated Colombian diplomat who cautiously reached an agreement with Hay, spoke in private of Roosevelt's "impetuous and violent disposition" which might predispose him to taking Panama by force. Hay urged restraint to President Roosevelt, who was becoming increasingly impatient with the Colombians whom he referred to as "jack rabbits" and "those bandits in Bogota."

The main stumbling block for Colombia was the $40,000,000 the French canal company was to receive from the United States. Colombia wanted to receive a portion of this payment as commission for

Dr. Manuel Amador was the leader of the U.S.-backed revolution in Panama and became the new country's first president.

allowing the transfer of the canal zone, but the French canal company did not agree and Cromwell was working hard behind the scenes to convince the American government that none of the agreed-upon purchase price should go to Colombia. Eventually a treaty was drawn up and signed in Washington by Hay and Herran, which granted the United States control of a canal zone six miles wide between Colon and Panama City, and which authorized the French company to sell its Panama holdings to the American government. In return, Colombia would receive a lump sum of $10,000,000 and, after nine years, an annuity of $250,000. The treaty's terms were not popular with Colombians, who believed they should be receiving more financial compensation, and the Colombian Senate refused to ratify it.

While Colombia equivocated, Panama conspired. A small group of prominent Panamanians began planning a revolution, led by 70-year-old **Dr. Manuel Amador** who, although born and educated in Cartagena, had lived in Panama since the California gold rush of 1848. The leaders of the movement all worked for the Panama Railroad and were in contact with Cromwell. These included Jose Agustin Arango, the railroad's attorney and a Panamanian senator, and the assistant superintendent Herbert Prescott, an American. In August 1903, Dr. Amador boarded a steamer bound for New York to drum up American support for their insurrection.

An intrigue of secret meetings and coded messages unfolded during Amador's stay in New York. Doublecrossed by a Panamanian businessman he had met while playing poker on the sea voyage to New York, Amador found himself getting nowhere with his American contacts until Bunau-Varilla arrived from Paris and, with characteristic efficiency, began organizing Amador's revolution down to the minutest detail, including the first draft of a Panamanian declaration of independence and a new flag his wife had quickly stitched together. While Amador waited in New York, Bunau-Varilla hurried by train to Washington where he was able to meet with Roosevelt and engage in an oblique conversation concerning a possible revolution on the Isthmus. By the end of their meeting, Bunau-Varilla was convinced Roosevelt was prepared to support an insurrection on the Isthmus. Back in New York, in his final briefing with Amador, Bunau-Varilla insisted the revolution take place on November 3 and provided the text for a telegram to be sent once the junta gained power, confirming Panama's independence and authorizing him to sign a canal treaty with the U.S.

When Amador returned to Panama, his cohorts didn't like the new flag and were nervous about staging a revolution based on the assurances of an unknown Frenchman. One influential member of the junta, claiming he was too young to be hanged, threatened to back out unless there was a tangible sign of support from the United States, namely an American man-of-war standing offshore. No one, not even Bunau-Varilla, was entirely sure of Roosevelt's intentions at this point, but a pending revolution in Panama seemed to be that year's worst-kept secret and anyone monitoring the situation would have noticed a small item in The New York Times reporting that the U.S. gunboat Nashville had sailed on the morning of October 31 from Kingston, Jamaica, its destination believed to be Colombia.

In the end, no less than 10 American warships would converge on both sides of the Isthmus, and it was undoubtedly their presence that decided the fate of Panama. Yet, it was the Panama Railroad and its superintendent, a 70-year-old American named Colonel James Shaler, who saved the day for the junta when a Colombian warship arrived at Colon only hours after the Nashville showed up on November 2. Commander Hubbard of the Nashville was there under the pretext of maintaining free and uninterrupted transit of the Panama Railroad, so he did nothing to stop General Tobar, the Colombian commander, from landing five hundred troops the next morning.

It was at the railroad wharf that the stonewalling began by Shaler, who had been notified of the troops' pending arrival and had shunted railcars away from the station. General Tobar and his senior officers suspected no hanky-panky when Shaler suggested they board a special car for Panama City, leaving their troops behind in Colon until more railcars were available. Away went Tobar and his officers, heading straight for a trap that was being set in Panama City, where a small garrison of Colombian troops was stationed. These soldiers had not been paid for months and their commanding officer, General Huertas, was known to be sympathetic to the revolutionary movement, so when he was approached by Amador and offered a small fortune if he joined the

Cathedral Square was renamed Independence Square after Panama revolted against Colombia in 1903 and became a separate republic

revolution and arrested Tobar, the young general reportedly hesitated for about a second before accepting the offer.

Back in Colon, a confidential telegram arrived for Hubbard, instructing him to prevent the landing of Colombian troops. Meanwhile Shaler was using delay tactics to prevent the movement of these same troops, insisting their fares be paid in full and in cash before they could ride on the railroad. At the other end of the line, Panama City buzzed with anticipation of an uprising slated for 5:00 p.m. in Cathedral Square. General Tobar and his officers, enjoying a fine lunch at Government House, still suspected nothing. But when his troops failed to arrive by mid-afternoon, Tobar began to grow anxious. With a crowd gathering in front of the military barracks, and an unsuspecting Tobar and his officers conferring on a bench near the gate to the seawall, Huertas issued the order. Armed with fixed bayonets, a company of soldiers marched out of the barracks and surrounded the seated general and his officers, demanding their surrender, which they did after beseeching some of the nearby sentries to come to the defense of their country. None came to their aid, and they were marched to the local jail.

While a jubilant crowd celebrated the success of their revolution in Cathedral Square, back in Colon the Colombian troops, under the command of a young colonel named Torres, were still trying to catch a train to Panama City. At noon the following day, over a drink in the Astor Hotel saloon, a Panamanian named Melendez told Torres what had happened the day before in Panama City. Torres flew into a rage and threatened to burn the town and kill all Americans if the Colombian generals were not released. No one took this threat idly, and after sequestering the town's American civilians to ensure their safety, Hubbard landed an armed detachment of sailors who barricaded the railroad's stone warehouse. He also moved the Nashville closer to shore, its decks cleared for action and its guns trained on the railroad wharf and on the Cartagena, which to everyone's surprise suddenly steamed out of the harbor. A tense few hours followed as the Colombian soldiers surrounded the warehouse, but no shots were fired and Torres eventually marched his troops to Monkey Hill (also called Mount Hope) where they camped for the night. The next day, driven off by mosquitoes, the Colombian troops marched back into town and Torres agreed to evacuate Colon in exchange for $8,000 which was paid in twenty-dollar gold pieces from the railroad company's safe. By evening he and his troops had boarded a Royal Mail steamer bound for Cartagena.

With the dispatch of Colombian troops and the arrival of more American gunboats at Colon and Panama City, all that remained was for the new Republic of Panama to sign a treaty with the U.S. According to the agreement reached between Amador and Bunau-Varilla in New York, the latter would have the diplomatic powers to act on behalf of the new nation, and act he did, in spite of receiving new instructions not to proceed until a small delegation led by President Amador arrived from Panama. Bunau-Varilla hurriedly revised the treaty Hay had drafted, making the conditions so favorable to the U.S. – including perpetual control of a 10-mile-wide canal zone – it couldn't possibly be rejected in the Senate. When the Panamanian delegation stepped off the train in Washington and were told by Bunau-Varilla that he had just signed a treaty on behalf of the Republic of Panama, one of the delegates responded by striking the Frenchman across the face.

Panama had to be content with the treaty and it was not such a bad deal for a new nation, starting out debt free, with a $10,000,000 surplus in the government coffers, a guaranteed annual revenue from its railroad and canal concessions, and the security of U.S. naval protection. Colombian troops did attempt to regain their lost province with an overland march through the Darien jungle but had to turn back. The loss of national income for Colombia, already burdened by a costly civil war, was crippling.

Panama's swift secession from Colombia was achieved without bloodshed, but Roosevelt was accused of acting impulsively in his "sordid conquest" of Panama. Roosevelt vehemently defended himself, claiming later in his autobiography that it was "by far the most important action I took in foreign affairs" and totally justified in the interests of national defence. Depending on a person's point of view, it had been gunboat diplomacy at its best, or its worst, tarnishing U.S. relations with Latin America for years to come. The mood of the American public was generally in favor of Roosevelt's actions, especially when Colombia made a desperate attempt following the revolution to accept the terms of the Hay-Herran treaty, proof in many peoples' minds that Roosevelt was right when he accused the Colombian government of extortion. The American President had, in his own words, "taken the Isthmus" and it was time now for the U.S. to make the dirt fly and build "that damn canal."

Colon was the scene of high tension when an American and a Colombian warship both arrived in port on the eve of the revolution.

THE WORLD'S LARGEST CONSTRUCTION JOB

When the United States took possession of the canal works at Panama on May 4, 1904, the scene was, at first glance, one of rot and despair – abandoned and rusted machinery, dilapidated buildings, filthy towns. On closer inspection, however, the amount of excavation already completed by the French was impressive, much of the equipment was salvageable and many of the buildings could be refurbished. Nonetheless, organizing the manpower and supplies needed to bring order and efficiency to the Canal Zone was a gargantuan task, made even more daunting by the establishment in Washington of the Isthmian Canal Commission which had to approve all requisitions received from Panama. It was headed by Walker, whose passion was to make sure no graft tainted the American effort in Panama. As a result, the first Chief Engineer appointed to Panama, **John Wallace**, was as bogged down in red tape as he was in mud. On top of these administrative frustrations was the weight of American public opinion, which wanted to see "the dirt fly" in Panama, prompting Wallace to commence digging right away at Culebra Cut.

There seemed to be no master plan in place, and morale among the workers, already low, plummeted with the outbreak of yellow fever. Panic swept the Isthmus and people couldn't leave fast enough. Even Wallace fled, under the pretext that he had important business to discuss with Secretary **William Taft** in Washington. Wallace was fired and a new man was quickly found to turn things around in Panama. That man was **John Stevens** who, at age 52, was widely considered the

John Stevens, the second chief engineer to lead the American effort at building a canal in Panama, was the man who turned things around and laid the groundwork for success.

best construction engineer in the country. Self-educated, Stevens had learned surveying on the job, working his way from track hand to chief engineer. He was gruff, physically tough and a legend among railroaders for discovering, in the dead of a Montana winter, the Mariah Pass over the Continental Divide. When Stevens met with Roosevelt, the two men hit it off immediately and the new Chief Engineer was told to do whatever was needed in Panama, which the President called a "devil of a mess.".

It took Stevens, upon arriving in Panama, less than a week to assess the situation. A hands-on and approachable man, he spent hours walking the Canal Zone, in any kind of weather, observing every detail and asking questions. He said little, just looked and listened. Then, six days after his arrival, on August 1, 1905, Stevens ordered all digging stopped. The equipment left behind by the French was not large or heavy enough, the undersized railroad so inefficient Stevens was astounded at how much the French had managed to accomplish. But the first problem to deal with, in Stevens' view, was the overriding atmosphere of fear due to yellow fever and other diseases plaguing Panama. Already at hand was the man best qualified to rid the Isthmus of the dreaded yellow fever, namely **Dr. William Gorgas**, a leading disease and sanitation expert who had rid Havana of yellow fever when sent there with the Army in 1898. Gorgas had been trying to replicate this success since his arrival in Panama a year earlier but with limited results. Few people, including members of the ICC, believed in the "mosquito theory." To spend thousands of dollars chasing mosquitoes seemed a waste of money to General Walker, who had refused to provide the resources Gorgas had repeatedly requested.

Dr. William Gorgas was a modest but tenacious man who rid the Isthmus of yellow fever. Born in Alabama, he met his future wife during a yellow-fever epidemic in Texas. Both fell ill, then fell in love during their convalescence and were hence immune to yellow fever, allowing the doctor and his wife to live in Panama without fear of the disease.

Stevens too was skeptical of the mosquito theory, but he had faith in Dr. Gorgas and he threw the weight of the engineering department at the doctor's disposal. Fumigation brigades, armed with buckets, brooms and scrub brushes, marched on Panama City and Colon where every single house was cleaned and fumigated. Sources of standing water, such as cisterns and cesspools were oiled once a week, and both towns were provided with running water, eliminating the need for fresh water containers. The results were immediate. The yellow fever epidemic ended within a month and, although it would take time for Panama to shed its reputation as a death trap, the tide was slowly turning. Malaria was also brought under control as brigades were dispatched to burn brush, dig ditches, drain swamps and clear the areas around the settlements being built along the canal route. The malaria-transmitting Anopheles mosquito is susceptible to strong sunshine and wind, so the open, sunny spaces surrounding the new towns were kept continually clipped and trimmed.

The key to successfully building the canal, Stevens had concluded, was the rail line. Not only was it a lifeline, transporting the needed manpower, machinery and supplies back and forth across the Isthmus, it would be the conveyer belt needed to haul away the huge amounts of dirt to be dug at Culebra Cut. His was not a complicated task, he claimed, but challenging for the massive scale of excavation required. So with a workable plan laid out, the man who had built railroads spanning hundreds of miles of rugged northern terrain, now focused his talents and tenacity on a narrow, 50-mile-long jungle corridor, and the transformation was nothing less than extraordinary.

Spraying all ditches and streams with oil was a key method of controlling mosquito larvae in Gorgas' sanitation campaign.

Stevens brought in experienced railroad men from across North America and proceeded to completely overhaul the existing rail line, installing heavier rails that were double-tracked and equipped with cars that were four times the size the French had used. He also recruited conductors, engineers and switchmen to operate the new rail line, while thousands of tradesmen and laborers were put to work building towns alongside it. A cold-storage plant was built at the Cristobal terminal and fresh food, arriving by steamship from New York, was distributed via the rail line, as were fresh loaves of bread from the new bakery.

Stevens was not just building a canal but a modern industrial state in the middle of an isolated tropical wilderness, and a complete infrastructure had to be put in place before the Canal itself could be built. This mammoth undertaking required both skilled tradesmen and unskilled laborers, and six months after his arrival Stevens had tripled the size of the labor force. A year later, by the end of 1906, nearly 24,000 men were working on the Isthmus. The labor force came from all parts of the world, but the majority of skilled white workers were American, representing forty different trades and specialties – from carpenters and bricklayers to cooks and plumbers. Many of the unskilled laborers were from the West Indies, specifically Barbados, where men lined up for the chance to go to Panama and earn a dollar day.

In early 1906, Stevens resumed digging at Culebra Cut, where he had devised an ingenious system of rail tracks which kept the steam shovels in constant motion as loaded dirt trains rolled out and a steady stream of empty cars rolled in. There was still no official decision regarding the type of canal he was supposed to be building, but Stevens had made up his own mind after watching the Chagres River flood its banks during the rainy season. He firmly believed a sea-level canal would be a "narrow tortuous ditch" plagued with endless slides and ships running aground in the shallow channel, whereas a lock canal could harness and utilize the floodwaters of the Chagres, creating a freshwater lake that would form a section of the canal and provide water to the locks. Stevens was summoned to Washington to lobby on behalf of a lock canal, and on June 19, 1906, the Senate voted by a narrow margin to build a lock canal.

Everything was now coming together, and in November of that year Roosevelt paid a visit to Panama, the first time a serving President had left the country while in office. Unlike de Lesseps, who twice visited Panama during the dry season, Roosevelt purposely planned his visit during the rainy season so he could experience Panama at its worst. Eager to see everything, Roosevelt set a pace that left Stevens and everyone else exhausted. His infectious enthusiasm was undampened by the driving rain as he cheerfully waved to bystanders from the back of his train and made impromptu speeches whenever the occasion presented itself. At one point, while touring the Cut, he climbed into the driver's seat of a 95-ton steam shovel where he was obviously delighted to be sitting at the controls while the engineer explained how it worked. He was always on the go and often not where the official schedule said he should be. On one occasion, he and his wife were expected at a formal luncheon in the Tivoli Hotel but they instead walked unannounced into one of the employees' mess halls and sat down to a 30-cent lunch.

No sooner did an exuberant Roosevelt return to Washington, confident of success in Panama, when a fly appeared in the ointment. Stevens, who had won Roosevelt's full confidence, was showing signs of cracking under the pressure. Suffering from insomnia, Stevens wrote what was interpreted as a letter of resignation to Roosevelt in late January 1907. Just as the French chief engineers had complained of the "disorder of detail", Stevens now spoke of the tremendous responsibility and strain he was under due to "the immense amount of detail". These complaints were likely not too startling to Roosevelt, but farther along in the letter came the clincher, wherein Stevens refers to the canal, Roosevelt's "future highway of civilization," as "just a ditch" and

President Roosevelt set a non-stop pace during his tour of Panama in 1906, shown in this famous photo at the controls of a steam shovel.

one of questionable utility at that. Stevens, who dreaded ocean voyages due to his seasickness, did not share Roosevelt's passion for naval supremacy and seagoing trade, but his personal reasons for resigning were never disclosed. Most observers concluded that the man was, quite simply, worn out. As for Roosevelt, he was profoundly disappointed in Stevens for his lack of commitment and sense of duty. To insure that the next man in charge of building the canal stayed on the job, Roosevelt declared he was turning the work over to the Army, to a corps of elite engineers trained at West Point Military Academy, its curriculum patterned after that of France's prestigious Ecole Polytechnique. These were engineering officers instilled with an honored tradition of serving their country. For them, the option of quitting was unthinkable.

The man Roosevelt appointed as chief engineer and chairman of the canal commission was a 48-year-old colonel named **George Goethals**. Born in New York of Flemish parents, Goethals was a model officer and specialist in coastal defenses. The line of authority in Panama had been streamlined at Stevens' request, and Goethals was now supreme commander of the Canal Zone. It quickly became apparent that he was a leader of unbending standards. His efficiency and command of details was unsurpassed, but he lacked the warmth and colorful personality of Stevens, whose departure from Panama was marked by a crowd of workers waving and cheering and singing 'Auld Lang Syne' as his steamer pulled away from the pier at Cristobal.

Goethals had big shoes to fill and his first months in Panama were ones of loneliness as he wrote long letters home to his son who was in his senior year at West Point. He soon earned the respect if not the affection of the canal workers and, despite his stern manner, was regarded as a benevolent despot by holding, each Sunday morning, a

George Goethals, the chief engineer who oversaw the completion of the Panama Canal, was not well-liked but he was widely respected and he got the job done, under budget and ahead of schedule.

court of appeal in his office where workers could voice their grievances and requests while he listened patiently. His decision on each matter was final and few questioned his authority.

Goethals also started a weekly community newspaper, called the Canal Record, which boosted morale and tied the settlements along the rail line together. Weekly excavation statistics for the teams operating the steam shovels and dredges were published, prompting an ongoing competition to capture that week's record. A healthy rivalry was also inspired by Goethal's reorganization of departments into three geographic units, with army engineers assigned to the Atlantic Division (handling design and construction of the Gatun Locks and Dam) and civilian engineers responsible for the locks and dams of the Pacific Division on the other side. The 32 miles of canal in between were called the Central Division, comprised of both army and civilian engineers, whose major challenge was the nine-mile stretch of Culebra Cut. Stevens had laid the foundations for building the canal, but engineers with expertise in hydraulics and the large-scale use of concrete were now needed to construct the colossal locks and dams, and their work would prove to be outstanding.

The American public, and the world at large, was fascinated with the canal's construction and tourists arrived by the shipload to view the proceedings. The biggest attraction was Culebra Cut, where men in straw hats and ladies with long skirts and parasols would watch from grassy bluffs the Herculean efforts of men and machines to claw a canyon into the earth's surface. There was much noise down below, but no confu-

A freighter passes through the Continental Divide between Gold Hill and Contractors Hill. The remains of the Cucaracha Slide are just behind and to the left of the container ship.

sion, only the continuous motion of drilling, blasting, shoveling and dirt hauling. The Cut, called Hell's Gorge by one steam-shovel man, was never silent and always hot and dusty, except when torrential rain turned the dust to mud and threatened to trigger yet another landslide.

While the work went ahead on the canal, a distinct class system emerged on the Isthmus, delineated by race and defined by the pay system which issued wages to the skilled whites in gold currency and to the unskilled blacks in silver currency. Living accommodations also reflected a person's "gold" or "silver" status. Simple barracks were built for the black workers and food provided in mess kitchens. However, most of the West Indians did not like the food or the regimentation of barracks life, and many opted to live in ramshackle huts in the jungle. Their living conditions appeared deplorable but were in fact better than what many of them had known before coming to Panama.

Those on the gold payroll lived in white clapboard buildings with screened porches and manicured lawns. These were divided into two or four apartments, each fully furnished and fitted out with plumbing, electricity and other conveniences, all at government expense. The size of a gold worker's apartment was determined by his salary, which entitled him to one square foot per dollar of monthly pay. To encourage married men to send for their families, wives were also entitled to one square foot per dollar of their husband's monthly pay. The top salaried,

Group of Italian laborers on dirt train at Culebra Cut. Thousands of Italians, Spaniards, West Indians and other nationalities were brought in to work on the construction of the Panama Canal.

married men lived in detached houses, while single men lived in one of the bachelor hotels, usually sharing a room with another man.

The average pay for white workers was $87 per month, plus free housing and medical treatment. A young graduate engineer was paid $250 to start, while a steam-shovel engineer received $310. The annual salary paid to Goethals was $15,000, half of what Stevens had made. These were generous salaries, but no one person or company grew rich building the canal. Salaries were set, there were no commissions, and the only work contracted out was the construction of the gates, which was handled by a Pittsburgh bridge builder, and the manufacture of electric motors by General Electric and of steel parts for the lock walls and gates, which kept 50 mills, foundries, machine shops and specialty fabricators busy in Pittsburgh.

As the years went by, "the work" gained momentum. Everyone took pride in their efforts – they were seeing results and knew they were working together to build something of great significance. They were making history, but the monumental task they faced no longer felt like a "war". In fact, most everyone seemed to be having a good time. The American families living in the Canal Zone enjoyed a strangely carefree lifestyle, one in which their basic needs and recreational pursuits were taken care of by the Commission. A friendly atmosphere and strong sense of community prevailed, along with an abundance of clubs and fraternities. Baseball fields had been built and leagues organized during Steven's' tenure, and other popular events included Saturday night dances, Sunday afternoon picnics and weekly band concerts. Life in fact appeared to be too good to some visitors, who saw the place as some sort of socialist utopia where workers were so completely taken care of, critics wondered how they would adjust to the 'real world' when the canal was completed and they returned to the United States. Others were concerned that the Canal Zone would become a breeding ground for political activists sold on socialism. Yet the zone was anything but political, with the people living there having no say in how things were run and their government located 2,000 miles away in Washington.

In 1912 the Gatun Dam was completed, causing water in the Chagres River to back up and overflow its banks, submerging the lower Chagres valley and creating an artificial lake. As the basin slowly filled, animals fled to high ground and native villages were relocated. Despite setbacks from slides and floods in the Cut, the work proceeded day and night. As dry excavations in the Cut neared completion, Goethals decided to finish the work with dredges doing wet excavation. The rail tracks in the Cut were taken up and all equipment removed. Then, with the workers all assembled at the north end of the Cut, at Gamboa, a charge was set off to remove the dike holding back the Chagres River, and its waters flowed into the Cut.

The Canal's historic opening day finally arrived on August 15, 1914, two weeks after World War I began in Europe and 10 years after the

United States had taken over the project. The Canal was ready for its first official vessel, and although there were numerous dignitaries on hand who were eager to go through on the first boat, Goethals decreed that only Americans who had worked at least seven years on the Canal would enjoy that privilege. A group of them and their families boarded the S.S. Ancon and entered the Canal from the Atlantic. They were lifted up in the locks, then transported across Gatun Lake, before entering the Cut where their vessel traversed the Continental Divide, passing between Gold Hill and Contractors Hill. By this point most of the men were in tears. The boat was then lowered back down to sea level in the Pedro Miguel and Miraflores locks, where it was set free to sail into the Pacific Ocean. The world's greatest shortcut was finally complete.

AFTERWORD

The Panama Canal was an American success story. Built under budget (total cost: $336,650,000) and ahead of schedule, the Canal was the 'moon launch' of the early 20th century. The massive locks, which raise and lower up to 40 ships a day, have worked with the precision of Swiss watches, and to this day a more efficient means of digging the canal could not be applied. Many of the talented men who worked on this engineering marvel went on to other projects, most notably the building of railroads in South and Central America, northern Canada and Alaska.

In 1921, after years of seeking redress, Colombia finally recognized the independence of Panama upon receiving financial compensation from the United States in a lump sum payment of $25 million. In 1939,

Panama's President Mireya Moscoso and former US President Jimmy Carter at the official handover of the Panama Canal in 1999.

the United States agreed to increase Panama's annuity to $434,000, an amount increased again in 1955 to $1,930,000. The United States also undertook to build a high-level bridge at the Pacific entrance to the canal, completed in 1962 and called the Bridge of the Americas.

There remained, however, ongoing grievances on the part of Panama, which sought greater control over the canal. In 1977 under the **Carter** administration, a new treaty was signed which ceded the Panama Canal Zone, now called the Canal Area, to Panama under joint U.S.-Panamanian control until the year 2000, at which time Panama would assume full control. A separate treaty guarantees the permanent neutrality of the canal. When Colonel Manuel Noriega, a known drug smuggler who had seized military control of Panama, gained the country's presidency in December 1989 and declared war on the United States, an American military force of more than 25,000 soldiers attacked Panama City and forced Noriega's surrender. Panama's legitimately elected president was sworn into office during the American invasion and Noriega was taken to the United States to face charges of drug trafficking. Found guilty, he remains in a Florida prison.

Politics have always plagued Panama, both at home and abroad. The opening of the Panama Canal, one of the world's most momentous events, was overshadowed by the outbreak of war in Europe. When the Canal was officially handed over to Panama at the close of the 20th century, the serving American President, **William Clinton**, chose not to attend the ceremony, his absence underlying the ambivalence of the American people regarding their retreat from one of their nation's grandest achievements.

Caribbean bound, a cruise ship enters the last of the Gatun Locks.

ART & ARCHITECTURE

Long before becoming part of Spanish America, regions of Central America and Mexico were inhabited by various agricultural tribes including the Maya. The Maya were an advanced society with an understanding of astronomy and engineering. They built their pyramidal structures oriented to the spring and fall equinoxes, and one of the world's earliest suspension bridges was built by the Maya in the seventh century in Yaxchilan, near Mexico's border with Guatemala. The Mayans also developed a hieroglyphic script, a numerical system and several calendars, some of which were accurate to within 20 seconds over a year.

They practiced agriculture and formed a hierarchical society based on patrilineal descent, in which kinship played a major role. There was no widespread political organization of the Mayans; each city state had its own internal structure of dynastic status and power. Their civic centers followed a pattern in which pyramidal structures and temples were built around a central plaza. Kilns were used to reduce the region's limestone into lime, which was mixed with white earth and water to create the mortar used in constructing the walls, corbelled arches and roof combs of these massive stone temples which were often decorated with elaborate carvings and ceramic paintings.

A common feature of their civic centers was a ball court with stone hoops. Opposing teams played with a heavy rubber ball which players kept in the air by bouncing it off any part of the body except the hands and feet. It's believed that these games were sometimes used as a peaceful means to settle disputes between leaders, with the loser giving up his land and followers to be assimilated with the winning team's people. Another theory is that the losing team offered a human sacrifice – often the team captain.

In poor, rural settlements, the Maya lived in small dwellings made of perishable materials, in contrast to the massive civic centers built of stone.

The Toltec ('master builders') dominated the Maya of the Yucatan when Tulum, a coastal trading center, was constructed.

Mayan civilization reached its height during the Classic period (AD 300 to 900), then went into a rapid decline during which the population plummeted. In the Yucatan, however, settlement persisted due to the arrival of the Toltec from Central Mexico. Also an advanced civilization, Toltec society was based on a warrior aristocracy. These master builders dominated the Yucatan's Maya from the 11th to the 13th century, at which time the nomadic Chichimec brought about the fall of the Toltec empire, soon to be followed by the rise of the Aztec.Toltec art depicts male nobility in feathered headdresses inspired by the brilliant plumage of the quetzal. A chief god of the Toltec and Aztec was Quetzalcoatl, who was identified with the wind and air and symbolized by a feathered serpent.

With the Spanish conquest came the introduction of Spanish art and architecture. The initial structures built by the Spanish, including cathedrals, were military in design and their style was massive and plain. This strain of simple, solid construction prevailed throughout the colonial period, as exemplified by the Spanish missions of California, but other styles were also introduced, including Moorish elements which had long been a part of Spanish design. The Moors occupied Spain for nearly eight centuries (710-1492), during which they built ornate palace complexes, their open courts adorned with a multitude of low arches and marble columns, and Moorish craftsmanship was famous for its glazed tiles, lacy wooden carvings, fine pottery and filigreed jewelry.

When Spanish styles fused with the inventiveness of the New World's native craftsmen, the result was a unique style of art and architecture. And, as Spain's artists made the stylistic transition from Gothic to Renaissance, elaborate design elements were introduced by their colonial counterparts, such as the Plateresque style of contrasting bare walls and ornamental doorways. (Plata is Spanish for silver, and the elaborate ornamentation of Plateresque is suggestive of silver plate.)

In Mexico, where native art was highly developed before the Spanish conquest, the region's art became known as Mexican baroque for its mingling of indigenous and European styles, and for the unique mellowness and richness of color displayed in its paintings. The Latin-American adaptation of Churrigueresque, a highly ornate form of Spanish baroque, is best represented by Mexico City's Cathedral of the Three Kings, which has been described as ultrabaroque for its profusion of opulent surface decoration.

(Opposite Page) 16th-century San Pedro Claver Church (top) and a Spanish colonial street (bottom), both in Cartagena. (Above) La Popa Monastery, Cartagena. (Below) The Aduana in Old San Juan is now a U.S. Customs House.

Common features of Spanish colonial houses, monasteries and other buildings include overhanging grilled balconies, inner courtyards surrounded by arched arcades, red-tile roofs and glazed tiles set in white or pastel adobe walls. Adobe is a brick or building material made of sun-dried earth and straw. The mountainside town of Taxco, founded in 1529 as a silver-mining community and an important stop between Acapulco and Mexico City during the era of colonial trade, is a prime example of the Spanish colonial town.

Mexico's architects have in recent times designed hotels with bold geometric lines and a dramatic scale inspired by past architecture, including the Aztec pyramids, Mayan temples and Moorish palaces. Some noteworthy examples are the Acapulco Princess Hotel and Vidatel Mayan Palace, and the Westin Regina Resort in Los Cabos.

The plant and animal life found in the tropics is unsurpassed in abundance, variety and beauty. Covering only 7% of the earth's land mass, tropical rainforests are home to half of the planet's species. In the dense jungles of lowland regions, where the humidity is high, rainfall is plentiful and temperatures remain hot year round, the foliage is luxuriant, from ground level to the tops of tall trees where interlaced branches form a dense canopy through which little sunlight can penetrate. Bromeliads (air plants) sprout from massive tree trunks, and include countless species of orchids thriving high in the forks of trees where they obtain moisture and nutrients from the air. Ferns grow at the tree bases and rapidly growing woody vines ascend to the canopy in search of light.

The brilliantly colored flowers found amid the verdant growth include the poinsettia, an ornamental shrub named for Joel Roberts Poinsett, an American diplomat who served in Mexico in the early 1800s and introduced this flowering plant to the U.S. A poinsettia is a type of spurge, and some of the other spurges produce poisonous saps which the natives used on arrow tips and to poison fish. The tropical hardwoods, such as mahogany, are deciduous but are considered evergreen because, rather than shed all their leaves at once, they do so sporadically throughout the year.

The widespread cutting of tropical rain forests to clear the land for agriculture has become a controversial practice due to the damage this causes to an area's watershed, where rainfall collects in rivers and lakes that depend on the surrounding forest for their survival. Tree roots prevent soil erosion during heavy rains, and when land is cleared for plantations, the absence of a vast forest to absorb the rainwater has detrimental effects on the area's water table. Trees also supply nutrients to the soil and are a vital source of oxygen.

In mountainous regions of the tropics, a montane (mist) forest grows on the upper slopes and ridges, and consists of small trees and ground vegetation of grasses and ferns. At the summits of the higher peaks is an elfin woodland of matted mosses, lichens and ferns which can survive in wet and windy conditions.

The massive trunk of this tropical tree is supported by buttress roots.

Palm trees grow throughout the tropics, their flowing crowns of frond leaves swaying in the breeze and providing welcome shade. Palms grow to heights of 100 feet or more, their smooth cylindrical stems marked by ringlike scars left by former leaves. The coco palm, from 60 to 100 feet tall, readily establishes itself on shorelines and small islands because its seeds, enclosed in a large buoyant pod, can float. Its fruit is the coconut, a hard woody shell encased in a brown fibrous husk, and a single coco palm can bear more than 200 nuts annually. A coconut has three round scars at one end, its embryo lying against the largest which is easily punctured to drain the nutritious juice inside. Copra, from which oil is extracted to make soaps, cooking oil and suntan lotion, is produced when a ripened coconut is broken open and dried.

(Above) Delicate orchids are plentiful in tropical forests. (Below) Coco palms thrive near beaches in the tropics.

Bananas, coffee and other crops were introduced to the West Indies and Central America for cultivation. Banana plants are widely grown, their leafy, palm-like aspect a familiar sight. The overlapping bases of the banana plant form a false trunk, from which emerges the true stem of a mature plant, bearing the male and female flowers. The latter develop into clusters of upturned bananas, called 'hands', with each banana a 'finger'. The plant is cut down for harvesting, since it bears fruit only the once.

The coffee tree, a small evergreen which yields clusters of fragrant white flowers that mature into small red fruits containing two coffee beans each, thrives at higher altitudes in the tropics, especially in fertile, well-drained soil of volcanic origin. The Spanish brought coffee beans to Spanish America from Africa 250 years ago and some of the world's finest coffee is cultivated in the highlands of Jamaica and Costa Rica where conditions are ideal.

Animal Life

The tropical rainforest is a habitat for hundreds of species of birds and butterflies, including macaws (parrots), quetzals, hummingbirds and keel-billed toucans, the latter a perching bird related to the woodpecker but with an enormous, tusk-shaped bill that is often brightly colored. In Costa Rica alone, some 800 species of birds live in its forests and are joined each winter by millions of birds that migrate from northern temperate zones to the tropics.

Animals inhabiting the tropical forest include monkeys, sloths and jaguars,

(Opposite Page) The wildlife found in a tropical rainforest includes the sloth (top), macaw (middle), toucan (bottom) and iguana (top, this page). Shore life includes crocodiles (middle) and flamingos (bottom).

these big cats becoming arboreal during flood conditions. Spider monkeys are agile acrobats who use their tail as a fifth limb and live in the forest canopy, as do howler monkeys whose bloodcurdling screams can be heard over six miles away. Sloths are about the size of a housecat and they hang upside down from branches while they sleep, eat and travel from tree to tree. Related to the sloth is the course-haired, collared anteater, which is less than two feet long and feeds on ants and termites, licking them up with its sticky tongue. The ring-tailed coatimundi, related to the raccoon, ranges from Peru to Mexico where it is often raised as a pet. An agile tree climber, the coati uses its long snout to grub for insects and roots, and also eats lizards, birds and fruit.

The large diverse iguana family includes species which live in trees along streams and those that inhabit the

(Top) The high-flying frigate bird. (Above) The brown pelican.

desert where they feed on cactus flowers and fruits. A herbivorous lizard, the cold-blooded iguana derives body heat from the sun and basks on rocks and tree tops for much of the day to maintain a body temperature high enough to digest the leaves and fruits it consumes. Peaceful and harmless, iguanas grow to three feet in length and can weigh over 400 pounds. The larger males are gray with a tall crest on the back, while the females retain the bright green body of a young iguana. The female burrows a nest in sandy soil, laying her eggs at the end of a tunnel which she then refills for concealment. When the young iguanas hatch, they dig their way to the surface where they are vulnerable to predators.

Crocodiles are large, carnivorous reptiles which live in swamps or on river banks, slipping into the water to hunt for prey with their powerful jaws. The eyes, ears and nostrils are on top of its head, with valves closing on the ears and nostrils when the crocodile submerges. The average length of a crocodile's flat body and tail is about 10 feet but the saltwater variety is often 14 feet long, sometimes growing to 20 feet. The American crocodile lives in both fresh and salt water in S. Florida, the West Indies and Central America, and does not attack humans without provocation.

Alligators, which are found in the southern United States, are generally less aggressive than crocodiles, have wider snouts and, unlike the crocodile, the lower fourth tooth does not protrude when the mouth is closed. Caimans are similar to alligators, growing to lengths of 15 feet, and are found in Central America.

Wading birds, found in coastal mangroves and lagoons, include the flamingo, a tall, tropical bird related to the stork and heron. The flamingo feeds in the shallow water of marshes and lagoons where it scoops water into its large bill, the serrated edges of which strain algae and shellfish from the water. The bird's pink color comes from its diet of shrimp and other crustaceans containing the pigment carotene. Flamingos build conical mud nests, one to two feet high and one foot across, with mates taking turns incubating the one or two eggs.

The Great Egret (also called Common Egret) is a type of heron that feeds in shallow water on small aquatic life. Threatened at the turn of the century when its white, silky plumage was used to adorn ladies hats, the egret is now a protected species. (See photo on page).

The magnificent frigate bird, also called man-o'-war bird, is the most aerial of the water birds with a wingspread of 7 1/2 feet – the largest in proportion to its body of any bird. Highly skilled fliers, frigate birds can be seen riding thermal updrafts along coastlines for extended periods of time. They feed mainly on fish they spot while in flight and they will harass other birds, such as pelicans, until they drop their catch which is then snatched in midair or retrieved from the water or beach. Its long tail, deeply forked and scissor-like, is opened only while maneuvering in flight.

The brown pelican, in contrast to the frigate bird, is heavy bodied with a long neck and large, flat bill. It too is a graceful flier as well as a skilled swimmer, and it will glide in circles in the air before suddenly diving straight into the water to scoop a fish into the large, expandable pouch hanging from its lower jaw. Brown pelicans nest on shore and the young feed from their parent's pouch.

CORAL REEFS

Some of the most unusual animal life in the tropics is found beneath the water's surface where coral reefs, formed by living organisms, are home to a fascinating variety of fish and other sea creatures. These underwater habitats are formed by soft, saclike animals called polyps. Smaller than a pea, each polyp secretes an exoskeleton of limestone. A colony forms by polyps budding new polyps, with all the buds remaining connected. These tiny polyps, each living inside its own limestone cavity, feed mainly at night on floating plankton which they trap with their extended tentacles. Microscopic algae grow within the polyp tissues and are collectively responsible for the coral colony's vivid colors. These symbiotic algae, called zooxanthellae, need sunlight and clear water to take up carbon dioxide and photosynthesize, thus providing an internal supply of oxygen and organic nutrients to the polyp.

When coral colonies die, their surfaces are recolonized by new corals or other types of invertebrates, such as sponges or soft corals. Layers of skeletal materials gradually accumulate over time to form a coral reef. Although corals live in temperate as well as tropical waters, coral reefs are found only in tropical waters, within 30 degrees of the equator, where the water temperature remains above 70 degrees Fahrenheit year round.

Coral reefs that extend from shore are called fringing reefs and those separated from shore by a wide lagoon are called barrier reefs. Barrier

Green Sea Turtle
Queen Angelfish
Moray Eel
Brain Coral

A Coral Reef Community

Some of the most unusual animal life in the tropics is found beneath the water's surface where coral reefs, formed by living organisms, are home to a fascinating variety of fish and other sea creatures.

Gray Angelfish

Trumpetfish

reefs rise like fortress walls from the sea floor and are habitat for tropical fish and large predators which feed here on the smaller fish. Fringe reefs, often within a few yards of the water's surface, serve as nurseries for hundreds of small tropical fish, as do mangroves which grow along shorelines. Their tangled roots and dense branches are saltwater tolerant, and they help stabilize coastlines by absorbing wave action.

Coral reefs also deflect incoming waves, their porous character allowing the absorption and dissipation of a pounding sea. In bays protected by strategically placed reefs, the steady shifting of particulate debris from the coral colony onto shore results in a beach of fine sand. Adjacent to reefs are seagrass beds, where sturdy stems and roots of underwater plants weave together to form a mat that stabilizes the shallow bottom and provides food for sea turtles, manatees, conchs and reef fishes. Seagrass beds also anchor sediments, helping maintain the water clarity required for a healthy reef which needs sunlight to survive.

Environmental pressures in the form of coastal development, water pollution, over fishing and increased recreational use have all threatened the survival of coral reefs. Excessive nutrients in the water, often caused by sewage and agricultural run-off, can trigger algal blooms that cloud the water and prevent sunlight from penetrating and activating photosynthesis in the corals' symbiotic algae. These unwanted blooms of algae can also attach to the surfaces of corals and grow until portions of the reef are smothered. Protective measures are being taken in the Florida Keys and other areas, which include the installation of mooring buoys so that no anchors are dropped from boats, and prohibiting snorkelers and divers from touching and taking pieces of coral.

Most reef-forming corals belong to the stony or hard group of corals. There are many different types of hard corals, some branch-like, others rounded, their distinctive shapes determined by the budding pattern of the various polyp species. Corals are often named for their appearance and some common hard corals include elkhorn, with its thick stocky branches, and staghorn, which has smaller branches. Other branching colonies include flower, finger, pencil and ivory corals. Pillar and ribbon corals grow upright in clusters, and brain corals grow in rounded shapes. Soft corals also help build the reefs, their feathery forms including sea fans and gorgonians in a variety of vivid colors. Sea anemones, unlike the corals, do not have a skeleton and often look like flowers when their feeding end is open and tentacles are fully extended. Brilliantly colored sponges, another aquatic animal, attach themselves to coral reefs, often in colonies. They vary in shape and size, and show little movement.

The shimmering tropical fish found along coral reefs come in an assortment of shapes, sizes, colors and markings which often change as the juvenile fish matures. Angelfishes are among the most beautiful of the small fish that inhabit shallow reefs, their flattened, disc-like shapes allowing them to slip through nooks and crannies as they feed on sponges and the ectoparasites of other fishes. Butterflyfishes are similar to angelfishes with yellow their dominant color. They travel in pairs, feeding on coral polyps, sea anemones, tubeworms and algae.

The size of reef fish can vary, the butterflyfishes growing to about 6 inches, the angelfishes ranging from one to two feet in length, and the tiny cherubfish, which prefers deepwater reefs, reaching less than three inches in size. Parrotfishes begin life as drably colored females then turn into males with gaudy green and blue scales. They have molar-like teeth with which they grind algae off the corals, producing sand in the process.

Other members of the coral reef community include the spiny lobster which hides in crevices by day and feeds at night, as does the moray eel - a snake-like fish which is harmless unless provoked. The tiny sea horse (ranging in length from 2 to 8 inches) is usually found swimming upright among the seagrasses, using its tail to hold onto a seaweed when resting. The seahorse, which utters musical sounds during the mating embrace, belongs to the same family as the pipefishes, with which it shares a unique breeding habit in which the female's eggs are forced into a pouch on the male's underside, where they are fertilized and nourished until expelled as miniature versions of the adult.

Coral reefs attract a variety of feeding creatures, including **sharks**, which are heavy fishes with skeletons made of cartilage. A shark must keep moving in order to breathe by taking water in through the mouth and passing it over the gills which form a line of slits down both sides of the fish. There are over 250 species of shark, ranging in size from 2 feet to 50 feet. Abundant in warm waters, not all sharks are predatory and few are interested in humans. Those considered harmless are the

A reef shark looks for prey near a barrier reef.

(Left) Southern stingrays are common in the Caribbean, living near shores and in bays. (Opposite page) The loggerhead turtle grows to 450 pounds and inhabits the subtropics. A 200-mile stretch midway along Florida's east coast is a popular nesting area for Atlantic loggerheads.

Nurse Shark, which grows to 12 feet in length, and the Caribbean reef shark, which grows to about 8 feet on a diet of reef fish, octopus, crabs and lobster. To detect their prey, sharks have electromagnetic senses on their snouts, which is why professional shark feeders wearing stainless-steel mesh suits and gloves can hypnotize a reef shark with a gentle stroke of the hand. Not so placid are the hammerhead and tiger sharks, which are predatory and dangerous to humans.

Rays are flat-bodied fish related to the shark. Shaped like a kite with winglike pectoral fins which propel it through the water, a ray also has a long whiplike tail. There are three basic groups of ray: mantas, eagles and stingrays. Mantas are the largest, up to 22 feet in width and 3,000 pounds in weight. Mantas and eagles are active rays whereas stingrays are bottom dwellers, lying like rugs on the sea floor as they dredge up shellfish and other small animals. The stingray's eyes and spiracles (breathing orifices) are on top of the head, its mouth and gill slits on the underside. Southern stingrays are common along Caribbean reefs, the female growing up to six feet in width. They have rows of spines along their tail which contain a poison that can inflict pain and be fatal to humans. Stingrays defend themselves against sharks by lashing with their tails but they rarely attack humans unless provoked or stepped on. They have no teeth, but their jaws are strong for grinding and sucking, which is why snorkelers at Stingray City on Grand Cayman will sometimes receive a hickey from a nuzzling stingray looking for food.

Turtles are the world's oldest surviving reptile, in existence since the time of the earliest dinosaurs some 200 million years ago. Equipped with toeless, oar-like legs, these ancient mariners can swim at speeds approaching 20 miles per hour, and some will travel thousands of ocean miles to reach their nesting sites. **Pacific loggerhead** turtles have been tracked crossing the Pacific Ocean from Yaku Shima in southern Japan to Baja California. The voyage for these 300-pound swimmers can take two to six years along a line in the ocean where cool water from the north and warm water from the south meets and where buoyant jellyfish, a favorite food of sea turtles, are trapped as the plankton-rich cooler water sinks beneath the warmer water.

Once a source of food for sailors, the green turtle is now protected by law, as are the hawksbill, olive ridley, leatherback and **loggerhead**, the latter named for its large head (up to 10 inches wide) and powerful jaws used to crush clams and crabs. The **green** turtle, named for the greenish color of its body fat, is a plant eater and can be seen grazing on seagrasses or sleeping under reef ledges. The **hawksbill** turtle, named for its narrow, pointed beak with which it pries sponges from coral reefs, was hunted nearly to extinction for its beautiful tortoiseshell, which was used in making jewelry. The **leatherback** has a rubbery dark shell and is the largest of all turtles, reaching lengths of eight feet and weighing up to 1,100 pounds. The **olive ridley** is one of the smallest with a shell length of 30 inches or less, and seabirds will sometimes hitch a ride on the back of an olive ridley as it swims across hundreds of miles of Pacific Ocean.

The female nests on beaches where the warm sand incubates her eggs. She drags herself onto shore in the night, selects a site and digs a hole in which 100 or more eggs are laid. After covering them, she returns to the sea having spent one to three hours on shore under cover of darkness. The two-inch-long hatchlings emerge two months later, again in the cool of the night, and crawl into the water. For years, the catching of females while they laid their eggs was a major factor in the marine turtle's decline, for as few as one in a thousand hatchlings survive to adulthood and it can take up to 50 years for some turtles to reach sexual maturity, their average lifespan being 150 years.

The olive ridley, and its Atlantic cousin the Kemp's ridley, are the only sea turtles that stage *arribidas* (arrivals), during which thousands of females laden with eggs will crawl ashore en masse and jostle for position as they dig their nests in the sand.

WHALES

Several species of large baleen whales frequent the warm waters off Mexico each winter, including the gray whale and the humpback. Baleen whales are filter feeders who eat schooling fish, plankton and other small organisms, which they catch by swimming with their mouths wide open. When the whale closes its massive mouth, it raises its tongue to force the scooped water out the sides where the bristles of its baleen plates trap the food.

Humpbacks feed on schools of small fish, the pleats on the sides of their mouths creating a pouch large enough to hold six humans.

Dolphins are highly intelligent, athletic and sociable, often seen travelling in large groups in the bow waves of ships.

The Pacific coast of Baja California is one of the best places in the world to sight **gray whales**. Each fall, an estimated 11,000 to 15,000 gray whales migrate south from their feeding ground in the Beaufort Sea to the Baja's warm-water lagoons where the females give birth and nurse their young from January to early April. A fully grown gray whale is 40-45 feet in length and weighs up to 40 tons. Strongly migratory but slow swimmers, gray whales travel near shore on their twice-annual migration between Mexico and the Beaufort Sea.

The **humpback** is about the same size as the gray whale, and it also migrates twice a year, spending the summer in Alaskan coastal waters, then heading south to breed and calve in tropical waters. December and January are the birthing months, following a 12-month gestation period. Cows give birth to a single calf weighing about a ton and measuring 12 to 15 feet in length. Calves are born without a blubber layer and nurse on their mother's milk which contains 50 percent butter fat. Humpbacks travel in threesomes - a female, her calf and a male escort. The male earns his position as escort by serenading the female with a repeated pattern of sounds at depths of 60 feet or more. If this doesn't win her, the male will challenge her current escort by smacking him with his fluked tail which packs 8,000 pounds of muscle and, studded with barnacles, is a humpback's most powerful weapon. No two humpback tails are alike and scientists identify each whale by the pattern on its flukes which are visible when the whale raises its tail high out of the water before making deep dive.

The **common dolphin**, a small toothed whale about eight feet long, is often seen travelling in large groups, riding the bow waves of ships. Wave riding is also a favorite pastime of the acrobatic **bottlenosed dolphin**, which averages 9 feet in length and weighs about 350 pounds.

These playful creatures swim in large groups and can reach speeds up to 30 mph. With a beak holding 200 teeth, the bottlenose feeds on small fish, crustaceans and squid. When pursued by a shark or killer whale, dolphins will try to out swim their predator or, as a group, they will try battering it to death. Bottlenosed dolphins communicate with an extensive array of sounds using the air sacs and valves in their blowhole, and these clicking sounds are used for echolocation (projecting a sound beam and listening to the echo) with which dolphins locate prey and avoid predators. The bottlenose likes inshore waters and is friendly to humans, often approaching close enough to be touched. Tales of dolphins rescuing people from drowning date back to Greek mythology.

In contrast to the gregarious bottlenosed dolphin is the reclusive **manatee**. Also called sirenian or sea cow, this large marine mammal descends from the same primitive group of land mammals as the elephant. The manatee spends its entire life in the water, surfacing to breathe at least every 15 or 20 minutes through nostrils on the upper surface of its snout which close tightly like valves when the animal submerges. Shy and completely harmless, manatees live in warm, shallow and sheltered waters where they consume up to 100 pounds of vegetation daily. The manatee can grow to 12 feet in length and weigh over 500 pounds, its thick, heavy body covered with hairless gray-brown skin. A sluggish, nocturnal bottom feeder, it propels itself with two weak flippers and a beaver-like tail. The female gives birth to one calf every two to five years and uses her flippers to hold the nursing calf to her chest. Both parents care for their young, one holding it while the other dives for food. An endangered species, the manatee has no natural predators but is vulnerable to injury from boat propellers, and is found in the coastal waters of Central America, the West Indies and Florida, where it's protected by law.

A pair of manatees surfaces in the coastal waters of Florida.

PART II

The Voyage and The Ports

The Caribbean
Gulf of Mexico
FORT LAUDERDALE
MIAMI
Nassau
BAHAMAS
Atlantic Ocean
0 150 300
Miles
N
COZUMEL
GRAND CAYMAN
CUBA
US VIRGIN ISLANDS
St. Thomas
DOMINICAN REPUBLIC
San Juan
Ocho Rios
Kingston
HAITI
PUERTO RICO
MEXICO
BELIZE
JAMAICA
GUATEMALA
HONDURAS
Caribbean Sea
ARUBA
CURACAO
BARBADOS
NICARAGUA
PACIFIC OCEAN
Panama Canal
Cartagena
TRINIDAD
San Jose
Limon
Colon
COSTA RICA
VENEZUELA
PANAMA
COLOMBIA
©OCEAN CRUISE GUIDES

CHAPTER ONE 

THE CARIBBEAN

The island-dotted Caribbean Sea is perfectly suited to a cruise vacation. No where else in the world can travellers visit such a diversity of destinations, in a tropical setting, and do so on any type of cruise vessel – from the dazzling new megaships to the small sailing ships which anchor off secluded beaches for picnic lunches.

Sailing vessels have long plied these tranquil waters, riding the constant trade winds which temper the region's heat and humidity. Then, in the 1960s, the concept of cruising was pioneered in the Caribbean when jet planes became the new mode of trans-Atlantic travel and shipping companies sought alternative roles for their ocean liners. Today the Caribbean is the most popular cruising area in the world. The beauty of its beaches is legendary and, with almost no tidal range, its turquoise waters remain warm year round – ideal conditions for swimming, snorkeling and other water sports.

Yet there's more to the Caribbean than white sand and swaying palm trees. The West Indies were once the most important colonial region in the world when sugarcane was cultivated here, and each island nation has its own history and local flavor, an exotic mix of African, European, Indian and Asian cultures called Creole. The African influence is most evident – in the people themselves, their love of rhythmic music and the bold use of color in everything from folk art and batik clothing to the colonial architecture, be it a canary yellow fort, a flamingo pink church or a lime green government building. West Indian homes boast bright wooden shutters and gingerbread fretwork, and the local fishermen paint their skiffs a combination of rainbow reds, yellows and blues, inspired no doubt by the aquamarine sea which shimmers across the colorful corals and tropical fish.

There is no mystery to the appeal the Caribbean holds for travellers yearning to escape the grey grip of winter. The senses are reawakened there, where the air is soft and warm, carrying the fragrance of flowers and sweet spices. Cruise ships often pull into port as dawn is breaking, treating their passengers to the magic of a seaborne arrival as the golden pink sun rises above a rippled sea and the verdant shores of a volcanic island draw ever nearer. The departure is equally special, the ship easing away from shore and heading out to sea as the setting sun casts its Caribbean colors across the sky. For a vacation of relaxation and romance, nothing surpasses a cruise to these islands of endless summer.

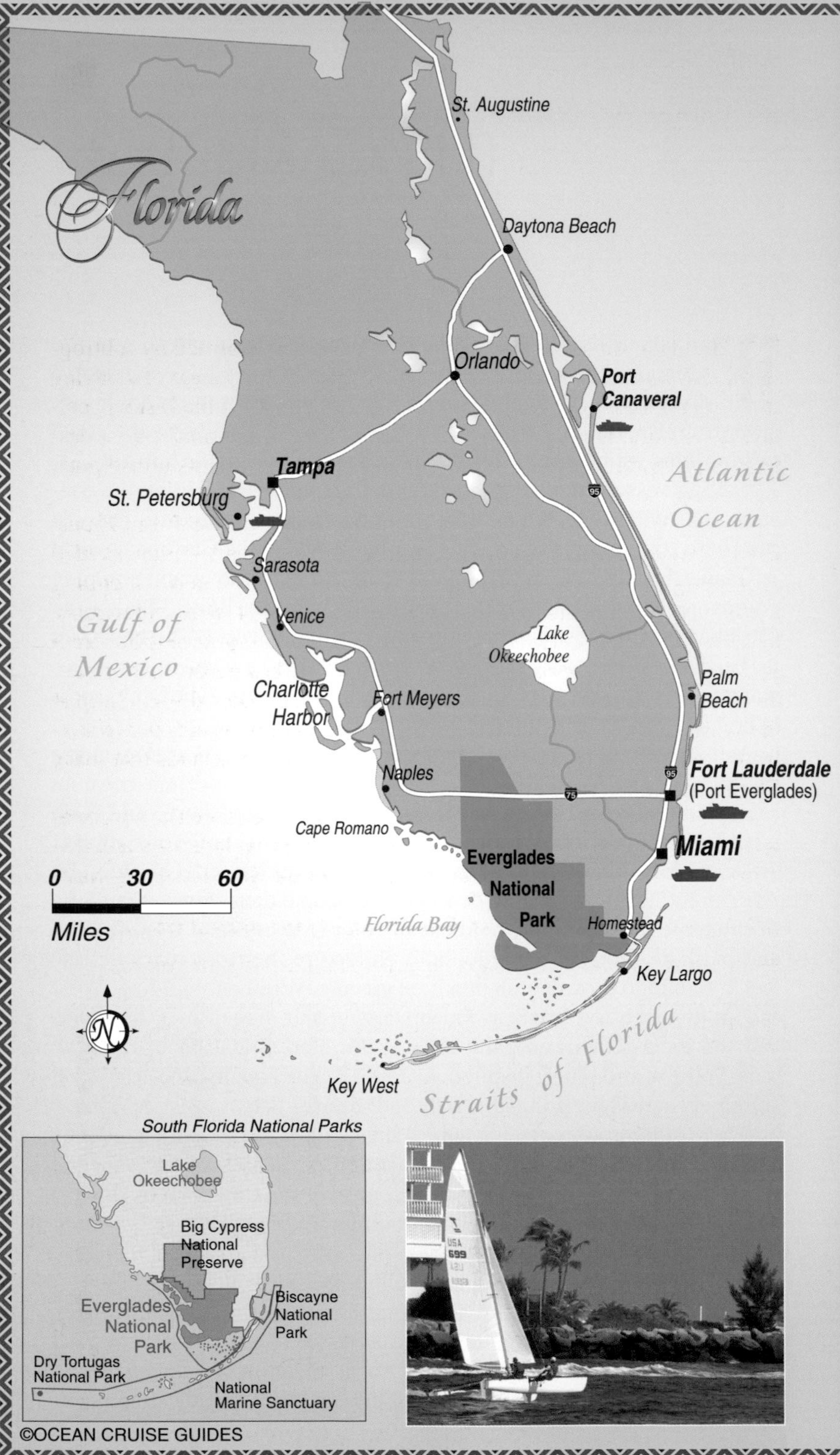
Florida
St. Augustine
Daytona Beach
Orlando
Port
Canaveral
Tampa
St. Petersburg
Atlantic
Ocean
Sarasota
Venice
Gulf of
Mexico
Lake
Okeechobee
Charlotte
Harbor
Fort Meyers
Palm
Beach
Naples
Fort Lauderdale
(Port Everglades)
Cape Romano
Miami
Everglades
National
Park
0
30
60
Miles
Florida Bay
Homestead
Key Largo
Straits of Florida
Key West
South Florida National Parks
Lake
Okeechobee
Big Cypress
National
Preserve
Everglades
National
Park
Biscayne
National
Park
Dry Tortugas
National Park
National
Marine Sanctuary
©OCEAN CRUISE GUIDES

FLORIDA

Florida is America's answer to the Caribbean. Warmed by subtropical waters, cooled by trade winds, this southern state of swaying palms and coral cays has much in common with the history, culture and natural habitat of the West Indies. An international tourist destination, Florida is also a gateway to the Caribbean, and its cruise ports are among the busiest in the world.

Florida counts its visitors, and cruise passengers, in the millions. Every conceivable 'fun in the sun' attraction is here – palm-shaded swimming pools, championship golf courses, tennis camps, shopping malls, sporting events and theme parks galore. Yet, it is water more than anything that defines Florida. The sea is readily accessible from any point in the state and some of the best beaches lie on barrier cays that line much of the splendid coastline. And the water doesn't stop at the seashore. Rivers and canals meander past cypress stands and waterfront homes, linking many of the lakes, lagoons and wetlands that make Florida an angler's paradise.

Lake Okeechobee is the largest of these lakes and is a chief source of water (along with Big Cypress Swamp) for the Everglades – a marshy, tropical savanna extending southward to Florida Bay. Covering more

Miami, a former trading post, is today one of the busiest cruise ports in the world, with luxury ships departing its harbor year round.

than 4,000 square miles, the Everglades is a unique wilderness region of slow-flowing water. Sawgrass and hammocks (island-like masses of vegetation) grow here in the solidly packed black muck which has formed over millions of years as vegetation decays in the nearly stagnant water. Everglades National Park includes Florida Bay and its many islets and islands, and contains a great variety of flora and fauna, including palms, pines and mangrove forests, and such endangered species as the crocodile, alligator, egret and bald eagle.

Birdlife abounds in Florida, where critical wetlands are now protected as wildlife refuges. A shoreline of seemingly endless beaches and holiday resorts has become dotted with parks, preserves and recreation areas. These conservation measures follow a century of unbridled development in which men with a passion for building – be it hotels, railroads, planned communities or theme parks – were attracted to Florida's broad, untouched landscapes.

The first 'developer' to arrive on Florida's shores was Spanish explorer Ponce de Leon. Seeking the fabled Fountain of Youth, he landed near the site of St. Augustine in 1513 during the Easter season (Pascua Florida) and mistook the long peninsula for an island, which he claimed for Spain. Turning south, he explored the coast to Key West, then headed up the west side to Cape Romano before retracing his route to Miami Bay and returning to his settlement in Puerto Rico where gold and slave labor had made him a wealthy man. The next year the Spanish king commissioned Ponce de Leon to colonize the 'isle of Florida' but it wasn't until 1521 that he returned with 200 men, farm implements and domestic animals, his two vessels landing in the vicinity of Charlotte Harbor.

The development-minded conquistador's plans were, however, thwarted by the Native Americans already living in the area. Called Caloosas, they built their dwellings on high rectangular mounds surrounded by waterways and boat basins. These terraced mounds were interconnected with ramps and shell-covered causeways and canals, some of which led to burial mounds and other midden mounds where waste was discarded. Temples, storehouses and leaders' homes were built on the tallest mounds. These people, their urban culture over 2,000

In 1513, the Spanish explorer Ponce de Leon landed near Cape Romano on Florida's Gulf Coast.

years old, did not take kindly to the sight of strangers attempting to subdivide their land, and they attacked the Spanish party, fatally wounding Ponce de Leon with a poisoned arrow. The Spaniards retreated, sailing immediately for Cuba where their leader died.

Spain abandoned any further plans to colonize Florida until the French began encroaching upon the area. St. Augustine was founded in 1565 to protect Spain's shipping route through the Straits of Florida. England, intent on expanding her American colonial holdings, was the next European country to threaten Spain's hold on Florida. At the end of the Seven Years War, England acquired Florida in the Treaty of Paris (1763), then returned it to Spain in 1783 at the conclusion of the American Revolution. But Spain's hold on Florida remained tenuous and in 1819 Florida was reluctantly ceded to the United States, with official U.S. occupation taking place in 1821. Andrew Jackson was appointed military governor and the next year Florida became a territory, with settlers from other states soon establishing cotton and tobacco plantations around the new capital of Tallahassee. The resident Native Americans – the Seminoles – resisted being displaced and a small band fled to the Everglades where their descendants live today on reservations near Lake Okeechobee.

Florida, a slave-holding state, was admitted to the Union in 1845, but seceded in 1861 to join the Confederacy. After the Civil War, Florida's new constitution provided for black suffrage and the state was readmitted to the Union in 1868. A decade later, New York financier Henry Flagler paid a visit to Florida's east coast. He envisioned the state as the perfect winter

The Breakers in Palm Beach was first built by Henry Flagler in the late 1800s and rebuilt in 1926.

Scenic Port Everglades is Florida's second busiest cruise port and a short drive from Fort Lauderdale's beaches and airport.

playground and proceeded to build a business empire of railroads, steamships and palatial hotels, while anonymously donating to the construction of schools, churches and hospitals. Another industrial tycoon, Henry Plant, built railroads and hotels on Florida's west coast. Sections of the Everglades were drained, starting in 1906, and land booms caused real estate prices to soar one year and plummet the next.

Following World War II, sustained growth came with manufacturing, especially in aeronautics after the opening of the John F. Kennedy Space Center at Cape Canaveral. Florida's population, now over 14 million, continues to grow with thousands of retired persons moving here. Nations of the Caribbean, most notably Cuba, are also a source of immigrants. In 1980, when Fidel Castro briefly opened the port of Mariel, more than 100,000 Cuban refugees were boat-lifted to Florida.

Florida's resources are diverse. A leading grower of citrus fruits, as well as vegetables, sugarcane and tobacco, the state also supports cattle

A passing pageantry of river vessels can be enjoyed along the pleasant pathways of Fort Lauderdale's Riverwalk.

and dairy farming, and the sea is a source of crab, lobster and shrimp. The state's timber is yellow pine, from which lumber and wood products are produced, and its mineral resources include phosphate rock, gravel and sand.

Florida is not without problems, however. Most pressing, many would say, is the degradation of the natural environment, with south Florida containing one of the most threatened wildlife habitats in the country. In the 1920s a ring dike was built around Lake Okeechobee to prevent water from blowing off the lake during hurricanes. This diking, along with land development in Big Cypress Swamp, disrupted the natural flow of water into the Everglades, and damaged plant and animal life. In the 1980s Florida instigated a massive conservation project which called for the reflooding of drained swampland and restoring to their natural state those areas previously cleared for agriculture and development. Sugar and vegetable farms have reduced the amount of phosphorus fertilizer discharged from their fields, and cleaner water is now running off their land into the imperiled Everglades ecosystem.

Tourism, which has contributed to Florida's environmental problems, may prove to be beneficial in the long run as areas of natural and cultural significance are preserved for the enjoyment of visitors, residents and, most importantly, for posterity.

FORT LAUDERDALE

The 'Venice of America', Fort Lauderdale is interwoven with more than 270 miles of natural and artificial waterways, including a navigable canal that connects with Lake Okeechobee. In neighborhoods crisscrossed with canals, both cars and yachts can be seen parked outside the palm-shaded homes.

Situated on the New River, this retirement and resort city of some 150,000 residents was settled around a fort built by Major William Lauderdale in 1837-38, during the Seminole War. Fort Lauderdale was incorporated in 1911 and the city grew rapidly during the Florida land boom of the 1920s. Its suburbs continue to expand, and today close to 4.5 million people live in the metro area. Fort Lauderdale has one of the most popular beaches in the country, one of the largest marinas in North America, and a cruise port that is fast becoming one of the busiest in the world.

Fort Lauderdale's seaport was originally a small lake used by recreational boaters. Locally known as Bay Mabel Harbor, it came to the attention of a developer and businessman named Joseph Young who moved to the area in the early 1920s, purchased 1,440 acres adjacent to the lake, and created the Hollywood Harbor Development Company. On February 28, 1927, expectant spectators gathered to watch an explosion that would remove the lake's rock barrier to the ocean. At the appointed time, President Calvin Coolidge pressed a detonator in the White House, but nothing happened. Nonetheless, the harbor was offi-

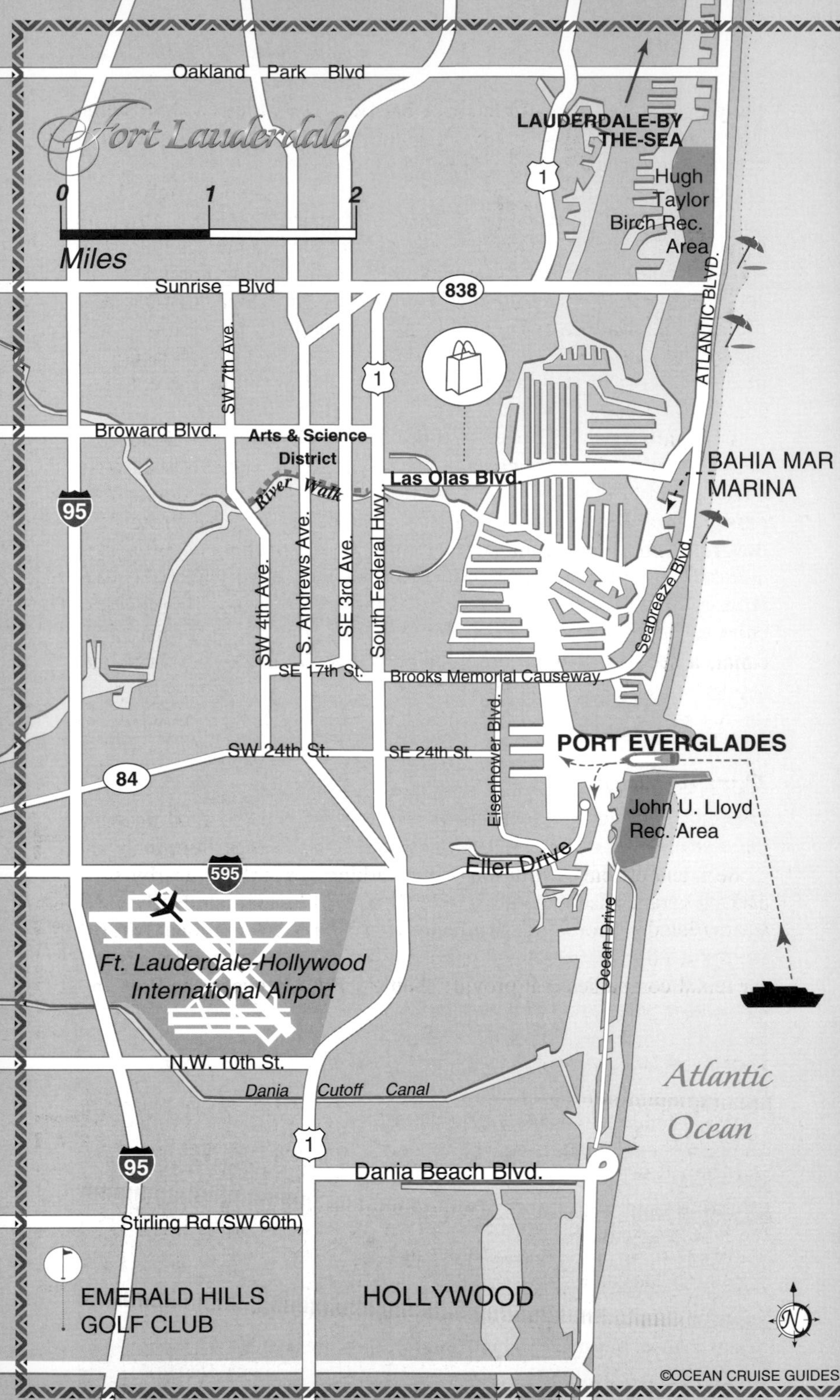

Fort Lauderdale
0
1
2
Miles
Oakland Park Blvd
LAUDERDALE-BY THE-SEA
Hugh Taylor Birch Rec. Area
1
Sunrise Blvd
838
ATLANTIC BLVD.
SW 7th Ave.
1
Broward Blvd.
Arts & Science District
River Walk
Las Olas Blvd.
BAHIA MAR MARINA
95
SW 4th Ave.
S. Andrews Ave.
SE 3rd Ave.
South Federal Hwy.
Seabreeze Blvd.
SE 17th St.
Brooks Memorial Causeway
Eisenhower Blvd.
PORT EVERGLADES
SW 24th St.
SE 24th St.
84
John U. Lloyd Rec. Area
Eller Drive
595
Ocean Drive
Ft. Lauderdale-Hollywood International Airport
N.W. 10th St.
Dania Cutoff Canal
Atlantic Ocean
1
95
Dania Beach Blvd.
Stirling Rd.(SW 60th)
EMERALD HILLS GOLF CLUB
HOLLYWOOD
N
©OCEAN CRUISE GUIDES

cially opened that day and the rock barrier was removed a short while later. In 1930, the new seaport was named Port Everglades – chosen from submissions to a naming contest.

The port is located opposite the **John U. Lloyd Beach State Recreation Area**, situated on 251 acres of barrier island separating the Intracoastal Waterway from the Atlantic Ocean. The park is named in memory of a local attorney whose efforts helped bring about its creation. The park is entered at its south end via Dania Beach Boulevard, and its broad flat beach – popular for swimming and sunning – is also one of Broward County's most important sea turtle nesting beaches. A jetty at the north end is excellent for fishing and watching the comings and goings of cruise ships and small sailing craft.

The park also contains an open-air Environmental Education Facility. This timber structure and adjoining waterfront boardwalk were built by Port Everglades in 1991 as part of a wildlife protection/awareness project which includes a comprehensive Manatee Protection Program. The Florida manatee is a protected species and in winter months these sluggish sea mammals frequent the Port where they are attracted to the heated effluent from the Florida Power & Light plant. When calving mothers were found to be utilizing the FPL discharge canal, a section of it became designated a 'Manatee Nursery' and access to it was restricted. Manatees and other marine life also frequent the mangrove-lined tidal waterway that runs down the middle of the John Lloyd park.

GETTING AROUND

Located south of downtown, Port Everglades is an artificial deepsea port with a short, straight entrance channel. Its passenger terminals are modern and efficient, with long-term parking available in nearby self-parking garages. Less than two miles from Fort Lauderdale/Hollywood International Airport (and 30 minutes from Miami International Airport via I-95), Port Everglades is serviced by a fleet of taxis and by several car rental companies that provide shuttle service between the Port and their rental lots.

Port Everglades viewed from John U. Lloyd Recreation Area.

Water taxis and tour boats are a popular way to explore Fort Lauderdale's scenic waterways. Water Taxi picks up at most waterfront hotels and restaurants north of the Brooks Memorial Causeway. Call 467-6677 for a pick-up; the one-way fare between two points is $7.50, the round-trip fare is $14; and an all-day pass is $16.

SHOPPING, DINING & STAYING

Las Olas Boulevard, the 'Rodeo Drive' of Fort Lauderdale, is lined with boutiques, galleries and several fine restaurants, including Mark's Las Olas and the Grill Room at the Riverside Hotel, a heritage property built in 1936. In Lauderdale-By-The-Sea, the Sea Watch serves superb seafood, and American cuisine can be enjoyed at Burt & Jack's, co-owned by movie star Burt Reynolds and situated on a scenic lookout near the passenger terminals of Port Everglades. The huge Sawgrass Mills Mall on Sunrise Boulevard contains more than a mile of shops and bills itself as the 'World's Largest Outlet Mall'.

Where to Stay – For a taste of 'Old Florida', the family-owned Riverside Hotel on Las Olas Boulevard is distinctly decorated with tropical murals and finely appointed rooms, with a pool area providing views of passing river traffic. The beachfront Lago Mar Resort Hotel & Club offers an elegant atmosphere with its bougainvillea-bordered swimming lagoon and luxurious lobby. Four restaurants, two swimming pools, tennis courts and miniature golf are among its extensive facilities. North of downtown, in Lauderdale-by-the-Sea, the wide array of comfortable motels includes A Little Inn By The Sea with its bright and airy rooms overlooking a beach-side swimming pool.

Beautiful beaches line the coasts of Florida, including this stretch of sand at Lauderdale-By-The-Sea.

Golf – There are more than 50 golf courses in the Fort Lauderdale area. The Emerald Hills Golf Club in Hollywood, about two miles south of the airport, is one of many open to the public.

Downtown – The **Greater Fort Lauderdale Convention & Visitors Bureau** is located at 200 E. Las Olas Boulevard. At the western end of Las Olas is **Riverwalk**, a lovely promenade on the north bank of the New River. Attractions in the Riverwalk area – also known as the **Arts and Science District** – include Esplanade Park which features outdoor exhibits on astronomy and navigation; the Museum of Art; a complex housing the Museum of Discovery and Science, and Blockbuster IMAX Theater; the Broward Center for the Performing Arts; and the Fort Lauderdale Historical Society Museum. The eastern half of Las Olas runs through an exclusive residential area of canal-lined streets called **The Isles**.

Beaches – Nearby is the Bahia Mar Marina and the International Swimming Hall of Fame. To the east lies Fort Lauderdale's famous stretch of beach which used to attract crowds of college students on spring break. They go elsewhere now, and the beach has been given a multi-million-dollar facelift which makes for a very pleasant morning stroll. A wave-themed beachfront promenade consists of wide walkways, crested gateways and neon lamp posts. Across the road from the beach is the Hugh Taylor Birch State Recreation Area with nature trails, picnic facilities and a museum.

The oceanfront boulevard proceeds north to **Lauderdale-by-the-Sea**, an inviting stretch of sand, restaurants and motels. Beyond is Pompano Beach, Hillsboro Beach and Deerfield Beach, and south of Fort Lauderdale are the beaches of John U. Lloyd State Recreation Area, Dania and Hollywood. There are 23 miles of beach in the Fort Lauderdale area, the shoreline punctuated by fishing piers.

NORTH OF FORT LAUDERDALE

The coastal drive north of Fort Lauderdale to Palm Beach follows a scenic highway, bordered by the Atlantic Ocean to the east and the Intracoastal Waterway to the west. Spanish River Park, in Boca Raton, provides access to an ocean beach and contains a lagoon, nature trails and picnic sites.

Palm Beach is where you'll see some of Florida's most palatial estates along Ocean Boulevard, including the Kennedy compound (President Kennedy's Winter White House) at 1095 North Ocean Boulevard which the family sold in 1995. For a taste of Old Florida, visit The Breakers (on County Road) – a luxury grand hotel originally built by tycoon Henry Flagler in the late 1800s. Rebuilt in 1926, the resort's Italian Renaissance architecture includes vaulted ceilings, frescoes and Florentine fountains outside the main entrance. Nearby, on Cocoanut Row, is Whitehall – a mansion built by Flagler in 1901 which is now a museum containing original furnishings and railroad exhibits.

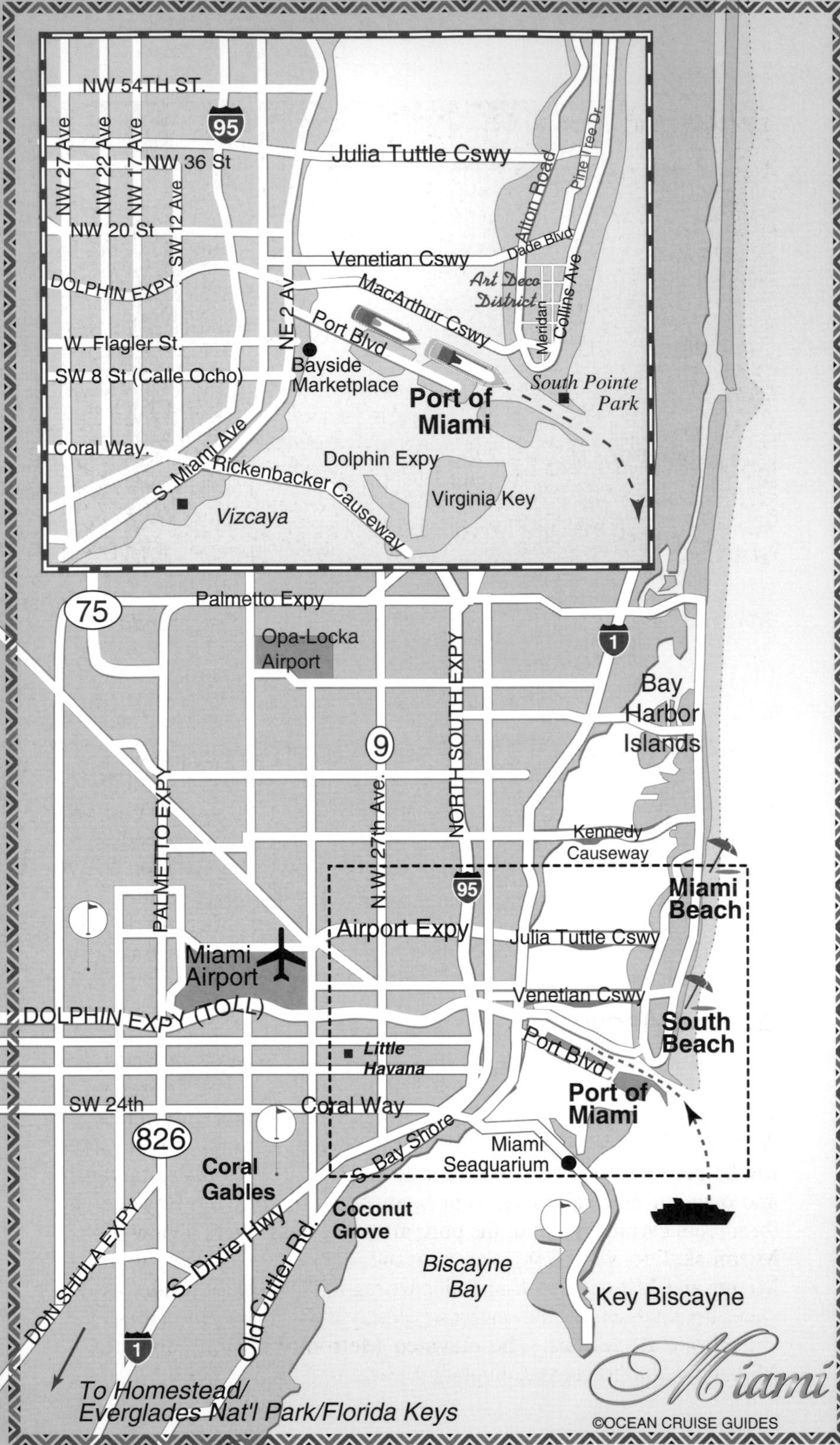

NW 54TH ST.
95
NW 27 Ave
NW 22 Ave
NW 17 Ave
NW 36 St
Julia Tuttle Cswy
Alton Road
Pine Tree Dr.
SW 12 Ave
NW 20 St
Dade Blvd
Venetian Cswy
Collins Ave
Art Deco District
DOLPHIN EXPY.
NE 2 Av
MacArthur Cswy
Port Blvd
Meridan
W. Flagler St.
SW 8 St (Calle Ocho)
Bayside Marketplace
Port of Miami
South Pointe Park
Coral Way.
S. Miami Ave
Rickenbacker Causeway
Dolphin Expy
Virginia Key
Vizcaya
75
Palmetto Expy
Opa-Locka Airport
1
Bay Harbor Islands
9
NORTH SOUTH EXPY
N.W. 27th Ave.
PALMETTO EXPY
Kennedy Causeway
95
Miami Beach
Airport Expy
Julia Tuttle Cswy
Miami Airport
Venetian Cswy
DOLPHIN EXPY (TOLL)
South Beach
Port Blvd
Little Havana
SW 24th
Coral Way
Port of Miami
826
S. Bay Shore
Miami Seaquarium
Coral Gables
Coconut Grove
DON SHULA EXPY
S. Dixie Hwy
Old Cutler Rd.
Biscayne Bay
Key Biscayne
1
To Homestead/
Everglades Nat'l Park/Florida Keys
Miami
©OCEAN CRUISE GUIDES

Miami Beach's revitalized Art Deco District is one of the trendiest hotel-and-restaurant strips in America.

MIAMI

Named for an American Indian tribe, Miami was a trading post when Henry Flagler, having built grand hotels at St. Augustine and Palm Beach, set his sights on this southern port. He made Miami a railroad terminus in 1896, the year it was incorporated, then proceeded to dredge the harbor to accommodate his fleet of steamships. Set on a low ridge overlooking Biscayne Bay, Miami is now the transportation and business hub of south Florida. It is also one of the busiest cruise ports in the world, with ships based here year-round for sailings to the Bahamas and the Caribbean.

GETTING AROUND

The Port of Miami's cruise port is a two-island complex in Biscayne Bay adjacent to downtown Miami. The port, consisting of a dozen passenger terminals, is located eight miles from Miami International Airport. It's a short taxi ride from the cruise terminals to Bayside Marketplace, a bustling waterfront development of shops, restaurants and open-air entertainment. Tour boats depart daily from Bayside on 90-minute narrated tours of the port, affording passengers a view of the Miami skyline, waterfront mansions and other sights. Trolley tours of Miami and Miami Beach also depart regularly from Bayside, as do water taxis which ply the waters of Biscayne Bay, stopping at various waterfront attractions. The elevated Metromover links downtown Miami's major hotels and shopping areas.

SHOPPING ,DINING & STAYING

Greater Miami has more than 500 hotels and motels providing over 50,000 rooms. The selection is extensive and includes a plethora of luxury properties. Yesteryear's elegance can be enjoyed at the Biltmore Hotel, built in 1926 as the centerpiece of Coral Gables. In a lovely setting of waterways, tennis courts and golf links, this is a classic grand hotel with a vaulted lobby and an opulent swimming pool/bar area. Nearby in Coconut Grove, is the modern Grand Bay Hotel overlooking Biscayne Bay. Luciano Pavarotti's two-level suite, which contains a baby grand piano and circular staircase, can be rented when he's not there.

In downtown Miami, the Hotel Inter-Continental Miami contains a stunning lobby that features a massive marble sculpture by Henry Moore. Across the bay, in Miami Beach, the Casa Grande is highly touted, as are several small, stylish establishments in the Art Deco District of South Beach. A few blocks up Collins Avenue, in North Beach, the restored art deco hotels are considerably less expensive.

The Bayside Marketplace is a popular spot for cruise passengers with a good selection of waterfront restaurants and shops. Other areas that offer a combination of shopping and dining are bohemian-flavored Coconut Grove, with its interesting shops, open-air bistros and sidewalk cafes along CocoWalk on Grand Avenue, and Coral Gables where its Miracle Mile – the main shopping thoroughfare on Coral Way between Southwest 42nd Avenue and Douglas Road – is lined with

The bustling Bayside Marketplace is located across the water from Miami's cruise port.

some of Miami's best restaurants. For a taste of Latin America and Miami's famous Cuban coffee, try one of the eateries on Calle Ocho in Little Havana.

For seafood lovers seeking a refined ambiance, The Fish Market (on Biscayne Boulevard at 16th Street) is recommended. In Miami Beach, the family-run Joe's Stone Crab Restaurant at 227 Biscayne Street has been a local favorite since opening in 1913. The South Pointe Seafood House in Miami Beach is a good spot to watch the cruise ships come and go, and for a sunset view of the Miami skyline, try The Rusty Pelican on Key Biscayne.

Golf – The Doral Resort near the Miami International Airport, has four 18-hole courses including one of the most challenging courses in the Miami area. The Links at Key Biscayne, one of the top-ranked municipal courses in the U.S., is built around lagoons and contains four waterside holes with views of the Miami skyline. The city-owned Biltmore Golf Course in Coral Gables opened in 1925 and was recently refurbished, and the Golf Club of Miami offers three different courses.

LOCAL ATTRACTIONS

Greater Miami encompasses the City of Miami, Miami Beach, Coral Gables, Hialeah and many smaller communities. About half of the City of Miami's population is Hispanic, many of Cuban descent, with hundreds of thousands of Cuban refugees moving here from the late '50s to early '70s, settling in the city's Little Havana section. Calle Ocho (Southwest Eighth Street) is the main thoroughfare and scene of an annual Hispanic festival that's held in March and stretches the length of 23 lively blocks of music and dancing.

Miami Beach, located on a barrier island in Biscayne Bay, was a mangrove swamp until connected to the mainland by a wooden bridge in 1913. Opulent hotels and huge estates were soon built here, while the South Beach area was sub-divided into smaller lots and developed as a middle-class resort of modest hotels and apartments. Many of these buildings went up during the Depression, when visitors came to Miami Beach to temporarily escape their worries. The area suffered a decline following World War II. Then, in 1979, South Beach's square mile area of Art Deco structures, built between the two world wars, was declared a national historic district – the first containing registered buildings less than 50 years old. Their style, sometimes referred to as Tropical Deco, consists of smooth lines and white exteriors trimmed with hot colors. During South Beach's revitalization in the late '80s and early '90s, many of the run-down hotels were refurbished and repainted in pastel colors. Today the area is one of the trendiest in America, where the steady stream of pedestrian and car traffic along Ocean Drive includes movie stars and fashion models frequenting the stylish eateries. The Art Deco Welcome Center at 1001 Ocean Drive is a good place to start a tour of South Beach. Points of interest include the Cardozo Hotel at

1300 Ocean Drive, which was featured in the 1959 film A Hole in the Head, starring Frank Sinatra.

Coral Gables, situated four miles south of downtown Miami, was founded in 1925 at the height of the Florida land boom which sparked an explosion of growth in the Miami area. A planned city designed by George Merrick, its Mediterranean architecture includes such highlights as the Venetian Pool – a huge municipal pool set in a coral quarry with caves, waterfalls and arched bridges. Merrick's boyhood home, a gabled plantation house on Coral Way, is open to the public. His dream city of canals, plazas and tree-shaded streets is also home to the University of Miami, where the Lowe Art Museum houses a permanent collection of Renaissance and Baroque art as well as Spanish and American paintings and artwork by North American Indians. The Orange Bowl Classic & Festival has been a major annual event in Miami since 1933 when the University of Miami played the Manhattan University.

Coconut Grove, on the waterfront east of Coral Gables, was settled in the late 19th century by New England intellectuals and Bahamian seamen. The conical home of founding father Ralph Munroe, a New York yacht designer, is called the Barnacle and is open to the public at 3485 Main Highway. Also in Coconut Grove is the **Vizcaya Museum and Gardens** (3251 S. Miami Avenue), a restored Italian Renaissance-style villa completed in 1916 as a winter residence for industrialist John Deering. The 34-room mansion, set in grounds of formal gardens and fountains overlooking Biscayne Bay, has been designated a National Historic Landmark. It contains Renaissance and Baroque antiques and artwork, and has been visited by such dignitaries as Pope John Paul II, Queen Elizabeth and President Clinton, who hosted the 1994 Summit of the Americas at Vizcaya.

A toll causeway links the mainland with Virginia Key, location of the Miami Seaquarium, and Key Biscayne, where the late Richard Nixon had a presidential retreat. Both islands contain parks, with a golf course and tennis stadium located on Key Biscayne.

SOUTH OF MIAMI

Homestead, south of Miami, is the gateway to Everglades National Park, Biscayne National Park and the Florida Keys. The center of Florida's fruit and nursery production, one of Homestead's major attractions is Coral Castle, which was built from massive blocks of coral by a Latvian immigrant who labored alone from 1920 to 1940.

Biscayne National Park, nine miles east of Homestead on SW 328 Street, is an undeveloped underwater park containing miles of coral reefs. Its shallow waters are very clear and warm – a natural habitat for sponges, crabs, manatees and more than 500 different kinds of fish. The park is primarily accessible by boat, with tour boats operating out of park headquarters at Convoy Point.

The **Florida Keys**, a chain of small coral islands extending 110 miles from the state's southern tip, are both exotic and all-American. Their sub-tropical vegetation, steady trade winds and coral reefs are quintessentially Caribbean, while Key West's clapboard houses and white picket fences are reminiscent of a New England coastal town. The Keys' reef-riddled waters supported a thriving salvage industry in the mid-19th century before modern lighthouses and steam vessels brought an end to the steady stream of ships that were snared by the reefs off Key West.

Key Largo, the largest of the islands at the 'top' of the Keys, is famous both as the setting for the '40s film classic Key Largo, starring Humphrey Bogart and Lauren Bacall, and as the location of John Pennekamp Coral Reef State Park – America's first underwater park, established in 1960. Over time, adjoining sanctuaries were established to protect the threatened reefs, and the Florida Keys National Marine Sanctuary now encompasses the entire length of the Keys.

Key West, the largest center in the Keys with about 25,000 residents, is the southernmost point of the continental United States and only 90 miles from Cuba. In 1912 the Keys became linked with the mainland with completion of Henry Flagler's railroad. The rail line was abandoned after sustaining hurricane damage in 1935 and replaced a few years later with the 123-mile Overseas Highway which includes 42 bridges. Despite this tangible and well-travelled connection to the rest of Florida, the Keys have retained an island ambiance and sense of seclusion, and Key West especially has long been an enclave for writers and artists, including Ernest Hemingway.

Scenes from the forties film Key Largo, starring Bogart and Bacall, were shot inside the Caribbean Club at Key Largo.

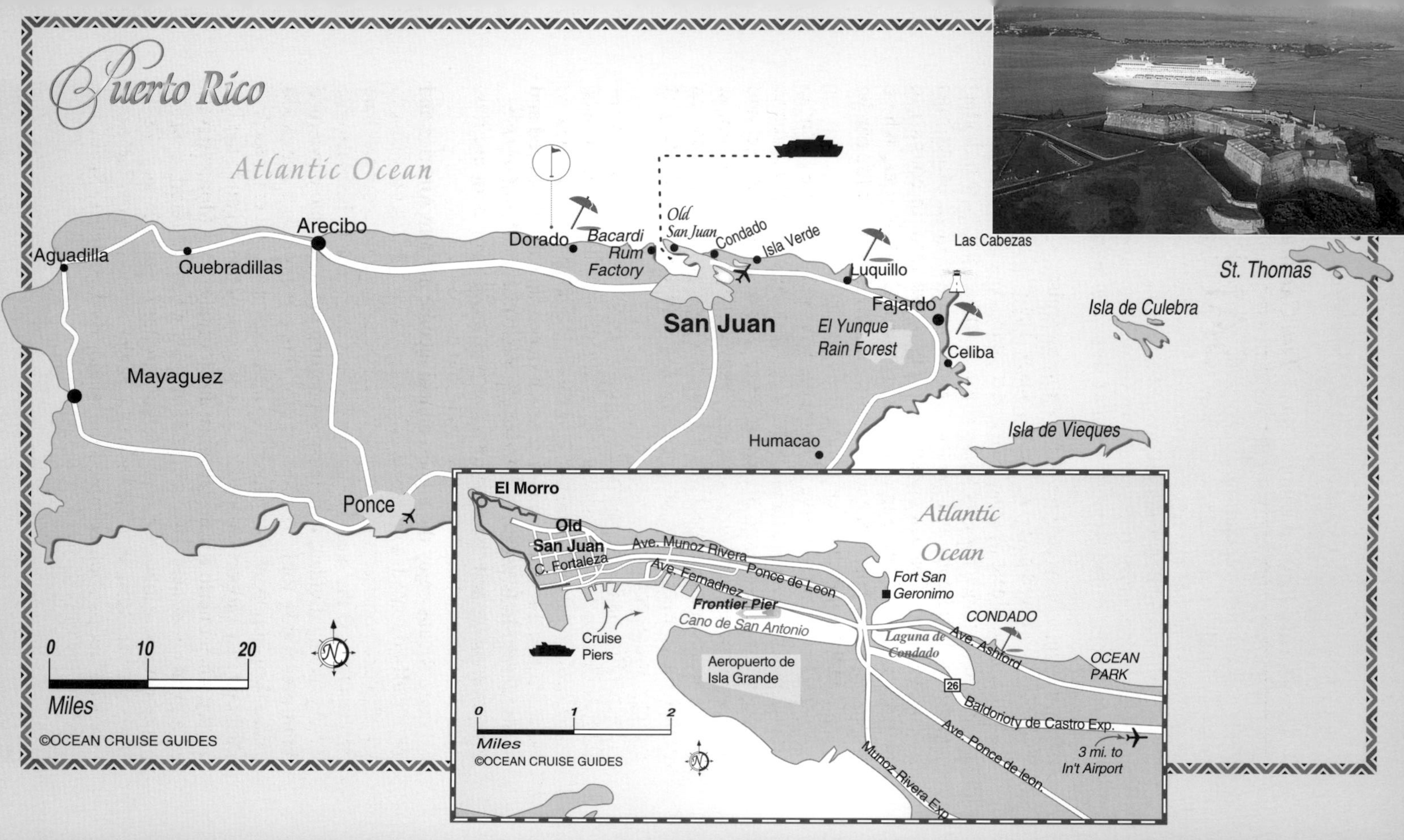

Puerto Rico
Atlantic Ocean
Aguadilla
Quebradillas
Arecibo
Dorado
Bacardi Rum Factory
Old San Juan
Condado
Isla Verde
Luquillo
Las Cabezas
St. Thomas
Fajardo
San Juan
El Yunque Rain Forest
Isla de Culebra
Celiba
Mayaguez
Humacao
Isla de Vieques
Ponce
0
10
20
Miles
©OCEAN CRUISE GUIDES
El Morro
Old San Juan
C. Fortaleza
Ave. Munoz Rivera
Ave. Fernadnez
Ponce de Leon
Frontier Pier
Cano de San Antonio
Atlantic Ocean
Fort San Geronimo
CONDADO
Laguna de Condado
Ave. Ashford
OCEAN PARK
26
Baldorioty de Castro Exp.
Ave. Ponce de leon.
Munoz Rivera Exp.
3 mi. to In't Airport
Cruise Piers
Aeropuerto de Isla Grande
0
1
2
Miles
©OCEAN CRUISE GUIDES

SAN JUAN

San Juan, a busy base port for Caribbean cruises, is also one of the best-preserved ports of colonial Spain. The walled city of Old San Juan, the oldest Spanish settlement under American sovereignty, is a World Heritage Site. Its cobblestone streets are paved with ballast from Spanish galleons and the impenetrable citadel of El Morro was once a symbol of Spanish domination in the Caribbean. In contrast to the historic feel of Old San Juan is the nearby Condado area, where modern high-rise hotels line the beaches and a sizzling night life can be enjoyed in the night clubs and casinos.

Puerto Ricans number over three and a half million and they refer to their Connecticut-sized island as the 'continent' of Puerto Rico due to its geographical diversity. Mountains here soar to over 4,000 feet and vegetation ranges from lush rainforests to low-lying mangrove swamps. Beautiful beaches line much of the coastline and, in the northwest, an extensive system of caves has been carved by one of the world's largest underground rivers.

Puerto Rico is a self-governing Commonwealth of the United States and its infrastructure includes a major airport, well-maintained roads, luxury resorts and championship golf courses. Industrialization came to Puerto Rico in the 1940s when Operation Bootstrap was introduced and its tax exemptions promoted American investment. Manufacturing, pharmaceuticals and the production of high-tech equipment are now major industries, along with agriculture and tourism.

Puerto Ricans enjoy the highest annual income in Latin America and are a well-educated work force. Few deny that the island's ties to America are beneficial and worth preserving, but an ongoing debate revolves around the 'statehood versus status quo' issue. The electorate is fairly evenly divided, with those supporting the status quo concerned about preserving their Spanish culture. Those supporting statehood accuse their opponents of 'wanting to have their cake and eat it too'. A small minority support independence, a movement that began in the last century when Puerto Rican statesman and journalist Luis Munoz Rivera led a growing demand for self government, which resulted in Spain granting its Caribbean colony some autonomy in February 1898. However, the Spanish-American war began a few months later and American troops soon occupied the island. By December, Spain had ceded Puerto Rico to the United States.

The massive fortress El Morro looms at the entrance to San Juan Harbor.

Puerto Rico remained under direct military rule until 1900 when Congress passed the Foraker Act, setting up a local administration with a U.S. Governor, an elected house of delegates and an upper chamber appointed by the U.S. President. Munoz Rivera, who had moved to New York where he published the Puerto Rico Herald before becoming the resident commissioner of Puerto Rico in Washington, was again a driving force for greater autonomy. In 1917 the Jones Act pronounced Puerto Rico a U.S. territory, granting its occupants U.S. citizenship and increased internal self-government.

While Puerto Ricans were making political gains, economic and social conditions were worsening. Much of their subsistence land was encroached upon by the establishment of large sugar plantations. The situation, aggravated by overpopulation, went from bad to worse when the sugar market fell in the 1930s. Recovery measures were taken under Franklin Roosevelt's presidency and the governorship of Rexford Tugwell. In 1948 Puerto Ricans elected their governor for the first time, and in 1952 the Commonwealth of Puerto Rico was proclaimed.

The smallest and easternmost of the Greater Antilles, Puerto Rico was originally inhabited by Taino Indians who called the island Borinquen. Christopher Columbus visited in 1493 and named the island San Juan Bautista (St. John the Baptist) but sailed on to Hispaniola to establish a settlement. Juan Ponce de Leon began the Spanish conquest of Borinquen, after finding gold there in 1508. He established a settlement on the shores of San Juan harbor, calling it Puerto Rico – rich port. The names were eventually switched, and rich is what Ponce de Leon became as governor of the island, with the lure of new conquests drawing him away from Puerto Rico from time to time.

In 1521, the Spanish colonists moved their settlement from a low-lying location across the bay to the present-day site of San Juan. Ponce de Leon was in Florida at the time, trying to establish a new colony, where he was felled by the poisoned arrow of a Native American. His party sailed immediately for Cuba where their leader died, his body returned to Puerto Rico for burial.

Meanwhile, hardship, disease and Spanish massacres had eliminated the Tainos and they were replaced with African slaves, first introduced in 1513. Once the island's placer gold deposits were depleted in the 1530s, the Spanish turned their attention to sugar plantations. Distractions came in the form of raids by Carib Indians and by British, French and Dutch pirates and roving corsairs, all of whom were attracted to this important outpost of the Spanish empire.

Twice a year two armed convoys were sent from Spain to collect precious gems, gold and silver. The Spanish ships entered the Caribbean Sea near Puerto Rico, one fleet heading to Veracruz to pick up Mexican gold and silver, the other heading to Cartagena to await treasures arriving from the Isthmus of Panama. The two fleets would then rendezvous at Havana for the return voyage to Spain. To protect her shipping interests, Spain established several military fortifications, the most strategic being San Juan harbor which Spain's King Philip II called 'the key to the West Indies'.

The famous **El Morro** fortress was built at the east side of the harbor entrance. It began as a round masonry tower which, over time and following various enemy assaults, was strengthened and expanded until it was a massive citadel. The main purpose of this fortification was to prevent Spain's European enemies from gaining possession of the port and using it as a base for attacks on Spanish settlements and trading ships.

Britain's Sir Francis Drake, justly feared by the Spanish and emboldened by his successful sackings of Santo Domingo, Cartagena and St. Augustine in Florida, was the first to test El Morro. In 1595 he forced the entrance to the harbor but was repulsed, with heavy losses suffered by the Spanish defenders. Three years later Britain's Earl of Cumberland successfully besieged El Morro, his brief occupation cut short by an outbreak of dysentery. The Dutch were next, in 1625, sacking and burning the town before being driven off by the Spanish.

In response to these attacks, Spain built several fortresses, making San Juan virtually impregnable. Massive walls of sandstone, some 50 feet high and 20 feet thick at the base, were raised around the town. A redoubt named San Cristobal was built about a mile east of El Morro to protect the town from a land-based attack. But it wasn't until the end of the Seven Years War (1756-1763), which left Spain and Britain the two powers in the Caribbean, that San Juan was transformed into the stronghold we see today. Thomas O'Daly, an Irish-born military engineer, was hired by Spain's King Charles III to oversee the completion of the wall, expand San Cristobal into the largest fortress built by Spain in the Americas, and turn El Morro into an impenetrable citadel. Hundreds of workmen were employed in this massive undertaking which took 20 years to complete. San Juan remained impregnable for more than a century and was one of Spain's last remaining holdings in the Americas when a revolution in Cuba sparked the Spanish-American War. A United States naval flotilla, in search of the Spanish war fleet, bombarded San Juan in May of 1898, and two months later American troops landed on the south coast of Puerto Rico. As soldiers advanced to the outskirts of San Juan, an armistice was signed. Spain's four-century rule of Puerto Rico had come to an end.

Getting Around San Juan

San Juan's main cruise port is located adjacent to the walled city; its secondary cruise pier **(Frontier Pier)** is two miles east of the main port. In between the airport and the cruise piers lie the hotel-lined beaches of Isla Verde, Ocean Beach and Condado, where the majority of passengers stay if spending extra time in San Juan before or after their cruise. Two **hotels** located right in Old San Juan are the El Convento (a former convent) and the new Wyndham Old San Juan Hotel on the harbor front. Tourist taxis are painted white and they offer fixed rates (per car) to and from tourist zones. The fare from the airport to Isla Verde is $8, to Condado is $12, and to the cruise piers in Old San Juan is $16. The fare from Isla Verde to the cruise piers is $16 and from Condado is $10. The fare from Frontier Pier to Old San Juan is about $10.

Parking is limited in Old San Juan and its streets are best explored on foot or by using the free trolley service which originates at the Covadonga parking lot, a block up from the cruise ship piers. Five trolley buses, equipped with wheelchair ramps, operate daily and cover two routes: a central one to Plaza de Armas and a northern route to the grounds of El Morro. Passengers can hop off and on at any stop.

To see some of the city's outlying districts and area attractions, such as the El Yunque National Forest, tours can be booked through the cruise lines' shore excursion office or at the tour desks of the major hotels. Another option is to rent a car. Rental agencies are numerous in the San Juan metropolitan area, including Avis, Budget and Hertz.

Spanish and English are the official languages. Spanish is predominant, but English is taught in school and is widely spoken. Long-distance phone calls can be made at 'Phones & More' located inside Pier 6 and other phones are opposite Pier 4. A post office is located opposite Pier 1 where San Justo intersects with Comercio.

Dining – San Juan has become a restaurant town, serving both traditional creole cuisine and the new Puerto Rican cuisine, which has taken

San Juan's inviting waterfront promenade leads from the main cruise port to the walled city.

traditional recipes featuring native Indian, Spanish and African foods, and enhanced them with new seasonings and presentation. A good place to sample some local fare is Amadeus, a popular bistro-style bar and restaurant across from the Plaza San Juan.

Shopping – San Juan has duty-free shopping at its airport and at several factory outlets in Old San Juan. The main shopping streets are Cristo, Fortaleza, San Francisco and Cristo, where the Polo/Ralph Lauren Factory Store is located. Numerous art galleries are located in the shopping area and on San Jose Street. Traditional items include cuatros (handmade guitars), bobbin lace (mundillo) and small wood carvings of religious figures called santos. Other local crafts include straw work, ceramics, hammocks and carnival masks. The Institute of Puerto Rican Culture operates the Popular Arts and Crafts Center, located at the bottom of Cristo Street near the Capilla de Cristo, where a variety of island crafts are displayed and offered for sale

(Below) The new Wyndham Old San Juan Hotel.
(Right) El Convento, a heritage hotel building.

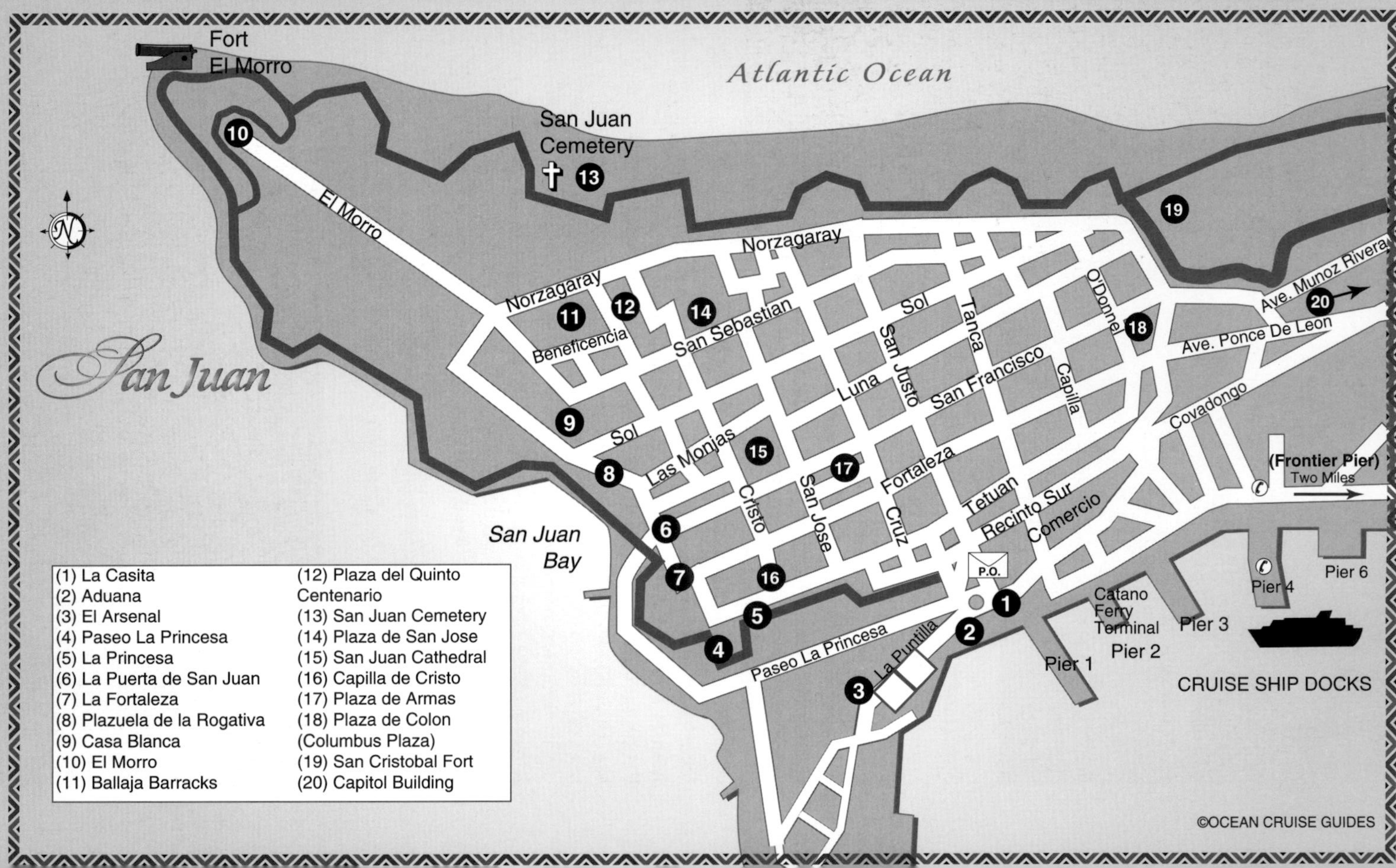
San Juan
Atlantic Ocean
Fort
El Morro
San Juan
Cemetery
El Morro
Norzagaray
Beneficencia
San Sebastian
Sol
Las Monjas
Cristo
San Jose
Luna
San Justo
Tanca
San Francisco
Capilla
O'Donnel
Fortaleza
Cruz
Tetuan
Recinto Sur
Comercio
Covadongo
Ave. Ponce De Leon
Ave. Munoz Rivera
(Frontier Pier)
Two Miles
Paseo La Princesa
La Puntilla
P.O.
San Juan
Bay
Catano
Ferry
Terminal
Pier 1
Pier 2
Pier 3
Pier 4
Pier 6
CRUISE SHIP DOCKS
(1) La Casita
(2) Aduana
(3) El Arsenal
(4) Paseo La Princesa
(5) La Princesa
(6) La Puerta de San Juan
(7) La Fortaleza
(8) Plazuela de la Rogativa
(9) Casa Blanca
(10) El Morro
(11) Ballaja Barracks
(12) Plaza del Quinto Centenario
(13) San Juan Cemetery
(14) Plaza de San Jose
(15) San Juan Cathedral
(16) Capilla de Cristo
(17) Plaza de Armas
(18) Plaza de Colon (Columbus Plaza)
(19) San Cristobal Fort
(20) Capitol Building
©OCEAN CRUISE GUIDES

Monday through Saturday. On weekends, local crafts can be purchased at an outdoor market beside La Casita information center and along La Princesa promenade. This market is also a popular venue for local musicians.

Rum is another Puerto Rican specialty, with free tours and samples provided at the Bacardi Rum Factory – reached by harbor ferry from the cruise ship pier. Gourmet coffee drinkers may want to purchase a pound or two of flavorful Puerto Rican coffee. If you're looking for fine cigars, there's a boutique catering to connoisseurs at El San Juan Hotel on Isla Verde. Shoppers looking for interesting books and souvenirs should check out the museum gift shops, such as the one at El Morro, where visitors can purchase replica gold and silver coins of the 16th century.

Beaches – Good beaches in the metropolitan area include Escambron Beach and Isla Verde Beach, both of which are balnearios (government-run beaches with facilities, lifeguards and security personnel). About 20 miles east of San Juan is highly popular and beautiful Luquillo Beach – rated one of the world's top ten by National Geographic. A favorite with children is Seven Seas in Fajardo at the northeast end of the island. More beautiful beaches lie west of San Juan at Dorado where a public beach is located near the hotel and golf resorts.

(Above) The cuatro is a traditional handmade guitar. (Bottom) Ocean Park Beach

Golf – Puerto Rico boasts a dozen public golf courses, including four at the Hyatt Resorts west of San Juan. Designed by Robert Trent Jones Sr., the par-72 East course at Dorado Beach contains a par 5 thirteenth hole, rated by Jack Nicklaus as one of the top ten in the world.

Viejo San Juan

(Right) Pablo Casals Museum (Bottom) Paseo La Princesa

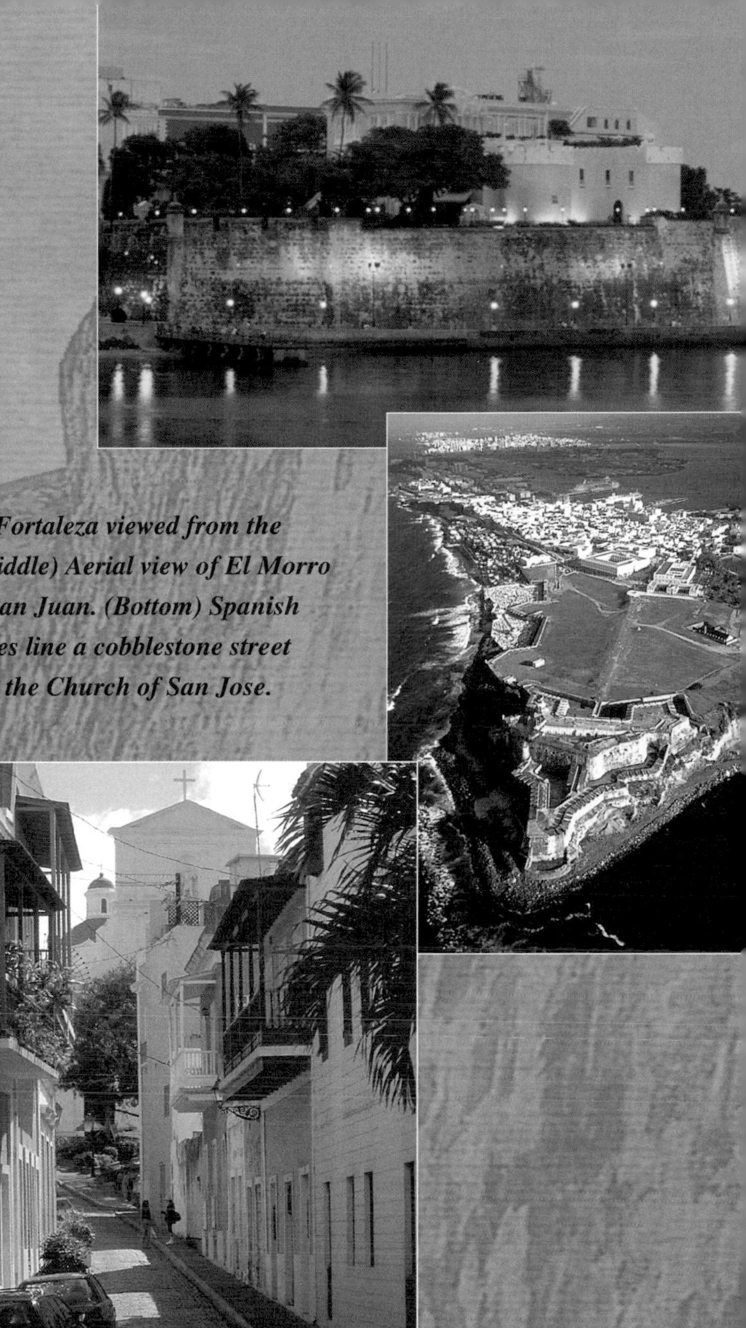

(Top) La Fortaleza viewed from the water. (Middle) Aerial view of El Morro and Old San Juan. (Bottom) Spanish townhouses line a cobblestone street leading to the Church of San Jose.

(Above) The waterfront promenade leads to San Juan Gate.

(Opposite) Children play in Small Plaza of the Religious Procession.

LOCAL ATTRACTIONS:

The cruise ships dock right at the doorstep of Old San Juan, a seven-block area packed with historical and cultural sights which include Gothic churches, restored colonial buildings, townhouses with inner courtyards and wrought-iron balconies, museums, art galleries, boutiques, plazas, fountains and gardens. An **information center** is conveniently located beside Pier 1 inside **(1) La Casita (the little house)** and is an ideal starting point for a self-guided walking tour of these historic streets and fortifications. Refreshments can be enjoyed along the way at various restaurants and sidewalk cafes, or from street vendors who sell bottled water and soft drinks. Piraguas (fruit-flavored snow cones) and helados (coconut and pineapple ices) are popular with the locals.

(2) Aduana, the beautiful pink building overlooking the harbor, is a U.S. Customs House. Nearby **(3) El Arsenal** was built in 1800 as a base for patrol boats and it currently houses Divisions of the Institute of Puerto Rican Culture. Three art galleries are located within the grounds. An elegant promenade, **(4) Paseo La Princesa**, runs parallel with the city wall and is where Spanish gentry of the 19th century once strolled. Restored for the Columbus Quincentennial, the esplanade is lined with palms and ornate street lamps, and features a large bronze fountain titled Raices (Roots), its human figures representing Puerto Rico's Indian, African and Spanish founders.

Paseo La Princesa leads past **(5) La Princesa**, a former jail, which has also been restored to its former colonial grandeur and is now the headquarters for the Puerto Rico Tourism Company, the island's official tourism body. The promenade curves along the waterfront at the base of the city wall, called La Muralla, which is guarded at strategic points by garitas (sentry boxes). **(6) La Puerta de San Juan (San Juan Gate)** is one of six heavy wooden doors once positioned along the wall and which, for centuries, were bolted shut at sundown to secure the fortified city from enemy attack.

Pass through this gate and make an immediate right on Recinto Oeste Street for a look at **(7) La Fortaleza (The Fortress)** which overlooks San Juan Bay. Built as a fort in 1540, its location proved poor for military defence and its role reverted to that of governor's mansion – the oldest one in use in the Western Hemisphere. The grounds are open weekdays to organized tours that start every hour in a small plaza beside the building.

A turn to the left upon passing through the San Juan Gate will take you to the top of a hill where **(8) Plazuela de la Rogativa (Small Plaza of the Religious Procession)** is a popular gathering place for local residents and the staging of children's puppet shows. A bronze sculpture here depicts an event of 1797 when Old San Juan was under attack by British ships. In desperation, the residents of San Juan, led by their bishop, marched through the streets one night carrying lit torches and praying for their safety. The British apparently mistook this parade of lights for Spanish reinforcements and retreated from the harbor. Opposite the Plazuela de la Rogativa is the Museo Felisa Rincon de Gautier (the former home of a popular mayor) and behind it the Museo del Nino (Children's Museum).

North of Plazuela de la Rogativa you will come to a fork in the road. On the left is Casa Rosada (Pink House) which was built in 1812 for the Spanish army. To the right an upper road leads past a plant-decked wall to a doorway from which steps lead into the lovely gardens of **(9) Casa Blanca (White House)**. Built in 1521 as the city's original fortress, this is the oldest Spanish colonial building in Old San Juan and has been modified over the years. It was a gift from Spain's monarch to Ponce de Leon for his settling of Puerto Rico. Ponce de Leon died the year the original wooden house was built, but his family resided there until 1779, when it was sold to the Spanish government. Following the Spanish-American war in 1898, the Commander of the U.S. Army lived at Casa Blanca until 1967. It was declared a National Historic Monument in 1968. Recently restored and furnished with authentic 16th- and 17th-century pieces, the mansion now contains two museums – the Juan Ponce de Leon Museum and the Taino Indian Ethno-Historic

(Above) A cruise ship approaches San Juan Harbor. (Bottom) Visitors approach El Morro from its landward side.

Museum. They are open Tuesday through Sunday, 9:00 a.m. to noon and 1:00 p.m. to 4:30 p.m.

Between Casa Blanca and the grounds of El Morro stand two impressive colonial buildings. Asilo de Beneficenica, its facade consisting of wrought-iron fencing and green shutters, contains the headquarters of the Institute of Puerto Rican Culture and several galleries which are open Wednesday through Sunday. The red-domed building beside it was built in the 1800s and now houses a school of fine arts.

One of the most popular attractions in Old San Juan is the dramatic fort of **(10) El Morro**, open daily from 9:00 a.m. to 5:00 p.m. Admission is free and a brochure map is available at the entrance.Administered by the National Park Service, El Morro's full name is Castillo de San Felipe del Morro or 'Castle St. Philip of the Headland'. The fort is reached by a long, straight path which leads across a broad grassy area called a glacis. This cleared land was smoothed and sloped by the Spanish so that attacking troops had no shelter from the fort's cannon fire. Beneath the ground are tunnels in which kegs of gunpowder were planted should enemy troops try to lay siege to the fort.

From this landward approach, the fort strikes a surprisingly low profile, so engineered to make it a small target for enemy troops approach-

ing by land. This was achieved by a dry moat which was dug along its length so the main wall could be sunk into the ground, yet still present a formidable height for scaling. The ocean side of the fort, in contrast to the landward side, consists of six tiers of batteries that loom above the water, protecting the fort from sea attacks. The lowest gun platform, the Water Battery, is washed by ocean swells while the uppermost ramparts – the Ochoa and Austria Bastions – stand 145 feet high.

Inside the fort, its entrance guarded by a drawbridge, are storerooms, gun rooms, troop quarters, a chapel and prison. These all open onto a central courtyard beneath which are cisterns. Tunnels and stairways connect different parts of the fort, and a museum is located in one of the bombproof vaults.

The El Morro lighthouse, which took a direct hit during the Spanish-American War, stands on the fort's fifth level. First constructed in 1846, it has been replaced three times since then. A working lighthouse, it helps guide ships entering one of the Caribbean's busiest ports.

Returning to the city streets, the next historic site is **(11) Ballaja Barracks** where Spanish troops and their families once lived. The Museum of the Americas is on its second floor. On the eastern side of the barracks is **(12) Plaza del Quinto Centenario (Quincentennial Square)**, constructed for the 1992-93 celebration of the 500th Anniversary of the discovery of the New World. This multi-level square affords a sweeping vista of El Morro and, from its upper western level, a view of the **(13) San Juan Cemetery**.

The steps of the square lead to **(14)**

(Top) Visitors check out one of Old San Juan's sentry boxes. (Bottom) Outdoor dining on Cristo Street, near Christ Chapel.

Plaza de San Jose where a statue of Ponce de Leon stands outside San Jose Church – the second oldest church in the Western Hemisphere, built in 1532, and the family church of Ponce de Leon's descendants. A beautiful example of Gothic architecture, the church was originally built as a chapel. Next to the church is the Convento de los Dominicos, containing the Institute of Puerto Rican Culture book and music store. Tucked in a corner townhouse of the plaza is the Museo de Pablo Casals, a small museum containing memorabilia of the famous cellist who spent his final years in San Juan. On the plaza's eastern side is Casa de las Contrafuertes (House of Buttresses), which contains the Museum of Latin American Prints and a Pharmacy Museum.

Cristo Street leads from Plaza de San Jose down the hill to **(15) San Juan Cathedral**. Built in 1540 with early 19th-century modifications, the cathedral contains the marble tomb of Juan Ponce de Leon. Two blocks south of the Cathedral, at the foot of Cristo Street, you will see **(16) Capilla de Cristo (Christ Chapel)** dedicated to the Christ of Miracles. It was built following a 1753 incident in which a youth was racing his horse down the hill at such a speed that rider and horse could not possibly stop before hurtling over the city wall. One legend is that both miraculously came to a halt just in time, another says the horse stopped but the boy flew over the wall, and a third version claims they both met their maker at this spot. Beside Capilla de Cristo is the small Parque de las Palomas (Pigeon Park) with a fine view of the harbor. Lying opposite is Casa del Libro (House of Books), a small museum and library with a collection of rare, pre-16th century books.

(Top) Quincentennial Square

(Left) San Juan Cathedral

(17) Plaza de Armas (Army Plaza) lies a block east of Cristo Street on San Francisco. Several government buildings surround the square, which was originally used for military drills, when built in the 16th century, and is now a social gathering place. City Hall, completed in 1789, stands on the plaza's north side and was designed to resemble its counterpart in Madrid; it contains a visitor information center. An administration building, at the west end of the plaza, and the provincial delegation building at its northwest corner, are fine examples of 19th-century neoclassical architecture. The century-old statues gracing the plaza represent the four seasons.

At the eastern end of Fortaleza Street, where it intersects with O'Donnel, you'll find **(18) Plaza de Colon (Columbus Plaza)** and Teatro Tapia, a 19th-century theatre. A few blocks north is the entrance to **(19) San Cristobal Fort**, open daily from 9:00 a.m. to 5:00 p.m. East of the historic quarter is the dome-roofed (20) Capitol Building.

AREA HIGHLIGHTS

El Yunque National Forest – A 45-minute drive from San Juan, this 28,000-acre tropical forest is one of Puerto Rico's natural wonders. Set in the Luquillo Mountains and named for anvil-shaped El Yunque peak, the park contains 240 species of tropical trees, flowers and wildlife, including ferns, orchids, parrots and tiny tree frogs called coqui. Cool and often rainy, the park's verdant forest contains a dozen hiking trails and a lookout tower. Its highest peak is 3,532-foot-high El Toro. A popular restaurant at the entrance to the park is Las Vegas where both Puerto Rican and American cuisine is served.

Las Cabezas de San Juan Nature Reserve **–** This peninsula at the northeastern tip of the island is often referred to as El Faro, which is the name of the 1882 lighthouse located here. Beautifully restored, El Faro now houses a scientific research center with an observation deck added to the building's exterior. The reserve, situated on land acquired by the island's Conservation Trust, encompasses a dry forest, mangroves, lagoons, beaches, reefs and offshore cays. Guided tours, by reservation only, are conducted in safari buses and include informative walks along trails and boardwalks to observe the various species supported by this diverse habitat.

El Faro Lighthouse

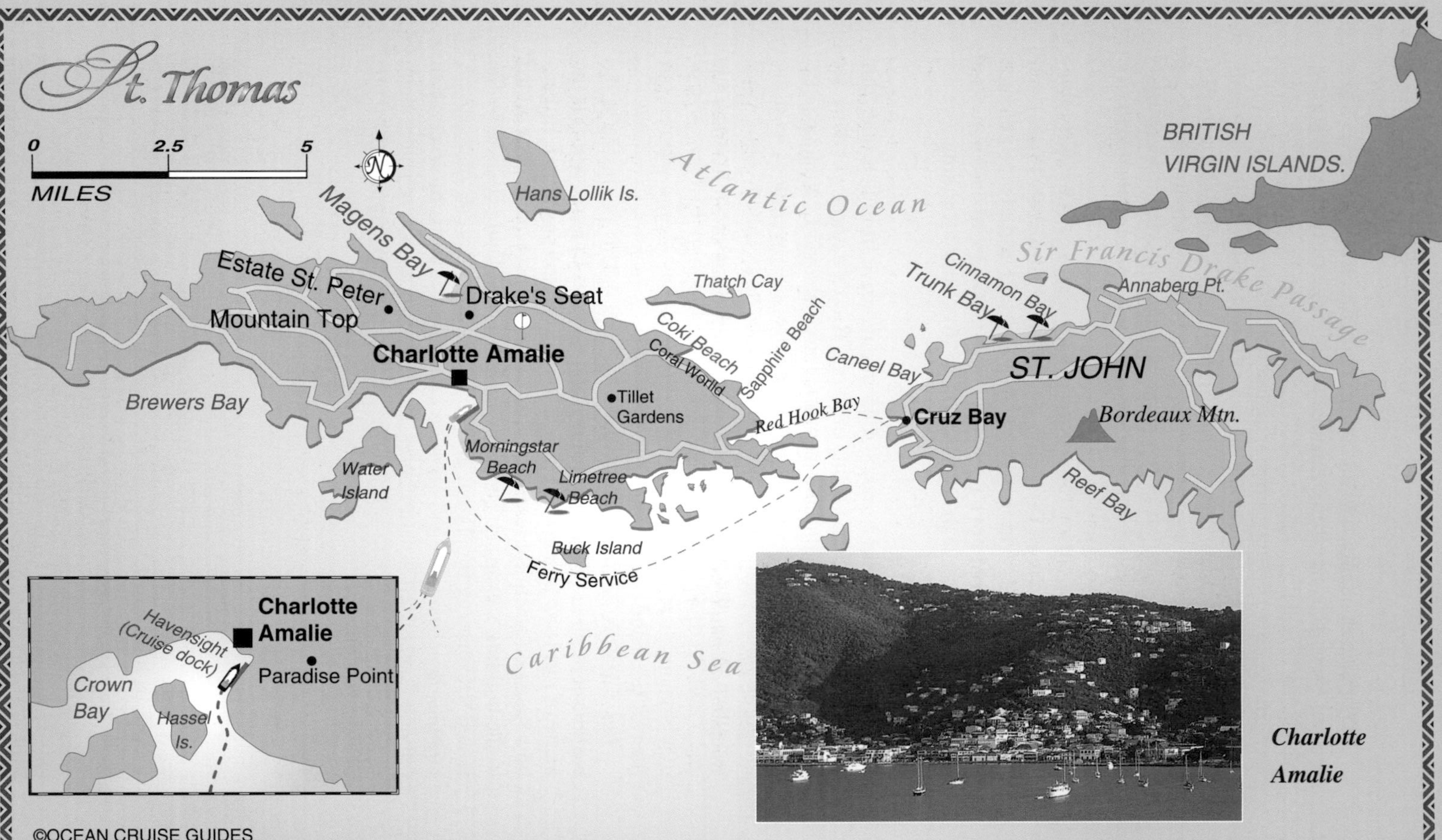

Charlotte Amalie

ST. THOMAS

The natural allure of the Virgin Islands prompted Christopher Columbus to name them, in 1493, for the legend of Saint Ursula and her 11,000 virgin martyrs. But not even Columbus could have predicted their potential as a tourist mecca. As recently as 1917, when the United States bought these tropical treasures from Denmark for $25 million, it was not for possession of their beautiful beaches and fragrant flowers but to protect America's shipping interests. At the time, after decades of economic decline, the Danish West Indies were valued mainly for their strategic proximity to the recently opened Panama Canal.

A 100-island chain, the Virgin Islands are divided into the U.S. Virgin Islands and the British Virgin Islands. The U.S. Virgin Islands consist of three principal islands – St. Thomas, St. John and St. Croix – and dozens of smaller islands. They contain many sheltered harbors and lie directly in the path of easterly trade winds, which made them an ideal stop-over point for trading vessels in the days of sail.

The capital of the U.S. Virgin Islands, Charlotte Amalie (pronounced *ah-mahl-ya*), is located on the south coast of St. Thomas and overlooks one of the finest harbors in the Caribbean. The downtown's narrow streets and colonial buildings look much as they did in the mid-1800s when Charlotte Amalie was one of the most important trading centers of the West Indies, bustling with the comings and goings of naval ships, whalers, merchant traders and fishing boats. Import firms flourished here, their warehouses lining the waterfront, and wealthy merchants lived on the surrounding hillsides where they enjoyed the sea breezes and magnificent harbor views.

Haagensen House, a restored 1820s townhouse in Charlotte Amalie.

Their gleaming white houses, set among terraced gardens and coconut palms, were rectangular in shape with hipped roofs designed to collect rainwater along the gutters. Inside these homes were polished mahogany floors and comfortable furnishings which included rocking chairs and a large sideboard for holding carafes of chilled drinks. Block ice was imported from Boston and stored in wooden ice houses, the spaces of their triple-layered walls filled with sawdust as insulation from the hot sun. The bedrooms contained huge four-poster beds from which hung mosquito netting. As a fire-safety precaution, the kitchen was contained in a separate building, as were the servants' quarters. Mode of travel around the island, up steep winding roads, was by horseback. Life on St. Thomas, however, centered around the town. As the 19th-century Danish naturalist A. S. Orsted wrote, "If you know the town, you know the whole island."

The town began in 1672 when the Danish West India Company established the first permanent settlement here. Fort Christian was completed in 1680 and the port quickly became a leading slave-trading center of the West Indies. Denmark allowed the Brandenburg American Company to operate here for a while and the town's four busy taverns soon earned it the name 'Tap Hus' (Beer Hall). In 1691 the settlement was officially declared a town and named Charlotte Amalie, in honor of the Danish Queen who was consort to King Christian V.

In 1717 the neighboring island of St. John was claimed by Denmark and a fort built at Coral Harbor. Neither St. Thomas nor St. John were ideally suited for agriculture, however, so in 1733 Denmark purchased St. Croix from France. That same year a slave rebellion took place on St. John and the rebels held the island for six months before French soldiers from Martinique helped the Danes recapture it. St. Thomas, meanwhile, was declared a free port and it became a thriving trade center and exporter of contraband trade from the strictly regulated Spanish colonies. It also became a refuge for pirates who sold their cargo here and often hid in the hills overlooking the harbor. The legendary Blackbeard is said to have holed up in a watch tower with a spyglass and supply of rum.

The islands became a Danish royal colony in 1754 and remained

Fort Christian

thus, apart from two British occupations – the first in 1801, when Denmark allied itself with Russia, and again from 1807 to 1815 when Denmark was allied with Napoleon. St. Croix was devoted to the cultivation and production of sugar, molasses and rum, its countryside covered with sugarcane fields and dotted with windmills. The island prospered and the port of Christiansted became Denmark's colonial capital. A town of well-planned streets and handsome buildings, it was protected by Fort Christiansvaern, built of yellow brick and dominating the harbor entrance.

Blackbeard's Castle

In contrast to the orderly development of Christiansted was the haphazard growth of Charlotte Amalie. Between 1804 and 1832, six fires swept through the town's narrow streets. Building codes were eventually enforced that banned frame construction in the commercial area along the waterfront. These masonry warehouses were fitted with fireproof roofs of tile or brick which were eventually replaced with corrugated metal due to hurricanes. Following emancipation in 1848, many freed slaves moved into town where existing residential lots were re-subdivided into smaller ones.

By the mid-1800s, the Danish West Indies had reached their zenith as colonial holdings. The price of sugar cane had dropped and, with steamships replacing sailing ships, St. Thomas was losing its importance as a stop-over point. Then a labor insurrection on St. Croix in 1878 prompted the remaining shipping companies in Charlotte Amalie to shut down. However, the protected harbors of St. Thomas and St. John were still of military value, prompting the purchase of the Danish West Indies by the United States in 1917 to prevent their being used as a German submarine base. The U.S. Navy handled initial administration of the islands, and residents were granted U.S. citizenship in 1927. Local government was established in 1954, with a governor and senate locally elected.

During World War II, the U.S. military constructed a submarine base, airfield, roads and housing on St. Thomas. Tourism began to

St. Thomas Harbor, viewed from atop Paradise Point.

flourish following the war, especially after the closing of Cuba to American tourists. A total of 26,650 visitors arrived at St. Thomas by ship or by airplane in 1950. Today that annual number is approaching two million. The U.S. Virgin Island, have established themselves as America's vacation paradise and Charlotte Amalie is once again the busiest free port in the Caribbean.

St. Thomas

Charlotte Amalie is serviced by two cruise ship terminals, the main one being the West Indian Company Dock which is located on the east side of the harbor, about a mile and a half by road from downtown. The other cruise terminal at Crown Bay is about two miles west of downtown. When ships anchor in the harbor, their passengers are tendered ashore to Kings Wharf on the downtown waterfront. The passenger ferry dock, with regular departures to St. John, is at the west end of the harbor, across from Hassel Island which is a national park. St. Thomas is fully geared for visitors with many of the island's 50,000 residents

Complimentary shopping shuttles run between the main cruise pier and nearby Havensight Mall.

employed in tourism-related industries. English is the official language and the U.S. dollar is the legal tender. Long-distance calls can be direct dialed to the U.S. mainland, and overseas service to Europe is excellent. A post office is located on Main Street, west of the Grand Hotel.

GETTING AROUND

St. Thomas is only 13 miles long and four miles wide, so the island's beautiful beaches are easily reached by taxi. A number of car rental firms operate on the island. Keep in mind that the roads are narrow and winding, and traffic keeps to the left. The port itself is usually busy with car traffic, and is best explored on foot. Open-air shuttle buses run regularly between the main cruise dock and downtown ($3 per person).

Officially licensed taxis carry a dome light and the letters TP on their license plates. Their rates have been set by the Taxi Commission

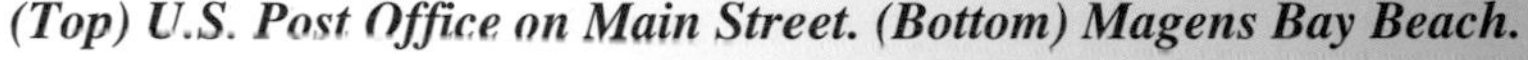

(Top) U.S. Post Office on Main Street. (Bottom) Magens Bay Beach.

and approved by the Virgin Islands' Legislature. Some sample fares per passenger: main cruise dock to downtown – $3.00; Crown Bay Dock to downtown – $4.00; Charlotte Amalie to: Magens Bay – $6.00, Morningstar Beach – $5.00); Red Hook ferry terminal (for ferry to St. John) – $8.00. **Paradise Point Gondola**, located across the street from Havensight Mall, whisks visitors up the mountainside for a sweeping view of the harbor. The complex contains a spacious sun deck, a restaurant/bar with umbrella tables, and a handful of gift shops.

Shopping – The Caribbean is famous for its duty-free shopping, and most famous of all is St. Thomas, where American visitors to the U.S. Virgin Islands can take advantage of a $1,200-per-person duty-free allowance. The prices in St. Thomas are generally 20% to 50% less than stateside and there's no sales tax. Imported liquor, jewelry, china, crystal, designer leather goods, watches and other items are all offered at substantial savings. Dozens of duty-free stores are housed in restored warehouses of the town's historic section, the shopping area concentrated along Main Street, the waterfront and the narrow, palm-shaded alleyways and pedestrian malls that connect these two busy streets. Additional duty-free shops, including branches of downtown retailers, are located at Havensight Mall beside the main cruise dock. The gift shop at Fort Christian sells locally made crafts including hand-carved mahogany rocking chairs, made to order.

Dining – For a taste of authentic Caribbean fare in a casual setting, try The Jamaican Ackee Tree & Bar, popular with local business people at lunch time and conveniently located across the street from Havensight Mall. Downtown, the Back Street (one block up from Main Street) is a good place to momentarily escape the crowds with a lunch stop at a number of good restaurants, including Cuzzin's at the corner of Back Street and Raadets Gade.

Beaches – Magens Bay, on the north coast, has been rated by National Geographic as one of the ten most beautiful beaches in the world. Admission is $3.00 and change facilities are available.

Other recommended beaches include Morningstar Beach and Limetree Beach southeast of Charlotte Amalie. On the northeast side of the island are Sapphire Beach and Coki Beach – good for snorkeling and adjacent to Coral World where change facilities are available.

Snorkeling & Diving – Off the island's south coast lie Cow and Calf Rocks, named for two humpback whales once seen at this dive site, which contains dramatic caves, archways and cliff overhangs from 25 feet. The Pinnacle (French Cap), about a mile offshore, consists of two stone pillars atop a seamount at 45 feet. Two miles out, at Buck Island, a World War I freighter is resting in 40 feet. Atlantis Submarine has a dive site at Buck Island, taxiing passengers by boat to the submarine which submerges to depths of 90 feet, providing views of the corals and fishes. On the north coast, the calm waters off Coki Beach

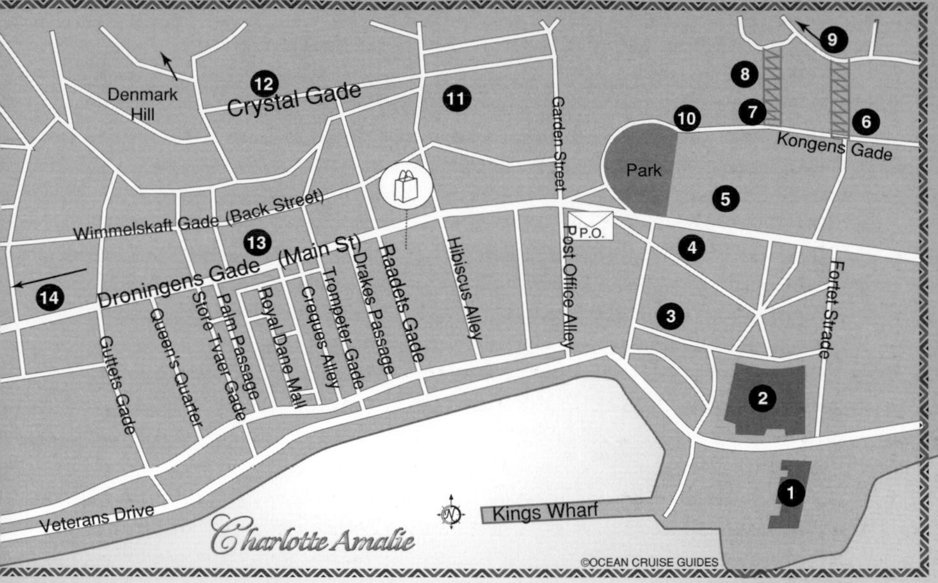

are excellent for snorkeling and beach dives, with a dive shop right on the beach. Lying opposite is Thatch Cay, another popular diving area.

Golf – Mahogany Run on the north coast is an 18-hole Fazio-designed championship course. Its famous 'Devil's Triangle' consists of three dramatic holes overlooking the Atlantic.

Downtown Charlotte Amalie

The **(1) Legislative Building**, a two-storey green building of Italian Renaissance design, is the seat of the U.S. Virgin Islands Senate. Built in 1874 as barracks for the Danish police, it was later used as housing for U.S. Marines Corps. It's open to visitors Monday through Friday.

(2) Fort Christian, built of red brick and rubble, is the oldest standing structure on St. Thomas. It was begun about 1666, completed in 1680 and altered in 1874 when the watch tower was removed and its north facade, with a crenelated clock tower, was added. The fort was later used as a jail, and is now a museum and National Historic Landmark.**(3) Emancipation Garden**, the site of many official ceremonies, commemorates the freeing of slaves in 1848 and contains a bust of Danish King Christian and a small replica Liberty Bell. A tourist information office (i) is located nearby at the corner of Tolbod Gade and Veterans Drive, opposite which is the open-air Vendors Market. The **(4) Grand Hotel**, originally called the Commercial Hotel & Coffee House, is a Greek Revival structure which occupied an entire block when built in 1840. Formerly three storeys tall, the top floor was presumably damaged by a hurricane sometime after 1896. The former hotel now houses a jewelry studio featuring designs by local artisans.

The **(5) Frederick Lutheran Church**, the official church of the Danish West Indies, was established in 1666 with worship services held in the homes of planters and soldiers, and then at Christensfort. The

the U.S. Virgin Islands

(Top) Government House
(Middle) Havensight Mall
(Bottom) A shopping street in downtown Charlotte Amalie

(Top) Legislative Building (Middle) Frederick Lutheran Church (Bottom) Charlotte Amalie's picturesque harbor

present building was built in 1793, gutted by fire in 1826 and damaged by a hurricane in 1870, after which the tower was added.

(6) Government House, completed in 1865, is a three-storey masonry building built in the neo-classical design. Its brick walls are painted white, as are the cast-iron verandahs that run the length of the first two storeys. Government offices are located here, including the Governor's Executive Offices. The Governor's official residence is the former Danish Consulate, an imposing two-storey mansion atop Denmark Hill. Two sets of stairs, the westerly one called **(7) The 99 Steps**, lead up the hillside behind Government House, past **(8) Haagensen House**, a restored 1820s townhouse which is now a museum. Standing atop Government Hill is **(9) Skytsborg** (Blackbeard's Castle), a five-storey conical tower constructed of rubble masonry by the Danish in 1678, with later changes. Now part of a hotel, the stone watch tower is said to have been used by the infamous pirate Blackbeard. **(10) Hotel 1829** (formerly Lavalette House) was built as a residence for a French sea captain and now houses one of Charlotte Amalie's finest restaurants. **(11) St. Thomas Reformed Church**, constructed in 1846, is a good example of Greek Revival building. **(12) Beracha Veshalom U'gemilut Hasidim**, built of cut stone and brick in 1833, is the second-oldest synagogue in the Western Hemisphere.

The **(13) Camille Pissaro Building** is where the famous impressionist painter lived above the family store in the 1840s. Born in a small Jewish community of Charlotte Amalie in 1830, Pissaro left St. Thomas in 1855 to study art in Paris. He became a teacher and friend of Gauguin and Cezanne, and died near Paris at the age of 73. The Pissaro building now houses the Tropicana Perfume shop and upstairs, above an inner courtyard entered off Main Street, is an art gallery.

(14) Market Square was, in 1946, officially named Rothschild Francis Square to honor the public service of this champion of civil rights and liberties. The square has long been a central meeting place where fresh produce, fish and spices are sold, with French farmers from the north side of the island bringing their fruits and vegetables to town by donkey. In the early 1900s, an open-air iron shed called the Bungalow was erected and the regular female vendors, called 'Market Women', each had their own spot under the shade of the bungalow – to the exclusion of any male vendors. The annual Carnival Food Fair is held here each April.

AREA ATTRACTIONS

West of Downtown – **Frenchtown**, founded as a fishing village by French Huguenots from St. Barts, lies west of Charlotte Amalie on the way to the Crown Bay cruise pier. Its restaurants and bars now create a lively night scene. The University of the Virgin Islands was founded in 1963 and the campus contains the Reichhold Center for the Arts where concerts and other events are held in its open-air amphitheatre.

East End – Coral World at Coki Point is a popular attraction with its underwater observatory, natural reef exhibit, aquarium and semi-submarine rides along a coral reef. Sharks, moray eels, stingrays and pink flamingos are some of the exotic creatures that can be seen here. Tillet Gardens, on the way to Coral World, is the site of an historic Danish cattle farm and a gallery featuring local arts and crafts.

North of Town – Drake's Seat, said to be used by Francis Drake as a lookout for Spanish ships while his fleet lay concealed in Magens Bay, offers breathtaking views of Magens Bay and the British Virgin Islands. **Estate St. Peter Great House & Botanical Gardens**, a former plantation estate, has been developed into a beautiful botanical garden with breathtaking ocean views from its mountainside location. The elegant, open-plan house is wrapped with white latticework and broad decks from which visitors can gaze at more than twenty offshore islands. Local art is on display and outside, on the lushly landscaped grounds, are more than 500 varieties of plants and trees.

A drive to **Mountain Top**, highest viewing point on the island, provides stunning views of St. John, the British Virgin Islands and Charlotte Amalie Harbor. Refreshments served here include the original banana daiquiri. The attractive complex includes Caribbean shops, an aviary and aquarium.

ST. JOHN

In contrast to bustling Charlotte Amalie, a shopper's paradise, is the peaceful island of St. John, a nature lover's paradise. Lush and mountainous, St. John is indented by numerous bays at the head of which lie some of the world's most beautiful beaches. The island is also a botanist's delight with its proliferation of tropical plants and flowers.

When A. S. Orsted, discoverer of plankton, travelled by barkentine to the Danish West Indies in 1845, he was so captivated by the plant life he found that he changed his field of study from zoology to botany. Born of an illustrious Danish family, Orsted was especially besotted with St. John where uncultivated slopes presented him with an array of indigenous plant species, including bamboo, guava berry, century plant and coconut palms. A century later, in the early '50s, Laurance Rockefeller paid St. John a visit. A member of the wealthy American family famous for its philanthropy, he too arrived by sailboat and he too was so impressed with the serene and natural beauty of the island that he purchased about two thirds of it, which he donated to the United States federal government for the establishment of the Virgin Islands National Park in 1956. The park has expanded since its inception and now covers about three-quarters of the island.

Residents of St. John, who number about 3,000, call their island 'Love City' and most visitors do fall in love with this protected paradise. Its highest point is Bordeaux Mountain at 1,277 feet, and the island's steep slopes provide dramatic vistas of distant islands and nearby cays where a deep blue sea fades to pale aquamarine at the head of beach-lined bays.

Getting Around

Cruise ships stopping at St. Thomas usually offer shore excursions to nearby St. John. Independent travellers can take one of the passenger ferries that connect St. John with St. Thomas, and these depart regularly from both Charlotte Amalie and Red Hook on St. Thomas for Cruz Bay on St. John. The Red Hook/Cruz Bay ferry leaves every hour on the hour both ways, is a 20-minute ride and costs $3.00 one way. The Charlotte Amalie/Cruz Bay ferry ride takes 45 minutes, costs $7.00 one way, and leaves Charlotte Amalie at one- to two-hour intervals throughout the day.

Cruz Bay is the main town on the island and open-air safari buses await here to transport visitors around the island. A Visitors Center at Cruz Bay provides information on the Park – its beaches, trails and activities, including organized hikes and historic bus tours.

Beaches – Inviting beaches line St. John's northwest coast, including the sugary white sands and clear turquoise waters of Trunk Bay – considered one the most beautiful beaches in the world. Excellent for swimming, Trunk Bay also has an underwater snorkel trail. On shore are shaded picnic areas and a snack bar. Cinnamon Bay has open-air dining and a watersports center that rents snorkel gear and beach chairs. Sailing and windsurfing

can also be enjoyed here, as well as National Park interpretive programs. Other lovely beaches include those at Hawksnest Bay and Caneel Bay, where a resort owned by Laurance Rockefeller is located.

Dive & Snorkel Sites – Cinnamon Bay has good snorkeling and a watersports center that rents snorkel gear. Trunk Bay has an underwater snorkeling trail with red, white and blue markers to guide snorkelers and identify the coral and marine life. Caneel Bay is recommended for the chance to view stingrays, green turtles, cushion sea stars, pipes-of-pan sponges and sargent majors. Popular dive sites are Steven's Cay, Carval Rock and Congo Cay.

Shopping – Cruz Bay is where most of the island shops are located, offering both duty-free goods and local arts and crafts. Mongoose Junction, across from the National Park Dock, is a pleasant shopping complex built of Caribbean stone. Its multi-level design of shaded terraces and tropical foliage contains fine shops, galleries and open-air restaurants.

Island Attractions – Points of interest on the island include the Annaberg Sugar Mill ruins, beautifully situated on the north side of the island overlooking Sir Francis Drake Passage. Also of note are the prehistoric petroglyphs at Reef Bay.

(Opposite, top) The ruins of Annaberg Sugar Mill. (Opposite, bottom) Cruz Bay is the main port on St. John. (Right) St. John's Trunk Bay is undoubtedly one of the world's most beautiful beaches, ideal for swimming and snorkeling.

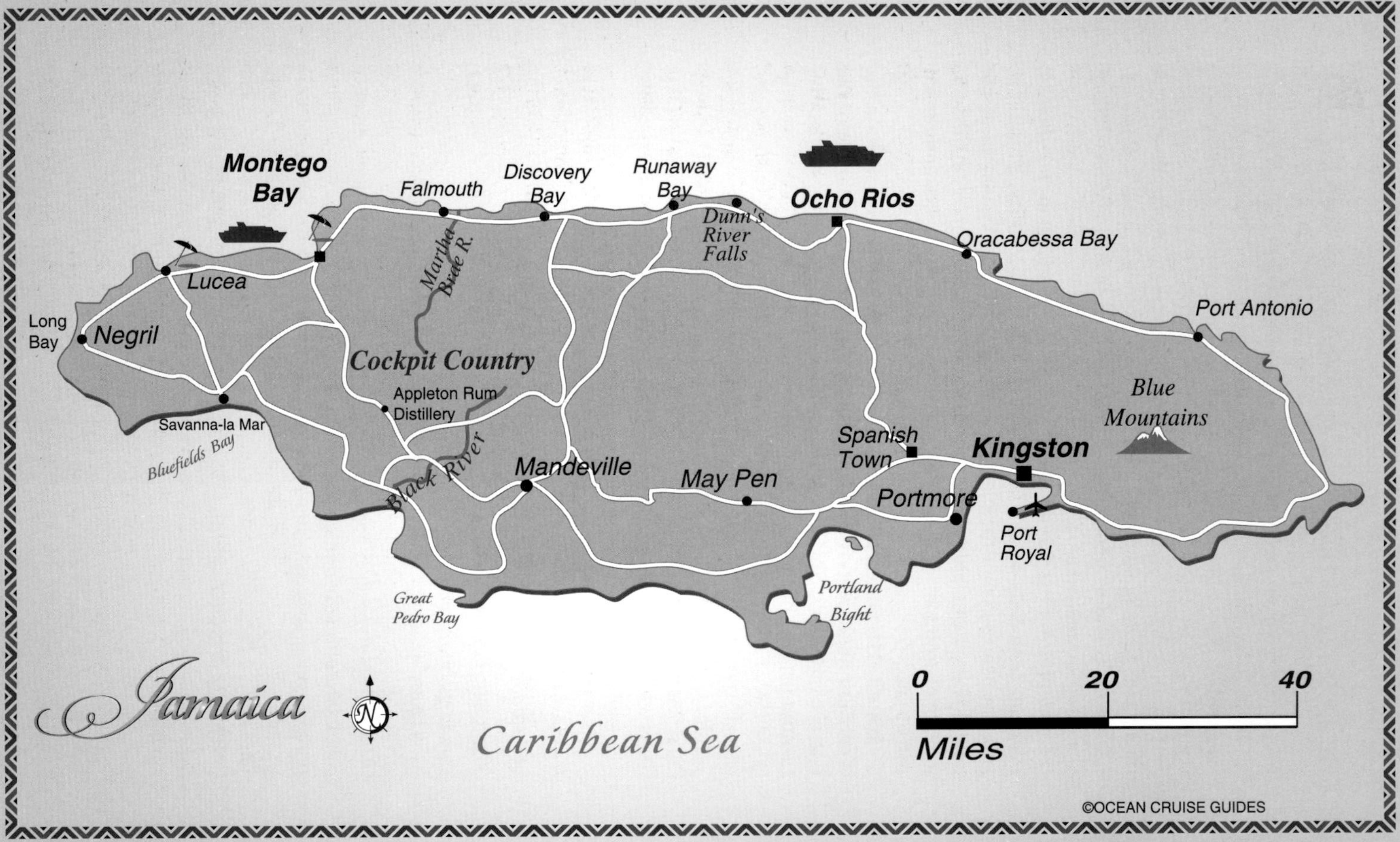
Montego
Bay
Falmouth
Discovery
Bay
Runaway
Bay
Dunn's
River
Falls
Ocho Rios
Oracabessa Bay
Port Antonio
Lucea
Long
Bay
Negril
Martha
Brae R.
Cockpit Country
Appleton Rum
Distillery
Savanna-la Mar
Bluefields Bay
Black River
Mandeville
May Pen
Spanish
Town
Kingston
Blue
Mountains
Portmore
Port
Royal
Great
Pedro Bay
Portland
Bight
Jamaica
N
Caribbean Sea
0
20
40
Miles
©OCEAN CRUISE GUIDES

JAMAICA

Jamaica, third largest island of the West Indies after Cuba and Hispaniola, is one of the most beautiful in the Caribbean. A lush and mountainous island where rivers rush to the sea and white beaches line sparkling bays, Jamaica has long attracted a diversity of peoples to its shores, from famous buccaneers to famous artists. The country's official motto is 'Out of Many, One People' – acknowledging the range of races and nationalities that have colonized this island nation. Its history is turbulent and social problems still exist, but a 'No problem mon' attitude sums up the buoyant spirit of Jamaicans.

A limestone plateau more than 3,000 feet above sea level, Jamaica has a mountainous backbone that rises at its eastern end to the Blue Mountains and the island's tallest peak at 7,402 feet. Narrow coastal plains lie on either side of the mountain chain where fertile slopes and broad river valleys support the country's export crops of sugarcane, bananas, ginger, citrus fruits, cocoa, pimento, tobacco and its famous Blue Mountain Coffee. Most of these crops are grown on large plantations while small farms grow subsistence crops such as yams, breadfruit and cassava.

Rainfall, abundant in the mountainous regions, diminishes westward across a rugged plateau of streams and subterranean rivers. The heart of this plateau, called the Cockpits, is used for livestock grazing. During Jamaica's colonial days, escaped or freed slaves – called maroons – fled to Cockpit country where they lived in villages and organized frequent uprisings against the European landowners.

Arawaks, an agricultural people, first inhabited the island about a thousand years ago and they called it Xaymaca – 'land of woods and streams'. The Spanish began colonizing Jamaica in 1509 under licence from Christopher Columbus's son, and the Arawaks soon died out under Spanish occupation. Captured by the British in 1655 and formally ceded to England in 1670, the island was a haven for buccaneers before becoming a major sugar producer in the 18th century.

Half of Jamaica's population is still rural with much of the work force employed in agriculture. However, the continuing trend is one of migration to the cities. Of the country's 2-1/2 million residents, about 600,000 live in the capital of Kingston. Situated on a deep, landlocked harbor, Kingston was established in 1692 after an earthquake destroyed Port Royal at the tip of the peninsula which forms the harbor. This British outpost and pirate haven suddenly sank 33 feet into the sea, tak-

Jamaica

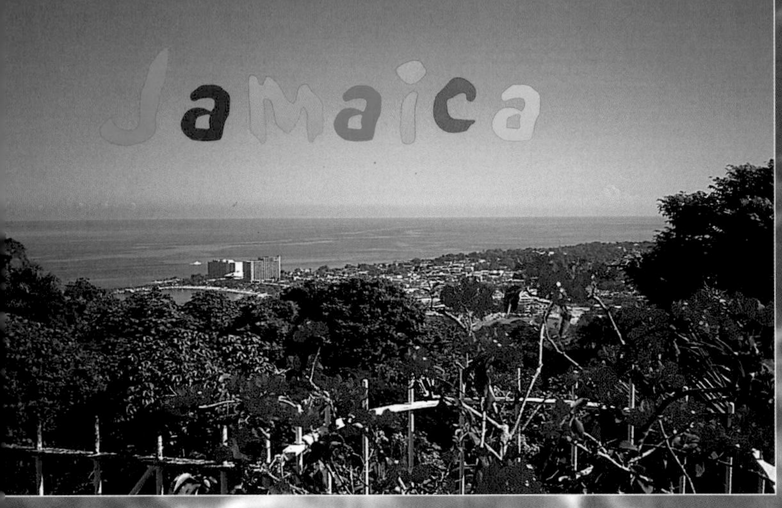

(Above) Jamaica's scenic north coast. (Below) River rafting on the Martha Brae. (Opposite Page, Top) Ocho Rios waterfront. (Middle) A resort at Turtle Beach. (Bottom) The tiered falls at Dunn's River.

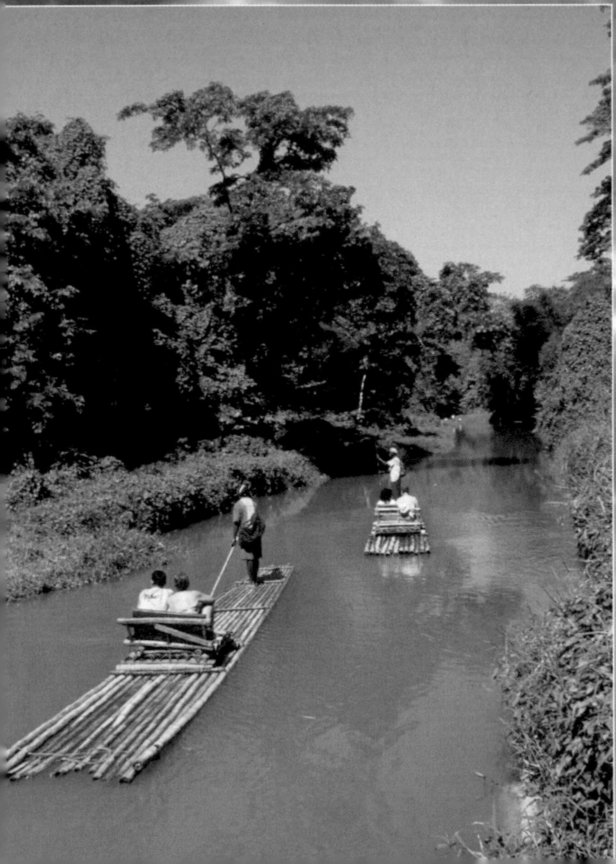

ing 2,000 inhabitants with it, and when a subsequent tsunami swept ashore, a British naval frigate was carried across the sunken townsite and desposited inland.

Plans are now underway to recreate 17th-century Port Royal, which wasn't property excavated until 1965, although some of its treasure was salvaged at once. The most famous name associated with Port Royal is Sir Henry Morgan, a Welsh privateer whose daring exploits included the sacking of Portobelo in 1668 and the capture of Panama in 1671. He was eventually arrested on charges of piracy and sent to England where, with war against Spain threatening once more, he was knighted and returned to Jamaica as deputy-governor.

The entire north coast, from Negril at its western end to Port Antonio at its eastern end, is dotted with beach-lined bays and palm-shaded resorts, including some of the most exclusive in the Caribbean. It also contains Jamaica's two main cruise ports – Ocho Rios and Montego Bay.

Many a famous person has spent time living or vacationing in Jamaica, beginning with Christopher Columbus who first stepped ashore in 1494 at Rio Bueno. On his fourth voyage to the West Indies in 1503, Columbus beached his damaged ships on the island's north shore and spent a year on Jamaican soil awaiting rescue. In more recent times, the swashbuckling movie star Errol Flynn pulled into Port Antonio in his private yacht to escape a storm and ended up building a home there on Navy Island.

For a relatively small country, Jamaica has had a far-reaching impact on the rest of the world with its music, dance and art. Jamaicans are international in outlook and many of its citizens have migrated to other countries, most notably Britain. Over 90% of Jamaicans are of West African descent with Asians and Europeans adding to the cultural tapestry of this dynamic island nation. Yet, the country's rich social fabric has at times appeared to be unraveling, with political tribalism resulting in election violence.

The People's National Party (PNP) was founded in 1938 by Norman Manley. His cousin, Sir Alexander Bustamante, founded the Jamaica Labour Party (JLP). These two parties, their roots in rival trade unions, have dominated Jamaican politics since 1944 when universal adult suffrage was introduced. Jamaica gained its independence from Britain in 1962 but remains a member of the British Commonwealth. The country's economy is one of the more prosperous in the West Indies, despite a recession that persisted throughout the 1970s and 1980s. After embracing socialism in the '70s, Jamaica now has a free market economy based on tourism, agricultural products and the export of bauxite, from which alumina is extracted.

Hurricane Gilbert caused widespread devastation when it swept the length of the island in 1988 and the country's tourism industry was crippled. The island has since regained its prominence as a popular Caribbean destination but many tourists stay at all-inclusive resorts. The government is trying to counter this insular attitude with a Meet the People program in which the tourist board will arrange for a visitor to spend time with a Jamaican host who shares a common interest.

Cruise passengers who are apprehensive about venturing ashore can simply book a shore excursion. Those who prefer to strike out on their own will find that Jamaicans, despite their reputation for aggressively selling their wares (including narcotics), are an outgoing people who will respond to a polite but firm 'No thank you' with a 'No problem mon' wave of the hand. Most Jamaicans have a good sense of humor and this, rather than anger, is usually the best way to fend off persistent advances.

Reggae & Rastafarianism

Rastafarianism is a religious-cultural movement that began in Jamaica in the 1930s when Haile Selassie (also named Ras Tafari) became Emperor of Ethiopia, as predicted by Jamaican hero Marcus Garvey. Selassie was hailed as the movement's messiah, Ethiopia was the promised land, and Garvey was considered a major prophet and early leader in creating black awareness and unity.

Reggae,which originated in the 1960s among the poor blacks of Kingston, is the protest music of the Rastafarian faith. Its sound is characterized by an off-beat rhythm that draws on American soul and traditonal African and Jamaican folk music. Reggae's most famous performer is the late Bob Marley, a Jamaican singer, songwriter and guitarist to whom a museum is dedicated in Kingston.

Born in 1945 and deserted by his white Jamaican father, Marley was raised by his mother in Nine Miles village on Jamaica's north coast. As a youth, he and his mother moved to the poor shanty area of Kingston where he worked in the welding trade while seeking success as a musician. Fame finally came to Marley in the '70s when his new group began playing reggae and their songs soared in the charts. When Marley died of cancer at the age of 36, he had achieved international stardom and received his country's highest public honor, the Order of Merit. The worldwide popularity of reggae is attributed in large part to Marley, whose songs supported his belief in non-violence and the Rastafarian religion.

Bob Marley, the 'King of Reggae Music'

Rastas, who object to shaving and cutting hair, wear their hair in long braids called dreadlocks – a symbolic connection with the Ethiopian lion. They are vegetarians who prefer natural foods and many of them smoke ganga, locally grown marijuana. Not everyone wearing dreadlocks is a Rasta and most 'real' Rastas are congenial, generally preferring the country to urban areas.

OCHO RIOS

The original Spanish name for Ocho Rios was Las Chorreras – The Waterfalls – an appropriate name for a port situated at the base of lush mountains where rivers and streams spill into the sea. A former fishing village, Ocho Rios has been developed as a tourist destination with high-rise hotels and condominiums lining the beaches to the east of Ocho Rios Bay. The local population numbers about 11,000 and residents speak an English-based patois. Ocho Rios Bay contains two piers – the Reynolds Pier and the new cruise ship pier which is joined by a jetty to shore where telephones, tourist information and a handful of shops are located.

GETTING AROUND

The cruise lines offer organized excursions to the major attractions, or you can hire a taxi. A visitor information booth is located in the terminal building and the taxi fares to various destinations are posted nearby. A dispatcher is also stationed there and, upon telling him where you want to go, he will hail you a driver whose car will carry the red Public Passenger Vehicle (PPV) license plates. If you want to visit a number of destinations, negotiate the fare with your driver before getting in. The fare is per taxi, so travelling in groups of four is the most economical. Some sample taxi tour rates for one to four persons: Dunn's River Falls – $20; Prospect Plantation – $30.

Shopping–Jamaica offers good buys in duty-free goods and great bargains in locally produced clothing, wood

(Left) Turtle Beach

(Opposite page) Cruise pier at Ocho Rios

carvings, coffee and rum. Beautiful, hand-carved walking sticks can be bought for $15 and tee shirts screened with unique Jamaican designs sell for as little as $5. More expensive are the beautiful batik cottons and silks. The exchange rate is approximately 45 Jamaican dollars for 1 US dollar, but there's no need to exchange money because American currency, travellers cheques and credit cards are widely accepted.

Within walking distance of the cruise ship pier are the **(1) Taj Mahal Centre** and **(2) Soni's Plaza**, or you can take a shopping shuttle which costs $2 per person. In between are the **(3) Old Market Craft Shoppes** and **(4) Craft Park**, where local artisans sell their wares. Excellent arts and crafts can also be bought at the Dunn's River Falls marketplace, and paintings by acclaimed Jamaican artists are on display at the **(9) Harmony Hall Gallery**, five miles east of the cruise port.

Best Beaches – Beautiful white sand beaches line the shoreline east of Ocho Rios Bay. Most of these are backed by hotels and have controlled access to protect tourists from pedlars. The admission fee is usually $1.00 per person. Closest to the pier is Turtle Beach, and an excellent beach lies on the other side of The Point at Mallards Bay.

Snorkeling excursions are available out of Ocho Rios to nearby shallow coral gardens, some of which have been damaged in recent years by hurricanes. Serious divers recommend going deeper to see an abundance of coral and sponge life. Wall diving is popular at Runaway Bay.

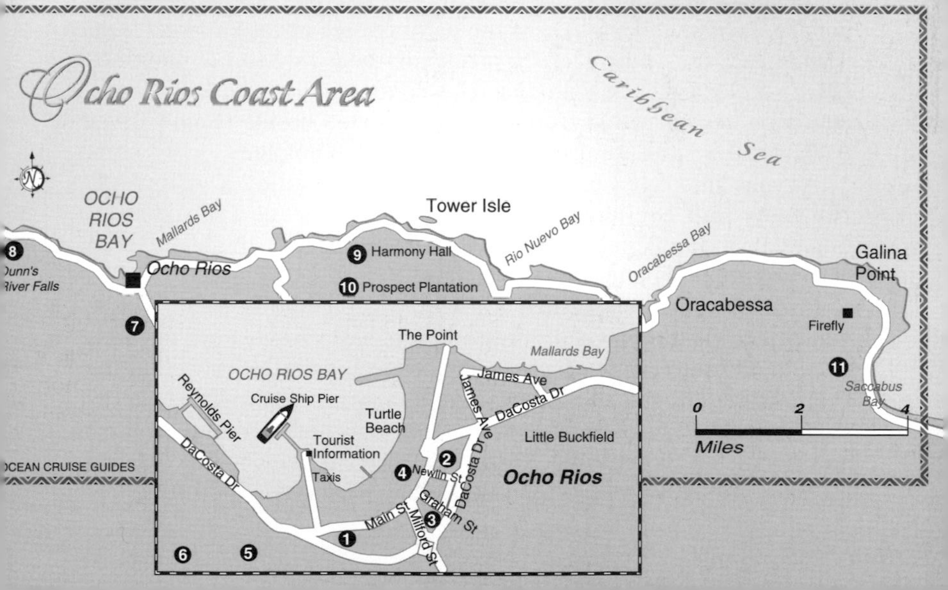

Ocho Rios Coast Area
Caribbean Sea
OCHO RIOS BAY
Mallards Bay
Tower Isle
Rio Nuevo Bay
Oracabessa Bay
Galina Point
Dunn's River Falls
Ocho Rios
Harmony Hall
Prospect Plantation
Oracabessa
Firefly
Saccabus Bay
0 2 4
Miles
The Point
Mallards Bay
OCHO RIOS BAY
Reynolds Pier
Cruise Ship Pier
Turtle Beach
James Ave
DaCosta Dr
Little Buckfield
Tourist Information
Taxis
Newlin St
Graham St
Main St
Milford St
Ocho Rios
OCEAN CRUISE GUIDES

Sandal's Golf & Country Club, overlooking Mallards Bay, is considered one of the most scenic in Jamaica, situated 700 feet up into the mountains. This 18-hole par-71 course was designed by P.K. Sanders and totals 6,500 yards.

Local Attractions

A botanical garden and bird sanctuary, **(5) Shaw Park Gardens**' hillside location provides panoramic views in a tropical setting. The Coyaba River flows through **(6) Coyaba Garden** where riverside paths and boardwalks lead past waterfalls and pools filled with koi carp and turtles. The museum contains pre-Columbian artifacts and the gallery displays creative works by Jamaicans.

Area Highlights

(7) Fern Gully, a former riverbed that went dry following an earthquake, is a three-mile stretch of road that winds into the Blue Mountains and leads, eventually, to Kingston on the other side of the island. The many species of fern that grow in this gully form a lush canopy for vehicles passing beneath it.

One of Jamaica's most popular attractions, **(8) Dunn's River Falls** consist of clear mountain water flowing seaward across a tiered limestone bed. Visitors are charged $5 US to enter the park area, which includes a guided climb up this stunning set of falls. Guides lead visitors, in single file, along a known route. Operators of the park are fairly insistent you remain part of a guided climb to prevent personal injury. For an additional $5, a guide will hold your camera and other belongings as you scramble up the falls. A pair of running shoes or aqua socks (which can be rented at the Falls) are recommended for the climb over slippery stones and rushing, knee-deep water. Dunn's Falls are about 1.5 miles by road from Ocho Rios and can also be reached by boat, a popular excursion being one of the party cruises aboard a large yacht that departs the cruise pier for a relaxing boat ride to the mouth of Dunn's River and back, with time allowed for climbing the falls. A new attraction has opened at Dolphin Cove, located beside Dunn's River Falls, where visitors can feed, pet and swim with dolphins.

Anyone interested in Jamaican folk art will enjoy a visit to **(9) Harmony Hall**, a restored Victorian great house. Set on a small plantation estate four miles east of Ocho Rios, it contains an art gallery, craft and book shops, boutique and restaurant.

(10) Prospect Plantation is a working plantation estate where guides take visitors on tractor-drawn jitneys past various flora and agricultural crops including bananas, sugar cane and coffee, as well as the White River Gorge and Sir Harold's Viewpoint, where Cuba can be seen on a clear day. Horseback tours are also available on each of three varied trails that traverse the 900 acres of grounds, which also contain a miniature golf course and a gift shop selling local crafts and souvenirs.

About 10 miles east of Prospect Plantation, **(11) Brimmer Hall** Plantation is another working plantation providing tours by tractor-drawn jitney. The beautiful grounds contain an 18th-century great house open for viewing, as well as a swimming pool, bar and shops.

Firefly, Noel Coward's "earthly paradise" set atop a plateau with a dramatic view of the surf pounding into Saccabus Bay, was the famous playwright's home for the last 25 years of his life and the place where he wrote some of his most celebrated works. Screen stars and British royalty would come to visit, but when Coward died in 1973 he asked that no fuss be made, and the site of his grave was where he often sat with friends sipping a pre-dinner cocktail while looking out to the sea. Coward's home and contents were bequeathed to Jamaica in 1975 and restored as a museum run on behalf of the National Heritage Trust by Island Outpost, which is owned by Chris Blackwell, the multi-millionaire founder of Island Records. However, Firefly failed to attract enough visitors and in early 2000 plans were made to auction many of Coward's belongings and rent the property out for private receptions.

At **Oracabessa** ("Golden Head" in Spanish), the road winds past Goldeneye, an estate overlooking a private cove which was the former winter retreat of the late Ian Fleming, who wrote his James Bond novels at this idyllic location. Noel Coward referred to Fleming's rather plain U-shaped house as the "Goldeneye, nose and throat clinic" while describing the cove's crescent beach of dazzling white sand as "unbelievable". Chris Blackwell's Island Outpost now owns the property and has converted it into a boutique-style luxury resort.

Other Excursions – Helicopter flightseeing trips can be taken from the heli-pad at Reynolds Pier. A 20-minute flight takes in the lush and varied coastal sights of the Ocho Rios area, including aerial views of Dunn's River Falls, sumptuous seaside villas, and beaches lapped by an azure sea.

River rafting on the **Martha Brae**, which lies between Montego Bay and Ocho Rios, is a popular attraction. On bamboo rafts carrying two people, the raft man uses a pole to guide the raft gently downstream past bamboo groves and chirping birds. The drive from Ocho Rios to Martha Brae takes 1-1/2 hours along the winding coastal highway, and the river ride is just over an hour in length. An organized shore excursion lasts about five hours, often with a stop at Columbus Park, near Discovery Bay, where Columbus first landed at Jamaica. Other notable places along this stretch of coastline include Nine Miles village, the birthplace and gravesite of **Bob Marley**, and the 18th-century Georgian town of Falmouth near the mouth of the Martha Brae, about 20 miles east of Montego Bay.

Greenwood Great House, located 16 miles east of Montego Bay, was built by relatives of poet Elizabeth Barrett Browning, and the stately mansion is furnished with antiques and contains a rare-book library.

A tour of Greenwood gives visitors an inside look at the privileged lives once enjoyed by plantation owners.

Rose Hall, a British mansion built in 1770, lies about 10 miles east of Montego Bay and is Jamaica's most famous great house thanks to a legendary mistress by the name of Annie Palmer. She lived here around 1820 and is said to have murdered three husbands and numerous slave lovers whom she controlled through witchcraft. According to one version of the legend, she was finally murdered by a lover who felt he was destined to be next on Annie's hit list.

MONTEGO BAY

Jamaica's second-largest city, Montego Bay is one of the Caribbean's most popular resorts, beautifully situated on a beach-lined bay surrounded by green hills. A commercial center and shipping port, it's a growing city of over 70,000 residents, many of whom live in shanty towns on the outskirts. On the lower slopes of the Miranda Hills are luxury hotels set in manicured grounds.

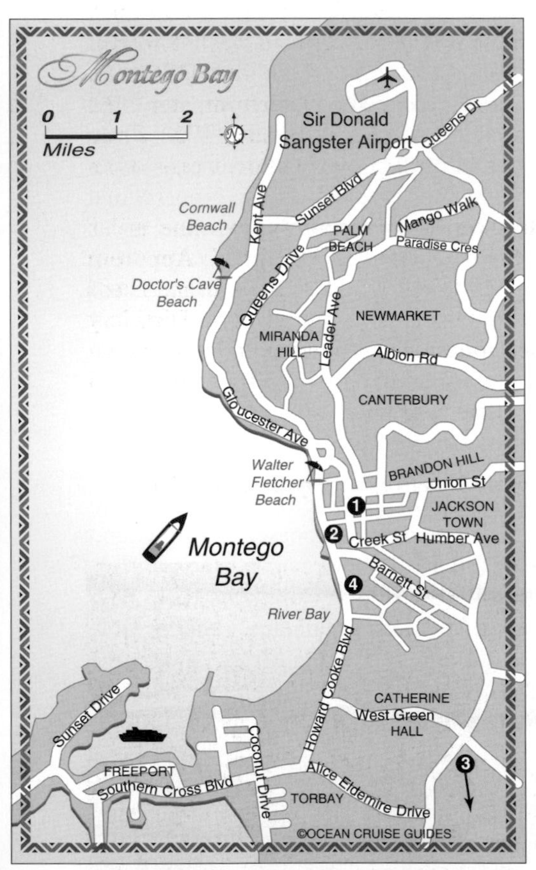

GETTING AROUND

The cruise ships dock at Freeport, about three miles west of downtown. An information booth and telephones are situated on the dock. Nearby is the Montego Freeport duty-free shopping area. The taxi fare into town is about $12 for up to four people, and only JUTA (Jamaica Union of Travellers Association) taxis and mini-vans should be rented.

Best Beaches – Doctor's Cave Beach, located just north of the town center, is Montego Bay's most celebrated beach. At the turn of the century it was a fashionable health resort and many distinguished visitors came to bathe here. Today it's Montego Bay's most popular beach, with an entry charge which includes change facilities. Other good stretches of sand are found at Walter Fletcher Beach, south of Doctor's Cave, and at Cornwall Beach which lies directly north of Doctor's Cave with a Jamaican Tourist Board office situated at its south end. Coral sea gardens can be viewed by glass-bottom boat in the clear, sheltered waters of Doctor's Cave, and snorkel and dive excursions can be arranged through local operators or your ship's shore excursion office.

A championship golf course (7,130 yards, par 72) is located at the **Half Moon Golf Course**, near the sea on the eastern outskirts of Montego Bay.

Local Sights & Shopping – The city's business district includes a few historic landmarks, most of them situated on or near **(1) Sam Sharpe Square** – named for a Jamaican hero who was hanged in 1831 for leading a slave revolt. On the southwest side of the square stands the Court House, an early-19th century colonial building. The Cage, a small building of the same period on the square's northeast corner, was used for detaining runaway slaves. Nearby, on Church Street, are a number of restored Georgian buildings including St. James's Parish Church which was rebuilt after suffering major damage in a 1957 earthquake. South of Church Street, near the water, is the colorful **(2) Crafts Market**. A few blocks to the north, along the waterfront, stand the remains of Fort Montego which was built by the British in 1752. From here Gloucester Avenue, the main shopping thoroughfare, wends north past the hotel strip.

Area Attractions – (3) Rockland Bird Sanctuary, nine miles south of Montego Bay, is popular with visitors, as is the **(4) Appleton Estate Express**, a train that departs daily from Montego Bay and heads into Cockpit Country, location of the famous Appleton Rum Distillery and the Ipswich Caves with their limestone stalagmites and stalactites.

East of Montego Bay are Rose Hall, Greenwood Great House and the Martha Brae River (see pages 163 and 164).

Famous beaches and British mansions are among the attractions at Montego Bay.

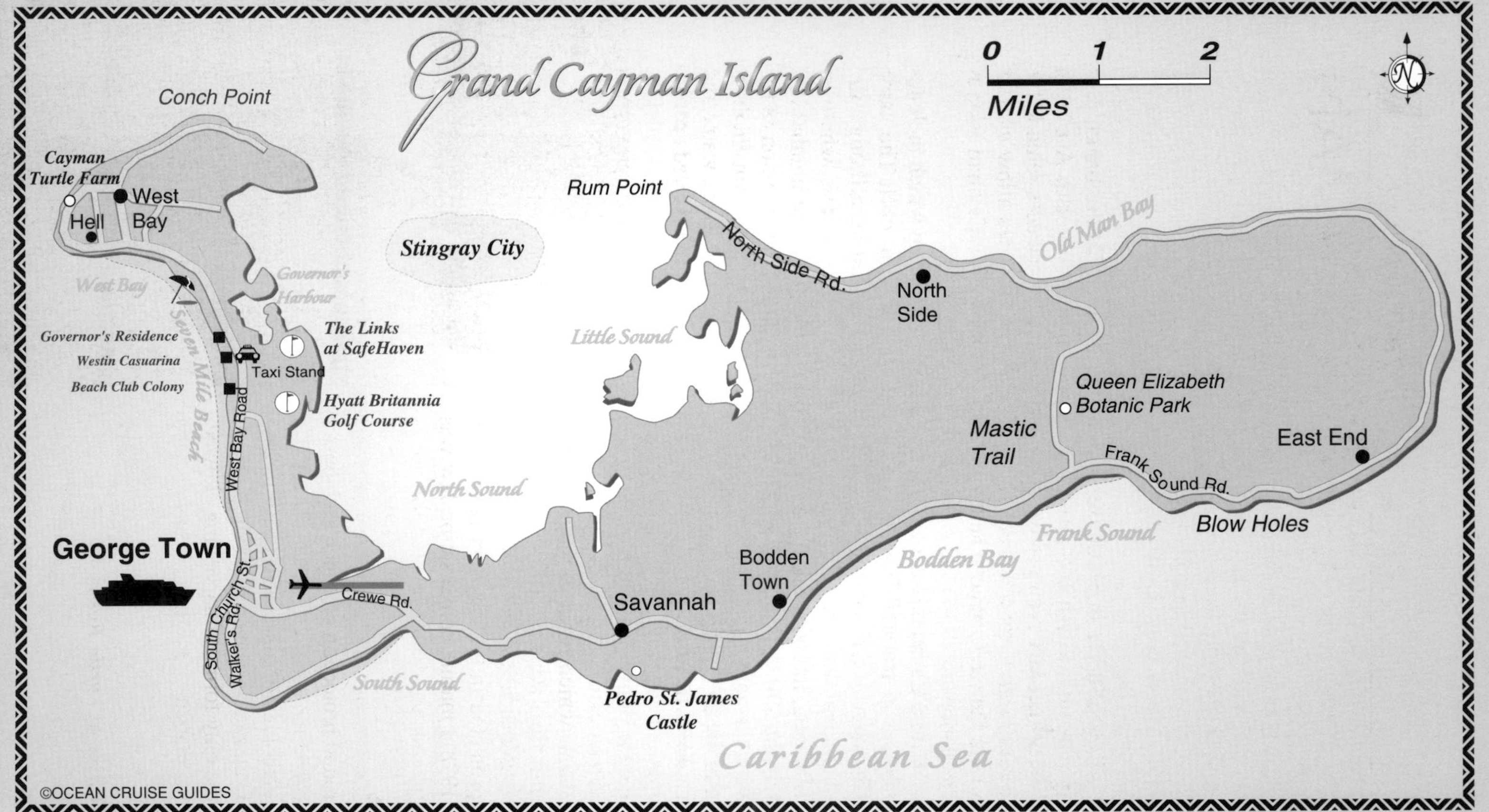
Grand Cayman Island
0 1 2
Miles
N
Conch Point
Cayman Turtle Farm
West Bay
Hell
Stingray City
Rum Point
North Side Rd.
Old Man Bay
North Side
West Bay
Governor's Harbour
Seven Mile Beach
Governor's Residence
Westin Casuarina
Beach Club Colony
Taxi Stand
The Links at SafeHaven
Hyatt Britannia Golf Course
West Bay Road
Little Sound
North Sound
Queen Elizabeth Botanic Park
Mastic Trail
East End
Frank Sound Rd.
Blow Holes
Frank Sound
Bodden Bay
Bodden Town
Savannah
George Town
South Church St.
Walker's Rd.
Crewe Rd.
South Sound
Pedro St. James Castle
Caribbean Sea
©OCEAN CRUISE GUIDES

GRAND CAYMAN

Grand Cayman, an international center for offshore banking, is one of the best-rated dive locations in the world. A person needn't even get wet to enjoy some of the island's remarkable aquatic sights, for a variety of vessels and observatories allow visitors to see the reefs, wrecks and marine life for which the Cayman Islands are famous.

Grand Cayman is the largest of a three-island group which includes Little Cayman and Cayman Brac – a Gaelic word for cliff. The name Cayman is derived from a Carib word for crocodile, although the Caymans were first called Las Tortugas by Columbus when he observed, in 1503, the hundreds of turtles living on these uninhabited islands. The Spanish paid these flat coral outcrops little attention as the soil was poor and there were no precious metals to mine, but English, Dutch and French ships pulled in regularly to take on fresh water and salted turtle meat. Today, the green sea turtle is an endangered species and in 1978 the United States banned the import of all turtle products, even those raised at the Cayman Turtle Farm, which releases young turtles into local waters.

Sea turtles are not the only species protected in the Cayman Islands. In 1978 a marine conversation law was passed, and four preservation zones were established in 1986. The Replenishment Zones provide year-round protection of conch and lobster breeding grounds, as well as every other kind of marine life. Line fishing from shore or beyond the drop-off are the only forms of harvesting allowed. Permanent moorings have been

Cayman Turtle Farm

Grand Cayman's tender pier is within easy walking distance of George Town's attractions and harbor-based sightseeing boats.

installed to protect the reefs which were becoming damaged by the anchors of dive boats. These progressive conservation measures have extended onto land with the establishment of animal sanctuaries and the opening of a botanical park by Queen Elizabeth. Grand Cayman's indigenous animal species include iguanas and parrots. Bird watching is popular here, with more than a hundred species of birds observed, including those on spring and fall migrations.

The Cayman Islands, a British Crown Colony since 1670, were a dependency of Jamaica when transferred from Spain to Great Britain under the terms of the Treaty of Madrid. Shortly thereafter the Cayman Islands were settled by a motley collection of British army deserters, shipwrecked sailors, retired pirates and African slaves who gained freedom when ships carrying them foundered on Cayman reefs.

Slavery was abolished by Britain in 1833, a year after a representative government was established on the Cayman Islands. When Jamaica opted for independence from Britain in 1962, a debate ensued among Cayman residents who eventually voted to remain a British Crown Colony. About 30,000 people live on the three islands, the majority on Grand Cayman. Of mixed origin and free of racial tensions, they descend from the English, Irish, Scottish and Africans who first settled the islands. With few natural resources on these mangrove-covered islands, the Cayman men traditionally made their living from the sea – turtle fishing, ship building and serving in the merchant marine. As recently as the 1950s, those working on foreign-owned ships were sustaining the local economy with the money they sent back home.

Grand Cayman remained an isolated backwater until 1954 when an airfield was built. But it wasn't until the island's troublesome mosquitoes were brought under control in the '70s that tourists began arriving in droves. The climate is ideal, the beaches are beautiful and the marine life prolific due to the varied underwater terrain which ranges from shallow coral reefs to submarine canyons. Meanwhile, Cayman's political stability and attractive tax laws make it an ideal environment for offshore banking interests. Some 70 financial institutions, six of which are clearing banks, operate on Grand Cayman where local services include offshore incorporation, company management and private banking. This thriving financial industry, which includes major accounting firms, is subject to strict government controls – which apply to both its banks and its customers. But professionalism and integrity do not provide good material for a Hollywood script, so Caymanians were more than happy to cooperate with Paramount Pictures when its film crew arrived at Grand Cayman to shoot scenes for *The Firm*, a movie of intrigue and corruption based on John Grisham's book and starring Gene Hackman, Tom Cruise and Jeanne Tripplehorn.

The movie's underwater scenes were shot at Soto's Reef and Rhapsody – two dive sites close to George Town. A sheltered cove on North Sound is where the fictitious 'Abanks Dive Lodge' was built, an attraction that will be left intact. The pool bar at the Grand Hyatt Hotel and the Holiday Inn's beachside bar were other film locations, as was Seven Mile Beach and a bank in George Town. A number of locals appeared as extras in the movie, including singer and songwriter George Nowak, who calls himself Barefoot Man.

GETTING AROUND

The cruise ships anchor off George Town and tender their passengers ashore. A visitor information booth and telephones are located at the north tender pier. The town's sights and stores are all within easy walking distance of the waterfront, and a shuttle bus takes visitors to Seven Mile Beach for a fee of $4 per person. A regular taxi ride beween George Town and Seven Mile Beach is $12. The Holiday Taxi Stand is located at

A cruise ship anchors off George Town where shore excursions include snorkeling and scuba diving.

the Westin Casuarina Resort

Ship-organized excursions cover most of the island, concentrating on its western end where Stingray City and Seven Mile Beach are located. Passengers interested in touring the island independently can hire a taxi (about $40 US to East End) or rent a car (approximately $40 a day plus $7.50 for a temporary driving permit) as well as mopeds, motorbikes and bicycles. Driving is on the left.

Shopping – A free port, Grand Cayman carries an assortment of duty-free goods. George Town, where the majority of shops are located (many of which are closed on Sundays), is very clean and orderly with no roadside pedlars. Local items to look for include numismatic jewelry, crafted from old coins retrieved from sunken vessels and featured in exquisite gold-and-diamond settings. Unique to the Cayman Islands are sculptures and jewelry made of an earth-toned, hard dolomite stone called caymanite that was discovered at East End.

The Cayman Island dollar equals about $1.25 US, but American currency is accepted throughout the islands. American and Canadian visitors should be aware it is against customs regulations to import turtle products into their countries.

Local Sights – Overlooking the pier area is the **(1) Cayman Islands National Museum**, housed in the former courthouse and containing displays on the islands' natural and cultural history, including artifacts of pirate lore. Cardinal, one of the main shopping streets, leads to the post office and the adjacent **(2) Elizabethan Square**. A few blocks west on Edward is the Public Library. Across the street is a small park containing a massive fig tree. At the intersection of Edward and Fort Streets is **(3) Clock Tower**, a monument to Britain's King George V. Fort Street leads down to the waterfront where the remains of Fort

The Cayman Islands National Museum is housed in Grand Cayman's oldest surviving building, a former courthouse.

George can be seen, built in the 17th century to protect the island from pirate attacks. Nearby, on Harbour Drive, is the restored 19th-century **(4) Elmslie Memorial Church**.

Best Beaches – The natural choice for cruise passengers is Seven Mile Beach, one of the finest in the Caribbean, which starts just north of George Town and stretches for about five miles along the island's western shore. Lined with hotels, this beautiful white-sand beach is free of pedlars and ideal for swimming, snorkeling and other water sports. Taxi vans run between George Town and Seven Mile Beach at a cost of $4 per person. The cruise lines often arrange with one of the hotels for their passengers to utilize its beach-front facilities for a small fee. Sailboards and other equipment can be rented at the Holiday Inn sports center located beside the public beach which is usually uncrowded. **Government House**, the Governor's official residence, is on the far side of the public beach area. Another way to visit Seven Mile Beach is by glass-bottom party boat, departing from George Town.

Seven Mile Beach

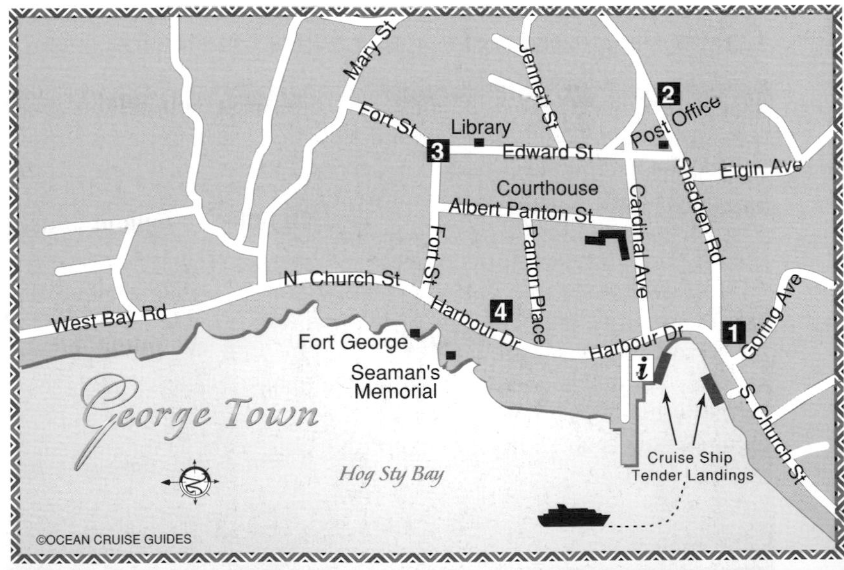

A diver swims with the tropical fish in Georgetown's harbor.

Dive & Snorkel Sites: Grand Cayman is the top of a submerged mountain and its offshore coral reefs form the famous 'Cayman Wall'. An estimated 60 miles of drop-offs encircle Grand Cayman where the underwater visibility extends to depths of 150 feet. There are more than a hundred dive sites surrounding the island, and they include numerous shipwrecks as well as coral gardens, grottos, caves and canyons which are habitat for rays, turtles, tropical fish and huge, colorful sponges. Whether snorkeling, shore diving or deep diving, Cayman Island offers crystal clear water, an abundance of marine life and a variety of underwater terrain.

This fascinating marine world can also be viewed from vessels that operate out of George Town, including a glass-bottom boat, a semi-submersible and a submarine. There are reefs and wrecks to explore right in Hog Sty Bay, such as Cheeseburger Reef and the wreck of the Cali. Other easily accessible dive sites include Eden Rock and Devil's Grotto, just south of George Town, as well as those along Seven Mile Beach. Dive boats take certified divers to the island's incredible drop-offs, such as the West Wall which lies about nine miles offshore. Atlantis Submarine operates out of George Town and offers non-divers the opportunity to view the famous Cayman Wall. Several dive and snorkel shops are located within walking distance of the tender pier, and the cruise lines also offer snorkel and dive excursions.

Golf: There are two golf courses on Grand Cayman, both a few miles north of George Town along West Bay Road. Closest to town is the Hyatt Britannia Golf Course, designed by Jack Nicklaus and offering three courses in one: a nine-hole championship course, an 18-hole executive course and one played with a special Cayman ball. The Links at SafeHaven is an 18-hole championship course and is reminiscent of those in Scotland.

ISLAND ATTRACTIONS

Stingray City, located in the protected waters of North Sound, has been described in National Geographic as "one of the most rewarding experiences in the undersea world." Visitors are taken by boat to this shallow sandbar where for decades fishermen used to clean fish, their discarded entrails attracting stingrays who would arrive at the sound of a ship's motor. In 1987, some divers began frequenting this spot, bringing squid for the normally shy stingrays, who gradually got used to their presence. Now 30 to 50 stingrays show up daily to be hand fed, stroked and held by humans. Visitors can watch from an observatory or snorkel with the stingrays.

Cayman Turtle Farm, a land-based attraction, is situated in a tidal creek of North Sound. Originally established in 1968 to raise and market turtle products, the farm now concentrates on research and breeding. Green sea turtles and hawksbill turtles are bred, hatched, raised and tagged before being released into Cayman waters. Tours of the facility are self-guided.

While many visitors like to stop at Hell so they can send a postcard, the real attraction is the weathered outcrop of iron shore which, although said to look like the charred remains of a hell fire, is actually made of black limestone about 1.5 million years old.

East of George Town the attractions include Bodden Town with its legendary Pirate Cave where pirates are said to have hidden their loot in a series of tunnels. Nearby is the Meagre Bay Bird Sanctuary and further east is the **Botanic Park**, officially opened by Queen Elizabeth in 1994. The park's 60 acres of grounds include a floral garden and an interpretive trail that winds through woodlands, wetlands, swamps and thickets. Adjacent to the park is the Mastic Trail, a restored 200-year-old footpath that winds for two miles through primary woodlands and mangrove swamps. The island's eastern shores contain **The Blow Holes**, saltwater geysers spouting from the coral rock as waves crash onto shore. East End is the oldest town on the island, founded in the late 17th century.

Stingray City is a highlight for visitors to Grand Cayman.

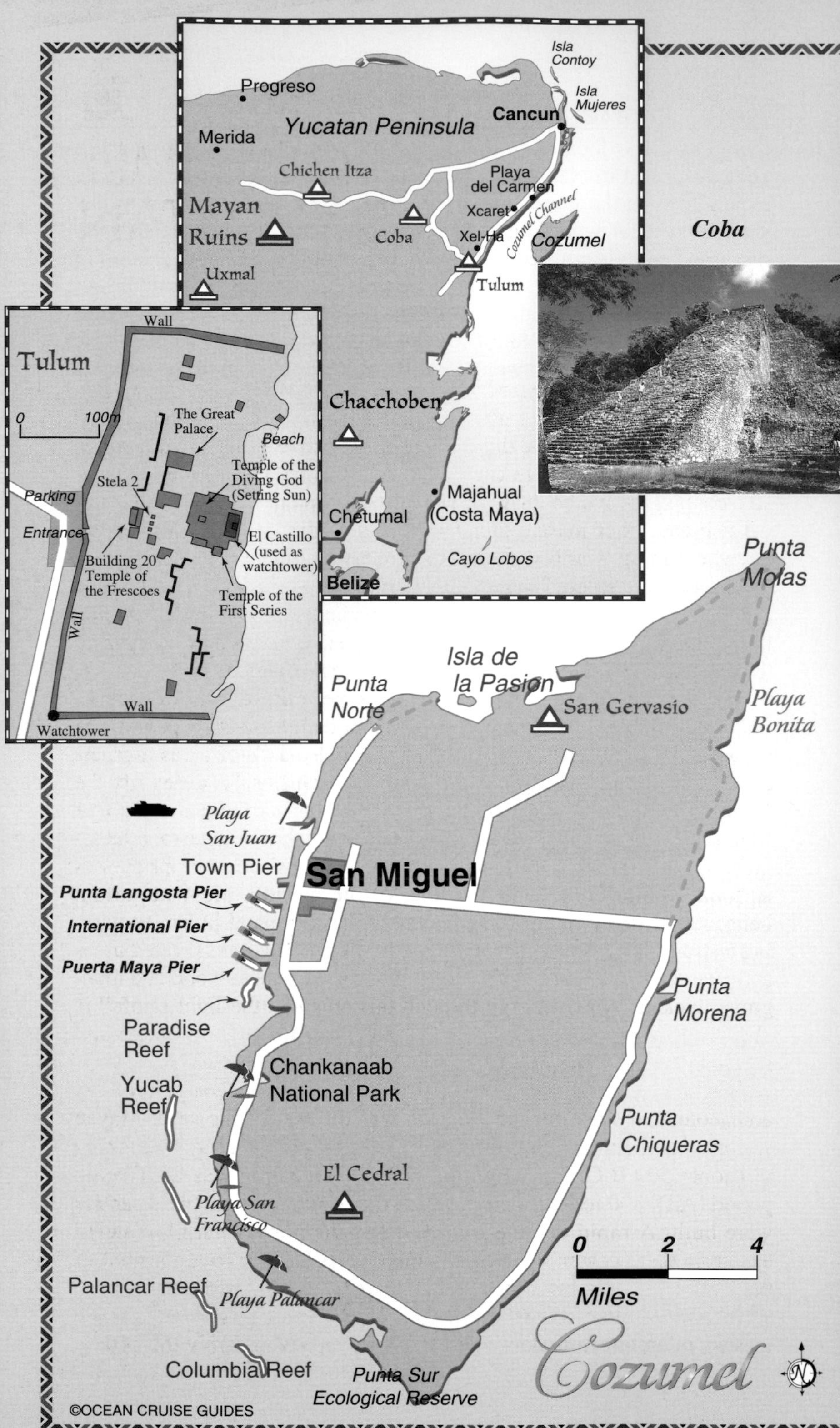

Isla Contoy
Progreso
Isla Mujeres
Cancun
Yucatan Peninsula
Merida
Chichen Itza
Playa del Carmen
Mayan Ruins
Xcaret
Coba
Cozumel Channel
Xel-Ha
Cozumel
Coba
Uxmal
Tulum
Wall
Tulum
0 100m
The Great Palace
Beach
Temple of the Diving God (Setting Sun)
Stela 2
Parking
Entrance
El Castillo (used as watchtower)
Building 20 Temple of the Frescoes
Temple of the First Series
Wall
Wall
Watchtower
Chacchoben
Majahual (Costa Maya)
Chetumal
Cayo Lobos
Belize
Punta Molas
Isla de la Pasion
Punta Norte
San Gervasio
Playa Bonita
Playa San Juan
Town Pier
San Miguel
Punta Langosta Pier
International Pier
Puerta Maya Pier
Punta Morena
Paradise Reef
Chankanaab National Park
Yucab Reef
Punta Chiqueras
El Cedral
Playa San Francisco
0 2 4
Miles
Palancar Reef
Playa Palancar
Cozumel
Columbia Reef
Punta Sur Ecological Reserve
©OCEAN CRUISE GUIDES

COZUMEL & THE YUCATAN

The coral-fringed island of Cozumel was a sleepy hideaway when Jacques Cousteau paid it a visit in the early 1960s and introduced the world to one of the Caribbean's top dive sites. The documentary Cousteau filmed here captured the brilliance of Cozumel's extensive coral reefs, which thrive in crystal clear waters teeming with tropical fish and other marine life. The clarity of the water is unsurpassed anywhere in the Caribbean, and the underwater caves and spectacular sponges are considered some of the best in the world. The island is also popular for its beautiful beaches and fascinating Mayan ruins which have attracted such notable visitors as Jacqueline Kennedy who came to Cozumel in 1968 while touring the area's archaeological sites.

The ancient Maya, from which Cozumel's inhabitants descend, named the island 'Land of Swallows' and dedicated it to Ixchel, the moon goddess of fertility. Remnants of temples and religious artifacts have been found throughout the island which lies 12 miles off the Yucatan Peninsula, separating the Caribbean Sea from the Gulf of Mexico. The Yucatan, low and flat like Cozumel, is a limestone tableland covered with thin topsoil which supports subsistence crops as well as tobacco and corn. It is also one of the world's most important henequen-growing regions, the leaves of these tropical plants containing a strong fiber used for making binder twine. The uncultivated areas are covered with a dense growth of scrub, cactus, sapete wood and mangrove thickets. No rivers run through this area and the light rainfall is absorbed by the porous limestone where it collects in underground rivers and wells (cenotes), and in surface pools called *aguadas*.

Scattered throughout the low hills are hundreds of pre-Columbian archaeological sites, for the Yucatan was the seat of the great Mayan civilization which flourished for more than two millennium, beginning in about 1500 B.C. The height of Mayan civilization was the Classic period (A.D. 300 to 900) during which many of their great civic centers were built. A rapid decline followed and the population plummeted except in the Yucatan, where settlement persisted due to the arrival of the Toltec ('master builders') from Central Mexico. Also an advanced civilization, Toltec society was based on a warrior aristocracy. These masters of architecture dominated the Yucatan's Maya from the 11th to the 13th century, at which time the nomadic Chichimec brought about the fall of the Toltec empire.

The first Europeans to arrive at the Yucatan were most likely a pair of survivors from a 1511 Spanish shipwreck. One man joined the Maya, the other was rescued by Hernan Cortes in 1519 and became his interpreter. Spanish battles with the Maya began in 1527, with Cozumel used as a staging base, and continued until 1546 when a Mayan revolt was crushed. However, resistance to Spanish (and later Mexican) rule continued into the early 20th century.

During the Spanish colonial period, administrative centers were established by Spaniards who imposed their own religious and political organization on the Mayan population. Assimilation, however, was far from complete. The indigenous elite were incorporated into the new colonial system but the rural peasants were left alone. The Spanish were disinterested in the Yucatan, due to its lack of mineral wealth and export crops. Its offshore islands of Cozumel and Isla Mujeres also were of little value to the Spaniards, but they did attract pirates such as Henry Morgan and Jean Lafitte, who hid in coves to lie in wait for passing ships laden with gold and other treasures.

In the late 18th century, a growing world demand for cordage and fibers prompted the establishment of huge henequen plantations throughout the northern Yucatan. The local Maya's village lands were expropriated and, as the plantations grew in size, former land owners were pressed into labor. Tensions reached a boiling point in the mid-1800s and sparked a rebellion in which the Maya tried to drive all Europeans off the Yucatan peninsula. They were unsuccessful, but the Spanish were never able to completely suppress the indigenous population, and isolated pockets located outside the plantation zone remained autonomous throughout the 19th century.

Mexico gained independence from Spain in 1821, but widespread political turmoil continued. The social order inherited from Spanish colonialists consisted of two groups: Spanish-speaking whites and ladinos who resided in the major towns and maintained control of the region's commercial interests, and the much larger group of Mayan-speaking farmers who lived in rural villages. Following the Mexican Revolution of 1910-17, a land redistribution program guaranteed the rural Maya would no longer have their village lands expropriated.

In the early 1970s, the Mexican government decided to build a world-class resort and once again the Yucatan Peninsula became the focus of outside interests. The location for a master-plan resort – carefully chosen for its white-sand beaches, Caribbean climate, clear waters and access to Mayan ruins – was Isla Cancun, lying off the northeast coast of the Yucutan Peninsula. Cancun and Cozumel were battered by Hurricane Wilma in October 2005, but rebuilding began immediately and within weeks cruise ships were again calling at Cozumel.

COZUMEL

Cozumel is a flat island, covered with scrub jungle, its highest point only 35 feet above sea level. The majority of islanders live in the town of San Miguel, located on the island's sheltered west coast overlooking Cozumel Channel. While no longer the quiet seaside town that greeted visitors back in the 1950s, San Miguel has retained much of its earlier charm. Safe and compact, the port is laid out in a grid pattern with streets running parallel and perpendicular to the waterfront. The locals, of Mayan descent, are generally shorter than the average Mexican and most speak Spanish as well as some English. The peso is the official currency (US$1 = approximately 10 pesos) but American currency is accepted.

A Mayan family sells crafts at a market outside Tulum.

GETTING AROUND

The three cruise ship piers are located one to three miles south of San Miguel. The closest, Punta Langosta, is within walking distance of the town. The southernmost pier, Puerta Maya Pier, is about a $5 taxi ride into town. In between is the International Pier. Ships that anchor off San Miguel transport their passengers by tender to the town pier, right

The Yucatan's magnificent Mayan ruins include Tulum, located across the channel from Cozumel.

in the heart of downtown opposite the main plaza. Some sample taxi fares from San Miguel: $10 to Chankanaab Lagoon; $15 to San Francisco Beach; $18 to Playa Palancar. A passenger ferry runs between Cozumel and Playa del Carmen on the mainland, which is a disembarkation port for cruise passengers taking organized shore excursions to the Yucatan's Mayan sites.

Shopping & Dining – Cozumel offers excellent shopping, with shops lining the streets leading from the main plaza. The local flea market is located off 5th Avenue between Calles 2 and 4, while the town's upscale boutiques are located on the waterfront's Avenue Rafael E. Melgar, as is a good selection of restaurants. All Mexican-made products are duty-exempt, and small discounts are often given for cash purchases, with most shops accepting U.S. dollars. Passengers taking organized excursions to the Mayan ruins on the mainland will have an opportunity to buy local crafts, including reproductions of Mayan artifacts, at outdoor markets. (For a description of Mexican handicrafts, see the Shopping section on page 274.)

LOCAL ATTRACTIONS

Located opposite San Miguel's town pier, **(1) Main Plaza** is pleasant to stroll through with its shaded areas, large gazebo, clock tower and a monument to motherhood.

(2) Museum de le Isla de Cozumel, located on the waterfront between Calle 4 Norte and Calle 6 Norte, is a welcome retreat from the busy streets and bustling boutiques. For a small admission charge, you can enjoy exhibits ranging from Cozumel's natural habitat to its Mayan and colonial history. A highlight is the replica Mayan house, set in a courtyard, with a garden outside and authentic tools and furnishings inside. A Mayan host demonstrates the various stone tools, identifies foodstuffs on display and generally brings to life the workings of a typical village home. An open-air restaurant on the museum's second floor provides a lovely view out to sea.

(3) **Cozumel Archaeological Park** contains full-size replicas of Mayan and Toltec stone carvings set in a jungle setting. A guided walking tour is included in the admission fee. Although there are numerous archaeological sites on Cozumel, none reach the scale and architectural significance of those found on the Yucatan peninsula. The most important island site is the Mayan temple of Ixchel at **San Gervasio**, about 10 miles by road from San Miguel.

(4) **Chankanaab National Park** is a natural underwater preserve featuring dozens of species of tropical fish in a beautiful lagoon filled with bright corals and connected to the open sea by underground channels. Surrounding the lagoon is a botanical garden where visitors can stand and watch the colorful fish. The lagoon itself is off-limits to snorkeling and swimming (to protect the marine life from harmful suntan lotions) but there is good snorkeling nearby along the reefs of Chankanaab Bay. Atlantis Submarine offers expeditions to Chankanaab Reef, descending to depths of 100 feet.

(5) **Punta Sur Ecological Reserve**, at the island's southern tip, is a large protected area encompassing the historic Celarain Lighthouse and Columbia Lagoon, which is a habitat for sea turtles.

Best Beaches – A few miles north of San Miguel is Playa San Juan, a good beach with shade and calm water just north of the Melia Mayan Hotel. The majority of beaches lie south of San Miguel, starting with Chankanaab Lagoon where a full-service beach offers water sports and a restaurant. Playa San Francisco, one of the island's most beautiful beaches, is a 3-mile stretch of sand with a bar and restaurant, beach chairs, umbrellas and water sports equipment. The island's southernmost beach, Playa Palancar, is a quiet beach with a local atmosphere and is serviced with a bar, restaurant, beach chairs and umbrellas.

Dive & Snorkel Sites – A strong current flows through Cozumel Channel, continually carrying food to the reefs, which is why the sponge growth is so spectacular and the marine life, including rays and sea turtles, is abundant. One of the Caribbean's most famous **dive sites** is Palancar Reef, with seven dive sites ranging from 35 to over 80 feet. Other good dive sites include: Colombia Reef with 50-foot coral pillars; Punta Sur with caverns and steep drop-offs; Santa Rosa Reef with huge coral mounds; San Francisco Reef's valleys and vertical wall; and Yucab Reef, an extensive and shallow dive site encompassing a variety of coral formations. Not far from Paradise Beach is Paradise Wall, which begins at depths of 50 feet and contains giant sponges.

The island's best **snorkel sites** are the shallow reefs at Playa San Francisco and at Chankanaab Bay. There is also good snorkeling at Palancar and Colombia Reefs, which are still in good condition after Hurricane Wilma. Snorkeling tours to these two reefs are available from Palancar and Paradise Beaches. These boat excursions are one- to two-hours long and cost about $30 per person.

COZUMEL & the YUCATAN

(Above & right) San Miguel's charming museum features a replica Mayan home. (Below) Tulum was an ancient trading center of the Maya and Toltec.

(Top) Chichen Itza is an important Maya-Toltec site on the Yucatan peninsula. (Middle) San Miguel's main shopping street is lined with lively restaurants. (Below) A cruise ship off Cozumel.

The Yucatan Peninsula

The lure of Mayan ruins and dazzling white beaches has prompted the construction of several cruise ship ports on the Yucatan Peninsula. **Progreso**, a tiny fishing village on the north coast, is now home to a cruise pier providing access to Merida (22 miles) and the Mayan sites of Uxmal (49 miles) and Chichen Itza (72 miles).

Merida – Once called the White City for its clean streets of gleaming white buildings where rooftop windmills are used to pump water from underground wells and streams, this Spanish colonial town was founded in 1542 by the Spanish conqueror Francisco de Montejo. Built on the site of a ruined Mayan city, Merida became the cultural center of the Yucatan peninsula, its Cathedral of San Ildelfonso completed in 1599. Today, as the Yucatan state capital with a population exceeding half a million, Merida's colonial heritage endures in its public buildings and the elegant old mansions of Paseo Montejo.

***Uxmal* (pronounced ooshmal) –** Situated in the Puuc hills, this important center of education flourished between 600 and 900 and is considered one of the finest examples of the Maya's Late Classic architecture. The site's impressive structures include the unique Pyramid of the Magician; the Governor's Palace, its facade decorated with some 20,0000 carved stone elements; and the Nunnery Quadrangle, the equivalent of a modern university.

***Chichen Itza* –** This well-restored and popular Mayan site was founded around two large cenotes (deep, natural wells) in circa 514 by the Itza – the last strong, independent Mayan tribe. A political and religious center, the site was occupied at various times until 1194 when it was abandoned for the last time. The buildings span two periods of Mayan civilization. The Classic style is reflected in massive structures and heavy, decorative sculpture; the Post-Classic period, with a strong Toltec influence, produced plainer buildings, columns and sculpture based on the Mexican feathered-serpent motif. The site's highlights include the Castillo temple, a ball court and, unusual among Mayan buildings, a round tower called the Caracol (snail shell) which was built in the Post-Classic period, probably as an astronomical observatory. Offerings, including human sacrifices, were thrown into Chichen Itza's sacred well which was a mecca for pilgrimages by other Mayan tribes of Central America and Mexico.

Cancun – Originally a Mayan settlement, its name meaning 'vessel at the end of the rainbow', Cancun consisted of a few hundred inhabitants before an international holiday resort was built on its offshore island in the early '70s. Long and narrow, the island is lined with powdery white beaches and connected to the mainland by a bridge at each end. Its hotel zone contains first-class hotels and recreation facilities which draw over two million visitors annually. The L-shaped island forms a lagoon where water sports can be enjoyed, and the outer beaches are sheltered by coral reefs. Isla Mujeres is a short ferry or water taxi ride from Cancun, and this tiny island of secluded beaches and lagoons contains the National Marine Park El Garrafon at its southern tip, where the underwater habitat attracts snorkelers and divers. Cancun embarked on an extensive rebuilding of its resorts after taking a direct hit from Hurricane Wilma in October 2005.

Coba **–** Dozens of stone roads and causeways once led to Coba – a commercial hub of the Maya which flourished from 400 to 1100. The largest settlement found to date, much of this site is still overgrown but those structures that have been excavated include the 80-foot-high 'Iglesia' temple-pyramid, the 'Crossword' pyramid, and the 'Nohochmul' pyramid which is the tallest on the Yucatan peninsula with 120 steps climbing to the top of its 138-foot-high face.

Calica is a cruise ship terminal located in **Punta Venado**, about six miles from Playa del Carmen (where the passenger ferry from Cozumel docks). Two natural parks are situated south of **Playa del Carmen**, the nearest being **Xcaret** ('little inlet'), an eco-archeological park built around the ruins of a Mayan ceremonial center where visitors can don life vests and ride the gentle currents along an underground river through caves illuminated by shafts of sunlight. The grounds also contain a botanical gardens, butterfly pavilion, turtle farm, swimming lagoons and restaurants.

Further south along the coast is **Xel-Ha**, touted as the world's largest natural aquarium. The park's limestone shoreline has been sculpted by the sea and freshwater springs, forming turquoise lagoons filled with tropical fish that can viewed from platforms above the rocky shore. Snorkelers can swim in the lagoons and along the Xel-Ha river. A footpath also leads to the river and into the jungle where two cenotes and the Cave of Miracles, a massive underground cavern, can be viewed.

Tulum **–** The only known walled city of the Maya, this ancient trading center is a stunning sight perched on the edge of a bluff overlooking the sea. Its stone buildings are surrounded on three sides by a stone wall that dates from 1200 AD and is said to be 16 feet thick in places. Tulum, 'City of the New Dawn', was the only Mayan city still occupied when the Spanish arrived in the early 1500s. The protected cove at the base of this site is ideal for swimming and snorkeling off its white sand beach.

Costa Maya – This cruise port at Majahual provides access to **Chetumal**, capital of Quintana Roo and home to one of the Yucatan's best museums on Mayan culture. The city is mostly modern, rebuilt after its destruction by a hurricane in 1955. Other excursions take in the ruins at Oxtankah and Chacchoben, both Mayan centers dating to the 4th century. **Banco Chinchorro**, a huge coral reef the size of Cozumel Island, lies offshore and provides good diving and snorkeling.

Chacmool statue.

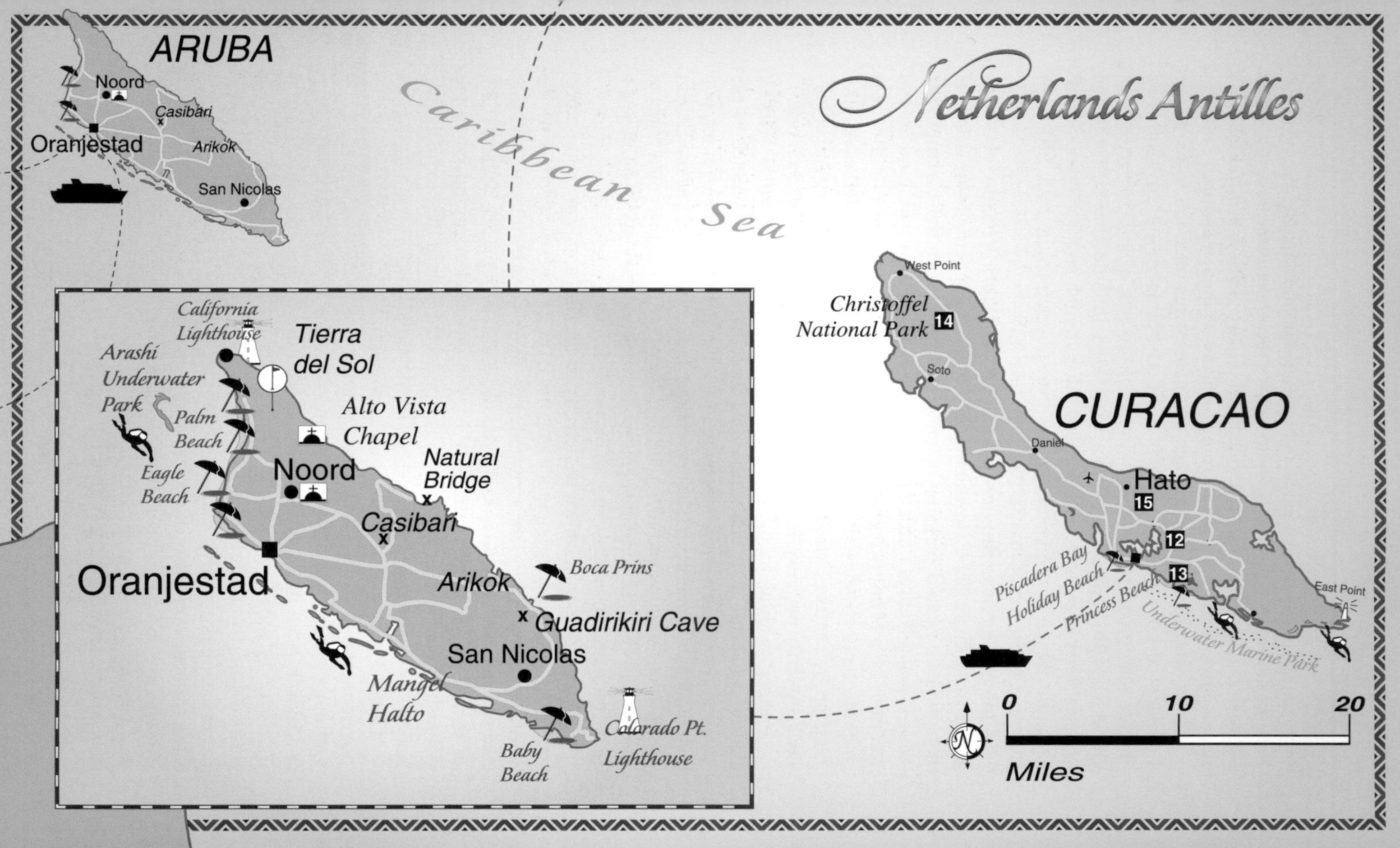
Netherlands Antilles
ARUBA
Noord
Casibari
Oranjestad
Arikok
San Nicolas
Caribbean Sea
California Lighthouse
Tierra del Sol
Arashi Underwater Park
Palm Beach
Alto Vista Chapel
Eagle Beach
Noord
Natural Bridge
Casibari
Oranjestad
Arikok
Boca Prins
Guadirikiri Cave
San Nicolas
Mangel Halto
Baby Beach
Colorado Pt. Lighthouse
West Point
Christoffel National Park
14
Soto
CURACAO
Daniel
Hato
15
12
13
Piscadera Bay
Holiday Beach
Princess Beach
Underwater Marine Park
East Point
0
10
20
Miles

ARUBA & CURACAO

The Dutch islands of Aruba, Bonaire and Curacao (the ABCs) lie off the coast of Venezuela, outside of the hurricane belt. Unlike the other Lesser Antilles, they receive little rain in summer, their vegetation consisting of drought-resistant cacti and divi-divi trees bent by the steady trade winds. Their stark landscapes of wave-eroded rock formations and brilliant white beaches are in contrast to the colorful ports where Dutch gabled, pastel-painted buildings line the waterfront.

The islands' semi-arid climate, interrupted by a brief rainy spell each winter, is one reason they were deemed 'useless' by the early Spanish explorers. They were inhabited at the time by Caiquetios, a tribe of peaceful Arawak Indians who lived in villages and caves, the walls of which contain pictographs they left behind. Their food came mostly from the rich bounty of the sea, the surrounding waters filled with colorful coral gardens and an abundance of fish. Other foodstuffs were obtained from mainland tribes in exchange for salt, one of the few natural resources found on these barren islands.

Located within 40 miles of the Venezuela coast, the ABCs are actually part of the Andes chain of mountains which snakes up the western side of South America and branches into smaller ranges at the north end of the continent. Underwater volcanic activity helped form the islands,

Colorful Dutch colonial architecture houses shops and businesses in Aruba's main town of Oranjestad.

which consist of batholith rock as well as younger limestone which formed before uplifting slowly brought the islands to the sea's surface.

The treasure-seeking Spaniards were the first Europeans to discover the ABCs when, in 1499, a Spanish sea captain en route to South America left some of his scurvy-afflicted sailors on one of the islands to die. When he returned less than a year later, he found them all alive and well. Hence the name Curacao – based on the Portuguese word for 'the cure'. Yet, despite its promising name, Curacao did not impress the Spanish for it was a dry, prickly place with no apparent gold deposits. Even the Valencia orange trees brought from Spain produced a bitter, almost inedible fruit when planted here.

It took the resourceful Dutch to see the potential of Curacao and make it an integral part of their trading empire. They seized the island in 1634, transferring the few Spanish settlers and Arawak Indians to the mainland, and took possession of Aruba and Bonaire a year or so later. Some Arawaks lived on Aruba where they maintained the cattle and horses that roamed freely on the island.

The Dutch West India Company was initially attracted to Curacao as a source of salt and hardwood, but it soon became a base for raiding settlements on other islands and the coastal mainland. Its sheltered harbor was fortified on either side at the entrance and, under the governorship of Peter Stuyvesant from 1642 to 1647, Willemstad became an important world port. With the soil unable to support sugar cane or other cash crops, Curacao's survival depended on trade, which came in the form of slaves. Throughout the latter half of the 1600s and well into the 1700s, Curacao was an enormous slave depot for the Caribbean and South America.

Meanwhile, Aruba was maintained as a vast cattle ranch, and corn was grown on Bonaire to feed the slaves passing through Curacao, which also became a commercial meeting place for pirates, American rebels, Dutch merchants and Spaniards from the mainland. As for those bitter-tasting oranges brought from Spain, it was discovered that their sun-dried peels contained

Fort Amsterdam was the center of the fortified town of Willemstad, Curacao.

an etheric oil which became the basis for Curacao's famous liqueur. The ABCs remained for the most part Dutch, briefly besieged by the British in 1804, and occupied by British troops from 1807 to 1814.

Slavery was finally ended in 1863 and the islands had to develop new resources. Trade with Venezuela became the mainstay of Curacao's economy and was helped greatly when the Dutch government lifted all import taxes on goods from the Netherlands, which local merchants could then exchange at a profit for Venezuelan products. On Aruba and Bonaire, the aloe plant became an important crop, its gel used in numerous pharmaceuticals, and the pods of the divi-divi tree were also exported for use in leather tanning.

In 1824, alluvial deposits of gold were found on Aruba and the island's mines, which operated for nearly a century, yielded more than three million pounds of gold. When, following World War I, oil was discovered at Lake Maracaibo in Venezuela the oil companies, seeking a stable place to locate their refineries and storage facilities, chose the nearby Dutch islands. When the demand for oil slumped, the islands developed yet another untapped resource which continues today – tourism.

Blessed with natural appeal – beautiful beaches, turquoise waters, colorful coral reefs, and a climate that's sunny and dry – the islands have added duty-free shopping, waterfront casinos and championship golf courses to their growing list of attractions. Their residents, who descend from a mix of races and cultures, are a people known for their racial and religious tolerance. They are also multilingual, learning Dutch – the official language – at school, and are often fluent in English and Spanish, as well as their native tongue of Papiamento, which is a lilting blend of Spanish, Portuguese, Dutch, English and African dialects.

All three islands are part of the Kingdom of the Netherlands but Aruba is no longer part of the Netherlands Antilles, of which Curacao is the capital and Bonaire is a member, along with the Leeward Islands of St. Maarten, Saba and St. Eustatius. Aruba, seeking more autonomy in connection with its oil revenues, became a separate entity in 1986.

Aruba

Once a cacti-studded cattle ranch, Aruba is today a holiday paradise with miles of blinding white beaches and crystal-clear turquoise waters. The island's first inhabitants, the Caquetio Indians, had established themselves at the mouth of Venezuela's Aroa River until repeated attacks by the Carib Indians prompted them to leave. Some of the tribe members moved to the shores of Lake Maracaibo and still bear the name Arubaes. Others moved to the island now called Aruba.

The island's southwest coast has beach resorts, shopping malls and casinos; its rugged northeast coast is where wave action has carved coral cliffs into dramatic sea arches. In between lies a hilly desert of

A ship docks at the Oranjestad cruise terminal.

caves, cacti and scrub. Splashes of color are provided by flamboyant trees, in bloom from June through August, and gardens of homes which often contain a variety of tropical flowers. Wells tap into the island's water table but a huge saltwater distillation plant at Spanish Lagoon, once a hideout for pirates, is the island's main source of fresh water.

GETTING AROUND

The cruise ships dock in the heart of Oranjestad, within easy walking distance of the shops and other attractions. Taxis are unmetered and rates are fixed, based on a carload of up to four passengers, but be sure to establish a fare before departing. People returning from the beach in wet bathing suits are usually refused, so be sure to dry off and take a cover-up. US currency is accepted, but not large bills (i.e. $50 or $100). The minimum rate to any destination is $4, and the hired rate per hour is $30. Some sample fares (in US$) from the cruise terminal: Eagle Beach ($7); Noord ($9); Mangel Halto Beach ($14).

Most major American car rental companies operate on Aruba, in addition to several local companies. Avis has an office at the cruise ship terminal. A valid driver's license is all that's required to rent a car. The island is 19-1/2 miles long by six miles wide, the main roads are paved, and driving is on the right. It's hard to get lost, and the divi-divi trees – bent by the trade winds – all point toward the island's leeward side where Oranjestad is located.

The official currency is the Aruban Florin (AWG) but US dollars are readily accepted island wide, and major credit cards are accepted at most establishments. The bank rate of exchange is fixed at 1.77 Afl. to $1 US (stores exchange at AWG 1.75 to $1 US).

Beaches – A string of fine beaches lie along the coast northwest of the cruise terminal, starting with Druif Beach (about 2 miles away),

which is adjacent to Manchebo Beach (where hotel facilities are available) which is adjacent to Eagle Beach, where watersports equipment is available. About four miles from the terminal is Palm Beach, considered one of the best beaches in the Caribbean and extremely popular for its good swimming, sailing and hotel facilities. Hadikurari is popular with windsurfers, where rental equipment is available. Arushi Beach, near the island's northern tip, is a wide expanse of sand dotted with beach huts and within sight of the California Light House. At the island's southeastern tip are Rodgers Beach and Baby Beach, the latter being ideal for young children with its calm, shallow waters and shady areas. Picnickers enjoy the romantic setting of Boca Prins, backed by sand dunes and pounded by the nearby surf, which makes swimming dangerous.

Dive and Snorkel Sites – The shallow waters and abundance of fish off Malmok Beach (8 miles from the terminal) make it an ideal spot for snorkelers but there are no facilities nearby. Another good snorkeling beach is Manguel Halto beach, with its nearby barrier reef. Arashi Reef and the Antilla, a German freighter destroyed during World

Numerous dive sites and powdery sand beaches beckon on Aruba. (Above) Palm Beach.

War II, are popular dive sites, and can also be viewed by semi-submarine and submarine, both available through ship-organized shore excursions. Seaworld Explorer transports passengers by bus to the north end of the island where their semi-submarine is boarded, while Atlantis transports passengers to and from their sub site by ferry from Seaport Village Marina.

Golf – An 18-hole course designed by Robert Trents Jones Jr is situated at Tierra del Sol near the island's northwestern tip. This par-71 course with water on two sides, has stunning sea views and is dotted with giant cacti and clusters of natural grasses.

Shopping – Shopping malls are located at the harborfront, in town and stretching northwest along the coast. **(1) Seaport Village Mall**, a five-minute walk from the cruise terminal, is Aruba's largest shopping and entertainment complex with dozens of stores, boutiques and a casino. The nearby **(2) Seaport Marketplace** is also popular with its shaded central walkway and sidewalk cafes. Oranjestad's main shopping street is Caya G.F. Betico Croes, with chic boutiques and shops.

International items to look for include cachet cosmetics and perfumes, designer fashions, china, crystal, fine jewelry, watches and cameras. There are also good buys in embroidered tablecloths, Spanish porcelain, Danish silver and pewter, Dutch cheeses, Austrian figurines, Peruvian hand-knit sweaters, Brazilian semi-precious stones, Venezuelan shoes and handbags, Colombian emeralds and leather, and locally made aloe vera products. Clay pottery and other local artwork is sold at outdoor stands along the waterfront.

Local Sights – (3) Fort Zoutman is the oldest building in Oranjestad, erected in 1796 and named for a Dutch Rear Admiral. Added to the fort in 1868 was King Willem III Tower which served as a lighthouse and now houses a heritage museum.

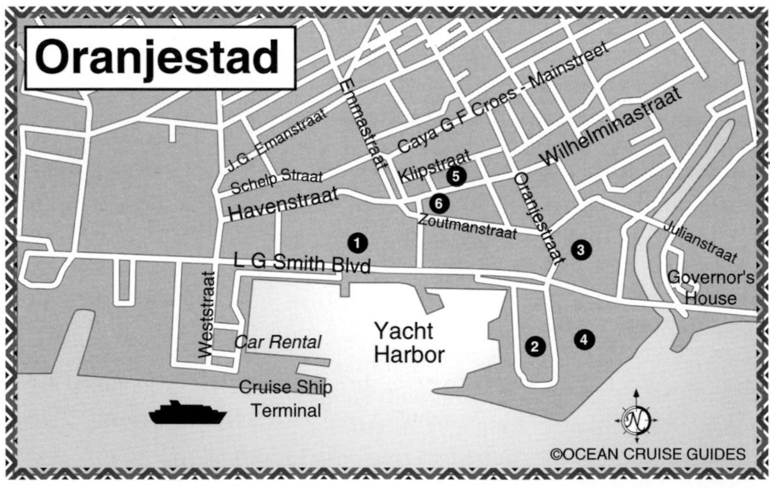

(4) Queen Wilhelmina Park, adjacent to the Seaport Marketplace, contains a marble statue of the former Dutch queen gazing toward the Governor's home. Wilhelminastraat contains interesting colonial architecture including the **(5) Protestant Church**, built in 1846. The (6) Archaeological Museum on Zoutmanstraat contains artifacts and pottery of the island's first Indian inhabitants.

Island Attractions – Santa Anna Church in Noord was built in the 1770s and its hand-carved oak altar, neo-gothic in design, won the exhibition award in Rome in 1870. The **Chapel of Alto Vista**, built by a Spanish missionary, is a place of pilgrimage situated on the north coast overlooking the sea. The interesting rock formations at **Casibari** can be climbed via some steps to the top for a view of the island and the Haystack. Aruba's famous landmark is the **Natural Bridge**, made of coral and carved by the sea on the island's windward coast. The arch is over 100 feet long and stands 23 feet above sea level.

Arikok National Park contains natural and man-made paths, a restored cunucu (countryside house), a traditional stone well and the Natural Pool, near Boca Keto, which is surrounded by rocks and filled with sea water. Several caves are situated along the north coast, including **Guadirikiri Cave**, its caverns containing stalactites and ancient drawings.

CURACAO

Few Caribbean ports of call can surpass the arrival awaiting passengers at Curacao. Here the Queen Emma Pontoon Bridge swings open to allow ships to enter the canal-like entrance of St. Anna Bay and glide past the waterfront buildings of colonial Willemstad. A centuries-old capital, its channel-side streets are lined with gabled buildings which were painted a variety of colors in 1817 when the Governor complained that the sun's glare off the stark white buildings was giving him headaches.

Initially founded as Santa Anna by the Spanish, the port's name was changed to Willemstad when Holland took possession of the island in 1634. Settlement grew on both sides of the channel with the eastern side called Punda and the western side Otrabanda ('other side').

Ferry boats have long transported residents across the channel but in the late 1900s the American consul, Leonard Burlington Smith, suggested a pontoon foot bridge be built. Fixed at one end so it could open whenever a vessel had to pass, the bridge was completed in 1888. A toll charge was based on each person's ability to pay – those wearing shoes were charged 2¢ and those walking barefooted were free. It's said that the poor would borrow shoes to prove their ability to pay, while the rich would take off their shoes to save 2¢. Today there is no charge for either the bridge or the passenger ferries which run continuously throughout the day.

ARUBA & CURACAO

(Top) A cruise ship departs Oranjestad, Aruba. (Above, left) A souvenir stand on the Oranjestad waterfront. (Above) Natural Bridge, Aruba. (Left) A shopping street in Oranjestad.

(Top) The Seaport Marketplace in Oranjestad, Aruba. (Middle) The Penha Building in Willemstad, Curacao. (Bottom) Dutch-gabled buildings line the canal-like entrance to Willemstad.

GETTING AROUND

Dutch charm and duty-free shopping await the visitor to Willemstad. The official currency is the Netherlands Antilles guilder (NAfl) but U.S. dollars are widely accepted. The cruise ships dock on the Otrabanda side of the channel and passengers can make their way to the Punda side on foot over the pontoon bridge, via the free passenger ferry which docks at Mathey Wharf, or by taxi (about $8 US) over the Queen Julianna Bridge which spans the harbor at a height of 185 feet. Taxis are unmetered and the fee should be agreed upon before departing. Sample fares, in US currency, from the cruise pier: Holiday Beach Hotel – $10; Piscadera Bay – $12; Princess Beach – $15; island sightseeing – $30 per hour.

There are several **tourist information booths** along the Otrabanda waterfront, and the main office is located on the Punda side at the east end of Wilhelminaplein. A post office is directly east of the Central Market.

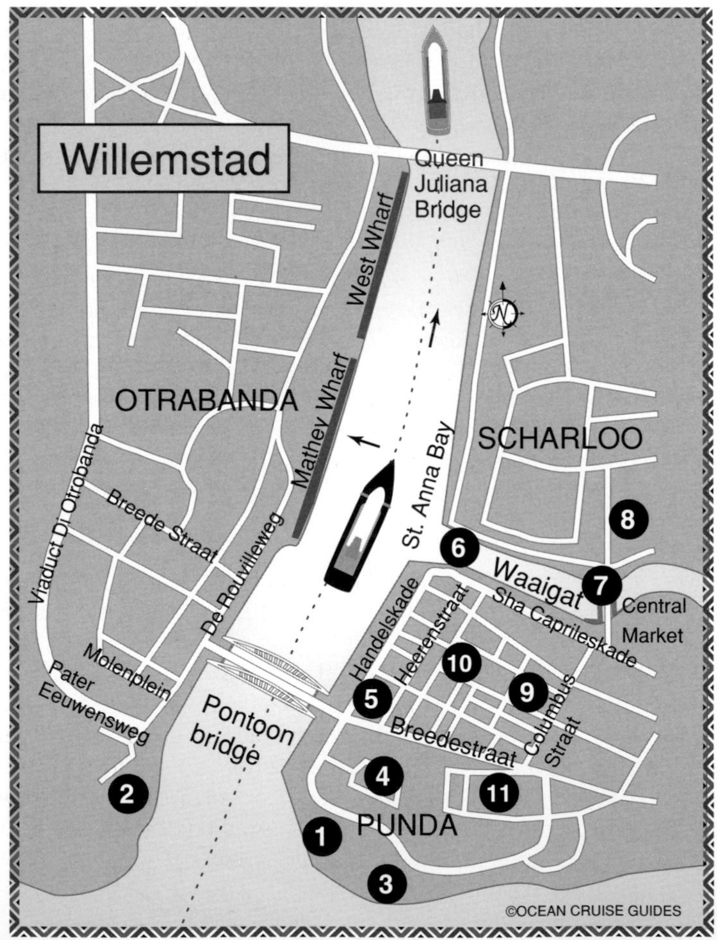

Organized ship excursions often include: a trolley train tour through the Punda section of Willemstad; an island tour with stops at the Curacao liqueur distillery and Curacao Seaquarium; a semi-submarine ride along coral reefs; and beach and snorkel excursions.

Beaches – Curacao's southern coast is indented with beach-lined bays and coves. Private beaches charge a small entrance fee, as do some of the hotel beaches. A popular hotel beach close to the cruise port is Holiday Beach. Farther west is the private beach at Blauwbaai (Blue Bay) – considered one of Curacao's best with its white sand, shady areas and change facilities. More hotel beaches are located at Piscadera Bay, including the Sonesta Hotel, Las Palmas and Curacao Caribbean. Fine beaches east of Willemstad include Princess Beach, where a hotel is located, and Seaquarium Beach and Santa Barbara Beach, both private beaches with change facilities and snack bars.

Dive & Snorkel Sites – Excellent snorkeling and diving are available all around the island with visibility of 60 to 80 feet, and sometimes up to 150 feet. The Curacao Underwater Park, ideal for both diving and snorkeling, protects 12-1/2 miles of unspoiled coral reef along which is an underwater nature trail and spectacular dive sites which include coral beds, sheer walls and shipwrecks. Klein Curacao, lying off East Point, is an uninhabited islet with beautiful beaches and good snorkeling and diving.

Golf – A nine-hole course with sand greens is open mornings at the Curacao Golf & Squash Club just north of the Willemstad Harbor.

Shopping – Duty-free bargains in Willemstad include brand-name jewelry, watches, European fashions, perfumes, crystal, china, electronics and cameras. Fine stores are located on Handelskade, Heerenstraat and Breedestraat, with more shops and boutiques located in the restored **(3) Waterfort Arches.** Local crafts are sold at the Central Market, located in a large circular building east of the **(6) Floating Market**, and at various shops in Punda such as Tropical Visions in the **(5) Penha Building**. Along the Otrobanda waterfront, facing the cruise pier, are a number of shops selling duty-free liquor and local handicrafts, including pottery at the Arawak Craft Factory opposite West Wharf.

LOCAL ATTRACTIONS

Located at the harbor entrance within the battlements of **(1) Waterfort** (built in 1634), and within hailing distance of ships entering the harbor, is the Van der Valk Plaza Hotel – one of only two hotels in the world that is covered by marine collision insurance. Still attached to the sea wall are iron rings once used to secure a chain that was stretched across the channel to prevent enemy ships from entering the harbor. During World War II, a steel net was stretched across the channel between Waterfort and **(2) Riffort** – built on the other side in 1838. Stretching east of Waterfort along the sea front are more old battlements, including the **(3) Waterfort Arches**, housing shops and restaurants.

(4) Fort Amsterdam with its mustard-colored walls, was the center of the fortified town from 1648 to 1861. Today it's the seat of the Netherlands Antilles government. Its inner courtyard, entered through an arched walkway, is formed by the Governor's Palace (facing the water), the Fort Church Museum (opposite), and government offices on each side. In case of siege, the church was built with a cellar for provisions and an adjacent water cistern. A cannon ball fired in 1804 by English troops, led by Captain Bligh of Bounty fame, remains embedded in its front wall.

The much-photographed **(5) Penha Building**, golden yellow with white trim, stands at the corner near the east end of the pontoon bridge. One of Curacao's oldest examples of Dutch colonial architecture, the building was formerly a social club with a gallery overlooking the harbor. Other waterfront buildings along this block resemble the canal houses of Amsterdam, one of which houses Gallery '86 – a showcase for the works of well-known artists of the Caribbean and Netherlands.

At the other end of the block is the **(6) Floating Market** where Venezuelan boats loaded with fruit, vegetables and fish sell their wares. At the east end of the market is the **(7) Queen Wilhelmina Bridge** which spans the Waaigat and leads to the former residential district of **(8) Scharloo** where wealthy merchants built opulent homes, their architectural styles ranging from 18th-century colonial to Victorian.

In 1651, a dozen Jewish families from Amsterdam arrived in Willemstad and by the early 1700s the local Jewish community numbered 2,000. The **(9) Mikve Emanuel Synagogue**, built in 1732 and similar in style to the old Portuguese one in Amsterdam, is today the oldest active synagogue in the Western Hemisphere. The Jewish

The Queen Emma Pontoon Bridge connects the two sides of Willemstad and can be accessed from the cruise docks.

Cultural Museum is entered off the synagogue's courtyard. Other museums in Punda include the **(10) Postal Museum**, housed in a 1693 building at the corner of Keukenstraat and Kuiperstraat, and the Numismatic Museum on Breedestraat.

The town's central park, **(11) Wilhelminaplein**, contains a statue of Queen Wilhelmina, as well as shaded benches and a playground. Opposite the park's east side is the former Jewish Reformed Synagogue Temple Emmanuel (the Temple Building) and City Gate, which marks the boundary of Willemstad when it was a fortified settlement.

Island Attractions (see overview map, page 184) – Outside of Willemstad the attractions include beautiful beaches, secluded coves, village churches and restored land houses which are former country estates situated on hilltops so the owner could watch his slaves and signal his neighbors if trouble developed. Popular attractions include the **(12) Curacao Liqueur Distillery**, located in the former colonial mansion of Chobolobo on the east side of Willemstad's harbor, and the **(13) Curacao Seaquarium** where visitors can view 400 species of sea life native to local waters, including various sharks and stingrays. Beside the aquarium is a full-facility beach of white sand.

At the north end of Curacao is **(14) Christoffel National Park**, a 4,500-acre nature reserve containing the island's highest point of Mount Christoffel (1,239 feet), Indian caves and trails. The prehistoric caves at **(15) Hato** were recently opened to the public, their limestone terraces containing fossilized coral that formed before tectonic uplifting brought the submerged island to the sea's surface.

The passenger ferry is another way to cross the channel running through the center of Willemstad.

South America to Panama
0
100
200
Miles
Caribbean Sea
Aruba
Curacao
Cartagena
Panama Canal
Panama
Limon
Colombia
Pacific Ocean
Avenida Santander
Old City / Centro San Diego
Avenida Venezuela
Avenida del Malecon
Cruise Pier
Cartagena
Boca Grande
Avenida Santander
Avenida Chile
El Laguito
1
2
3
4
5
6
7
8
9
11
12
©OCEAN CRUISE GUIDES

CARTAGENA

Cartagena (pronounced kar-ta-hay-na) is an historic walled city of shady plazas, Iberian-style palaces and narrow cobblestone streets. Founded by the Spanish in 1533, Cartagena de Indies was named for an important Mediterranean port in Spain which was established in ancient times by the Carthaginians.

For two centuries, from the mid-1500s to the mid-1700s, Cartagena was one of Spain's most prized New World ports. Two fleets would sail from Spain each August, one heading to Veracruz in the Gulf of Mexico, the other calling at Cartagena to load gold and silver arriving from Portobelo. When Spanish ships pulled into port loaded with goods from the home country – wines, cheeses, books, clothing and porcelain – Cartagena took on a circus-like atmosphere. The townspeople would crowd the docks where bankers, merchants, agents, pedlars and prostitutes all sought a piece of the action. Bidding wars for Spanish products often ensued, with local merchants paying fantastic prices. A few months later the fleet would sail for Havana, its ships now loaded with gold, silver and precious gems, where it would rendezvous with the other fleet for the journey back to Spain.

A series of forts and massive stone walls, which now divide the Old City from the newer part, were built over time to defend the port against marauding pirates and enemy fleets. Its history is a bloody one of sieges and sackings, starting with its fall to the English privateer Sir Francis Drake, who took Cartagena in 1586, after doing the same to its Mediterranean namesake the year before.

Fort San Felipe

The Spanish built fortifications at the entrance to Cartagena's harbor to help protect it from enemy attack.

Drake's successful attack and pilfering of Spanish treasures in the Caribbean prompted an enraged King Philip II to hire an Italian engineer named Antoneli whose task for the next 20 years was to make sure it didn't happen again. A series of forts were built to defend Cartagena from sea approaches and the city remained impregnable for more than a century, until the famous French buccaneer Jean Du Casse arrived in 1697 with 700 men and direct orders from the France's King Louis XIV to go ahead and attack. After a fierce battle, the Spanish surrendered to the joint force of French pirates and soldiers, the latter collecting the loot of gold and silver, then refusing to share it with the pirates who turned back to the city and sacked it again.

In 1741, an unsuccessful British siege was led by Edward Vernon who was able to storm the harbor but whose troops, including a regiment led by George Washington's half brother, succumbed to dysentery, malaria and yellow fever before a final assault could be staged.

The view of Cartagena and its cruise port from atop La Popa Hill.

(Right) Cartagena's famous cathedral. (Middle) La Popa Monastery. (Bottom) A local woman in traditional dress poses for photos in the Old City.

Independence was declared here in 1811, the first city in Colombia and Venezuela to officially defy Spain's rule. It became known as the Republic of Cartagena, a base from which Simon Bolivar launched his military campaign to liberate Venezuela. The walled city built by Spanish colonists was, ironically, besieged and captured by Spanish forces in 1815, but the rebel forces regained Cartagena in 1821 and the former treasure city of the Spanish Main was incorporated into Colombia. Its importance waned until the 20th century when oil refining brought newfound wealth to the city. In addition to oil, other commodities shipped out of Cartagena's busy port include coffee, bananas, platinum and gold.

Today Cartagena, with a population of about 850,000, is considered an island of peace in a country plagued by civil war and drug violence. The Spanish colonial architecture of the city's walled quarter has earned it United Nations World Heritage Site status, and visitors continue to enjoy Cartagena's historical highlights.

GETTING AROUND

The entrance to Cartagena harbor is nine miles long and worth viewing as your ship approaches or leaves this historic port. The entrance used to be much shorter, until it was blocked by boulders following Admiral Vernon's attack in 1741. Cruise ships enter Cartagena Bay south of Isla de Tierra Bomba and most of them dock at the cruise ship pier in residential Manga.

From the pier there are three options for seeing the city – a ship-organized tour, hiring a bilingual guide or taking a taxi.

Ship-organized city tours are conducted on buses that load at the dock. Passengers wishing to hire a bilingual guide can identify the 'tour guides' by their blue caps with a licence number on the front. They line up on the dock and some drive their own cars while others have a taxi driver with whom they work. If you simply want to take a taxi, the drivers who work alone are generally dressed in brown and speak limited English. They too are lined up in the dock area. Agree on a price with your guide or cab driver before setting off, and be sure to avoid anyone offering you a trip for 'one dollar'.

The dock area is patrolled by port police (dressed in green uniforms) who control smuggling, theft and drug pushing. Passengers should not be intimidated by their presence, but are advised to take reasonable precautions before heading ashore which includes refraining from wearing any expensive jewelry, especially showy necklaces.

Shopping – Cartagena is not a duty-free port but local products worth shopping for include leather goods, ceramics, silver jewelry, semi-precious stones and, of course, emeralds. The world's finest emeralds are mined in Colombia and sold throughout the Caribbean at impressively low prices. Emeralds, like diamonds, are sold by weight but the cut of the stone is less important than its color. The darker the emerald, the higher its value, yet a person should buy the color they personally prefer. All emeralds are flawed and be suspicious of someone offering you a dark green stone with no visible flaws at a low price, for it might be a fake. Also, a green oil is sometimes rubbed on an emerald to hide its flaws and deepen its color – until the oil wears off – so it's important to buy an emerald from a reputable dealer.

Colombia is the world's leading producer of emeralds and those sold at Cartagena are unique in that centuries-old goldsmithing techniques are used to create handcrafted items of jewelry.

The **(1) Pierino Gallo Shopping Center** at El Laguito is the place to shop for quality merchandise. A number of reputable jewelers are located here, including Greenfire, Colombian Emeralds International and H. Stern. The center's other stores carry fine leather goods, pre-Columbian art including beadwork and ceramic pieces, gourmet coffee products, pottery, hand-painted plates and appliqued t-shirts.

Gourmet Colombian coffee is a popular item with shoppers.

In downtown Cartagena, an interesting shopping experience can be had bartering with street vendors or at boutiques housed in medieval dungeons. The Portal of Sweets, located in the arches facing the **(2) Clock Tower**, is a noisy passageway filled with white candy stands as well as newsstands, shoeshine boys and watch repairers.

Local Sights – The Old City was laid out in the traditional Roman grid scheme with one property often stretching an entire block, its owner's name given to the street out front. **(3) Plaza Bolivar** is the center of the Walled City. Here you will find the main Cathedral, the Palace of the Inquisition with its museums, and the Gold Museum with an excellent collection of pre-Columbian gold work. Nearby is the **(4) Church of Santo Domingo** – the oldest in the city – and the **(5) Church of San Pedro Claver**, named for a Jesuit monk who was canonized 200 years after his death in the mid-1600s for his life's work of defending the African slaves.

East of Santo Domingo Church is **(6) Plaza de la Aduana** and the **(2) Clock Tower**. Following the waterfront, you will see **(7) Parque del Centenario** to your left, the **(8) Cartagena Theatre** straight ahead and to your right, on the waterfront, is the **(9) Convention Center**. Other highlights of a city tour include the fortifications at **(10) Las Bovedas** and a visit to **(11) San Felipe de Barajas**, a fort dating back to 1657, which provides an excellent view of the city, as does the 17th-century monastery at **(12) La Popa Hill**. A winding road leads up the hillside to the monastery, devoted to Saint Monica, and each February 2nd (Saint Monica's Day) the faithful of Cartagena climb up this road on an annual pilgrimage.

Cartagena's beach and hotel strip, the **Boca Grande**, is directly south of the city's historic core. The upscale **Pierino Gallo Shopping Center** is at the far end of the strip, in between the Hotel Las Velas and the **(13) Hotel Cartagena Hilton**.

(Above) Schoolgirls file past the 16th-century Church of San Pedro Claver. (Right) Spanish colonial architecture is well preserved within the walls of the Old City.

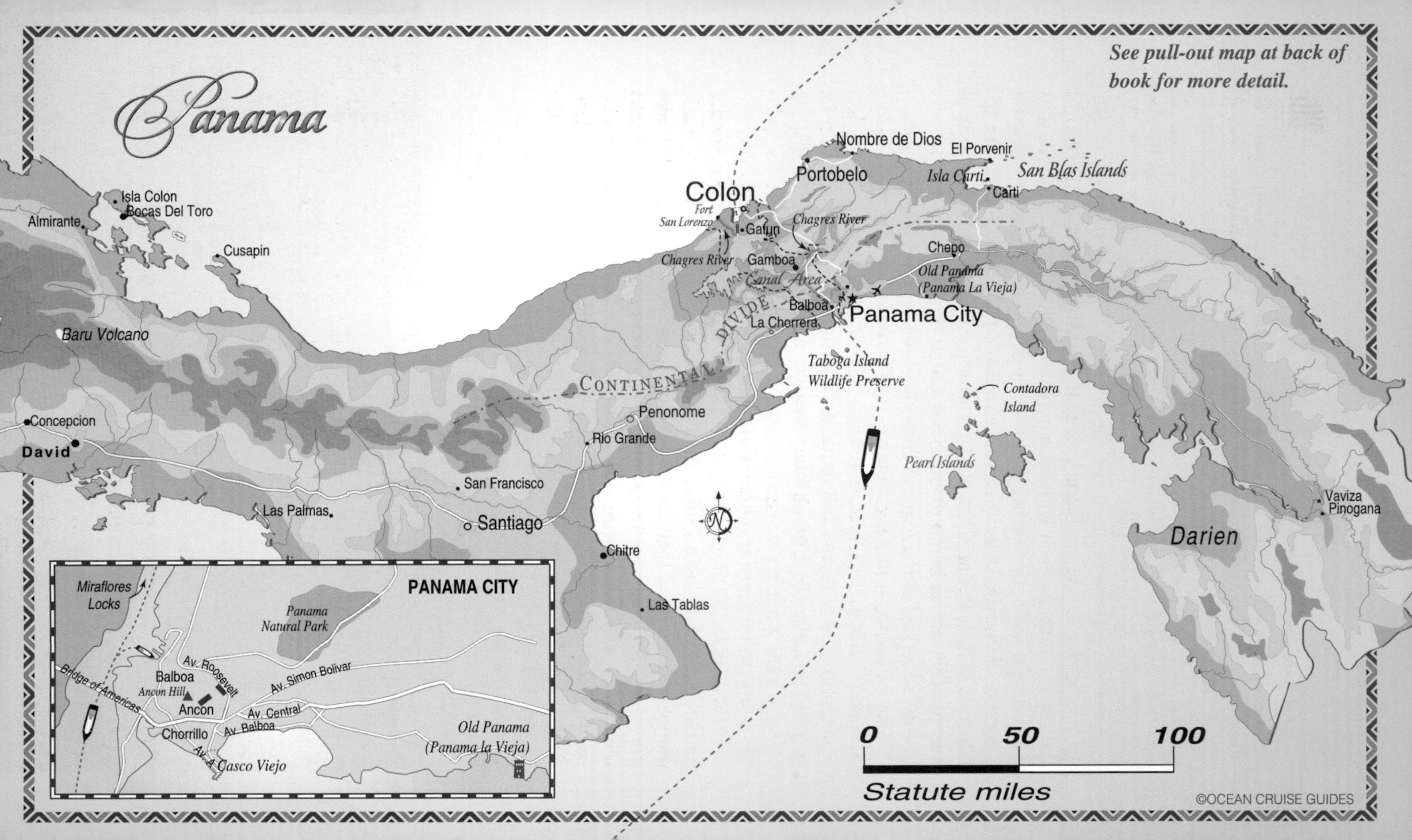
Panama
See pull-out map at back of book for more detail.
Nombre de Dios
El Porvenir
Portobelo
Isla Carti
San Blas Islands
Carti
Colon
Fort San Lorenzo
Chagres River
Gatun
Chepo
Chagres River
Gamboa
Canal Area
Old Panama (Panama La Vieja)
Balboa
Panama City
Continental Divide
La Chorrera
Isla Colon
Bocas Del Toro
Almirante
Cusapin
Baru Volcano
Taboga Island Wildlife Preserve
Contadora Island
Penonome
Concepcion
David
Rio Grande
Pearl Islands
San Francisco
Las Palmas
Santiago
Vaviza
Pinogana
Darien
Chitre
Las Tablas
PANAMA CITY
Miraflores Locks
Panama Natural Park
Av. Roosevelt
Balboa
Bridge of Americas
Ancon Hill
Av. Simon Bolivar
Ancon
Av. Central
Chorrillo
Av. Balboa
Old Panama (Panama la Vieja)
Av. A
Casco Viejo
0
50
100
Statute miles
©OCEAN CRUISE GUIDES

CHAPTER TWO

PANAMA – THE CANAL & THE PORTS

For centuries mariners had to face the tedious reality that for only a mere fifty miles of mountains, they would have to sail thousands of miles out of their way around the dreaded Cape Horn. Once it was known the narrow neck of the Isthmus of Panama was all that separated merchants from lucrative Far East markets, the dream of a canal was born. At completion of the Suez Canal in 1869, many investors believed the dream of a Panama Canal was one whose time had come.

The Panama Canal represents one of the world's greatest peacetime endeavors. As an engineering achievement it is unparalleled and has contributed significantly to human progress and civilization. With its unique and central location between the world's two largest oceans, the Canal provides a relatively inexpensive passageway and, since its opening in 1914, has had a profound influence on world trade patterns.

As the first approach wall of the Canal comes into view, a passenger on the upper decks of a cruise ship can see the scale of this man-made miracle – somehow, locks will lift your ship 85 feet to a beautiful lake in the middle of a tropical rainforest and, somehow, another set of locks will set you gently back down on a new ocean. Even for seasoned cruisers, it's an exciting moment. This is a voyage along one of the modern wonders of the world and the beauty of this perpetual motion machine is its simplicity, using Panama's abundant rainfall and Earth's gravity.

A ship completes the lifts at Gatun Locks and moves into Gatun Lake, 85 feet above sea level.

PANAMA AT A GLANCE

The Republic of Panama has a population of 3 million and its capital and largest city is Panama City, at the Pacific entrance to the Canal. The official language is Spanish, although English is widely understood in the urban centers. Panama's monetary unit is the Balboa (equal to the US dollar) with American paper money used throughout Panama. Coins are identical in shape and value to US coins but are printed with a bust of Balboa, except for the penny which carries a bust of Uraca, an Indian folk hero. American and Panamanian money is completely interchangeable.

The climate of Panama is pleasantly tropical, and temperatures are fairly uniform the year round, ranging from 73 to 83 degrees Fahrenheit in coastal areas. The heat, however, can be stifling at mid-day when your ship is passing through the Culebra Cut – the temperatures often in the 90s. Panama averages 65 inches of rain on the Pacific side and 120 inches on the Atlantic side, most of this falling during the wet season from May to December when you can expect a shower about once a day with an occasional all-day rain. During the dry season the trade winds blow steadily from the southeast.

For some, a transit of this famous canal might be seen as eight hours of slow steaming through a hilly tropical jungle. And, in a way, that was what the creators of the Canal wanted – a routine, safe and efficient passage from sea to sea, without incident or delay, and with hardly a thought of the thousands of miles saved in just a few hours.

One of the many intriguing aspects of the Panama Canal is its configuration. The Isthmus, which connects Central and South America, is actually S-shaped. As a result, a cruise ship travels in a southeasterly direction when going from the Atlantic side to the Pacific side. On exiting the canal at Balboa, a ship is actually 23 nautical miles further east than when it started at Limon Bay. When viewed from the Canal, the sun rises over the Pacific and sets over the Atlantic.

Since the locks first opened on August 15, 1914, more than 850,000 vessels have transited the 50-mile-long Canal. Currently about 14,000 vessels transit the Canal each year, almost 40 a day, and of these about 30 percent are PANAMAX-sized vessels, the largest vessels the waterway can accommodate. In April 2001, Royal Caribbean's *Radiance of the Seas* broke the toll record, paying $202,176.76 to get through the Canal. This 88,000-ton ship was within inches of the allowed maximum size of 965 feet in length and 106 feet in width. The lowest toll ever charged was 36 cents, paid by

Richard Halliburton when he swam through the Canal in 1928. Cruise ships' transit tolls are prepaid to Panama through the cruise line's agent.

With its handover by the United States at the end of 1999, the Panama Canal became an inalienable patrimony of the Panamanian nation – it can't be sold, assigned, mortgaged, or transferred, and the permanent neutrality of the Canal is guaranteed. The United States has retained the right to defend the waterway in the interest of national security, but Panama has assumed full responsibility for the administration, operation and maintenance of the Canal. Solely responsible for fulfilling these duties is the Panama Canal Authority (ACP), an autonomous entity of the Panamanian government whose 9,000 workers are now mostly Panamanian.

Panama has made some changes to the former Canal Zone, now called the Canal Area, where investment in tourism has soared and numerous companies now offer tours throughout the Canal Area, notably to the Soberania Parks and the area around Gamboa. Both the government and private investors are developing eco-lodges and tourist facilities, and the upgraded port facilities at Colon and Balboa (Fort Amador) are being developed as attractive stops for cruise passengers. President Mireya Moscoso has made the clean-up of Colon a priority, along with improving the lot of the many poor in that city.

COLON

Built on a swampy island near the Atlantic entrance of Panama Canal, Colon owes its existence to both the Panama Rail Road and the Canal. The town was first called Aspinwall in honor of William Aspinwall, one of the founders of the railroad. Colombia changed the name to Colon (after Christopher Columbus) in 1890 and during the French years the city was often scourged by yellow fever, a situation that

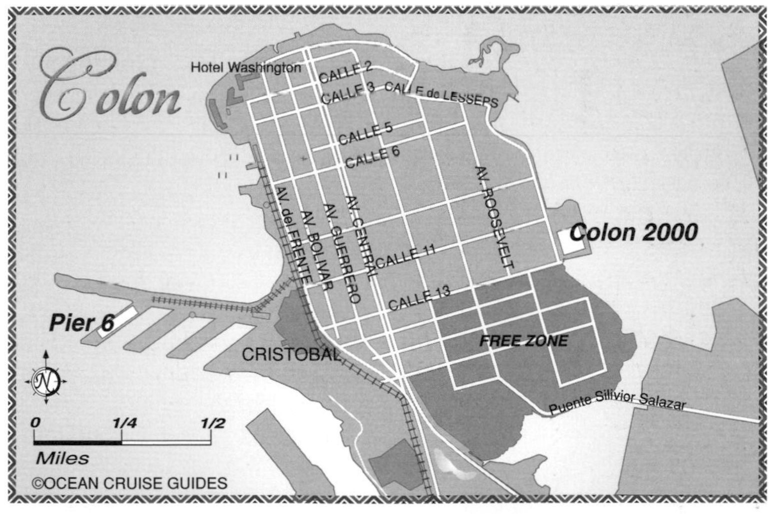

endured until sanitary work (closing sewers and paving streets) was completed by the Americans.

A fire in 1885 destroyed most of the city, which was rebuilt in the French colonial style, and many buildings from this period still exist. After the Canal was built and thousands of workers returned home, Colon went into a protracted economic depression. In an attempt to revive investment, the southeast part of the city in 1948 was turned into a Free Zone. Here traders from around the world buy and sell at wholesale and avoid paying taxes. Although this has made Colon the world's second busiest free port after Hong Kong, Colon's poor have not benefited and a large part of the city is a slum.

Colon's population of 140,000 makes it the second largest city in Panama but, for tourists, Colon remains unsafe. Reports of daytime muggings have persisted although in the last two years there have been serious attempts by the government to clean up the city and reduce the

(Top) Fort San Lorenzo. (Bottom) Embera natives on Gatun Lake.(Right) Kayaking on Gatun Lake.

EMBERA NATIVES

The majority of Panama's Embera Indians live in Darien Province to the south, but a substantial number live along Gatun Lake. Their houses are built with cone-shaped roofs made of palm leaves and erected on stilts about 10 feet above the ground to escape pesky night critters. The Embera build superb dugout canoes, called piraguas, with very shallow drafts and the Panama Canal Authority has purchased a number of these piraguas to access the upper reaches of the Canal's watershed. The U.S. Air Force has also recruited Embera natives to teach jungle survival to its pilots and astronauts at Fort Sherman near Colon.

level of crime. Be sure to check with the front desk or shore excursion personel before going on a stroll into Colon. If you do so, it might be a good idea to travel with a group.

Ships will stop at one of two dock facilities. **Cruise Terminal Pier 6**, on the west side of the town, is adjacent to Cristobal, a suburb to the south of the Colon. The port facilities here have been recently upgraded to accommodate cruise ships with some shopping facilities and access to tours. The new **Colon 2000** pier, located on the east side of Colon just outside the Free Zone, features a shopping mall with duty free products and tours to local attractions.

SHORE EXCURSIONS

With improvements at Pier 6 and the completion of Colon 2000, cruise lines now see Panama as more than just a canal. The country has much to offer and for passengers whose ships are stopping in Colon, there are some excellent shore excursions available. Tours currently are designed for ships on loop cruises out of Florida which spend a half day on Gatun Lake and dock for the afternoon at Colon. Tour operators will normally pick up passengers from ships on Gatun Lake, proceed to the tours and return them to the ships at one of the docks in Colon.

Some tours include a visit to the observation areas at Gatun Locks the workings of the locks can be viewed up close. Usually these tours are combined with other attractions such as a tour of an Embera native village, located on Gatun Lake or boat tours and kayaking expeditions also on the lake. Perhaps, for history buffs, one of the most intriguing attractions has to be a visit to the nearby Spanish forts of San Lorenzo or Portobelo. Fort San Lorenzo, which guarded the entrance of the Chagres River, was built in the late 16th century during the reign of Philip II. In 1671 Captain Henry Morgan captured this fort after three days of fighting, then continued along the Chagres River to Old Panama, which he sacked and destroyed. Portobelo was the main shipping port for Spanish gold up to 1747. Other Colon area tours include exploring the nearby islands and viewing wildlife or on to the Gamboa aerial tram to see some of the most renowned rainforest canopy in Central America.

THE FRENCH ATTEMPT

For over a decade France was caught up in the venture of building the Panama Canal. The attempt was flawed yet heroic, for in the face of death and despair the young French engineers stayed on the job and did not flee. Conditions were appalling, even unimaginable to those back home. The nastiest of insects, the deadliest of snakes and a suffocating heat combined with a tropical humidity and torrential rainfall, made conditions hellish for the workers. Floods prevailed during the wet season, and the French engineer Bunau-Varilla reported inspecting the rail line by canoe after one storm and floating past tree tops that were "black with millions of tarantulas." Death stalked the workers in the form of tropical diseases, including cholera, dysentry and, more common, malaria and the dreaded yellow fever. Despite the great courage shown by the French in continuing to work in such menacing conditions, the loss of life (especially among laborers from the Caribbean) was staggering. In just 10 years some 20,000 workers died.

The French were frustrated for many reasons. Begun in 1880 and led by Ferdinand de Lesseps, it was long on enthusiasm but short on the technology needed for such a massive project. The steam shovels used were only a fraction of the size of the later American Bucyrus. At the rate the French were digging, it's been estimated they would have taken 50 years to dig a sea-level canal. The excavated earth and rock (called spoil) was hauled by undersized cars on light-gauge rail to dumping areas too close to the canal, contributing to the slides, and much of the unloading was done by hand. Medical advances were still years away from dealing with the ongoing decimation of its work force by yellow fever and malaria. Perhaps the biggest obstacle was the mindset of de Lesseps, who insisted on building a sea-level canal. Had a lock system been adopted at the beginning in 1880, as was suggested by French engineer Godin de Lépinay at a canal congress in 1879, French

The unstable soil vexed the French as well as the Americans, and slides were a fact of life for those working on the Isthmus.

prospects would have improved. But even then, the canal would have been quickly obsolete because of the small lock size (a width of only 59 feet) the French engineers were contemplating.

When the United States bought out the French concession to build the Canal for $40 million they got a partly-dug canal from which about 30 million cubic yards of spoil had been removed – about one tenth of the finished canal's total excavation, which was 264 million cubic yards. The French had dug a canal 25 feet deep and 70 feet from Colon to Bohio, a distance of 11 miles. They had also lowered the Culebra Cut saddle by over 160 feet and had excavated a small channel from Miraflores to the Pacific. American engineers arriving at Panama marvelled at how much had been accomplished by the French.

In many ways the United States was destined to build this greatest of the world's canals. The completion of the Panama Canal meshed with the confident mood and military interests of America, not to mention the expanding economy and ability of the United States to underwrite such a large venture. And, as is often the case, the right man – President Theodore Roosevelt – came at the right time to make it all happen.

AMERICA CHOOSES A HIGH-LEVEL LOCK CANAL

At first the United States wasn't sure what kind of canal should be built. The French had focused their efforts almost entirely on a sea-level canal – similar to their success with the Suez Canal. Digging a long ditch or strait to connect the two oceans would eliminate the need for locks lifting ships up to an intermediate lake. However, as American engineers pondered the task, it became obvious that the effort required to dig a sea-level canal was just too enormous. Chief Engineer George Goethals at one point said that there wasn't enough money in the world to build a sea level canal at Panama. There was simply too much earth to excavate, the task was too immense. Early estimates predicted it would take double the time and money to built a sea-level canal and, it was emphasized, there was no guarantee a safe navigable canal would be the end result. Even if the ongoing slides were manageable, the final canal would be a narrow, tortuous channel. And, it was pointed out, at least one lock would be necessary to deal with the difference in water levels due to the large tides of the Pacific Ocean.

Of far greater significance, however, was the Chagres River. This was "the lion in the path" of any canal according to one Panama governor. Chief engineer John Stevens stated during Senate hearings, "The one great problem in the construction of any canal down there is the control of the Chagres River. That overshadows everything else." During the wet season, frequent heavy rains often resulted in spectacular flooding, with the river rising as much as 40 feet in a single day. Such conditions would obliterate canal banks, making navigation difficult, and the strong river currents would make the passage extremely dangerous for ships transiting the tight twisting channel.

A sea-level canal was the favorite in the public mind – on a map the isthmus looked so narrow and easy to gouge out a trench out of. But to field engineers wading through the sawgrass and the heat, it was an impossible and impracticable dream. The vote in favor of a lock canal was very close in the Senate (36 to 31), but this momentous decision proved to be the right one.

How the Canal Was Built

Although the scale of the project was huge and many of the needed technologies were in their infancy, the mood was upbeat among both American engineers and the general public. However, as American workers arrived in Panama under the leadership of John Wallace (who brought his wife and two metal caskets to Panama), the first steps were tentative. The sheer scale of the project bore down on the engineers who were unsure how to begin or where to start. Within a year morale was low. Panic set in when an epidemic of yellow fever broke out in 1905 and terrified workers filled the ships leaving for the U.S.

At the dismissal of John Wallace, President Theodore Roosevelt found an ideal replacement in John Stevens who inspired workers and turned the situation around. Stevens was on the scene just a few days, reviewing the canal's progress, when he abruptly ordered all work to stop and began sending thousands of employees home. Stevens, the railwayman who discovered the Marias Pass over the Continental Divide in the Rocky Mountains, saw the challenges he was facing – proper planning and engineering of the project, eradicating disease, and building a smooth organization to execute the plans.

There were two types of slides workers had to deal with – gravity slides, such as this one near Culebra, and break slides.

On this last point, Stevens reorganized everything. His first goal was making the canal a "fit" place to live. He built thousands of new houses, mess halls, apartments, offices and warehouses. He brought in shipments of fresh food and sold it to workers in stores or mess halls at cost. Eggs, fresh fruit, even ice cream were available to workers. The health of the workers became a priority and he gave the Sanitation Department carte blanche in ridding the Canal Zone of tropical diseases. Stevens' direct manner and sense of purpose calmed the men and, with morale improved, the planning of the canal's construction moved ahead.

The engineering challenges were enormous and included the biggest excavation ever attempted by man which, in time, would equal three Suez Canals. Also, the canal would require the construction of the largest earth dam ever built; designing and building the most massive canal locks ever built; constructing the largest gates ever swung; and solving watershed problems of enormous proportions.

By early 1906, with the organization in place and diseases in check, Stevens began calling men from the United States back to the Canal. Excavation resumed and, with the United States Senate approving a lock canal in June 1906, the dirt finally began to fly. The planned canal would lift ships 85 feet in three locks, or steps, to a summit-level lake and then lower the ships again to sea level in three more locks.

Plans included a mammoth lake extending from the town of Gatun (six miles south of Colon) to halfway across the Isthmus. Because this would be the largest man-made lake (Gatun Lake) ever attempted at that time, the building of an earth dam to hold back the water was con-

John Stevens solved the riddle of Culebra Cut with an ingenious rail system that always kept empty cars in front of steam shovels.

sidered the most serious challenge. It turned out it wasn't – the construction of the dam went like clockwork. The major headache would be breaching the Continental Divide at Culebra Cut. As slides continued, estimated excavation at the Cut nearly doubled to 100,000,000 cubic yards – an unprecedented excavation, comparable to drilling a 12-foot-square hole through the center of the earth. Nothing like this had ever been attempted in the engineering history of the world.

The saddle or low point of Culebra Cut was 335 feet above sea level, at a point just north of Gold Hill which the French had whittled down to a depth of 200 feet. There was still an estimated 60 million cubic yards of tedious digging to be done throughout the length of the nine-mile-long Cut to lower the canal bed to 40 feet above sea level. Engineers first designed this gorge at the saddle to be 200 feet wide at the bottom and about 670 feet wide at the top. The bottom width was increased to 300 feet and the top, over time, had to be widened to more than 1800 feet to attain the necessary angle of repose for the adjacent hillsides.

Stevens saw the problem of the Cut as one of efficiently removing the spoil – making sure there was a continuous, smoothly running conveyor of dirt flowing from the cut to safe dump sites. With decades of experience in rail construction in Canada and the U.S., Stevens developed an efficient working "plant" of spoil removal. Flatbed cars were specially designed for ease of loading and unloading. These were brought uphill to the steam shovels where they were loaded and departed downhill. On any given day during peak excavation, up to 200 trains a day were running in and out of the Cut. Engineers, track switchers and traffic managers all ensured the system ran smoothly so there was

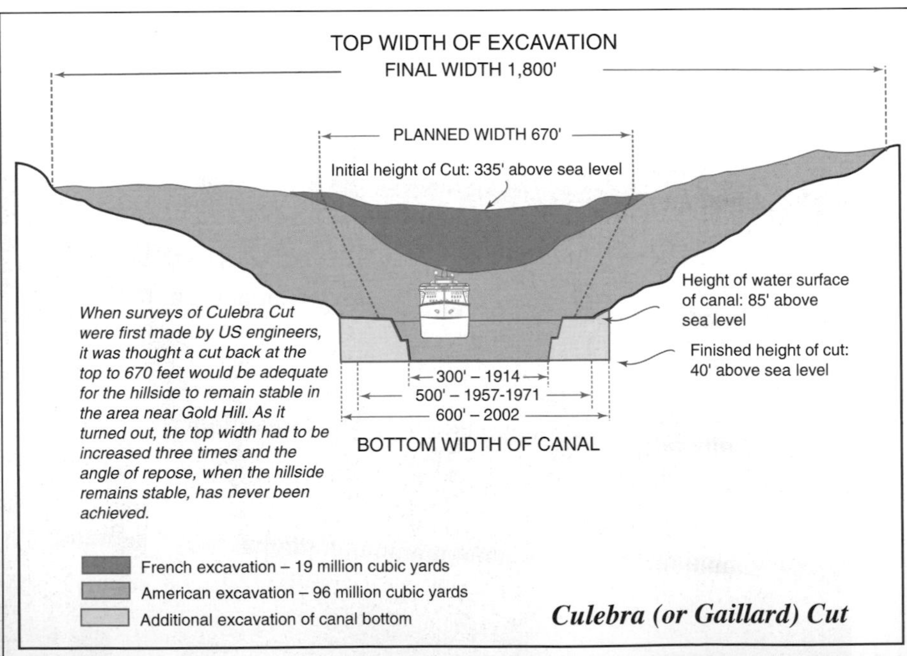

Culebra (or Gaillard) Cut

no delay of empty trains arriving at the steam shovels. Many of the dump sites became building sites, the spoil used to construct the earth dam at Gatun, the breakwaters on both sides of the canal and the relocated tracks of the Panama Rail Road.

Once the problem of spoil removal was solved, Stevens realized other engineering challenges still lay ahead, namely the design and building of the massive locks, and the complex machinery required for their operation. Even more daunting, perhaps, to a man who had little experience with hydraulic engineering, was the construction of the world's largest earth dam at Gatun to maintain the Gatun Lake level at 85 feet above sea level and to tame the wild Chagres River.

It was at this point, in late 1906, when real progress was apparent and shortly after the successful visit to the Canal by President Theodore

(Above) Culebra Cut on a Sunday. Noise levels in the cut were said to be deafening during work days. (Below) The cement ship SS Ancon marked the official opening of the Canal in 1914.

PILOTS AND THE CANAL

Every ship and boat transiting the Panama Canal requires a pilot, and large ships will often have two on board throughout their lock transits. Pilots normally board the ship near the ocean entrances – at the breakwater near Colon on the Atlantic side and at the end of the channel near Naos Island on the Pacific side. The ship's captain and the pilots work together, but it's the pilot who gives the helmsman all navigational orders. While in the locks, the pilot is in constant contact by radio to the locomotive operators and, working in tandem with the ship's captain, tries to ensure the ship does not "touch" the side walls of the locks. (You can usually see the pilot and captain on the bridge wings at this point.) Even the slightest jar of the ship's hull against the concrete walls will scrape off chunks of paint, adding an extra cost to the already expensive Panama transit.

With the help of a laptop computer, electronic charts and the Global Positioning System (which works by satellite), the pilot can tell exactly where the ship is throughout its transit of the Canal. The Maritime Traffic Control Center in Balboa sends information about all ships in the Canal to the pilot's computer, allowing him to view a "live" map showing the position of all transiting vessels. The pilot can easily find out the time and meeting point with other vessels. Pilots can also monitor the ship's speed, and the distances to the canal banks, to other vessels, and to the locks.

Pilots use laptop computers which show the exact position of the ship during the canal transit.

Roosevelt, that Stevens resigned. The reasons for his resignation remain a mystery but it seems most probable that the workload had become too much. President Roosevelt put Army engineer Colonel George Goethals in charge, whose great attention to detail saw the Canal to completion. But Goethals always credited Stevens with laying the great foundation for building the canal.

Stevens was right about one very important aspect of the canal and that was turning the Chagres River from terrible adversary to useful ally. Whereas the French envisaged digging channels to divert the Chagres away from the canal, or even over the Continental Divide to the Pacific, the Americans understood all this water could be used instead to create a huge man-made lake upon which ships could travel most of the way across the Isthmus. The Chagres became the key to the success of the project or, in Stevens' words, the "servant, instead of the master of the situation." Without Panama's legendary rainfall, without its massive watershed of over 1300 square miles, without its annual supply of new water flowing down the Chagres and its 20 odd tributaries, through some of the wettest real estate in the world, the Panama Canal could have remained a dream even to this day.

On August 3, 1914, the Cristobal was the first oceangoing ship to complete a transit of the Canal. By a bizarre twist of fate, World War I broke out the same day and the official opening of the Canal two weeks later, with the *SS Ancon*, was something of an anticlimax, the news buried on the back pages behind reports of the war in Europe.

GATUN LOCKS

When George Goethals replaced John Stevens as Chief Engineer in 1907 he partitioned the work into three divisions – the Atlantic, Central and Pacific. The Central Division was charged with clearing a path through the Continental Divide, while the Atlantic and Pacific

Water from Gatun Lake floods into the lock chambers through 100 holes which reduces turbulence when lifting ships.

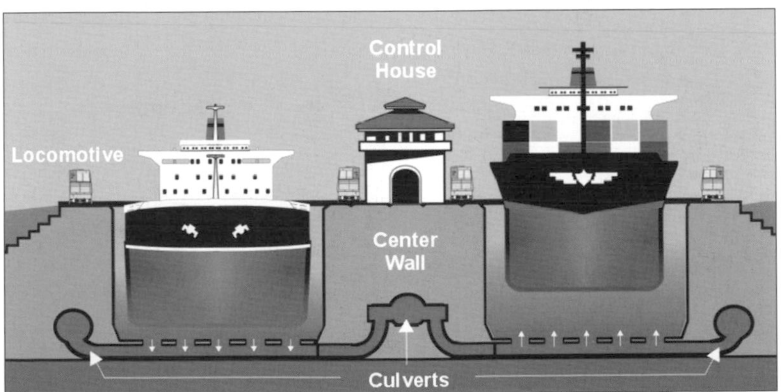

Divisions were assigned the job of building the massive concrete locks and steel gates needed at each end of the Canal. Goethals placed an army engineer, Major William Sibert, in charge of the Atlantic Division and a civilian engineer, Sydney Williamson, in charge of the Pacific Division. As Goethals anticipated, an intense competition developed between the two to see which could be most efficient and competent in the completion of their tasks. In the end, the match proved to be a draw, as the results at both ends of the canal were excellent.

Although the Gatun Locks is a unique triple set of locks and is the largest and longest set of locks in the world, it has in many aspects in common with the other locks such as the gates and operating mechanisms. Each lock is 110 feet wide and 1,000 feet in length and were built in pairs to accommodate passing traffic. Each lock can hold a ship up to a maximum of 106 feet in width and 965 feet in length, and each also has the ability to section itself into a smaller lock depending on the size of the ship. Each lock also uses the same type of miter gate but the one variation between the Atlantic and Pacific locks is the height of gates. The Pacific side locks were built to accommodate the tidal range of 20 feet. Ships that existed in 1909, when the locks were designed, had plenty of room, but today's large cruise ships clear the lock walls with just inches to spare.

The side wall of the Gatun Locks compared to a six-storey building. Publications at the time emphasized the scale of the construction.

The locks, whether on the Pacific or Atlantic side, use water from Gatun Lake; no pumps are needed – the whole system is gravity-fed with lake water entering huge 18-foot-high culverts running the length of the center and side walls of each lock. The water leads into a system of cross-culverts under the lock floors to rapidly fill the lock. Each cross-culvert has five openings for a total of 100 holes in each chamber floor for water to enter or drain, depending on which valves are opened or closed. This large number of openings distributes the water evenly over the lock floor to control turbulence while the lock is being filled.

All movement of water is handled by the operators in the red-roofed control building in the center of each of the locks. Here a control board with a waist-high working representation of the locks shows the operator what is taking place in the locks. Everything that happens in the locks happens on the control board at precisely the same time. The switches to work the lock gates are located beside the representation of that device on the control board. To lift a huge ocean-going ship in a lock chamber, the operator has only to turn a small chrome handle. Another ingenious part of the system are elaborate racks of interlocking bars below the control board to make the switches mechanically interlock. Each handle must be turned in proper sequence or it will not turn. This eliminates doing anything out of order or forgetting a step, ensuring safe operation.

(Above) Weighing hundreds of tons, every lock gate is nearly bouyant in water. (Below) View of a lock during maintenance

Whether you enter the Panama Canal from the Atlantic or Pacific side, your ship is raised by water which has already lifted two other ships through the two locks ahead of you. To save water from Gatun Lake, it is reused by draining into each successive lock, lifting a ship each time. At Gatun, each lock or step, is about a 28-foot rise and it takes about 10 minutes to bring a ship up to the next step or lock in the system. For large cruise ships, 52 million gallons of water is used to transit the canal – equivalent to a one-day supply for a city of 100,000.

One of the great innovations of the locks was the use of electricity in operating motors, valves, lock gates and the unique electric towing locomotives (known as mules) which maintain complete control over ship movement in the locks. Designed by Edward Schildhauer, the locomotives work on tracks built atop the lock walls. Operating at a

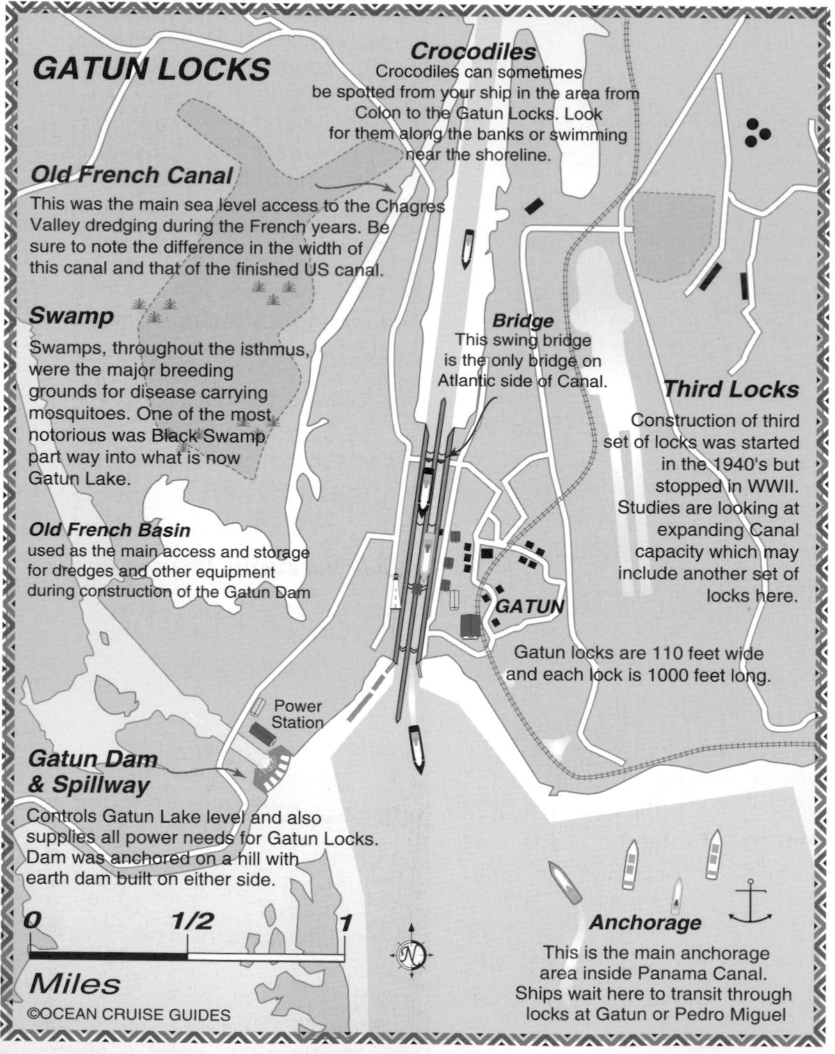

speed of about 2 miles per hour with a towing pull of 70,000 pounds, these locomotives were specially designed to travel the 45-degree incline between the lock chambers. The original cost for each one was $13,000. Today, new mules cost $2 million each.

During construction, the site of Gatun Locks was of great interest as critics raised concerns about the foundation on which the massive triple-lock structure would rest. Built with over two million cubic yards of concrete, each 1000-foot-long lock is a huge structure which, if stood on end, would compare with the tallest buildings of the modern world. Even lying flat as they do, the walls of the locks are taller than a six-storey building. Each lock floor is between 12 and 20 feet thick and the total length of the Gatun triple locks, with the center guide walls, is over a mile. If any uneven settling had taken place, the locks may have cracked.

Numerous borings were taken in the area and it was found the underlying shale-like material was superb as a base for the locks. Chief Engineer Stevens said early in the construction that "if nature had intended triple locks there she could not have arranged matters better." It was crucial for the integrity of the entire canal that the bedrock extending from Gatun Locks to the hills west of Gatun Dam be absolutely stable and impervious to water and this, fortunately, turned out to be the case.

It took four years to build the locks once the first concrete was poured at Gatun on August 24,

WEIGHING IN ON CONCRETE

Until the late 1800s, concrete had been little used in building, and then mostly for floors and basements. There was still a great deal to be learned in the science of concrete production, which requires specific, controlled measurements of water with cement and sand. The concrete work in Panama was an unprecedented challenge that would stand unequalled in total volume until construction of the Boulder Dam in the 1930s. So much cement was used, Goethals estimated saving $50,000 just by shaking out each bag. In spite of the newness of the science, the results were extraordinary. After nearly 90 years of service, the concrete of the locks and at Gatun and Miraflores dams remain in excellent condition, a fact regarded by modern engineers as one of the most astounding aspects of the entire Canal.

Huge cantilevered cranes were used at the Pacific Division to pour concrete.

(Above) Arrow confirms lane to pilot. (Middle) Mules pull ship forward; (Bottom) Water flowing from Gatun Lake lifts the ships.

1909. These were four intense years of planning, preparing the site, building steel and wood forms to mold the thousands of tons of concrete, and organizing a complex overhead system of pouring the concrete into the molds. The gravel came from Portobelo, where a large crushing plant was built, and the sand from the infamous Nombre de Dios, the bay where Sir Francis Drake, after dying from dysentery, still lies in a lead casket.

A small automatic railway brought the appropriate amounts of gravel, sand and cement to a location near the Gatun spillway where the concrete was mixed. When the concrete was ready to be poured, large buckets carrying six tons of concrete were whisked upwards by an overhead cableway. Suspended 85 feet above the ground and travelling at a speed of 20 miles an hour, the buckets were raced to the locks and lowered to the men below who would evenly spread the concrete. The whole system – the gigantic cableway towers and large steel forms – was on tracks and as the work progressed, the entire structure was moved forward.

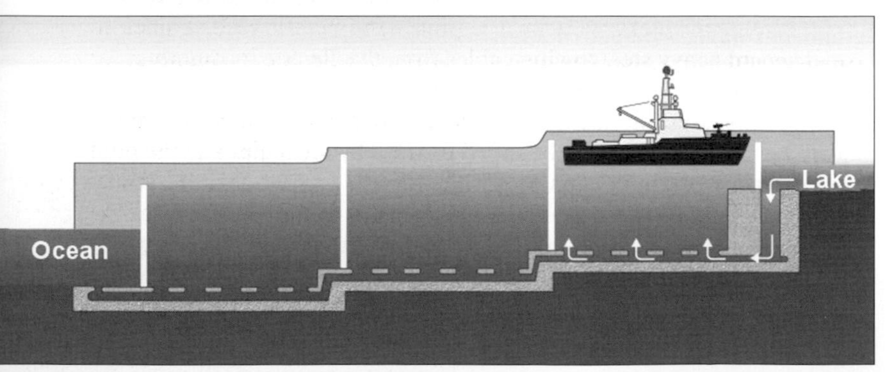

The electric locomotives (mules) used in the locks have tremendous pulling power.

The reason a total of three locks are used at each end of the Canal (rather than one or two) is to reduce the lift in stages to provide a wide margin of safety. A single lock holding back a 130-foot-high head of water (depth of channel plus 85 foot height of Gatun Lake) would be dangerous. If the gates ever gave way, through a fault in the structure or by a ship collision, the results would be catastrophic for the ship, those on board, and the entire Canal. The risks of gate failure are greatly reduced by having three locks and each with the added precaution of double gates.

The gates, the Canal's most dramatic moving parts, swing like double doors, closing in a shallow V with the pressure of the rising water helping to seal the gates. The gates weigh several hundred tons each but are nearly weightless in water due to the lower half being a hollow watertight compartment. Not only does this greatly reduce the strain on the gate hinges but requires only a small 40 horsepower electric motor to open and close each gate leaf. The leaves are 65 feet wide by 7 feet thick. However, they vary in height from 47 to 82 feet, depending on their position. The lower gates of Miraflores Locks are the highest due to the extreme variation of Pacific Ocean tides.

Upon approaching the Gatun Locks from the Caribbean, a ship is directed to one of the two canal lanes by a large green arrow at the front of the center wall facing the bow of the ship. This arrow is a visual confirmation of orders the pilot receives for which lane the ship is to take for transiting the locks. Rowboats approach the ships to receive lines to send aboard heavy steel towing cables from the electric locomotives, or mules, which are then attached to the ship.

The ship eases into the first lock and by this point will be secured to six to eight mules. It is slowly pulled forward by the mules and the pilot and captain work in tandem to position the ship in the lock during its upward lift. When the water in the first lock equalizes the level of the next lock, the gates slowly swing open and the ship is pulled into the next lock. After being "locked" three times, a cruise ship has been lifted 85 feet to Gatun Lake, which marks the start of a beautiful cruise past the tropical rainforest that surrounds the lake.

Gatun Dam and spillway are in the upper center area of photo.

GATUN DAM

The engineers who designed the Panama Canal's locks and dams had to overcome numerous challenges, but they also had a bit of luck pertaining to the location of the Gatun Locks and Dam. Extending westward from Gatun Locks across the Chagres Valley, the dam connected to hills a mile and half away. A small solid hill right in the middle of the Chagres Valley provided the anchoring point for the concrete portion of the dam with a spillway laid in a cut made through the hill. This spillway is half a mile from the locks and easily spotted as you are leaving or just approaching Gatun Locks. This spillway controls the height of Gatun Lake and also provides most of the power for the canal.

As with the Gatun Locks, some politicians and the public were apprehensive about the dam's strength during its construction. Just 20 years earlier, the Johnstown Flood disaster in Pennsylvania had claimed 2,200 lives after an earthen dam gave way. The Gatun Dam was huge, over 8,000 feet long and 105 feet high, making it the largest earth dam on record, but the engineers were confident this dam would hold and testified in great detail as to the dam's strengths. Extensive rock "toes" half a mile apart ran along the front and back edge of the dam. Hydraulic fill, a clay-like material impervious to water, was laid on top and thousands of trainloads of spoil from Culebra Cut were dumped on top of this to bring the final height of the dam to 105 feet above sea level – 20 feet above the normal level of Gatun Lake.

During construction, one senator wondered if Gatun Dam would be strong enough to bear the water pressure from the wide expanse of Gatun Lake. It was explained to him that water pressure is due to the height of the water and not to its width. Otherwise, it was pointed out, how was it that the dikes in Holland hold back the Atlantic Ocean.

In 1977, the Canal Commission initiated dam inspections under the coordination of the Engineering Division, with assistance from the

For its time, Gatun Dam was unprecedented in size and its construction created the world's largest man-made lake.

Corps of Engineers, to assure that all three dams – Gatun, Miraflores and Madden – remain in good, safe working condition. Gatun Dam is presently being monitored for the effects of vibrations caused by recent tremors. So far, the dam continues to show no sign of instability.

GATUN LAKE

In 1912, upon completion of the Gatun Dam, the Chagres River began to slowly fill its valley. It took almost two years for the water level to reach its planned height of 85 feet above sea level, with the new Gatun Lake covering an area of 164 square miles, equal in size to Barbados.

Gatun Lake became the largest man-made lake in the world and it extended from Gatun to the Pedro Miguel Locks – a distance of 32 miles. Dozens of small villages vanished and scores of small islands were created. Today, there are over 30 man-made lakes bigger than Gatun but it was over 20 years before it had to give up its title.

When the lake first started to form, Canal workers warned local natives of the dangers but many refused to leave their homes and eventually had to be evacuated. In one case, a flood caused a rapid rise and a police launch was sent to a house near Lion Hill. The house was almost entirely covered by water and police approached an elderly native and his family resting in a cayuca moored to the roof. "Don't you know that the lake is going to cover your house," the anxious police asked. The old man, unperturbed, replied, "that is the same old story the French told my dad thirty years ago."

Damming the Chagres Valley greatly diminished the cost and effort of excavation north of the Continental Divide and it also tamed the wild "lion" which had been the nemesis of the French. With the dam in place, the Chagres could rage and flood all it wanted for the additional water merely flowed into the huge Gatun Lake which might increase a foot or more in height, but could be easily regulated at the spillway of the Gatun Dam. In addition to supplying the means for ships to cross the Isthmus, Gatun Lake (and Madden Lake) provides for the electrical needs of the Canal, and drinking water for the cities of Panama and Colon. Keeping a close eye on water levels, ACP has monitoring stations throughout the lake after the effect of the El Nino weather phenomenon in 1998 caused the worst drought in the history of the Canal. Draft restrictions (the depth of the ship below water level) were established to ensure no ships would run aground in the Canal.

Ensuring adequate water for the Canal is essential and increasing the capacity of the lake by making it deeper is one measure that's been taken in the past. In the early 1980s the channel through the lake was deepened by three feet and currently an eight-year project will deepen the Canal another three feet. Other actions include recent legislation defining the boundaries of the watershed to guarantee its conservation and management.

As you transit Gatun Lake, you will likely spot a variety of birdlife and occasionally an alligator, which likes fresh water and provided sport for canal workers during the days of construction but is now a protected species.

Black Swamp – This infamous nemesis of pirates trying to cross the Isthmus to Panama City was reported to be bottomless. During construction of the Panama Rail Road a large amount of fill was needed to create a secure railbed (bottom was finally found at 185 feet below ground surface). Despite the best efforts of the rail line, the roadbed kept sinking and required yearly maintenance. The canal goes right over the former Black Swamp just south of Tiger Island.

Orchid Island – The most beautiful orchids in the Panama rainforest grew near the top of the largest trees and were difficult to reach. As Gatun Lake rose, however, workers and their wives would row out in small boats to the dying trees and pick off the pretty orchids. Orchids are plentiful on this island.

Bohio – Originally known as Bohio Soldado or "home of the soldier," this site about 11 miles south of Colon was first considered by French and American engineers for a dam to stop the Chagres River. The French excavated a canal, 25 feet deep and 70 wide, from Gatun to this point and the underlying rock looked promising. Engineers thought, however, the location at Gatun was better both for the conditions of the bedrock and because the resulting lake would be far larger, providing more capacity for controlling the Chagres.

Barro Colorado Island – About eight miles south of the Gatun Locks, this largest of the lake islands is an important living laboratory for the Smithsonian Institute of Tropical Research. Almost 400 bird species live here as well as 102 mammal species and 1,316 plant species. Previously only research scientists were allowed on the island, but now tour operators take visitors on day trips along its nature trails.

Soberania National Park – This tropical rainforest is a major recreational park covering over 50,000 acres and extending about half way across the Isthmus. Among the many hiking trails is a part of the old Las Cruces Trail used in early Spanish times to transport gold and supplies between Panama City and Nombre de Dios and Portobelo. The park is home to numerous species of birds and other wildlife

Barbacoas Island – At this point, 23 miles south of Colon, the terrain of the Canal begins to close in as the elevation rises. Barbacoas, a native Indian word meaning bridge, was an important point in the transit of the Isthmus in the days of the Panama Rail Road. A massive wrought-iron bridge 600 feet in length had been erected on stone piers to carry the rail line across the Chagres River at the southwest side of what is now Barbacoas Island. However, during Ferdinand de Lesseps' first visit to Panama in 1879, this bridge was washed out and he and his entourage, where forced to cross what was left of the bridge on foot. Although this should have been a clear warning to de Lesseps about the power of the Chagres, he made no mention of this to his investors back in France when he reported on his trip.

Malachin – Chinese rail workers, suffering the melancholia effects of malaria, committed suicide here "en masse" in the mid-19th century.

Gamboa – This small town remains an important hub for canal and tug maintenance, and in recent years has become a vibrant tourism destination for its nearby rainforest. This is where the Chagres River enters Gatun Lake and you can easily see the rail and highway causeway cross the mighty Chagres near the Canal. Two of **the world's largest industrial cranes**, confiscated from Nazi Germany after World War II, are perched at the edge of the town by the Canal and attract mechanical engineers from around the world. Just to the south of the Chagres causeway is where a large earth dike was built to divert the river away

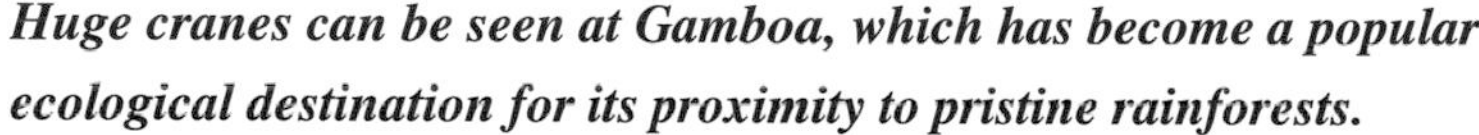

Huge cranes can be seen at Gamboa, which has become a popular ecological destination for its proximity to pristine rainforests.

GATUN LOCKS & LAKE

(Top) A cruise ship nears the entrance to Bohio Reach where a dam location for the canal was first proposed. (Middle) A view from the ship's bridge shows the close proximity of the shoreline. (Below, left) A ship rounds the east side of Barro Colorado Island. (Bottom) Balcony cabins provide good views of Gatun Locks.

(Right) Pacific-bound cruise ships leave Gatun Locks. (Middle) Looking north to channels leading to Gatun Lake from Tabernilla. (Bottom) Lush vegetation on islands in Gatun Lake are indicative of the dense jungle workers had to deal with.

from the excavation work in Culebra Cut. On a few occasions during the wet season, the river would breach the dike and flood the canal, leaving equipment, steam shovels and rail track under many feet of water. In October 1913, upon completion of the dry excavation at Culebra Cut, President Woodrow Wilson pushed a button in Washington and through a signal relayed by telegraph wire from Washington to Panama, the dike was blown apart and the canal flooded so that dredges could complete the final excavation.

Madden Dam – Built in 1935, this dam was constructed to further assist in the control of the Chagres and provide additional electrical power for the Canal. The large reservoir behind the dam also helps maintain the water level in Gatun Lake during dry season. Located on the Chagres River approximately 12 miles upstream from the Canal and 25 miles from the City of Panama, the dam is 974 feet long and 223 feet high. It was named in honor of Martin B. Madden, a former member of the U.S. House of Representatives from Illinois.

Canopy Tower – During the Cold War, the United States Air Force built a three-storey cylindrical tower as part of its intercontinental defense. The tower is now used by the ACP as a communications outpost and a popular eco-lodge. It includes a small museum devoted to the local wildlife and the history of the former military site. The tower has great views over the Canal and some of best rainforest in Panama. Canopy Tower is rated by Audubon Magazine as one of the top eco-lodges in the world.

Summit Botanical Gardens & Zoo – A few miles beyond Gamboa is this important refuge for the endangered harpy eagle, Panama's national bird. This is one of the largest members of the hawk family, reaching a height of 38 inches. Known by the Aztecs as the "winged wolf," the harpy eagle eats macaws and sloths, and was named after the winged monsters of Greek mythology. The botanical gardens were created in 1923 to introduce tropical plants from around the world to Panama and contains some 15,000 plant species.

CULEBRA CUT

This nine-mile section, from Gamboa to Pedro Miguel locks, was the main engineering challenge throughout 40 years of effort by the French and Americans. Culebra, meaning snake, referred to the Rio Obispo valley north of Gold and Contractor Hills and represented the best pass across the Continental Divide from Gamboa to the Pacific. The actual saddle of the Continental Divide would today be approximately in line between Gold Hill and Contractors Hill. Water north of this point drained into the Atlantic Ocean and south of this point (where the Canal follows the valley of the Rio Grande to Miraflores) all water drained into the Pacific Ocean.

Culebra Hill itself is an ancient volcanic core of solid basalt and the soil along the valleys is an unstable mix of granite, sedimentary rock,

The famous Cucaracha Slide kept delaying the Canal's completion.

shales and many forms of clay which had the tedious ability to stick to everything – especially shovels. The clay when wet, however, would turn into a substance like putty or peanut butter and could flow like a glacier down the slopes and bury months of work in just a few days. The worst of these gravity slides occurred just south of Gold Hill at Cucaracha where, on one occasion in 1907, 500,000 cubic yards slipped into the canal. Hundreds of miles of track could be lost in such a slide, and steam shovels could be buried with only the tips of their cranes visible. By 1912, Cucaracha had dumped some three million additional cubic yards of material into the canal, all of which had to be painstakingly removed.

Break slides, however, were even more destructive. These resulted from unstable rock formations losing the lateral support of earth which had been excavated. The first sign would be cracks in the

LET'S WORK!

Men from all corners of the globe came to Panama to work in the Cut and one description reported in 1908 in The Saturday Evening Post captures this: "The man who ran the steam shovel, who had charge of the engine and maneuvered it, was an Irishman. The man on the crane, who attended to the dumping, was an American. The two stokers at the engine behind were Jamaican negroes, and the six members of the 'move up' crew, the men who leveled the ground to where the shovel stood and placed the tracks so that it could move forward and keep its nose to the bank, were Sikhs who wore white turbans on their heads and worked like automatons."

Bottom right of photo shows junction of Chagres River & Canal near Gamboa. To the left is Bas Obispo Reach – the start of Culebra Cut.

ground along the rim of the Cut. What was so unnerving about these slides was that there was no telling when the next stage would commence. It might be weeks, months or even years before an entire slope might suddenly heave or collapse – sometimes in a matter of a few hours. The worst of these "break" slides was on the west bank of the Cut where some six million cubic yards of earth dropped into the canal over the summer of 1912.

Work in the bottom of the Cut was hell. In the dry season, temperatures were usually in the range of 100 degrees Farenheit and in the wet season everything was mud. The noise of steam shovels, trains and blasting was deafening. More dynamite was used during construction of the Canal than in all previous wars of the United States combined, and many workers were killed by premature detonations, one of which killed 23 men.

Since the completion of the Canal, Culebra Cut has been widened in straight sections from 300 to 500 feet, and further increased to 600 feet in 2002. The Cut is also widely known as Gaillard Cut, named in honor of the Central Division's Chief Engineer, David du Bose Gaillard, who, in 1913, suddenly became incoherent while on the job and, upon returning to New York, died of a brain tumor a few months later.

Empire – Situated on the west bank overlooking Culebra Cut, Empire was the location of Central Division headquarters during construction. Every piece of equipment – train cars, steam shovels and even the rock drills – was co-ordinated with the use of a large map. Schools and most of the housing for the division were located here.

Culebra Reach – East Culebra Slide is to the immediate left and the dark shape ahead is Gold Hill. (Below) At the Continental Divide.

Culebra – Called "brains hill" by one Panama governor, this was an employee townsite where the main corps of engineers lived during the construction of the Canal. At the completion of the Canal, Culebra was dismantled and the buildings moved to Ancon.

Gold Hill – In the words of Major Sibert, "Gold Hill is a hard trap rock with a volcanic neck extending down to an unknown depth and is there to stay." This hill, the highest point of the eastern side of Culebra Cut, got its name from the assertion of the French canal company that the hill was full of gold, enough to pay for the total cost of the canal's construction. There was no gold, although cruise passengers can still see streaks of rust along the face of this hill which may have prompted its naming. The hill today, with its terraced slopes, looks like a jagged tooth in the landscape – a lasting reminder of the hard-fought battle.

In the depths of the Continental Divide in 1913. More dynamite was used in Culebra Cut than all previous wars of the U.S. combined.

Contractors Hill – On the west side of Culebra, or Gaillard Cut, Contractors Hill got its name from the early days of French excavation when, despite many attempts by numerous contractors, paid large amounts of money, the hill never seemed to lessen in size. This hill was the high point on the west side of Culebra Cut and was connected to Gold Hill with a saddle-like ridge. Over the years both this hill and Gold Hill have been cut down to try and lessen slides. Since 1915, about 40 feet have been removed from the top of this hill which is now about 370 feet above sea level.

Ships navigate past Gold Hill after the East Culebra Slide in 1915. This shot is looking north between Gold and Contractors Hills.

Paraiso – Originally a native village, this was the site of many slides – one of which fell so suddenly the grass was still intact on top of the slide as it landed on the bottom of the canal.

Pedro Miguel Lock (See Gatun Locks for detail about the lock operations.) – U.S. engineers first thought the Pacific locks would be built in an area near present-day Balboa – adjacent to Sosa Hill. As events transpired it was found that the substrata was not adequate and it was also thought the locks would be vulnerable to enemy ships. So for both engineering and military reasons the Pacific locks were moved some three miles further north to Miraflores and Pedro Miguel.

Pedro Miguel is about a mile and a half from Miraflores Locks, separated by Miraflores Lake, and is a single lock. It is unique in that the lock lift here is 31 feet as opposed to 28 feet at each step of the Gatun Locks and 27 feet each (without tide consideration) at the two steps at Miraflores. The additional

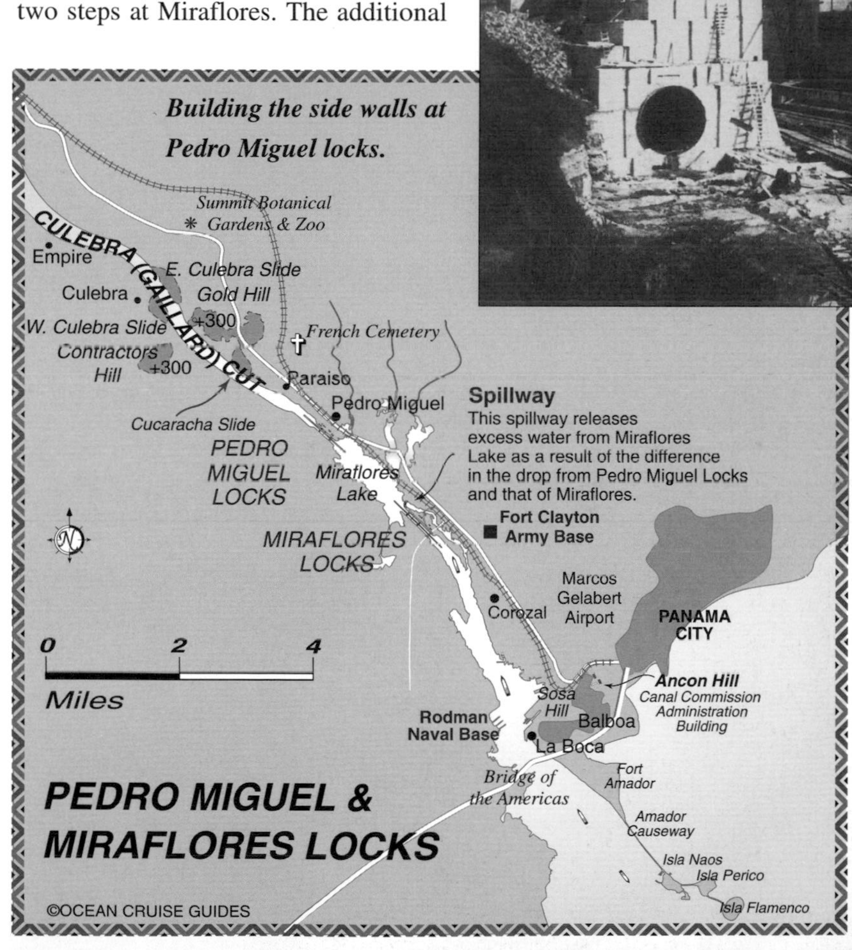

Building the side walls at Pedro Miguel locks.

CULEBRA CUT TO THE PACIFIC

(Top) The Pacific Ocean side of Miraflores Locks has the tallest gates of all the locks. (Above) Pedro Miguel Locks. (Bottom) A solid core tusk is all that remains of Gold Hill.

(Top) Panama City has grown 20-fold since the time of the Canal's construction.
(Right) Pilot and Captain shake hands after completing a smooth transit of the Canal.
(Bottom) All transiting vessels are monitored at the Panama Canal Authority Administration building on Ancon Hill near Panama City.

water volume from this lock is discharged over the spillway at Miraflores. The terrain at Pedro Miguel and Miraflores is not open, like that at Gatun, so during construction a suspended cable way wasn't possible for the pouring of concrete. Pacific Division Engineer Sydney Williamson instead used enormous cantilever cranes, so large they could be seen for miles distant, which could move about on tracks inside the locks and were used to pour 2.4 million yards of concrete.

There has been some conjecture whether it was a blunder not to combine all three locks at Miraflores, similar to that at Gatun. But Goethals concluded the bedrock was not adequate for triple locks and the additional concrete needed was too costly. Critics have since said that this has resulted in a bottleneck at this side of the canal, although ACP statistics point to the biggest backups at the Atlantic side.

Miraflores Lake – the small depression between Pedro Miguel and Miraflores became an intermediate lake and was planned as a temporary anchorage. Although ships occasionally do anchor here, almost all traffic continues straight on to the Miraflores Locks. An important filtration plant is located here, supplying drinking water for the city of Panama. The lake is about a mile and a half long and half a mile wide.

Miraflores Dam and Spillway – Located just east of Miraflores Locks, this concrete structure was built in 1914 to control the excess discharge from Pedro Miguel Locks and the runoff from the Cocoli River which is on the west side of the Miraflores Lake. The dam extends from the locks west to the river.

Miraflores Locks (See Pedro Miguel and Gatun locks for more detail.) – These southernmost double locks can have the biggest lift of any of the Canal locks because of the extreme tidal fluctuations of the Pacific. The maximum lift for these locks can be as much as 65 feet at a low tide. Miraflores' lower lock gates are the heaviest and largest to accommodate the Pacific tides – each gate weighs 745 tons and is 82 feet high. This lift can be either the largest in the Canal, up to about 38 feet, or the least at about 18 feet. A viewing platform at Miraflores gives tourists, and local citizens, a chance to see the locks in action and is especially busy on Sundays. There is a swing bridge at the south end of the locks which was opened in May 1942 and provided cars and trucks with a permanent way to cross the Canal.

Balboa – During Canal construction some 22 million cubic yards of fill was dumped into a swamp below Ancon Hill resulting in a reclamation of 676 acres. This site was actually named La Boca right up to 1909 when a visiting ambassador from Peru suggested to Goethals that he honor the discoverer of the Pacific by renaming the town Balboa, and Goethals promptly complied.

The permanent **Administration Building** was located at Balboa, and the best buildings from Culebra and Empire were moved around it. Balboa continues to serve as the main fueling and maintenance yard not only for Canal vessels but occasionally for cruise ships which may refuel here on cruises from Alaska to the Caribbean.

Bridge of the Americas – Almost a mile in length, this bridge provided a highway connection between Panama and Central America. Built in 1962, the bridgedeck is almost 400 feet above the Canal.

Panama City – After the destruction of Old Panama in 1671 by Captain Henry Morgan, the Spanish moved their city to a location below Ancon Hill which is surrounded by water on three sides. This small city was almost forgotten by the Spanish in the 18th century when, after too many pirate attacks on Portobelo, they gave up on their trans-Isthmian route and began shipping gold directly to Spain via Cape Horn. Upon completion of the Canal, the city population was about 30,000 – about what it was at the time of Morgan's visit.

Since 1915 Panama City has grown more than 20 times and its present population of 700,000 resides in an area extending from the Canal in the west to the old city, about seven miles to the east. The original city core, Casco Viejo (meaning old compound) includes 17th-century Spanish architecture, notably the Santo Domingo church with its famous flat arch. At the time of French involvement in Panama, some influence carried over to the city's architecture as evidenced by the canal administration building, now the Interoceanic Canal Museum. This building faces the famous Plaza de la Independencia which was the scene, on November 3, 1903, of Panama's peaceful revolution and birth as a country.

Old Panama (Panama La Vieja) has very little left from the days of its pillage at the hands of Captain Morgan. There is a church and tower but most of the city was built over by sprawling residential structures in the 1950s and it wasn't until the mid 1970s that the government protected the ruins by declaring them a protected historic site.

Casco Viejo, the old part of Panama City, still charms visitors.

Ancon Hill – Both the French and Americans located their hospitals for sick workers here. With some ocean breeze, the rooms were relatively cool but the French hospital was a notorious breeding ground for mosquitoes and an unlikely place to get better. Ancon Hill was also where rock was quarried and crushed for use in concrete mix for the Pacific locks. Its conspicuous bald top can be seen for miles out at sea.

Naos Island and Causeway – This breakwater and causeway constructed in 1912 connected four small islands to the mainland about two miles away. The purpose of the breakwater was to prevent the Canal's Pacific entrance from filling in with silt due to prevailing currents. Because of the bay's soft bottom, ten times the projected amount of fill was needed before the breakwater finally connected with Naos island. Causeways eventually connected all four islands of this group which includes Naos, Culebra, Perico and Flamenco.

These four islands were once the most fortified position for the United States leading up to World War II. Fort Grant was established in 1913 to guard the Pacific entrance to the Canal. In the late 1920s two 14-inch guns with a 30-mile range were mounted on rail carriages and, in the event of an attack, could be quickly moved to either side of the Isthmus. The tracks for moving the guns are still visible on Culebra Island. In their efforts to attract more cruise business, Panama's investors are developing the Fort Amador Cruise Port on Flamenco Island which is the most seaward island of the four. Plans call for a large hotel and shopping mall complex with transportation links to the Panama Rail Road and Panama City.

Taboga Islands – These fairly large islands are located just to the west of the Pacific Ocean entrance. During the time of French efforts in Panama, it was believed that yellow fever was caused by the corruption

Built in the early 1960s, the Bridge of the Americas is the only highway link between North and South America.

of vegetation, so workers who contracted malaria or yellow fever were removed to a large sanitarium built on the largest of these islands. Many of these patients were soon moved from hospital beds to graves in the large cemetery on the island.

Before the French, the islands had a rich history. Inhabited by natives until the arrival of the Spanish in 1515, they were used as a base for numerous pirates who raided Panama, including Morgan and Drake. The second oldest church in the Western Hemisphere is located in the town's small square and was built in 1550. During World War II the islands were used by the U.S. military which installed anti-aircraft guns and bunkers. Today, with sparkling beaches and prolific wildflowers, the islands are a popular spot for locals and tourists.

Pearl islands – This beautiful archipeligo may one day become a cruise destination and currently some ships spend a day in the Gulf of Panama cruising by these islands, one of which (Contadora) was once home for the exiled Shah of Iran in 1979.

San Blas Islands – Lying just off the north coast of Panama, this archipelago of some 400 small, low-lying islands is an infrequent but unique port of call for cruise ships. When American engineers were building the Canal, they stopped at one of these islands and found the kind of sand they were looking for to make cement. However, the local Kuna Indians said their sand was a gift from God and not for sale. Little has changed since then, for the Kuna remain indifferent to modern industrialization, living in thatch-roofed houses and retaining primitive customs. Their handicrafts are coveted by tourists who can buy colorful embroidered clothing and gold jewelry, including arm and ankle bracelets, with U.S. dollars even though coconuts are still the principal currency. Ships drop anchor off Isla Carti and tender passengers ashore.

Kuna natives are renowned for their bright colored textile crafts.

Central America
Yucatan
MEXICO
Belize City
BELIZE
Roatan Is.
Bay Islands
JAMAICA
Kingston
GUATEMALA
Guatemala
HONDURAS
Tegucigalpa
San Salvador
Puerto Quetzal
EL SALVADOR
NICARAGUA
Mosquito Coast
Caribbean Sea
Managua
San Juan del Sur
San Jose
Puntarenas
Puerto Limon
Puerto
Caldera
COSTA RICA
Colon
Panama
PANAMA
Cartagena
COLOMBIA
Pacific Ocean
0
200
400
Miles
N
©OCEAN CRUISE GUIDES

CHAPTER THREE

CENTRAL AMERICA

The two great continents of North and South America are joined by a mountainous land bridge where verdant jungles and misty volcanic peaks have long fascinated the rest of the world. Hidden waterfalls, exotic birds and fragrant flowers all flourish in the region's tropical rainforests, as do brilliant butterflies, tree frogs, spider monkeys and jaguars. Called Central America, this region encompasses seven small nations and a variety of ecosystems – from coastal mangroves to cloud-covered summits – and was once part of El Mundo Maya (The Maya World), which thrived for 3,000 years, its territory extending from Mexico's Yucatan peninsula down through Belize and Guatemala into areas of El Salvador and Honduras. This great empire was destined to fall, along with other indigenous communities of the region, to the Spanish conquest.

In 1522, the conquistador Gonzalez de Avila set out from Panama to conquer Nicaragua, and the next year Pedro de Alvarado began his conquest of Guatemala where the Maya-Quiche eventually toppled. Although the Spanish found little gold, a prosperous colony was established in the area, its food cultivated in the fertile soil and its wealth generated by Spanish trade. The first capital was located at Ciudad Vieja in the southern highlands of Guatemala, and the region was governed by a captaincy general. As in other parts of Spanish America, the dreaded encomienda – a plantation system of forced labor – was introduced throughout the area, with the exception of Costa Rica, where most of the native inhabitants died at the hands of the Spaniards or of European diseases, depriving their conquerors of slave workers for their haciendas.

Costa Rica and Nicaragua remained under the governorship of Guatemala until 1821, when Central America gained independence from Spain and was briefly annexed to the Mexican Empire before forming the Central American Confederation. This loose federal state never succeeded due to political and personal rivalries between liberals and conservatives – a condition that would plague Nicaragua and Guatemala for decades to come. Yet, in spite of tensions between these neighboring nations and a tendency to interfere in one another's affairs, they are joined by a common geography and history, and in 1960 the

(Above) The preserved Spanish colonial architecture of Antigua has earned the city World Heritage status. (Below) A Mayan woman sells flowers at the market in Chichicastenango.

Central American Common Market was formed to promote economic integration and trade among its members. Agriculture remains the largest employer, the chief crops being bananas, coffee, cocoa and sugar cane, but the economies of these countries are slowly diversifying as their industrial and service sectors develop.

Minor Cooper Keith – Adventurers, archeologists and entrepreneurs have all left their mark on Central America, but none more so than the American magnate Minor Cooper Keith. Born in Brooklyn in 1848, Keith founded the Costa Rican port of Limon on the Caribbean in 1871, then proceeded to build a railroad across the mountains to San Jose, a daunting project that took nearly 20 years to complete. Meanwhile, Keith's experimental banana plantations near Limon became a prosperous industry, so he established the first steamship service to transport this fruit to the United States. He soon dominated the banana trade, gaining control of other plantations in Panama and Colombia, and in 1899 he combined these holdings with a West Indian enterprise (called the Boston Fruit Company), thus forming the United Fruit Company. Returning to railway building in 1912, he organized the International Railways of Central America. Although he had completed an 800-mile railway system by the time of his death in 1929 at the age of 81, he failed to realize his dream of a line running from Guatemala to the Panama Canal.

William Walker – Of the colorful characters associated with Central America's volatile politics, the American filibuster William Walker is one of the most memorable. (The word 'filibuster' is from the Spanish filibustero, meaning 'freebooter', and referred to foreigners who engaged in the mid-19th century practice of fomenting insurrections in Latin America.) A trained doctor, lawyer and journalist by the time he was 24, the Tennessee-born Walker decided he wanted a more adventurous career and so became a filibuster. Walker's first filibustering expedition, an invasion of Baja California in 1853, failed miserably. Tried for violating neutrality laws, but acquitted by a sympathetic jury, Walker next set his sights on Nicaragua, where he planned to build a transisthmian canal using slave labor. Backed by one of the country's revolutionary factions, Walker captured Granada and declared himself president in July 1856. He was received with hostility by the other Central American states and, having lost the support of his former friend, Cornelius Vanderbilt, who controlled Walker's supply lines with his transit company, Walker soon surrendered to the U.S. navy. Widely regarded as a hero by his fellow Americans, Walker was again acquitted of violating neutrality laws and again he made an attempt, in 1860, to conquer Central America, this time from a base in the Bay Islands of Honduras. Forced to surrender to the British Navy, Walker was shot by a Honduran firing squad on September 12, 1860, at the age of 36.

Volcanic peaks surround the deep waters of Lake Atitlan, Guatemala.

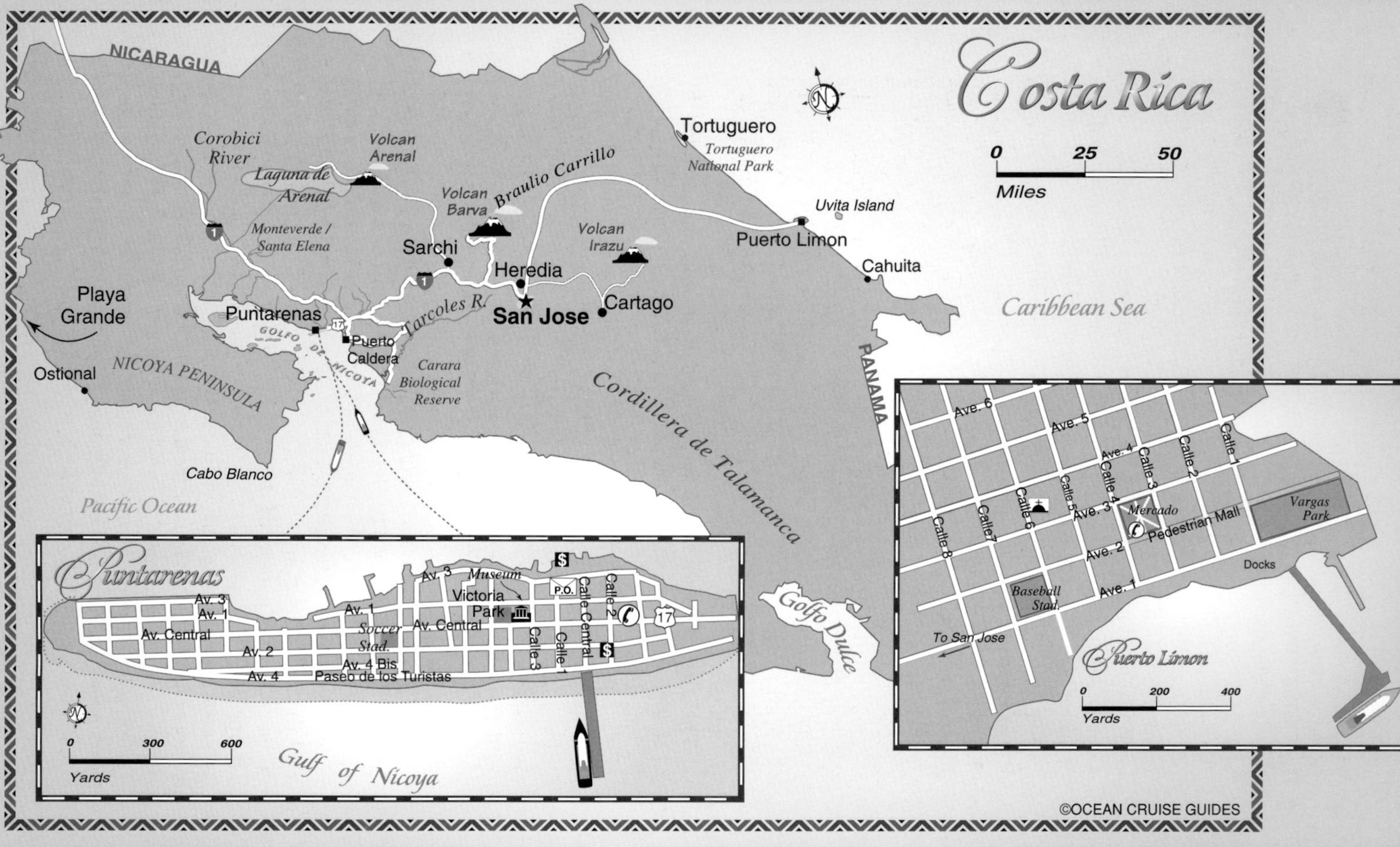
Costa Rica
0 25 50
Miles
NICARAGUA
Corobici River
Volcan Arenal
Laguna de Arenal
Monteverde / Santa Elena
Volcan Barva
Braulio Carrillo
Tortuguero
Tortuguero National Park
Uvita Island
Puerto Limon
Cahuita
Volcan Irazu
Sarchi
Heredia
San Jose
Cartago
Tarcoles R.
Playa Grande
Puntarenas
Golfo de Nicoya
Puerto Caldera
Carara Biological Reserve
Ostional
Nicoya Peninsula
Cabo Blanco
Pacific Ocean
Caribbean Sea
PANAMA
Cordillera de Talamanca
Golfo Dulce
Puntarenas
Av. 3
Museum
Victoria Park
P.O.
Calle Central
Calle 2
Av. 1
Soccer Stad.
Av. Central
Calle 3
Calle 1
Av. 3
Av. 1
Av. Central
Av. 2
Av. 4 Bis
Av. 4
Paseo de los Turistas
0 300 600
Yards
Gulf of Nicoya
Ave. 6
Ave. 5
Ave. 4
Calle 1
Calle 2
Calle 3
Calle 4
Calle 5
Calle 6
Calle7
Calle 8
Ave. 3
Mercado
Pedestrian Mall
Vargas Park
Ave. 2
Docks
Baseball Stad.
Ave. 1
To San Jose
Puerto Limon
0 200 400
Yards
©OCEAN CRUISE GUIDES

COSTA RICA

Costa Rica may be a tiny country (about the size of West Virginia) but it holds three mountain ranges and supports such an abundance of flora and fauna that nearly one quarter of its total land area is preserved by national parks or private reserves. Situated within the massive cordillera running the length of the country is a central plateau, several thousand feet above sea level, where the climate is perennially springlike and coffee is cultivated. This fertile plateau is the heart of this agricultural country and the majority of Costa Ricans reside here, many of them living in the modern capital of San Jose or the nearby towns of Alajuela (the country's capital in the 1830s) and Heredia, founded in the 1570s and today a center of the coffee and cattle industries.

The first ship to cruise past Costa Rica was commanded by Christopher Columbus in 1502. He paused near present-day Puerto Limon, noted the native inhabitants were wearing gold decorations and dubbed the area *costa rica* (rich coast). Colonization began four years later, but the impenetrable jungle and guerrilla attacks by bands of Indians hampered the invasion, as did the region's tropical diseases. Several failed attempts were made to colonize Costa Rica and it wasn't until 1563 that Juan Vasquez de Coronado successfully founded a permanent settlement, called Cartago, in the central highlands where the climate is healthy.

Few indigenous people survived the European diseases introduced by colonists, so the Spanish worked the land themselves. Settlements sprang up throughout the highlands, including San Jose in 1737, but the promise of gold for which Costa Rica was named never materialized, and the colony was, ironically, one of the Spanish Empire's poorest. Then coffee was introduced from Cuba in 1808, and an oligarchy began to emerge as the profits from coffee exports brought wealth to some of the growers. Their domination ended with the seizing of power by the army general Tomas Guardia. In the course of his military dictatorship, from 1870 to 1882, Guardia exiled the country's leading families whose destructive Liberal-Conservative rivalry was threatening to tear Costa Rica apart. Guardia's regime, although repressive, laid the groundwork for democracy, which has endured to this day.

Costa Rica

(Top) Puntarenas is a pleasant port of call on Costa Rica's Pacific coast.
(Middle) Costa Rica's national flower.
(Bottom) Musicians entertain visitors to Sarchi.

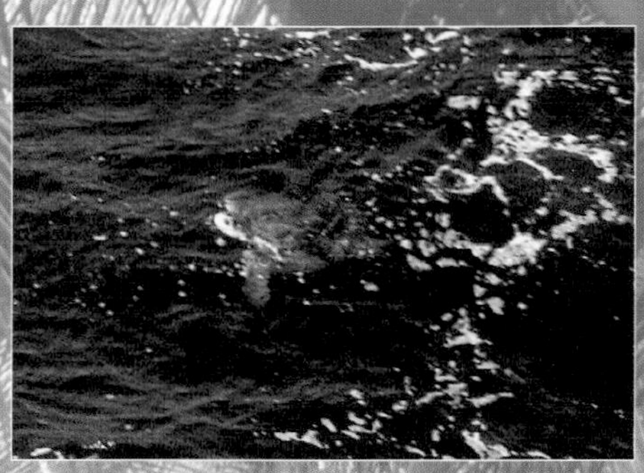

(Top) Bird life is abundant on the Tarcoles River.
(Middle) Migrating sea turtles can be seen from the ship along the Pacific coast, from Costa Rica northward to Mexico.
(Bottom) The colorful carreta is a national symbol of Costa Rica.

The country's pattern of political stability was briefly broken in 1917 when the elected president was overthrown, and again in 1948 when a disputed presidential election sparked a six-week civil war. Once peace was restored, the country's army was disbanded (eventually replaced in 1992 with a civil guard) and a new constitution was adopted. Despite economic downturns and natural disasters, such as droughts and volcanic eruptions, Costa Rica retains its tradition of orderly democracy.

Today, Costa Rica provides its 3.5 million citizens, who are mainly of Spanish descent, with a public health system considered the best in Latin America and one of the top 20 in the world, with an average life expectancy of 75.9 years for men and 79.8 years for women. The literacy rate is over 90% and although Spanish is the official language, English and French are taught in schools. Voting is compulsory and the president, upon completing a four-year term, cannot be immediately reelected.

The country's natural beauty and protected parkland have made it one of the world's premier eco-tourism destinations, and for nature lovers who flock to Costa Rica to see the abundant variety of birds and other wildlife, the country is indeed a "rich coast." Sea turtles nest on both coastlines, with the largest green turtle rookery in the Caribbean located at **Tortuguero National Park**. On the Pacific side, **Playa Grande** on the **Nicoya Peninsula** is a winter nesting site for the leatherback, while thousands of olive ridley converge on a half-mile of beach at Ostional each fall. There are threats to the survival of Costa Rica's sea turtles, including the illegal harvesting of their eggs which are prized in Latin America as an aphrodisiac and energizing protein. Yet through public education and involvement in turtle preservation, Costa Rica is protecting this threatened species.

Costa Ricans call themselves Ticos, and have a passion for soccer, the national sport. The most popular Costa Rican dish is gallo pinto, made with rice and black beans, and Ticos will jokingly explain that for breakfast they eat rice and beans, and for lunch they eat beans and rice. This traditional dish is, however, prepared dozens of different ways and for breakfast is accompanied by eggs and corn tortillas. At lunch, plates of rice and beans also include fried plantains, hearts-of-palm salad, cheese, diced vegetables and a choice of meat, chicken or fish. A variety of tropical fruits are grown in Costa Rica, along with some of the finest coffee in the world.

GETTING AROUND

Costa Rica is a small country, and many of its interior attractions can be accessed from both its Caribbean port of Puerto Limon and its Pacific ports of **Puntarenas** and nearby **Puerto Caldera**. Puntarenas means "sandy point" and is a traditional fishing village situated on a narrow peninsula. A friendly town, it has new pier which opened in 1998, and shuttle vans transport passengers to the end of the pier. A few craft stands are situated ashore near the pier, but there's not a great deal to see in town, and most passengers promptly head to one of the region's nature reserves or to the capital of San Jose, which is a two-hour drive. Red-colored taxis congregate at the pier and fares are approximately $20 to $30 per hour. Most drivers speak limited English and you should agree on a fare before setting out. Some sample, round-trip fares (per cab, 1-4 passengers) from Puntarenas: San Jose – $160; Carara Biological Reserve – $90; Sarchi – $100. The fare to Caribbean Village Fiesta Resort (where there is a swimming beach of black volcanic sand) is $7 one way. The new port of Puerto Caldera is located 11 miles (18 km) southeast of Puntarenas.

Puerto Limon, on the Caribbean coast, is the leading port of Costa Rica from which bananas, cocoa and timber are exported. Although not considered a tourist town, it does have a pleasant waterfront park (Parque Vargas) and a colorful market. The offshore island of Uvita is where Columbus landed in 1502, and Columbus Day (October 12) is celebrated in Limon with street parades and other festivities.

There are 80 national parks, protected zones, and biological and forest reserves in Costa Rica, and several of these can be visited by ship-organized shore excursion – a recommended way to view a tropical forest, for it's not advisable to hike into the jungle without an experienced guide who is able to spot and identify the flora and fauna as well as watch out for everyone's safety.

Beaches – Many of Costa Rica's beaches consist of black volcanic sand. On the Pacific side, passengers can enjoy a swimming beach and other resort facilities at the Caribbean Village Fiesta Resort, where a day pass is $38 per person. On the Caribbean side, some beautiful swimming beaches can be found at Cahuita, 27 miles south of Limon, where a long black-sand beach lies at the north end of the village and a white-sand beach lies at the other end within a national park.

Shopping – Costa Rica is considered the Bordeaux of coffee-growing countries, and its most famous brand is Cafe Britt, grown and roasted on a plantation near Heredia where visitors can purchase bags (or cases) of fine coffee. Wooden handicrafts include salad bowls, jewelry boxes and miniature replicas of colorfully painted oxcarts which are sold at the Chaverri Oxcart Factory in Sarchi. Costa Rica's official currency is the colon, but U.S. dollars are widely accepted. The approximate exchange: $1 US = 300 colones; $1 CDN = 200 colones.

AREA ATTRACTIONS

***San Jose* –** Founded in 1738 and the capital of Costa Rica since 1823, San Jose is the cultural center of the country and a transportation hub, connected to both coasts by a railroad and highway. The city's mixture of Spanish and North American architecture includes colonial mansions fronted by expansive lawns and gardens. The National Museum is housed in the country's former military headquarters which

(Above and left) The National Theatre in San Juan is Costa Rica's most beautiful building.

were converted into a cultural center when Jose Figueres Ferrer abolished the Army in 1948, and its exhibits include pre-Columbian pottery and artifacts, and colonial furniture and religious art. The Teatro Nacional (National Theatre) is Costa Rica's most beautiful building, designed in the 19th-century neo-Classical style with an opulent interior of gold leaf, marble accents and murals.

Heredia – The colonial town of Heredia, founded in the 1570s, has retained much of its colonial character. Spanish-style buildings can be seen at Parque Central, north of which is a colonial fortress. East of the park is the 18th-century La Immaculada Concepcion church, which has withstood earthquakes due to its squat design and thick walls. The colonial village of Barva, 1.6 miles north of Heredia, is an historic monument. Also in Heredia is the famous Cafe Britt coffee plantation, where daily tours are held.

Sarchi – The oxcart, one of the main means of transportation during colonial times, became an art form a century ago in the town of Sarchi when a local peasant painted his cart with bright, geometrically patterned colors. These gaily decorated wooden carts, called *carretas*, are now a national symbol and Sarchi is the place to watch artisans at work,

Exhibits at the National Museum include a pre-Columbian granite boulder and a ceremonial table from around 1500 AD.

handcrafting multi-colored wooden carts and other ornaments.

Monteverde Cloud Forest/Santa Elena Reserve – This biological reserve began as a watershed for the Quaker community of Monteverde and is now one of the country's most popular rainforest hikes. The Monteverde Conservation League, formed in 1985, continues to expand the protected area. In 1988, it launched the International Children's Rainforest project, by which school groups the world over have raised funds to save rainforest lands adjacent to the reserve. Santa Elena Reserve was created in 1989 to relieve some of the visitor pressure on Monteverde.

A crocodile rests on a mudflat at the mouth of the Tarcoles River.

Arenal Volcano – Northeast of Monteverde is Costa Rica's most active volcano, Arenal, its perfect conical shape rising to 5,356 feet (1633 m). It erupted in 1968, killing several dozen people, and continues to discharge red-hot lava, its degree of activity varying from week to week. The nearby Tabacon hotsprings are popular with visitors seeking a quick soak in naturally heated mineral waters.

Braulio Carrillo National Park – The Puerto Limon-San Jose highway runs though this park which protects a virgin forest ranging from the Caribbean lowlands to the top of Barva Volcano. The rainforest aerial tram is just outside the park, its 6-person cars whisking passengers through the forest canopy for a unique view of this ecosystem.

Parque Nacional Volcan Irazu – The American astronaut Neil Armstrong once described Irazu Volcano as a desolate landscape resembling the surface of the moon. Vapor constantly rises from one of the craters and its cool summit is often shrouded in mist. Irazu is one of Costa Rica's most active volcanoes, destroying Cartago with an eruption in 1723 and blanketing San Jose with ash in 1963. The volcano is 11,260 feet (3,430 m) high and a paved road leads to the summit where, on a clear day, a person can see the Pacific Ocean, the Caribbean Sea, and Lake Nicaragua.

Carara Biological Reserve – This area of lowlands covers 11,750 acres of tropical forest where hiking trails wind beneath a canopy of giant trees. The birds and animals frequently sighted here include macaws, monkeys, coatis, iguanas and colorful butterflies.

Tarcoles River – Located near Carara Biological Reserve, the mouth of the Tarcoles River and its estuaries are home to a large colony of crocodiles and a variety of birds which live among the mangroves and tidal flats. A highly recommended tour involves boarding a covered Mawamba boat for a cruise along the shoreline while an experienced guide points out various species of bird and the odd crocodile swimming in the river or lying along its banks.

Rio Corobici – Costa Rica is filled with rivers spilling through narrow gorges and jungle-clad valleys, and river rafting on the Corobici River in the province of Guanacaste is one way to view the monkeys, parakeets and other birds which live along its banks while you drift and paddle downstream in a large rubber raft.

Tortuguero – This park is situated on the Caribbean coast, about 50 miles (80 km) north of Limon, and is an important nesting site for green sea turtles which arrive from July to early October, peaking in late August. The leatherback (February to July) and hawksbill (July to October) also nest here, but in much smaller numbers. In addition to turtle, Tortuguero contains three species of monkey and over 300 species of birds. Sightings can be made on the park trails or during boat trips on the river, which is home to caimans (similar to alligators), crocodiles, basilisk lizards and freshwater turtles.

NICARAGUA

The least densely populated Central American nation, Nicaragua is a land of outstanding natural beauty, its rivers and lakes providing a much-coveted trade route between the two oceans before the completion of the Panama Canal. Named for Nicarao, the leader of an indigenous community that inhabited the shores of Lake Nicaragua at the time of the Spanish conquest, Nicaragua soon attracted British and Dutch buccaneers, who preyed on Spanish shipping and would rendezvous in Bluefields Bay at the mouth of the Escondido River on Nicaragua's Caribbean coast. Called the Mosquito Coast for the region's indigenous inhabitants, the Miskitto, this sultry, swampy coastal belt, about 40 miles wide and never exactly delineated, became a British protectorate in 1678 with Bluefields its capital. Britain retained its foothold in Central America until pressured in the mid-1800s to relinquish the Mosquito Coast.

Following Nicaragua's independence from Spain in 1821, the country's politics became polarized between Liberals and Conservatives, centered respectively in the colonial cities of Leon and Granada. A new capital, Managua, was founded in 1855 as a compromise. Meanwhile

The colonial city of Granada was founded by the Spanish in 1523.

British interests in the region had come head to head with those of the United States, which was interested in building a transisthmian canal across Nicaragua, and the two countries' grievances were settled by an 1850 treaty. The Mosquito Coast gained its autonomy from Britain but was forcibly incorporated into Nicaragua in 1894 under the dictatorship of Jose Santos Zelaya, its northern part finally awarded to Honduras in 1960 after decades of dispute between the two countries.

A Nicaraguan canal was never built, but in 1916 the United States paid Nicaragua $3 million for an option in perpetuity to build a waterway as an adjunct to the Panama Canal, its projected route to generally follow the San Juan River, pass through Lake Nicaragua near the southern shore, then cross the narrow isthmus of Rivas into the Pacific Ocean. This agreement was terminated in 1970 amid a growing Liberal

Visitors to active Masaya Volcano can view its smoking crater.

opposition to U.S. intervention in Nicaragua where the Somoza regime had held power since 1937 and was finally overthrown in 1979 by the Sandinista National Liberation Front. Upon seizing power, the SNLF moved rapidly to the political left and the United States withdrew financial aid, imposed a trade embargo and funded a counter-revolutionary military force. In 1990 a coalition party gained power and a more conciliatory political environment finally prevailed.

The majority of Nicaraguans, who number about 5 million and are Spanish-speaking mestizos, live along a volcanic belt lying between the Pacific coast and two large lakes. Lake Managua, the smaller of the two, drains into Lake Nicaragua, which is the largest lake in Central America and drains into the Caribbean Sea via the San Juan River. These two lakes lie in a lowland region, called the Nicaragua Depression, which was once part of the ocean. When the land lifted, the lakes formed. Several islands and volcanic peaks dot Lake Nicaragua, which contains fish normally found in saltwater, including sharks, which have adapted to the lake's fresh water.

The cruise ships dock in San Juan Del Sur, a scenic horseshoe-shaped bay surrounded by mountains where a tranquil fishing village sits at the base of sandstone cliffs. During the California gold rush, this port was the Pacific terminus of Cornelius Vanderbilt's transit route across the isthmus, his customers travelling by steamboat up the San Juan River and by coach from Lake Nicaragua to San Juan Del Sur. Today the port, connected by railroad to the commercial center of Rivas, handles export shipments of coffee, sugar and cocoa. It is also a leading holiday resort with its white sand beaches and warm waters.

Shopping – Items to look for in Nicaragua include basketry, cotton hammocks and woven mats. Nicaraguans are also noted for their ceramics, woodcarving, leatherwork and goods made of reptile skin, including snake and crocodile. Nicaragua's official currency is the cordoba, but U.S. dollars are widely accepted. Approximate exchange rates: $1 US = 13 cordobas; $1 CDN = 8.5 cordobas.

(Top right) Steps lead to the summit of Masaya Volcano. (Bottom right) Pre-Columbian stone sculptures are displayed at the San Francisco Convent in Granada.

AREA ATTRACTIONS

Granada – The colonial city of Granada, founded in 1523 on the shores of Lake Nicaragua, was repeatedly raided by British and French pirates, and captured in 1855 by the filibuster William Walker during its bloody rivalry with Leon, the city of the liberals. Today this city of 120,000 attracts tourists to its Spanish colonial architecture, including the beautiful cathedral and Culture House, and the San Francisco Convent, housing a large collection of pre-Columbian stone sculptures. The city's main plaza sets the stage for music and folk dancing, with a nearby marketplace selling native crafts. Casa de los Leones, adjacent to the square, features unique gardens.

Masaya – Sitting on the edge of a crater lake with Masaya Volcano towering above it, this well-known artisans center features markets selling a huge selection of both local and country-wide handicrafts. Nearby Volcan Masaya National Park offers visitors the opportunity to observe an active volcano. A paved road leads from the park entrance to the top of the volcano where steps can be mounted to the summit for a breathtaking view of the entire region and a look inside the volcano's crater, which periodically smokes and steams. The Spanish first placed a cross here, believing the volcano was an entrance to hell – which it was in pre-Columbian times for young Indian women who, according to legend, were tossed into the boiling lava at the bottom of the crater to appease their goddess of fire.

THOSE OF THE "LITTLE WARS"

Guerrilla is a Spanish word meaning 'little war' and the term was coined to describe the resistance fighting by Spanish partisans against the armies of Napoleon I when they invaded Spain during the Peninsular War (1808-14). The expression spread to Latin America where legendary figures of guerrilla warfare include the Argentinian Ernesto "Che" Guevara, who trained originally to be a physician but whose revolutionary zeal was awakened in 1952 when he participated in riots against the dictator Juan Peron. The following year, Che Guevara joined Guatemala's pro-communist regime but soon fled to Mexico where he met Fidel Castro and other Cuban rebels.

Nicaragua's best known guerrilla leader was a revolutionary general named Augusto Cesar Sandino, who was a farmer and mining engineer before joining a liberal revolution in 1926 against a conservative regime. From 1927-33 Sandino conducted campaigns against U.S. marines, who were backing the government, but he was never captured. After the marines withdrew, Sandino returned to farming and headed a cooperative. In 1934, General Somoza (soon to be dictator) set a trap for Sandino, inviting the former guerrilla to a meeting at which he was seized and executed. His name was adopted by a subsequent revolutionary group, the Sandinistas.

GUATEMALA

There are 33 volcanoes in Guatemala, which means 'House of Fire' in Indian dialect – an apt name for a country that has been plagued throughout its history with volcanic eruptions, floods and earthquakes. Equally turbulent have been the country's politics, beginning with its conquest in 1523 by the brutal Spanish conquistador Pedro de Alvarado. A chief lieutenant of Hernando Cortez in the conquest of Mexico, Alvarado governed Guatemala with an iron fist until he was killed in 1541 while putting down an Indian uprising in western Mexico. Alvarado's young and ambitious wife, Beatriz de la Cueva, manipulated her own election as her husband's successor, becoming the only woman to hold such a position of power in colonial Spanish America. Her governorship, however, was short-lived. Within weeks of her assuming office, disaster struck when, after several days of earthquakes and relentless rain, a wall of water swept down the volcano Agua's slopes, destroying the capital of Ciudad Vieja at its base and drowning more than a thousand townspeople, including Cueva.

The survivors of this devastating flood built a new capital nearby, naming it Antigua. Dominated by three volcanoes, including Agua, the capital thrived despite being continually subjected to volcanic eruptions, floods and earthquakes. As the capital of Spanish Guatemala, it became one of the richest cities in the New World and by the 18th century, with a population nearing 60,000, Antigua was a center of the arts and learning with a university, churches, convents, monasteries, public buildings and private resi-

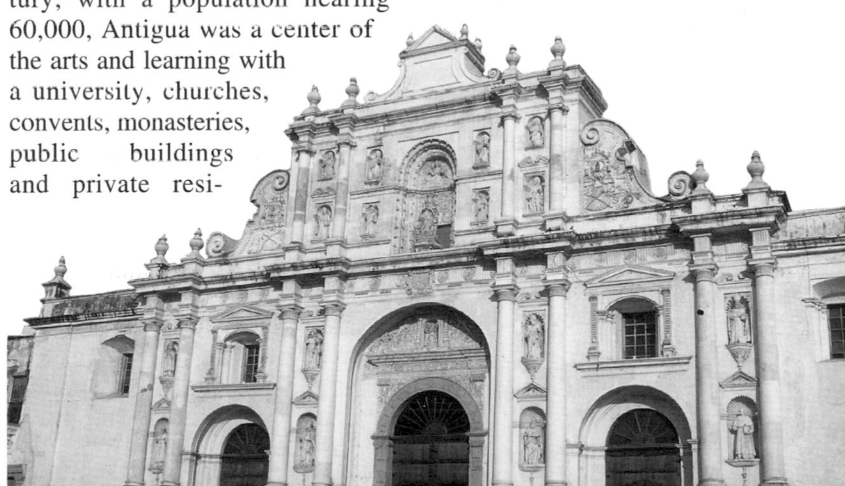

dences all built in an opulent style. The end came in 1773 when Antigua was leveled by two earthquakes. This time the capital was moved to a highland plain supposedly free of seismic disturbances. Founded in 1779 and named Guatemala City, it too was hit by earthquakes in 1917 and 1918, but was completely rebuilt.

Guatemala's repressive dictatorships of the 19th century were followed by volatility and violence in the 20th century as the country seesawed back and forth between economic reform and reaction. Ruled by the military and plagued with ongoing terrorism by both the political right and left until a peace treaty was signed in 1996, the country was also hit by a devastating earthquake (7.6 on the Richter scale) in 1976 which killed close to 23,000 people. Most of the country's population, which is evenly divided between Maya Indians and mestizos, lives in the southern highlands where a rugged range of mountains includes the inactive volcano Tajumulco (13,816 ft/4,211 m), the highest point in Central America.

The northern half of the country is covered by a vast tropical forest, called El Peten, where the magnificent temples of Tikal, the largest and possibly oldest of the Maya cities, rise above the surrounding jungle. Tikal was abandoned by about 900 AD, but Guatemala's modern Maya continue their distinctive mode of life in the highlands between Chichicastenango, an ancient trading center, and Quezaltenango, where the capital of the ancient Maya-Quiche kingdom once stood. The Quiche (kee-chay) was the most important group of ancient southern Maya, having attained a high degree of learning at the time of the Spanish conquest, and is today the largest of Guatemala's contemporary Indian groups, numbering about 300,000. More than 20 Amerindian languages, including Quiche, are still spoken by 40% of Guatemalans, who number close to 11.4 million, while the remaining 60% speak Spanish. Courses in Spanish have become popular with foreign visitors, who have long been drawn to Guatemala's famous sites.

Cruise ships visiting Guatemala pull into Puerto Quetzal, situated east of Puerto San Jose, which was the country's major Pacific port from 1853 until well into the 20th century when it was supplanted by the more modern Puerto Quetzal. Major attractions are located a considerable distance from the cruise port, so ship-organized shore excursions are recommended for Guatemala.

Shopping – Mayan craftsmanship includes elaborate weavings, decorative stitching and ceremonial masks – all of which can be bought at markets in Antigua, Panajachel and Chichicastenango. The official currency is the quetzal, but U.S. dollars are widely accepted. Approximate exchange rates: $1 US = 7.5 quetzals; $1 CDN = 5 quetzals.

AREA ATTRACTIONS

***Antigua* –** Founded in 1542 and now a United Nations World Heritage Site, Antigua is one of the loveliest colonial towns in Central America. In addition to several beautiful churches, the town's central plaza (Plaza de Armas) is fronted by the Palace of the Captains General with the coat of arms of Spain's King Charles III displayed over the portal. The Cathedral of San Jose features an original ornate facade and tiers of intact arches, while the enormous San Francisco Church, destroyed in 1773 and reconstructed in 1960, contains many fine frescoes, paintings and statues. One of the city's most famous buildings is La Merced Church, which is richly decorated with lacy white stonework.

A vendor heads to market with her wares in Antigua.

Lake Atitlan – This high-altitude lake, its sparkling waters surrounded by volcanic peaks, is a flooded caldera (a volcano's collapsed cone) in which the water reaches depths exceeding 1,000 feet. Panajachel is the 'gateway' to the lake, which is best toured by boat for views of waterfalls cascading down high cliffs and visits to traditional lakeside villages whose inhabitants descend from the various Mayan tribes of the region. At the village of Santiago Atitlan, Mayan women can be seen weaving on looms outside their thatch-roof houses which line the main street leading from the lake to the local church. The nearby town of Solola holds a traditional Mayan market on Tuesdays and Fridays which is second only to the marketplace in the mountain village of Chichicastenango.

Chichicastenango (often shortened to 'Chichi') – Situated in the heart of the highlands, this ancient trading town became a spiritual center for the Quiche following the Spanish conquest. The Spanish called the town Santo Tomas and founded a Dominican monastery in 1542. It was here that the famous Popul-Vuh manuscript of Maya-Quiche mythology was discovered. This sacred document, in which the Quiche recorded their history, mythology and other subjects, was destroyed by Alvarado but rewritten in Spanish shortly after the conquest by a converted Quiche. Chichi is today considered quaint and charming, its maze of winding streets surrounding the main plaza which is the scene of one of the most colorful town markets in Central America.

Tikal – Built during the Classic Period (AD 300-900) deep in the jungle of El Peten, this famous archeological site is the largest (500 acres) and possibly the oldest of the Mayan cities. A United Nations World Heritage Site and part of a national park, Tikal stands on limestone hills surrounded by swamps and lush tropical vegetation, its nine groups of courts, plazas, pyramids and temples interconnected with bridges and causeways. These ruins were once a hub of the Mayan

High roof combs are an impressive feature of Tikal's soaring temples.

world, where traders would bring fish and shells from the Caribbean and Pacific, and jade and obsidian (a volcanic glass) from the mountains. At its height in the 8th century, Tikal was home to 100,000 people before falling into decline at the end of the 9th century. When the Spaniards marched past Tikal in 1525, they did not see the abandoned city concealed behind the tropical foliage, and not until 1848 was this magnificent site discovered.

Situated an hour's drive from the airstrip at Flores, Tikal is surrounded by 222 square miles of rainforest and is an impressive site as the Great Plaza comes into view, its two facing temples rising above the treeline. Temple of the Grand Jaguar (Temple I) contains the tomb of one of Tikal's greatest rulers, and a replica of this elaborate tomb can be viewed in the Tikal Museum near the Visitors Center. Temple of the Masks (Temple II) stands opposite, and Temple IV, standing at the end of causeway leading from the Great Plaza, is the site's tallest structure at 229 feet. It's a Tikal ritual to climb the wooden stairs leading to the base of this temple's roof comb for a sweeping view of distant temples poking through the green canopy of the jungle.

Copan – Rivaling the ruins of Tikal in Guatemala are those of Copan, just across the border in Honduras. Although smaller in size than some of the other great Maya sites, Copan's monuments were the most artistically embellished, the profusion of carved images providing archeologists with clues to the society's nobility and royal succession. Dotting the Great Plaza are tall stelae carved with depiction's of Copan's rulers, and the site's famous Hieroglyphic Stairway is comprised of 63 steps covered with nearly 2,000 glyphs recording the history of the royal house of Copan. The site also contains the Temple of the Inscriptions, its walls covered in superb relief, and the second-largest ball court in Central America.

A center of learning, where astronomy was most accurately applied to chronology, Copan covers about 75 acres and was extensively restored from the mid-1930s to the '50s. Artifacts unearthed at the site are displayed in the nearby village museum of Copan Ruinas, a classic Spanish-American village of cobblestone streets, white adobe buildings with red-tiled roofs and a central plaza. A colonial church stands on one side of the square, facing the museum, and a market is just down the street from the museum.

The Mayan site of Copan is renowned for its profusion of carved images.

Mexico
Los Angeles
California
San Diego
Arizona
New Mexico
Texas
USA
New Orleans
Baja California
Laguna Ojo de Liebre
Laguna San Ignacio
Bahia Magdalena
Sea of Cortez
Chihuahua
Sierra Madre Occidental
Rio Grande
MEXICO
Topolobampo
La Paz
Durango
TROPIC OF CANCER
Cabo San Lucas
Mazatlan
Gulf of Mexico
Marias Islands
Tepic
Delores Hidalgo
Guadalajara
Merida
Puerto Vallarta
Yucatan
Mexico City
Veracruz
Manzanillo
Sierra Madre del Sur
Tabasco
Belize City
BELIZE
Ixtapa
Zihuatanejo
Petatlan
Oaxaca
ACAPULCO
Huatulco
Gulf of Tehuantepec
GUATEMALA
Pacific Ocean
0
200
400
Miles

CHAPTER FOUR

MEXICAN RIVIERA

Washed by the Pacific Ocean and known as the Mexican Riviera, this thousand-mile-long stretch of rocky headlands and dazzling beaches is dotted with resorts rivaling the best the world has to offer. Acapulco led the way when discovered by the post-war jet-set crowd, followed by Puerto Vallarta – forever immortalized as the love nest of Richard Burton and Elizabeth Taylor when John Huston filmed *Night of the Iguana* here in 1963. Sleepy fishing villages were transformed into tropical resorts and new ones were developed to serve North Americans' insatiable appetite for sun, sand and watersports – all of which the Mexican Riviera is famous for.

MEXICO'S PAST & PRESENT

Centuries before Spanish conquistadors landed on the beach-lined bays of Mexico's rugged sea coasts, the country's tropical lowlands and temperate highlands supported ancient civilizations whose stone ruins and jade carvings testify to their advanced artistry and social organization. The Aztecs were the last to hold power in Mexico, and their magnificent capital of Tenochtitlan, founded in 1344, was one of the architectural wonders of ancient America. It stood in the Valley of Mexico, part of a central plateau bounded by mountain ranges, and was called

The remote fishing village of Zihuatanejo is a popular port of call.

(Above) Mexico's colonial cities are filled with baroque churches and magnificent plazas. (Below) Traditional costumes reflect the Spanish influence.

Anahuac ('near the water') by the Aztecs, who built their huge and elaborate stone temples on an island in Lake Texcoco. The country's capital, Mexico City, now stands on this ancient site, which was razed by the Spanish conquistador Hernando Cortez in 1521 after he defeated the last Aztec emperor, Montezuma II. Serving as the capital of New Spain for three centuries, Mexico City is today a growing metropolis with a population approaching 25 million, nearly one-quarter of the country's total.

Mexico is the world's largest Spanish-speaking nation and the country's colonial past is readily apparent – in the overhanging grilled balconies, the arcaded courtyards, the colorful fiestas. Cities and towns invariably contain a central square (*zocalo*) overlooked by a church or cathedral, and Roman Catholicism is the dominant religion, encompassing 97% of the population, the great majority being of mixed Spanish and Native American descent. Yet a sizeable minority is pure Indian and speaks only Indian tongues, most notably Nahuatl – a lan-

guage descended from the now extinct Aztec which is still spoken by close to one million Mexicans. The folk arts, notably weaving, pottery making and silver work, have flourished since the beginning of Mexico's long history, and the country's indigenous foods, such as chili peppers and cornmeal, form the basis of authentic Mexican cuisine.

The land is rich in minerals, and the mountains of the Sierra Madre ranges dominate the landscape. Only 20% of Mexico's total land area is arable, with river water used to irrigate crops of cotton, coffee, tomatoes and sugar cane. These foodstuffs, as well as shrimp, are exported, along with sulfur, zinc and petroleum, the latter bringing a boom to the economy in the 1970s, followed by a bust in the 1980s when oil prices fell. Foreign-owned factories in the north, along the border zone with the United States, have since diversified the economy, which is benefiting from the 1992 North American Free Trade Agreement between the United States, Canada and Mexico.

While petroleum reserves are Mexico's single greatest asset, its other important source of foreign exchange is tourism. The natural beauty of the land, especially the seaside resorts, has made Mexico a popular tourist destination, as has the country's rich cultural heritage. As far back as 1300 BC, the Olmec peoples inhabited the coastal states of modern-day Veracruz and Tabasco. Food was grown on the fertile flood plain and huge pieces of basalt, weighing as much as 40 tons, were floated on rafts to riverine settlements where skilled sculptors carved colossal human heads out of the volcanic rock. The Olmec, whose anatomical knowledge of the human heart rivalled that of the Ancient Egyptians, influenced other Mesoamerican civilizations, most notably the Maya, who occupied Mexico's Yucatan Peninsula and adjacent parts of Central America. Well known for their civic centers containing pyramids, ball courts and other stone structures, the Maya were masters of abstract knowledge. They developed a system of writing for recording chronology, astronomy and religion, and were centuries

Ancient traditions included carving colossal heads out of basalt rock.

ahead of Europe in the field of mathematics, measuring the 365-day Mayan year with more accuracy than the Gregorian calendar.

When the 34-year-old Cortez set sail from Cuba in 1519 with instructions to conquer Mexico, his expedition began in the Yucatan, where he rescued a shipwrecked Spaniard who had learned the Mayan language. This was followed by a victory over the natives living in Tabasco, where he acquired the services of a female slave who knew both Maya and Aztec. Proceeding up the coast, Cortez founded Villa Rica de la Vera Cruz and befriended the coastal Totonacs, from whom he learned of the incessant warfare plaguing the Aztec empire under the despotic rule of Montezuma. Declaring himself no longer accountable to the governor of Cuba, who had sent him on his Mexican mission, Cortez scuttled his ships to prevent any Spanish dissenters from returning to Cuba and began his famous march to Tenochtitlan. Received by Montezuma as a descendant of the god Quetzalcoatle, Cortez seized the Aztec emperor as a hostage, making him a puppet ruler. The Aztecs soon revolted, forcing the Spaniards from their capital, but Montezuma was killed in the battle and Cortez returned a year later, taking Tenochtitlan after a three-month siege.

With the Aztec empire defeated, Cortez extended his conquest by sending expeditions over most of Mexico, including the Pacific coast where people lived in villages, farming the land and fishing in local waters. They excelled in colorful beadwork, and their social activities included a form of *ulama*, the ball game for which the Maya built stone playing courts. Meanwhile, the Portuguese navigator Ferdinand Magellan, after rounding the perilous southern tip of South America, led the first Spanish squadron of ships westward across the Pacific Ocean to the Philippines. Other Spanish expeditions across the Pacific followed, and in 1565 the Philippines, named for King Philip II, became Spain's base of operations in the Far East, with Manila established as a center of trade.

In exchange for silver, Chinese merchants provided exquisite items made of porcelain, ivory, jade and silk, all carefully wrapped in bales to survive their sea voyage across the Pacific to Acapulco, which became an important Spanish port with its secure harbor and convenient location.

(Left) A cannon on display at San Diego Fort in Acapulco.

Pre-Columbian artifacts are displayed at the Acapulco Historical Museum in Fort San Diego.

Loaded with silver from Peru, the Manila galleons that departed Acapulco would pick up the prevailing northeast trade winds to the south and ride these to the Philippines. It was a relatively easy three-month voyage compared to the return trip, which covered 8,000 miles, took about six months and entailed crossing the stormy North Pacific to Cape Mendocino, near San Francisco, where the ships sailed down the coast to Acapulco.

The sturdy Manila galleons, built of teak, were so heavily sheathed as to be impervious to cannon shot. Pirates attacking these galleons as they were about to make port in Acapulco would often run out of ammunition trying to hole one of these vessels, which were also armed for defence and difficult to board from another ship. Those who did succeed in capturing a Spanish treasure ship were instantly wealthy. In November 1587, after six hours of hard fighting, the English privateer Thomas Cavendish captured the treasure-filled *Santa Maria* off the coast of Baja California, and in 1708 the British privateer Woods Rogers intercepted a Spanish galleon

Manila galleons transported Far East treasures across the Pacific to Acapulco.

heading to Acapulco, its cargo of silks, bullion and precious stones worth a fortune. To protect its Manila galleons, which sailed the Acapulco-Philippines route from 1565 to 1815, Spain built San Diego Fort overlooking the harbor in Acapulco. But the main enemy was scurvy, an ever-present threat to crew and passengers on the long sea voyage, the most horrific example being that of the *San Jose* which was sighted near Acapulco in June 1657, nine months after leaving Manila. When a boarding party reached the ship, which was sailing closehauled under shortened sail, corpses litted the decks. All on board had died of scurvy or starvation.

Whenever a Manila galleon pulled into port at Acapulco, there was great rejoicing. The news spread quickly to Mexico City, where church bells rang and prayers of thanksgiving were offered before residents hurried to Acapulco and its galleon trade fair. Many a fine house in Mexico City became furnished with superbly crafted Chinese wares. The bulk of the ships' precious cargo, however, was hauled by pack animals over the Sierra Madre mountains to Veracruz for shipment to Spain, along with vast quantities of silver mined in Central Mexico.

The Spanish governed the viceroyalty of New Spain, as Mexico was then called, with an iron fist. The *encomienda* system of land ownership was forced upon the natives, who were "granted" land by the Spanish crown, for which they paid tribute and provided services to the local conquistador in return for military protection and instruction in

TEQUILA

The national drink of Mexico, tequila is made by redistilling mescal which is a colorless liquor distilled from the fleshy leaves of the maguey plant. Maguey is a Mexican name for the American aloe, also referred to as an agave plant. Mexico's agave plants were plagued by a fungus in 1997 which, combined with overharvesting to meet a growing demand for tequila, has drastically diminished its population. The agave plant cannot be quickly replenished, for it needs at least eight years to mature. The Aztecs revered mescal as a gift of the gods but it wasn't until 1795, in the town of Tequila, that the Spanish applied a distillation process to mescal which produced a potent drink they called *vino de mezcal* and became known as tequila. To fully enjoy tequila, aficionados recommend licking some salt off the hand and squeezing some lime juice on the tongue before taking a shot. The worm in the bottom of the tequila bottle comes from the agave plant and is added as a sign of quality.

DAY OF THE DEAD

The pre-Lenten Carnival celebrations held throughout Mexico are well known for their exuberant festivities, but one of the country's most anticipated religious festivals is the Day of the Dead (*Dia de los Muertos*), held on November 1 and 2, when plazas are elaborately decorated and families hold nocturnal, candle-lit picnics at the gravesides of loved ones. This celebration of souls follows weeks of preparation, which includes making decorative candles and special dishes of food to place at household altars. Thousands of sugar skulls and papier mache skeletons are handcrafted for the event, its rituals rooted in the Aztec belief in the afterlife. Celebrations commence with the tolling of church bells on the night of October 31, heralding the arrival of the spirits.

the Christian faith. This oppressive system of forced labor met with great resistance and the Spanish had difficulty establishing control. Eventually a society evolved, consisting of three distinct classes – Spanish, Native American and Mestizo (mixed Spanish and Native American). Spain also imposed a rigid mercantilist system, designed to drain its colonies of wealth, which forbid manufacturing, forcing the local populace to depend on shipments from Spain for many of their goods. The social discontent was widespread, not only among the disgruntled laborers who worked the land and the silver mines, but within the privileged Spanish class, its members differentiating between those who were born in Spain and those, considered inferior, who were born in America and called *criollos* (creoles).

Various priests and missionaries tried to help the Native Americans by petitioning the Spanish government for reforms, but the status quo

A Mexican beach umbrella or roof thatched with palm leaves is called a palapa. (Below) La Paz waterfront.

prevailed until the start of the 19th century when a revolutionary fervor gripped Europe and spread to Spanish America. Inspired by the democratic ideals of the French Revolution, a Creole priest, intellectual and social activist named Hidalgo Y Costilla, while serving in the parish of Dolores, launched Mexico's revolution on September 16, 1810, when he boldly issued the *Grito de Dolores* (Cry of Dolores) in the village square, a decree calling for racial equality and redistribution of land. He quickly raised an immense army of Native Americans, which was soon joined by radical creoles. After some initial victories against the royalist forces, Hidalgo's ill-organized army was crushed and their leader executed. But the independence movement continued under new leadership, and in September 1821 Spain accepted Mexican independence.

Vestiges of Spanish colonialism remained, however, and amid the ongoing corruption and social disparity there was a frequent turnover of dictatorial governments. In the 1840s, a dispute with Texas led to an all-out war with the United States, in which Mexico lost 40 per cent of its territory. In 1864, following a civil war, Mexico sought foreign aid from France's Napoleon III, who installed the Hapsburg prince Maxmilian to oversee his new colonial empire, which toppled within three years. A century later, despite revolutionary reforms and the establishment of democratic institutions, Mexico was still struggling with widespread poverty and corruption. It was not until the election of Vicente Fox to the presidency in the year 2000 that decades of authoritarian one-party rule were finally ended. The problems facing Fox include Mexico's powerful drug cartels, which make billions of dollars trafficking cocaine from Colombia to the United States and which flourish due to the bribes accepted, and now expected, by Mexican army generals and government officials. At the other end of the pay scale, Mexican laborers seeking work continue to slip across their country's northern border into the United States, where Hispanics have become America's largest ethnic minority.

Against this centuries-old backdrop of political turbulence and social unrest, the arts in Mexico have thrived. Highly developed before the Spanish conquest, Mexican art became a hybrid of native and European styles, especially in its paintings which achieved a serenity and richness of blues and reds for

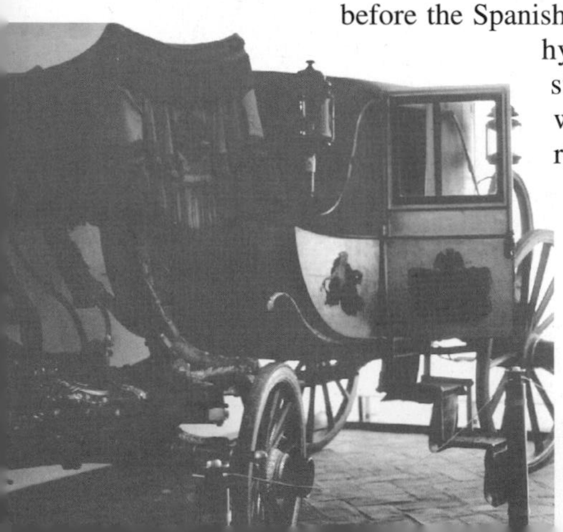

(Left) A carriage built during the brief reign of the Hapsburg prince Maxmilian is on display at Fort San Diego in Acapulco.

(Above) Decorative plates on display in an Acapulco shop window.

which they became known as Mexican baroque. Religious themes eventually gave way to revolutionary ideals and for most of the 20th century Mexican artists have enjoyed generous government patronage. Contemporary painters and sculptors continue to create an outstanding array of prized works while modern architects carry on their country's age-old tradition of melding Mexican stylistic elements, such as bold

HOLLYWOOD SOUTH

From the 1940s to the 1970s, Mexico was a favored location of Hollywood film directors who were attracted to the varied terrain of jungle-clad mountains and semi-arid plains, the latter used as backdrops for dozens of westerns. Then, for two decades, Mexico fell off the movie-making map as other countries competed for Hollywood's business and Mexico's reputation for corruption kept film producers away. That tide has turned since the establishment in 1995 of Mexico's National Film Commission, which promotes Mexican locations and the reliability of Mexico's American-trained film crews. Hollywood producers have rediscovered Mexico and movies recently shot here include *Blow* in Acapulco and *Pearl Harbor* in Baja California, along with *Titanic, The Mask of Zorro* and *Tomorrow Never Dies.* Mismaloya Bay, shown here, is where scenes from *Night of the Iguana* were filmed in 1963.

geometric lines and dramatic scale, with European and North American techniques. The folk arts have not been left behind, and throughout the country its local artisans produce high-quality crafts in styles reflecting both the Spanish influence and the traditions of the Maya, Aztec and other ancients who long ago inhabited the land we now call Mexico.

TRAVEL TIPS

Currency – The unit of currency is the Mexican peso, but American currency is widely accepted. ATM machines are found throughout most major resort areas and these accept cards with Cirrus, Plus and NYCE systems. The Mexican peso is worth approximately 9¢ US (12¢ Cdn) and $1 US = 11 pesos ($1 Cdn = 8.5 pesos)

Dining – Tex-Mex fast-food cooking has little to do with traditional Mexican cuisine, its regional dishes based on native recipes that have been modified by Spanish, French and Italian cooking styles. Examples of authentic Mexican foods are ceviche (raw seafood marinated in lime juice, chili peppers, tomatoes, onion and cilantro) and mole (a rich, slowly simmered sauce made of chili and various ingredients such as tomatoes, bananas, raisins, sesame seeds and onions). Mole is used to flavor chicken and meats, which are often served in tamales – cornmeal steamed in a corn husk.

Shopping – Mexican handicrafts are among the finest in the world and most coastal resorts have shops and open-air markets selling crafts from all over Mexico, including Taxco silver jewelry and black pottery from Oaxaca. The assortment of ceramics, tiles, pottery, copperware, glassware and whimsical hand-painted wooden animals is impressive. Quality leather goods include wallets, belts, sandals and cowboy boots, while hand-woven products range from baskets, rugs and hammocks to embroidered blouses, fine beaded tapestries and colorful woolen shawls called *serapes*. Gold and silver filigree (intricate ornamental work) is another Mexican specialty, creating exquisite earrings, necklaces and bracelets. When buying expensive jewelry, it's prudent to do so at reputable stores recommended by the cruise lines rather than at flea markets where there is no guarantee of quality. Most Mexican ports have an open-air artisans' market where tourists can barter for local handicrafts and souvenirs. The larger ports also have a municipal market where the locals shop for food and other items.

Taxis – Available at all ports of call, taxis are unmetered and a fare should be agreed upon before hiring a driver. US dollars are widely accepted.

Telephone Calls – Long-distance calls can be made at public phones marked TELMEX and charged to a calling card. Personal calling card access codes: AT&T 001-880-462-4240; MCI 001-880-674-7000; Sprint 001-880-877-8000; CANADA DIRECT 01-800-123-0200.

BULLFIGHTING

Bullfighting, a controversial but important part of Spanish culture, was introduced to Spain by the Moors who fought bulls from horses and killed them with javelins. This Moorish practice evolved into the sport of bullfighting, which was brought by the Spanish to Mexico where the first bullfights were held in town plazas. The modern bullfight, held in a large outdoor arena called the plaza de toros, unfolds in three ritualistic parts. First, toreros wave capes at the bull and mounted picadors thrust at it with lances. The next stage involves banderillos who, while on the run, poke short barbed sticks into the bull's withers. Finally the matador, holding a small cape and a sword, makes daring passes at the bull who eventually stops charging and succumbs to the matador's dominance. When the bull strikes a stationary stance, with its four feet square on the ground and its head hung low, this is the moment when, according to ritual, that matador must shove his sword into the bull's heart. Fighting bulls are specially bred, and successful matadors are highly paid and admired for their skill and courage. A bullfight demonstration (in which the bull is not killed) and rodeo show can be seen in Puerto Vallarta.

A brass band greets ship passengers arriving in Acapulco.

HUATULCO

Until the early '80s, the small fishing village of Santa Cruz, set on the edge of the Gulf of Tehuantepec between mountains and sea, was surrounded by jungle. Today it's surrounded by resort development, but of a unique nature. Situated on one of nine beach-ringed bays lying along 20 tropical miles of pristine coastline, Santa Cruz is now part of the Mexican government's first eco-tourism resort, called Huatulco (pronounced wa-tool-ko). Features of this ecologically sensitive plan include strict building codes that specify the architectural styles of new hotels, their heights limited to six storeys. To preserve the natural allure of this jungle paradise, the government's master project has designated 70% of this 50,000-acre area be held as ecological reserves. Although the entire resort will not be completed until 2020, several bays now have resort and visitor facilities, including a marina and 18-hole golf course. For the time being, however, golden beaches and countless coves far outnumber Huatulco's sprinkling of luxury resorts.

Getting Around – The cruise ships anchor off Santa Cruz and tender passengers ashore to the local marina where a fleet of sightseeing boats await and taxis are available. Huatulco's original fishing village, Santa Cruz (Holy Cross) has two waterfront plazas, each surrounded by shops and an artisans marketplace. Boat trips depart from the local marina on tours of the Nine Bays of Huatulco, including El Organo Bay with its natural rock formation in the side of a cliff, dubbed 'stone face.'

Beaches – There are 36 beaches lining the bays of Huatulco, the closest being Playa Entrega in Santa Cruz and those in adjacent Chahue Bay which offer pleasant swimming in a moderate surf. Other popular beaches include those of Tangolunda Bay where the Sheraton and other luxury resorts allow visitors access to their facilities for a small fee (70

Passengers visiting Huatulco are tendered ashore to Santa Cruz

or more pesos). A public beach (Tangolunda Beach Park) is situated on the bay's eastern shore and provides changing facilities, showers and toilets. Quieter beaches are found at Bahia Conejos (the bay just beyond Tangolunda) or in the opposite direction, past Santa Cruz, at Cacaluta Bay.

(Top) One of Huatulco's pristine ocean beaches. (Right) A local sells beach snacks. (Bottom) La Crucesita was designed to resemble a Spanish colonial town.

Dive & Snorkel Sites – Local waters provide opportunities to see such reef inhabitants such as angel fish, parrotfish and other tropical species, as well as sea turtles. Good snorkeling can be enjoyed in the clear waters off Playa Entrega and off Playa Maguey.

Shopping – Santa Cruz offers a small selection of shops while La Crucesita features a bustling market and plenty of shops bordering the central plaza. Look for handcrafted items from the interior town of Oaxaca, its artisans' works among the best in Mexico, including hand-wrought gold and silver filigree, black pottery, hand-woven rugs and shawls, and alebrijes (whimsical hand-painted wooden animals).

LOCAL ATTRACTIONS

Tangolunda Bay – The bay's Zapotec name means "place where the gods live" and its five beaches are now home to seven luxury low-rise resorts, including a Club Med which is the largest of its kind in the Western Hemisphere, as well as an 18-hole golf course, a shopping area and several restaurants.

La Crucesita – A mile inland from Santa Cruz is a fascinating faux village, built in 1986 to resemble an authentic colonial settlement with a central plaza, bandstand, Art Deco cathedral and municipal market.

Copalita River – The trails along the banks of this river afford the perfect opportunity for tropical birding and wildlife viewing. The region's 200+ bird species include the egret, falcon, parrot and hummingbird, while land animals include the iguana and armadillo.

Finca de Pacifico – High in the hills behind Huatculco, this 120-hectare coffee plantation is an organic operation producing a rich, aromatic coffee which can be sampled in the hacienda restaurant.

***Oaxaca* –** A hundred miles inland from Huatulco is the state capital of Oaxaca (pronounced waha-ka), one of Mexico's most historic cities. Founded by the Aztecs in 1486 in a valley surrounded by low mountains, Oaxaca was taken by the Spanish in 1522 and is today a small commercial and tourist center noted for its colonial churches and beautiful gardens, as well as its thriving artistic community.

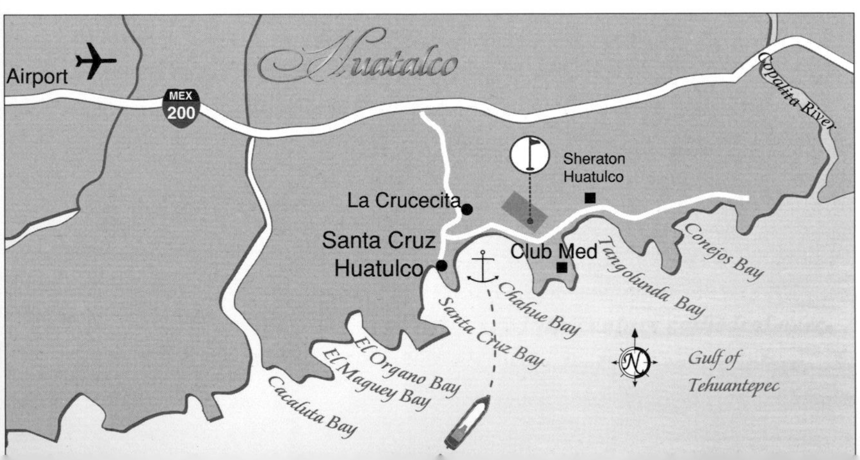

ACAPULCO

The world once came to Acapulco. An international playground attracting the rich and famous to its beautiful crescent-shaped bay and sizzling nightlife, Acapulco became Mexico's premier beach resort in the 1960s. John and Jackie Kennedy honeymooned here in a private villa in 1953, but it wasn't until direct international air service to Acapulco began in 1964 that this scenic resort, strung like a necklace at the base of the Sierra Madre mountains, was fully discovered by the international jet set. Hollywood stars and European aristocrats arrived in their ready-to-wear Pucci designs, ready to party into the night as the setting sun turned the bay a burnt orange and the twinkling lights of hillside villas cast a magical glow on the gentle surf below.

Those who flocked to Acapulco included the dashing Florentine fashion designer **Emilio Pucci**. His comfortable yet chic lines of summer clothes were often inspired by native motifs, including dresses designed in bold Aztec prints, and they were the perfect 'resort wear' favored by the glamorous starlets who frequented Acapulco. As the first and still the most popular resort in Mexico, Acapulco has it all, although some would say it has too much. Too many hotels lining its famous beaches, too many taxi drivers vying for fares, too many peddlars trying to sell their wares. Yet this cosmopolitan city of 2 million residents continues to draw 3.5 million visitors annually and, to regain some of its lost allure, Acapulco began a beautification program in 1994, improving its public areas, cleaning its beaches, renovating several hotels and building new ones beyond Acapulco Bay.

The magic of Acapulco is easy to understand when it is experienced from the deck of a cruise ship. A pre-dawn arrival is the best, when the city surrounding Acapulco Bay is a display of sparkling lights, and approaching cruise ships are sometimes escorted by dolphins into the Boca Grand, the mouth of bay. Late evening departures are equally magical, as the ship slips its moorings and draws away from the bay's glittering shoreline while passengers dance to the ship's band on the upper decks.

GETTING AROUND

The cruise ships tie up beneath the ramparts of El Fuerte de San Diego, the Spanish-built fort that once protected the port from pirates. Taxi drivers congregate outside the cruise terminal, but only the specially licenced drivers are allowed into the building and it's one of these you should hire if you're planning to explore the town by taxi. Fares are posted inside the terminal and a dispatcher is on hand to answer questions. **Sample fares one-way from the terminal, are:**

Cliff Divers	**$8**	**Papagayo Park**	**$6**
Las Brisas	**$15**	**Princess Hotel**	**$25**

Many sights are within walking distance, such as the streets of Old

A view of the Acapulco cruise terminal from the nearby beaches.

Acapulco, the fort, and the beaches which stretch eastward from the cruise terminal. Just be prepared to walk a gauntlet of eager cabbies on the street immediately outside the terminal entrance.

Shopping – Several excellent shops selling handmade jewelry and silverware are located inside the cruise terminal. Little Margarita's provides free transportation to its main store – Joyeria Margarita – in Old Acapulco, which offers an array of leather goods, handmade jewelry, dolls, T-shirts and unique arts and crafts. B&B also has a larger store, called the B&B Marketplace and Factory, located in Papagayo Park – within walking distance or a 10-minute taxi ride – where visitors can enjoy free margaritas while shopping for handcrafted jewelry and Mexican handicrafts. Plaza Taxco, located near La Quebrada, contains an extensive selection of gold, silver and gemstone jewelry where designers can create a customized piece of jewelry upon request.

Beaches – The curved shoreline of Acapulco Bay extends for more than four miles and is lined with beaches. Easiest to reach are those just east of the ship terminal. Playa Tamarindo, Playa Hornos and Playa Hornitos are where fishermen haul in their catch and locals like to swim in the moderate waves or enjoy a game of soccer on the beach. An umbrella and two chairs can be rented for 5 pesos. Further along, where the hotel zone begins, La Condesa beach is popular for its amenities and watersports. West of the cruise terminal, on the far side of the peninsula, are several smaller beaches, including Playa Caleta, which is also popular with the locals.

Golf Courses – One of Mexico's finest courses, designed by Robert Trent Jones, Jr., is part of the Pierre Marques resort on the east side of Acapulco Bay. The nearby Acapulco Princess also has an 18-hole

Pleasant walkways lead west from the cruise terminal. past shops, a central fountain and waterfront views of the bay.

course, as does the Mayan Palace. For more information, consult with the ship's shore excursion manager.

LOCAL ATTRACTIONS

(1) The Zocalo – Old Acapulco's central plaza, this tree-shaded square is a gathering place for locals and is overlooked by the Nuestra Senora de la Soledad, the city's unusual-looking cathedral of stark design with Byzantine towers. The most pleasant route for reaching the square is along the waterfront, where a tiled walkway winds past a cluster of boutiques selling Mexican handicrafts. White, wrought-iron benches flank the promenade as it leads to a central fountain, at which you turn right and head into the center of Old Acapulco where the *zocalo* is located.

(2) La Quebrada – No visit to Acapulco is complete without watching the spectacular cliff diving at La Quebrada. The men who perform these heartstopping swan dives and pike somersaults have spent years training for their 136-foot plunges down the face of a jagged granite cliff into a narrow gorge where the water is only 12 feet deep. The six divers pray at a small shrine before climbing to a small rock ledge called La Punta where, poised on the edge, they wait – in pairs – until just the right moment, timing their dives to coincide with an approaching wave as it washes into the gorge below.

The walk to La Quebrada takes about 15 minutes from the cathedral. Follow Lopez Mateos, the road to the left when facing the church entrance, which ends at the top of a very steep hill. By taxi (much less strenuous) it's about a 10-minute ride from the terminal. The daily show times are 1:00 p.m., 7:15 p.m., 8:30 p.m., 9:30 p.m. and 10:30 p.m. The view is best from the upper area beside the ticket booth. Admission fee is $2.00.

(3) Fuerte de San Diego – For a hands-on look at the history of Mexico's Pacific coast, Fort San Diego is well worth a visit. Built in 1783, replacing the original structure (1615) which was destroyed by an earthquake in 1776, this pentagon-shaped fortress was designed using advanced military engineering concepts of the period. Defensible on all flanks and surrounded by a dry moat, the fort could hold up to 2,000 troops and stock enough provisions and ammunition for a year-long siege. The fort was attacked by revolutionary forces in 1810, withstanding repeated attacks and a two-year siege before it was taken. In 1986 the fort became the Acapulco Historical Museum, its vaulted rooms entered off the central courtyard now housing Spanish colonial exhibits, including The Manila Galleon Room, the Pacific Piracy Room and The East Trade Room, with treasures from the Orient on display.

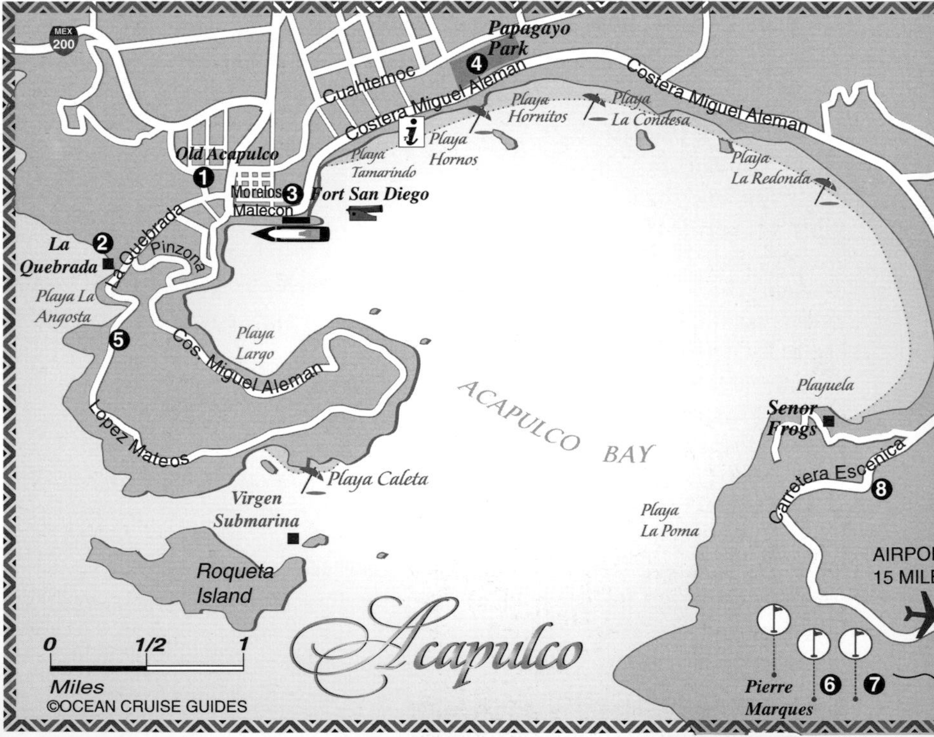

Reaching the fort entails crossing the busy Costera Miguel and climbing up a few flights of steps to the entrance. The entrance fee is $4.00 and opening hours are 10 a.m. to 6:40 p.m., Tuesday through Sunday.

(4) Papagayo Park – This 52-acre municipal park is filled with attractions, including a botanical garden, a replica of a Manila galleon and the B&B Marketplace and Factory where tours allow you to see designers crafting pieces of gold and silver into beautiful jewelry.

Famous Resorts – Several of Acapulco's resorts are attractions in themselves, where visitors can stroll the grounds and public areas, and perhaps pause to enjoy a refreshment or a light repast. **(5) Los Flamingos**, an art deco-style hotel built in the 1930s overlooking the Pacific, was the former hideaway of movie legend John Wayne and his Hollywood cronies, including Johnny Weismueller, the star of that era's Tarzan movies. At the other end of the bay is the world-famous **(6) Acapulco Princess Hotel** which is shaped like an Aztec pyramid, and the **(7) Vidatel Mayan Palace**, built in the shape of a Mayan temple and featuring lovely gardens. **(8) Las Brisas**, on a hillside overlooking Acapulco Bay, is considered one of the finest resort hotels in the world, its individual *casitas* (bungalows) offering luxury, a private pool and a stunning view of Acapulco Bay. This view can be enjoyed at the Chapel of Peace, erected as a memorial to two children who perished in a plane crash.

Papagayo River – Situated a 50-minute drive from the cruise terminal, this spectacular river can be enjoyed on an exciting Shotover Jet boat ride which whisks passengers through narrow, twisting canyons, past untouched flora and fauna.

The entrance to Fort San Diego, built by the Spanish to protect the Manila galleons arriving in port with treasures from the Far East.

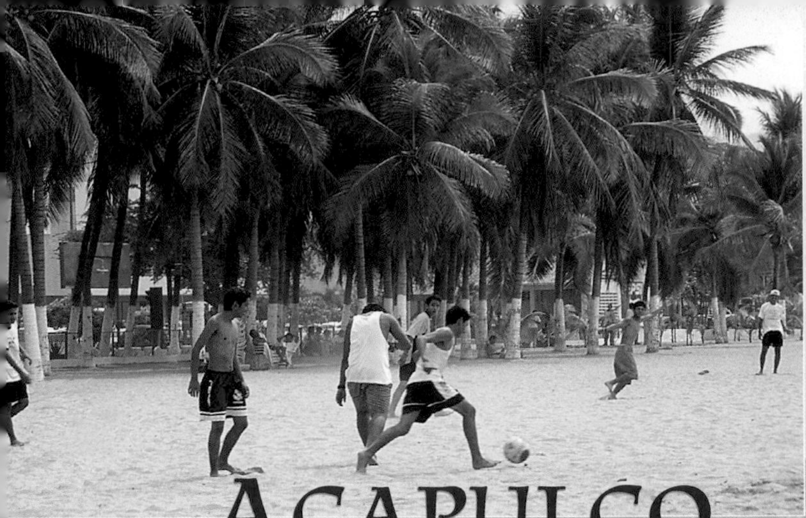

ACAPULCO

(Above) A soccer game unfolds on Playa Hornos. (Below) Fishing skiffs dot the sands of Playa Tamarindo. (Opposite) Spectators gather at La Quebrada to watch Acapulco's famous cliff divers perform their heartstopping swan dives into the shallow waters of a narrow gorge.

ZIHUATANEJO

One of the Mexican Riviera's most relaxing ports of call, the fishing village of Zihuatanejo (*zee-wah-tah-nay-ho*) is situated at the base of mountains on a sheltered bay ringed with beaches. The tidy village is easily explored on foot with time left to lounge on a local beach or visit nearby Ixtapa, a planned tourist resort where high-rise hotels line a 2.5-mile stretch of spectacular beach. Stone carvings and stelae have been unearthed in the area, indicating an indigenous civilization dating back to antiquity whose nobility used Zihuatenejo as a sanctuary. In more recent history, Zihautanejo was an isolated fishing port when, in the 1970s, the Mexican government developed neighboring Ixtapa into a world-class tourist resort.

Getting Around – The ships anchor in Zihuatanejo Bay and tender passengers ashore to the municipal pier. Ixtapa is four miles away by highway; public minibuses run between Zihuatenejo and Ixtapa, and taxis are plentiful and reasonably priced.

Sample taxi fares (per person, one-way) from Zihuatenejo are:

La Madera Beach – $1.50
La Ropa Beach – $2.00
Ixtapa – $4.00
Playa Linda Beach (on the far side of Ixtapa) – $5.00

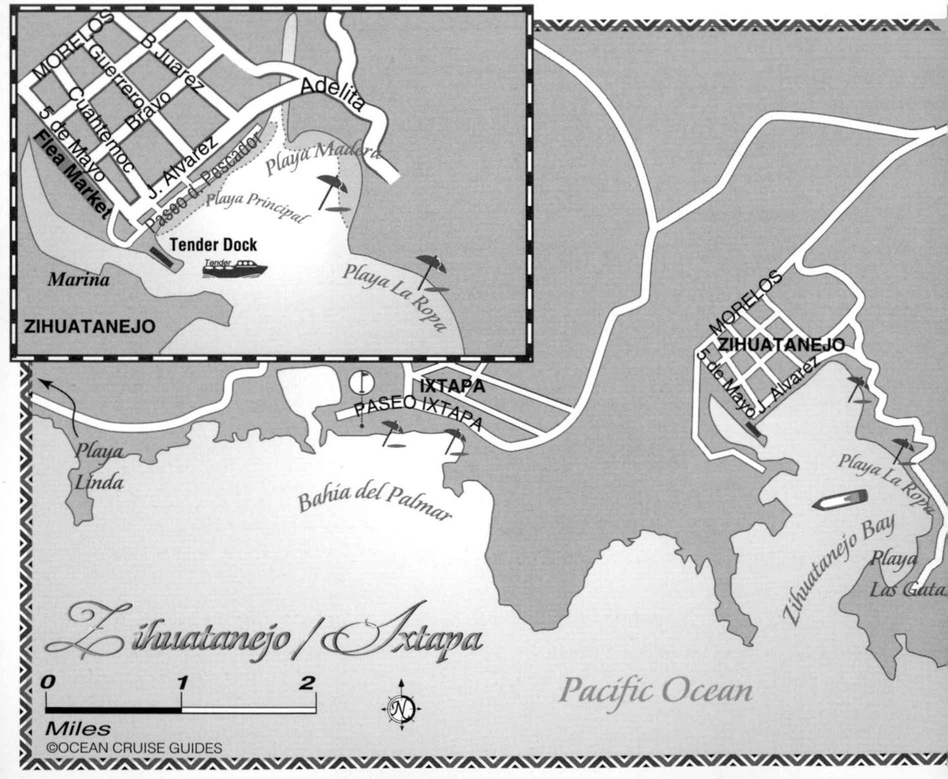

The water taxi to Las Gatas Beach, which departs from Zihuatenejo's municipal pier, is $4 round-trip per person and departs every 30 minutes.

Shopping – Zihuatenejo's artisans are widely known for their bright ceramics and carved wooden fish and masks. The vendors here are less aggressive than those in the larger ports, so this is the place to leisurely browse for local crafts. The tourist flea market is a short walk from the pier along Avenue 5 day Mayo. The town's main street is Avenida Cuauhtemoc, where shops carry such noteworthy items as handmade pottery and silver jewelry from the mountainside town of Taxco, a famous center of silversmithing since colonial times.

Zihuatanejo Beaches – Playa Principal – Good for people-watching, this municipal beach beside the pier is busy with local fishermen and families. La Madera Beach – Once used for loading fine hardwoods (hence its name which is Spanish for 'wood') this swimming beach of fine sand and gentle surf is overlooked by some hillside hotels.

La Ropa Beach – Lying at the base of a cliff in the center of the bay, this is the town's longest beach and, although popular with surfers, has an uncrowded feel due to its length. Ask your taxi driver to drop you off at La Perla restaurant and arrange for a pick-up time.

Las Gatas Beach – Reached by a 10-minute water taxi ride from the pier, this beach is recommended for snorkeling, with equipment rentals available. A stone wall parallels the beach, believed to have been constructed as a shark barricade by a Purepecha king so his family could safely bathe here. Over time, the stone barrier has become encrusted with coral and attracts an abundance of marine life.

Ixtapa Beaches – Playa Del Palmar Beach – Ixtapa's main beach and lined with hotels, it can be accessed by public path at either end. Open to the Pacific, this stunning stretch of sand is washed by a continous surf.

Playa Linda – This tranquil beach, and adjacent Quieta Beach, are ideal for swimming. The pier at Playa Linda provides water taxi service to tiny Isla Ixtapa which offers picturesque beaches, good snorkeling, and scuba diving on its ocean side.

Snorkel & Scuba Sites – Excellent snorkeling can be enjoyed at Las Gatas Beach (see above) in Zihuatanejo, and at Isla Ixtapa off Playa Linda (see above).

Local Attractions – Paseo del Pescador – This beachfront road leads from the municipal pier past a pleasing assortment of shops and seafood restaurants, and provides lovely views of the bay and the ship at anchor. A tourist office and archeological museum are also found along this street.

***Petatlan* –** Located in the foothills southwest of Zihuatenejo, this place of pilgrimage is famous among Mexicans for its local church where miracles have been linked to the patron saint, Father Jesus of Petatlan.

Ixtapa / Zihuatanejo

Zihuatanejo's stunning setting and beautiful beaches.

(Top & bottom) The charming streets and hillside homesof Zihuatenejo. (Middle) Ixtapa's main beach.

PUERTO VALLARTA

A person could be forgiven for thinking that Puerto Vallarta was a creation of Hollywood. Legendary motion picture director John Huston, who was especially fond of Mexico, had already shot *The Treasure of Sierra Madre* in the Michoacan village of San Jose Purua when he brought a star-studded cast to Puerto Vallarta in 1963 to film *Night of the Iguana*. Ava Gardner and Richard Burton played the film's leading roles, but Elizabeth Taylor provided the off-screen drama when, still married to Eddie Fisher, she accompanied Burton to Puerto Vallarta. Their scandalous love affair drew reporters to the seaside town, who were immediately enamored of this exotic hideaway nestled at the base of the Sierra Madre mountains. Whitewashed buildings with red tile roofs lined the cobblestone streets, bougainvillea spilled from wrought iron balconies, and the waterfront Hotel Oceana – where Burton and Taylor were staying – provided sweeping views of a sapphire blue sea.

Puerto Vallarta's tropical setting is one of jungle-clad hillsides and rugged cliffs overlooking Banderas Bay (Bay of Flags), so named by a Spanish conquistador in 1541. Sailing ships dropped anchor here when making long voyages along the coast but it wasn't until 1851 that a townsite, called Puerto de Penas, was established as a port for shipping silver and supplying salt to the silver mines on the Rio Cuale. In 1918, the village became a municipality of the state of Jalisco and its name was changed to Puerto Vallarta in honor of the state's governor. The bay's shoreline is 25 miles long, and from October through April this wide bay is frequented by humpback whales, who spend their winter breeding season in tropical waters.

Puerto Vallarta's transformation from a remote fishing village to one of Mexico's most popular resorts has resulted in today's city of a quarter-million population which receives 1.5 million visitors a year. Yet the original town center has retained its Old Mexico character, and bylaws are in place to preserve this ambiance – new houses must be painted white and parking lots paved with cobblestone. Some say the

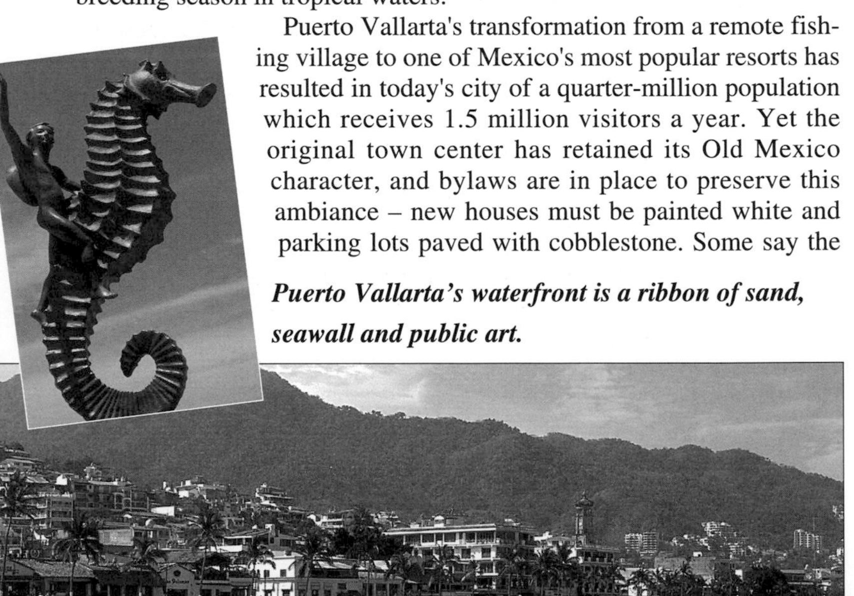

Puerto Vallarta's waterfront is a ribbon of sand, seawall and public art.

place has become too prettified, yet a stroll along the back streets reveals a Mexican colonial town that's as authentic as the brilliant blue bay it overlooks.

Getting Around – The ship docks about three miles north of the town center, next to Playa Del Oro. Taxi cars and vans are available outside the terminal gate. Taxi vans transport groups of passengers between the cruise terminal and town center for $2 per person. To return to the ship from town, take a yellow Nissan taxi for $5 per carload. **Other fares, per car, one-way: Gringo Gulch $6; Playa de los Muertos $6; Mismaloya Beach $15.**

Shopping – Items to look for in Puerto Vallarta include glassware, pottery, stoneware and fine beaded tapestries. Shops selling quality jewelry and leather goods face the *malecon*, while the flea market (on the north side of the Cuale River) is a good place to barter for local handicrafts. For fine Mexican Indian art, the Galeria Indigena on Juarez Street (a block south of the main square) features ceremonial masks, Aztec-style etchings and bead-and-yarn art by the local Huichols. Seven blocks north of the town square, at Juarez and Leona Vicario, is Mexico's first and largest jade workshop and gallery (called Jades Maya Gallery) where archaeological reproductions are on display and jewelry and other gifts can be purchased.

Beaches – The beaches begin on either side of the cruise port where hotels line the waterfront. In the town itself, the most popular beach is Playa de los Muertos (Beach of the Dead) where another strip of hotels is situated. Watersports are available here and on adjacent Playa de Olas Altas (High Waves Beach). A gay beach is situated on a small section of Muertos Beach near its southern end. South of town is the beautiful crescent beach of Mismaloya. Further south along the coast are secluded beaches accessible only by sea, such as the one at Las Caletas, John Huston's former hideaway (see below), and the twin beaches of Las Animas and Quimixto.

Snorkel & Dive Sites – For both snorkeling and diving, Los Arcos National Underwater Park contains a cluster of rock islands, some hollowed out in places by wave action, which provide a habitat for tropical and subtropical fish, marine mammals and sea birds. Islas Marietas is one of the area's best dive sites, featuring reefs and underwater caverns, and is an hour-long boat ride from town. Las Caletas also includes good snorkeling opportunities.

Golf – Marina Vallarta Golf Course is an 18-hole 6,500-yard championship course dotted with lakes, ponds and lagoons. Although designed as a private golf club, it is open to cruise passengers who can book a package through the ship's shore excursion office.

LOCAL SIGHTS

Malecon – The Old Town of Puerto Vallarta is pleasant for strolling, especially along the beach-fronted malecon (seawall) which is

(Top) Playa Mismaloya. (Above & left) Cathedral of Our Lady of Guadalupe.

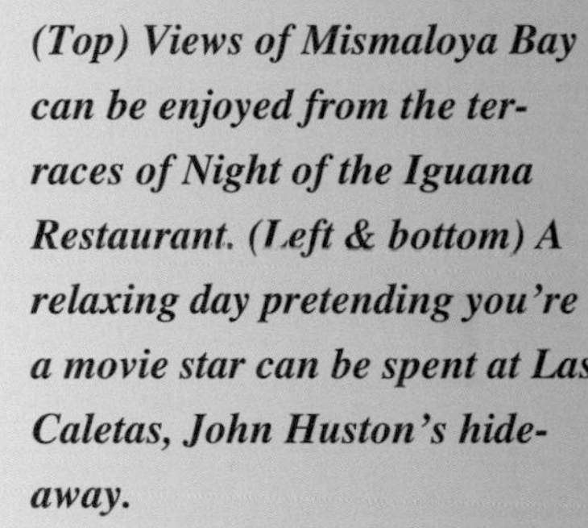

(Top) Views of Mismaloya Bay can be enjoyed from the terraces of Night of the Iguana Restaurant. (Left & bottom) A relaxing day pretending you're a movie star can be spent at Las Caletas, John Huston's hideaway.

dotted with benches and sculptures. Opposite the Seahorse Statue, at the foot of Calle Galeana, stands the Hotel Oceana (where Burton and Taylor stayed) and which now houses Tequila's Restaurant & Bar. A few blocks south along the malecon is the Old Town's central square, with some shaded benches and a statue of Don Ignacio Luis Vallarta.

Cathedral of Our Lady of Guadalupe – Rising above the town square is the landmark steeple of the Cathedral of Our Lady of Guadalupe (1906), which is topped with a huge replica of the crown worn by the empress Carlotta, whose husband Maximilian was emperor of Mexico from 1864-67. Part of this crown toppled during an earthquake in October 1995. The Virgin of Guadalupe, Mexico's patroness, is honored nationwide on December 12, with millions of pilgrims converging at the Basilica de Guadalupe in Mexico City. On a smaller scale is Puerto Vallarta's multi-day festival.

Gringo Gulch – Narrow streets behind the cathedral lead up the hillside to the wealthy Zaragoza neighborhood, better known as Gringo Gulch. Richard Burton and Elizabeth Taylor each owned a villa here with beautiful views of the bay and these were joined by a footbridge spanning the street in between. Now a bed & breakfast hideaway called Casa Kimberley, these two villas also house the Taylor-Burton Museum (Zaragoza 445) which is filled with original furniture and mementos. Visitors can gain admission ($6.00) by ringing the door bell.

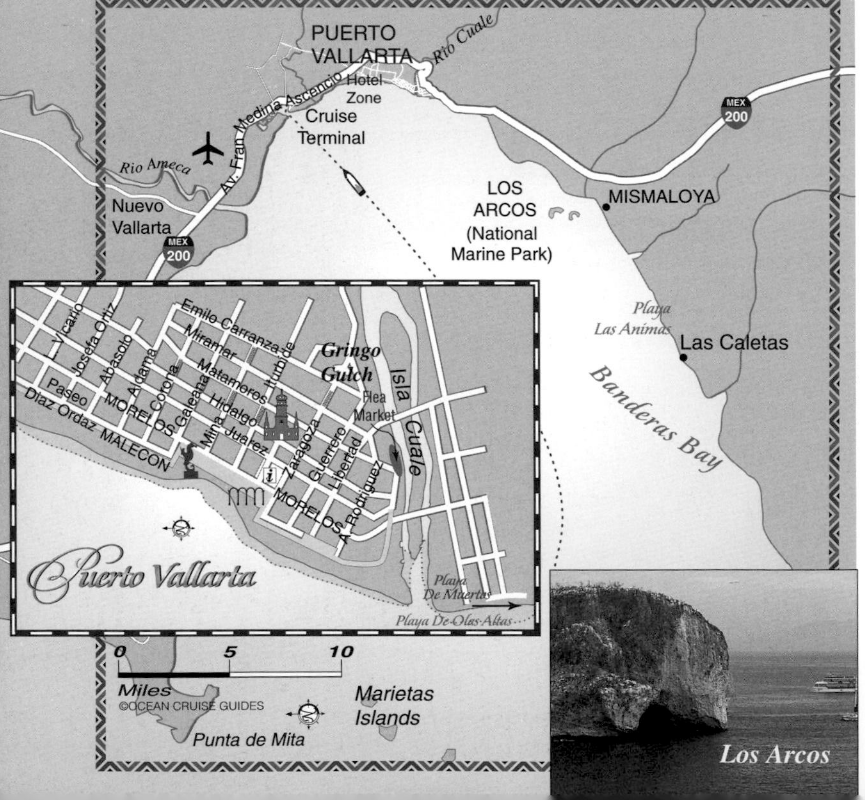

Isla Cuale – This island lies in the middle of the Cuale River, which divides Old Vallarta from the town's Romantic Zone where a bohemian atmosphere can be enjoyed at the many sidewalk cafes and beachside bars. A museum, boutiques and restaurants are located on the lushly overgrown river island.

Playa Mismaloya – The coastal drive south of town to Mismaloya winds past luxury hotels and homes overlooking the bay, including a villa owned by Steven Spielberg. Lying offshore are the rounded rock islets of Los Arcos, and just beyond is Mismaloya Bay where scenes from *Night of the Iguana* were filmed. A modern resort now stands at one end of the crescent beach and at the opposite end, atop a rugged hillside, is the Night of the Iguana restaurant where palm fringed views of the beach and bay can be enjoyed from the outdoor patio.

Las Caletas – A visit to this tranquil retreat is available as an all-inclusive day-long excursion involving a scenic 45-minute boat trip each way and a relaxing day spent at this isolated cove where visitors can lounge on the palm-fringed beach, snorkel or kayak in the clear water, and enjoy a buffet lunch featuring local cuisine. The grounds contain a range of facilities in the tile-roofed pavilions and palapa-style beach huts, including a restaurant, complimentary bar and John Huston's Museum with a small collection of the movie director's memorabilia on display. In describing his Mexican hideaway, Huston said, "Las Caletas faces the sea and its back is to the jungle so for this reason one thinks of it as an island."

Surrounding Area – The foothills surrounding Puerto Vallarta can be explored on several ship-organized excursions, including a drive past traditional Mexican villages and farms, or by horseback along jungle trails.

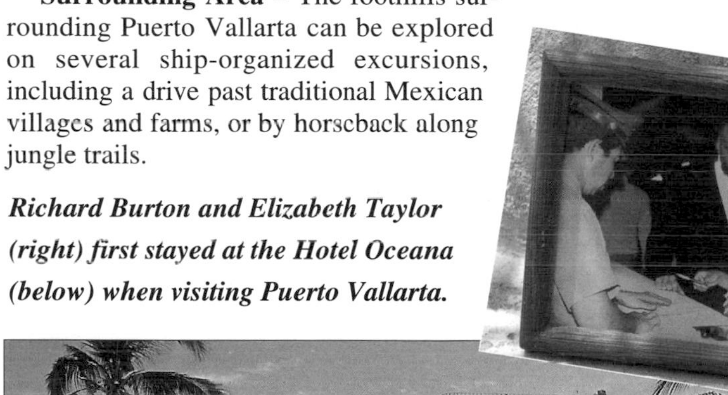

Richard Burton and Elizabeth Taylor (right) first stayed at the Hotel Oceana (below) when visiting Puerto Vallarta.

MAZATLAN

The heart of a port city is the dock area, and cruise passengers arriving at Mazatlan are provided with a close-up view of its industrial heart. As the sun rises over Isla Chivos and the ship slips through the stone breakwaters into the harbor, early risers can watch from the ship's rail the waterfront activities of docked freighters and moored fishing vessels. A city of some half-million people, Mazatlan is a major cargo port, connected by rail with Mexico City and the United States, and by ferry to Baja California. Its fishing fleet nets large quantities of shrimp and tuna, while marlin, swordfish and dorado are also plentiful.

First inhabited by nomadic tribes who fished and hunted, Mazatlan derives its name from a Nahuatl word meaning 'place of deer'. The Spanish conquistador Don Nuno Beltran de Guzman landed here in 1531 and called his newly founded settlement 'The Islands of Mazatlan' for the three offshore islands that were a natural landmark and navigational aid for Spanish merchant ships, as well as the English buccaneers who sailed these waters. Spanish colonial trade with the Philippines stimulated the growth of Mazatlan after gold and silver deposits were discovered nearby in the Sierra Madre mountains. Today the city hosts a growing number of tourists lured by the beautiful beaches and superb sportsfishing.

Getting Around – The ship docks at the commercial dock where complimentary trams whisk passengers to and from the terminal which contains telephones,

Mazatlan, home to the Pacifico beer brewery, is a fishing and cargo port.

restrooms and a handful of shops. Outside is a flea market and taxis. The fare, per taxi (up to four people), to the Golden Zone (where the beachfront hotels are located) is about $10.00. For a drive along the malecon, with stops at scenic outlooks and a visit to Plaza Machado to view the cathedral before returning to the port, a reasonable fare is $12.00 to $15.00 per taxi. Small open-air vehicles (similar to golf carts), called *pulmonia*, are available for hire on the street outside the terminal gates.

Shopping – The shops are concentrated in the Golden Zone (tourist zone), between Rodolfo Loaiza

(Top) El Faro lighthouse. (Middle) The pilot boat heads back to port during a cruise ship's dawn arrival at Mazatlan. (Bottom) Dancers perform at the Aztec Theater.

and Avenue Cameron Sabalo. Items to look for include Huichol beadwork and embroidery, and the Mexican fire opal, a bright red translucent stone.

Beaches – Mazatlan's beaches begin in the Old Town, with the surfing beach of Playa Olas Altas (Beach of Tall Waves) and Playa Norte where the locals swim. Next is the Golden Zone, the city's tourist area, where waterfront resorts and restaurants overlook lovely stretches of sand, one of the best lying in front of Los Sabalos Resort at the south end of the Zone. Another popular beach with watersports rentals is Playa Las Gaviotas, where the Royal Villas Resort is located. Offshore lie the 'three islands', named Bird, Deer and Goat. Deer Island (the middle one) is an ecological reserve offering good swimming and snorkeling, and can be visited by water taxis available at several hotels, including one that departs from the beach next to the El Cid Mega Resort.

Sportfishing – The marlin and sailfish caught off Mazatlan routinely break records, and the local swordfish, caught in March, are considered one of sportfishing's most challenging catches. The sportfishing docks are located in a bay southwest of the cruise ship dock.

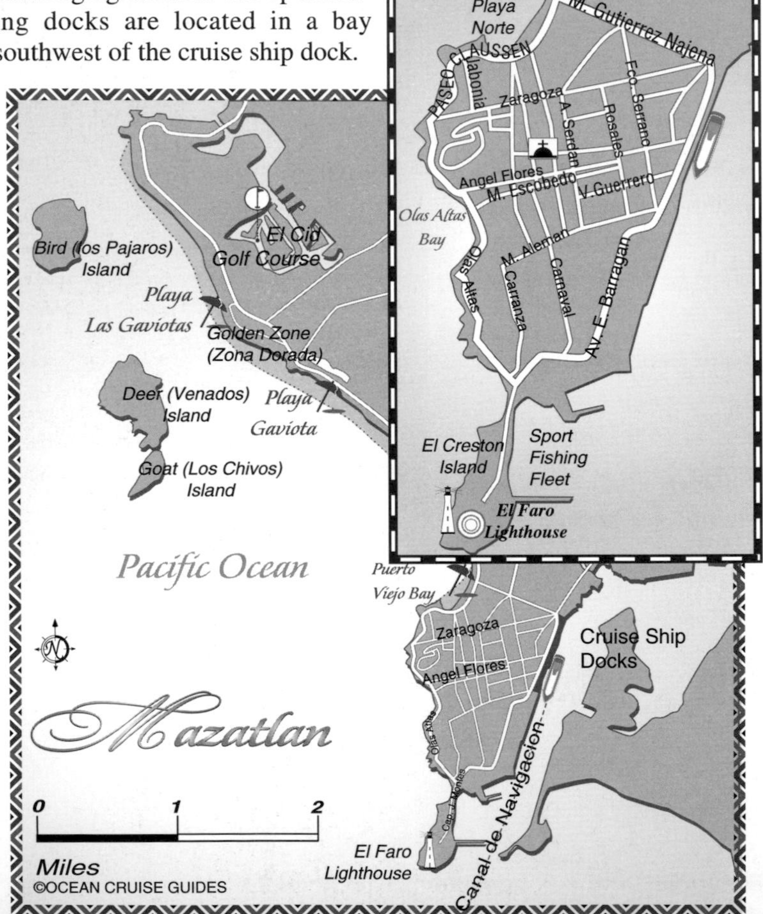

Golf – An area of lagoons beside the Golden Zone has been transformed into an upscale residential community of custom-built homes and a new 9-hole golf course designed for the El Cid Golf & Country Club by Lee Trevino.

LOCAL ATTRACTIONS

El Faro – Mazatlan's most prominent landmark and the world's second-tallest natural lighthouse (after Gibraltar), El Faro stands atop a 500-foot hill near the entrance to the port. It takes about half an hour to hike from its base to the top for sweeping views of the city and surrounding area.

The Malecon – This waterfront promenade, backed by Icebox Hill, runs for 13 miles along the edge of the bay and provides vistas of Mazatlan's ruggedly beautiful coastline. Public art graces the wide walkway, one of the largest sculptures being the Fisherman's Monument. At Cliff Diver's Park a diving platform has been built on a large rock outcropping from which a trained diver takes the plunge for the benefit of tourist groups. On the landward side of the malecon is haunted Devil's Cave where a murder once took place, its entrance sealed by a locked, wrought-iron gate.

Plaza Machado – The city's Moorish-style cathedral, built in 1856, overlooks the central square where locals gather to peddle their wares or enjoy the shade of its ornate gazebo, built during the regime of Porfirio Diaz (1876-1911) who admired the lavish splendor of French Second

(Above, right) The Papantla Flyers. (Below) The Moorish-style cathedral at Plaza Machado.

Empire architecture, a style introduced to Mexico during the brief (1864-67) reign of Emperor Maximilian. Nearby is the open-air public market where fresh fish, produce and local crafts are sold. Two blocks south of the plaza is the 19th century Angela Peralta Theatre, recently restored to its original grandeur.

Aztec Theater – Situated in the Golden Zone, this open-air theater presents daily shows of Mexican folkloric dancing and a daredevil routine by the Papantla Flyers who reenact a Totonac Indian ritual called "The Dance of Those Who Fly". Highly entertaining, the show features talented and traditionally attired dancers performing festive numbers, including the well-known Mexican Hat Dance.

Sierra Madre Mining Towns – Several colonial towns are located a short distance into the foothills of the Sierra Madre Occidental. The nearest is Concordia, 28 miles from Mazatlan, which was founded in 1565 and is noteworthy for its 17th-century stone church and local crafts, including handmade pottery and furniture. Farther afield, 15 1/2 miles from Concordia, is the town of Copola where the 16th century Church of San Jose overlooks the town's cobblestone streets and colonial houses.

CABO SAN LUCAS & SEA OF CORTEZ

Known as 'the other Mexico,' Baja California is distinctly different from the Mexican mainland. Geographically an extension of the California coast, the Baja peninsula – the longest in the world – was formed some 20 million years ago when seismic activity along the San Andreas Fault created a depression in the earth's surface that extends inland to the Coachella Valley in Southern California. Sea water flooded in, creating the Gulf of California, which initially encompassed the Imperial Valley and the Salton Sea until they were cut off by the growth of the Colorado River delta.

(Above) Morning light warms the granite sentinels at Land's End.

The peninsula's long, craggy coastlines were first explored in the 1530s by Francisco De Ulloa and other Spaniards, who named it Baja (Lower) California. This arid region of scrub-covered mountains lacked gold or silver deposits and was of limited interest to the Spanish crown, so it was left to missionaries to colonize. The first Jesuit mission was established in 1697 at Loreto, on the Baja's east coast, and was the first of a chain of Spanish missions eventually established the length of the Californias. These modest settlements were protected by small military garrisons while the missionaries converted the local natives to Catholicism.

In the mid-1700s, the Franciscans, followed by the Dominicans, continued the mission work begun by the Jesuits, but diseases introduced by the Spanish were decimating the Indians whose numbers plummeted from more than 50,000 in the 17th century to less than 500 today, and the missions were eventually abandoned. During the Mexican War (1846-48), American troops marched on La Paz and San Jose del Cabo, but the Baja remained with Mexico when a peace treaty

(Opposite page) El Arco, the massive sea arch at Land's End.

(Below) Lover's Beach can be reached by water taxi.

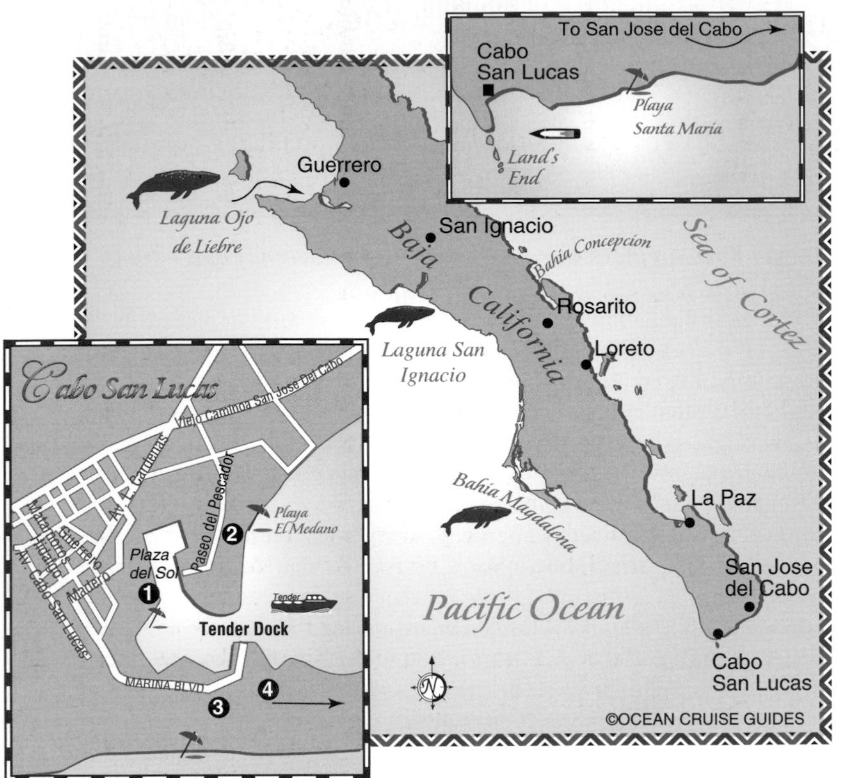

was signed and Alto (Upper) California, along with Texas and New Mexico, were ceded to the United States in return for $15 million.

The Baja's semi-isolation and sparse population made it a paradise for naturalists and archaeologists who come to study the region's indigenous plants, animals and marine life. The Gulf of California (also called the Sea of Cortez) deepens from north to south, and nutrient rich upwellings from the sea floor support a wealth of marine life, including sponge and oyster beds, as well as some 800 species of reef fish. John Steinbeck, the Nobel-winning American writer from California, harbored a great interest in marine biology and, after accompanying the marine biologist Edward Rickets on a collecting expedition to the area, he co-wrote with Rickets *The Log from the Sea of Cortez* (1951).

At the southern tip of the Baja peninsula, where the Sea of Cortez meets the Pacific Ocean, the waters off Cabo San Lucas contain underwater cliffs where depths drop off to 1200 feet. One submarine canyon, discovered in 1960, was filmed by Jacques Cousteau for its unique spectacle of sand cascading over its edge into an abyss of darkness. Cousteau's son Jean-Michel, continuing his late father's cause of preserving the earth's oceans, has spoken out about the deteriorating condi-

(Above) Pelicans perched on rocks are often seen during a glass-bottom boat ride to Land's End (below).

tions in the Sea of Cortez, where the deepwater coral has been depleted and overfishing by Asian trawlers, licensed to longline for shark and squid but apparently are also scooping up other species, is slowly clearing out what has long been regarded as the world's greatest fish trap.

Visitors eager to experience the Baja's famous sportfishing and pristine beaches arrive in ever-increasing numbers by air and by land, following the Transpeninsular Highway which was completed in the late 1960s. The best arrival, however, is by sea. As the Mexican sun rises above the Sea of Cortez and casts its glow on the granite sentinels at Land's End, this timeless sight is the reward for rising early and being at the ship's rail as the anchor goes down in the bay of Cabo San Lucas.

Cabo San Lucas

In November 1587, the English privateer Thomas Cavendish pulled into the bay of Cabo San Lucas where he deposited 190 crew and passengers from the *Santa Maria*, a treasure-filled Spanish galleon he had captured off the coast of Baja California. After transferring 122,000 pesos of gold, along with silks, perfumes, pearls and preserves, onto his two small ships, Cavendish burned the *Santa Maria* to her waterline, and departed. At that time, the southern tip of Baja California was a desolate wilderness of rocky headlands and hostile natives, and it was with some urgency that the Spanish crew salvaged their ship's burned-out hulk and sailed her to safety across the Sea of Cortez.

Today's half-million annual visitors to Cabo San Lucas are in no hurry to leave, for the stark scenery is among the world's most dramatic. At Land's End, where the Pacific Ocean meets the Sea of Cortez, the pounding surf has carved a massive sea arch into one of the rocky pinnacles which stand like silent sentinels in the swirling wash. Granite cliffs guard secluded beaches, and all day long the azure blue bay buzzes with sightseeing boats and sailing craft, including parasailers soaring high above the spectacular sea stacks off Land's End.

Getting Around – The seaside resorts of Cabo San Lucas and nearby San Jose del Cabo are referred to as Los Cabos ('The Capes') and their atmosphere is part Mexico, part California. American hotels and golf courses overlook the beaches that dot the 19 miles of coastline between the two capes, and the U.S. dollar is the preferred currency. Cabo San Lucas is a booming tourist town while San Jose del Cabo offers the more languid pace of a Spanish colonial village.

Passengers are tendered ashore to the marina at Cabo San Lucas where dozens of docks accommodate the many tour boats providing excursions from the waterfront, including glass-bottom boat rides to El Arco ($7-$8) (45 minutes round trip) which also serve as water taxis to Lover's Beach. The town can be reached on foot, along the waterfront, in about 15 minutes. Taxis are located near the tender pier, behind the flea market, and are usually eight-seater vans. A taxi ride into town costs about $3 per person. Other fares, per person, are: Playa Medano ($3 – $4); Palapa Beach Club ($2-$3).

(Left) A parasail soars above Lover's Beach. (Below) A ship's tender returns from the marina at Cabo San Lucas.

The view of the Bay of Cabo San Lucas from Giorgio's Restaurant.

Shopping – A flea market selling Mexican crafts is located near the tender pier, while the town's jewelry shops are situated on or near Marina Boulevard.

Beaches – Closest to the tender pier is the excellent beach in front of **(1) Plaza Las Glorias Hotel**. **(2) Medano Beach**, where watersports equipment can be rented, stretches east along the bay from the marina and is backed by several hotels and beachfront restaurants. **(3) Palapa Beach Club** at Hotel Finisterra provides access to a Pacific beach which is fine for sunbathing and strolling, but not swimming due to its strong currents. **(4) Playa del Amour (Lover's Beach)**, reached by water taxi (see above), is a stunning swath of pristine white sand lying at the base of cliffs near Land's End. Swimming and snorkeling are popular here on the Gulf side of the beach but not the Pacific side where strong currents can be treacherous.

The dawn came quickly now, a wash, a glow, a lightness, and then an explosion of fire as the sun arose out of the Gulf.
A passage from John Steinbeck's parable, *The Pearl* (1948), set in Baja California Sur.

Dive & Snorkel Sites – The rocky foreshore and clear waters off Cabo San Lucas are an ideal environment for tropical fish, as well as starfish, sea fans and sponges. Pelican Rock Cove and Lover's Beach at Land's End offer good snorkeling, as does Playa Santa Maria which lies 8 miles east of Cabo San Lucas (accessible by road or by boat) and is considered the area's best snorkeling beach. Snorkel gear can be rented in town. One of the area's best dive sites is Playa Barco Varada (Shipwreck Beach), located 5.5 miles west of San Jose del Cabo, where a sunken tuna boat lies in depths of 80 feet (27 meters). The submarine trench in Cabo San Lucas Bay also attracts an abundance of tropical and sub-tropical species of fish.

Golf – There are five championship golf courses in Los Cabos, all with ocean views. For more information, consult with the ship's shore excursion manager.

Local Attractions

El Arco – This massive sea arch at Land's End has become the symbol of Cabo San Lucas. It can be viewed up close by glass-bottom boats that depart regularly from the marina, the trip is also an opportunity to view the underwater life, as well as pelicans perched on rocks and the resident sea lion colony.

***San Jose del Cabo* –** An Old Mexico atmosphere endures in this colonial town, its main street a wide pedestrian boulevard lined with lovely gardens and interesting boutiques, galleries and restaurants. The town's Spanish colonial architecture includes a handsome Municipal Palace, mission church and tree-lined plaza.

A 19th-century cathedral overlooks La Paz's central plaza.

Sea of Cortez

***La Paz* –** With a population of 200,000, La Paz (meaning 'peace') is the largest city and capital of the state of Baja California Sur, which comprises the southern half of the Baja peninsula. Situated at the head of a bay and first settled in 1811, the town was famous for its pearl fishing – evocatively described in Steinbeck's parable *The Pearl* – until disease destroyed the oyster beds in the middle of the 20th century. The palm-lined *malecon* provides lovely views of sailboats at anchor, its waterfront square a popular gathering place for locals as the sun sets over the bay. Plaza Constitucion, the city's central plaza, is graced with a 19th-century cathedral (Cathedral de Nuestra Senora de la Paz) and the Palacio del Gobierno. The port is located on the Pichilingue peninsula, which forms the bay's eastern shore and is lined with beautiful beaches. The unspoilt islands of Espiritu Santo and Partida, the latter a seal sanctuary, can be visited by boat from La Paz and are popular with divers.

Loreto – The region's oldest permanent settlement, Loreto was founded by Jesuit missionaries in 1697. This quiet town of 12,000 residents has been hard hit in the past by hurricanes and earthquakes, but the mission church has been beautifully restored, its cloisters containing a museum recounting the local histories of the three religious orders – Jesuit, Franciscan, Dominican – which colonized the region when it was part of New Spain.

Nearby **Isla Corondos** offers superb swimming beaches and snorkeling, as does Bahia de la Concepcion, about 40 miles north of Loreto, where crystal-clear waters and breathtaking beaches lie at the base of stark cliffs.

Santa Rosalia – Unlike the Baja's mission settlements, Santa Rosalia was strictly a company town, built in 1868 by French interests on the slopes of a mountain containing rich deposits of copper ore. The streets are lined with weatherboard houses, with company officials living on the upper slopes and the workers housed below on the lower slopes. The French colonial style is seen in overhanging fretwork balconies and the town's cast-iron church, designed by a contemporary of Gustave Eiffel and exhibited in Paris before being shipped to Santa Rosalia in 1895.

Inland from Santa Rosalia is the oasis town of ***San Ignacio***, situated atop an underground supply of fresh water, its shady central plaza graced with colonial buildings such as the mission church, built by the Dominicans in 1786 to replace an earlier one built of adobe by the Jesuits. Nearby is the Sierra de San Francisco, where archaeologists have discovered caves containing pre-historic wall paintings.

Sportfishing is popular in Cabo San Lucas and the Sea of Cortez.

California
San Francisco
LA
OREGON
REDWOOD NATIONAL PARK
Shasta Lake
COAST RANGES
SIERRA NEVADA
Reno
Lake Tahoe
Coloma
Sonoma
Napa
Sacramento
Berkeley
San Francisco
Oakland
YOSEMITE NATIONAL PARK
Mono Lake
Monterey
Carmel
SEQUOIA NATIONAL PARK
DEATH VALLEY NAT. MONUMENT
NEVADA
MOJAVE DESERT
Sierra Madre Mts.
Santa Barbara
Santa Clarita
Hollywood
Malibu
Los Angeles
JOSHUA TREE NAT. MONUMENT
Long Beach
San Juan Capistrano
Santa Catalina Is.
CHANNEL ISLANDS
Salton Sea
San Diego
Tijuana
USA
MEXICO
5
15
10
0
100
200
Miles
©OCEAN CRUISE GUIDES

CHAPTER FIVE

WEST COAST PORTS

California is America's third largest state in land area but second to none in terms of natural beauty and diversity. The state's northernmost coastal region is home to huge cathedral-like redwood forests containing some of the world's tallest trees, over 300 feet tall. In stark contrast is arid Death Valley, in eastern California, where less than 2 inches of rain falls annually on the lowest point in the Americas where some of the world's hottest temperatures have been recorded. A hundred miles northwest of Death Valley, in the glacier-scoured valleys and mountains of Yosemite National Park, is North America's highest waterfall, Yosemite Falls. And in Sequoia National Park, the giant pines are as impressive as the jagged peaks of the High Sierras, among them Mount Whitney, the highest mountain in the U.S. outside Alaska. Yet it's the Pacific beaches of coastal California that most often come to mind when people think of life in the Golden State – those beaches of wave-washed sand and rugged headlands where seals and sea lions lounge on rock outcroppings while movie stars lounge on the decks of their beach houses.

With a population exceeding 30 million, California is the most populous state in the U.S. and more than 90% of its residents live in metropolitan areas. Cities and beach communities line the west coast, their growing populations showing no signs of abating as people flock to California just as they first did in 1841, when overland American immigrants began arriving in large numbers despite the granite barrier presented by the Sierra Nevada mountains and the fact that California was still part of Mexico. Ceded to the United States by Mexico in 1848, California entered the Union in 1850. By the turn of the century, the state was thriving. It was, in fact, a land of plenty, with its fertile soil and a long growing season for cultivating a wide variety of produce, including avocados, oranges and grapes for wine. By the end of the 20th century, California's economy was the most productive of any state, dominated by manufacturing and the new field of high-tech electronics. Other important industries include petroleum, motion picture and television production, and tourism, the latter drawing visitors by the millions.

SAN DIEGO

Few cities seem to be as perfectly situated as San Diego. The sub-tropical climate is ideal for enjoying the city's ocean beaches, and the excellent natural harbor, at the downtown's doorstep, makes San Diego a cruise port of undisputed appeal. The second-largest metropolis in California with a population of 2,725,000, the city that attracts artists and retirees is also home to a third of the U.S. Navy's Pacific Fleet. San Diego became an important naval base during World War I, and other branches of the military soon established bases in the area, their presence giving rise to a booming aerospace industry. When Charles Lindbergh completed the first solo, nonstop transatlantic flight from New York to Paris in 1927, the plane he flew, Spirit of St. Louis, was built by the Ryan Aeronautical Company in San Diego.

Shipbuilding is another important industry in San Diego, and yachting is a popular pastime. In 1987, the San Diego Yacht Club won the America's Cup for the United States and successfully defended the Cup in 1992. The first sailing ship to pull into San Diego Bay was commanded by Portuguese-born Juan Rodriguez Cabrillo, who landed at Point Loma in 1542 and claimed what he saw on behalf of Spain. In 1769, San Diego became the first Spanish settlement in Alto (Upper) California when Junipero Serra established a Franciscan mission and a fort was built. San Diego, like the rest of California, eventually joined the United States, but the city's Spanish past and close proximity to Mexico remain part of the cultural vitality of this Pacific port.

Getting Around – The San Diego International Airport (also known as Lindbergh Field) is a 10-minute drive from downtown and the adjacent cruise ship terminal on San Diego Bay where miles of waterfront parks, hotels, restaurants and marinas line the shores. South of the terminal is the city's spectacular Convention Center with its glass-enclosed lobby and landscaped outdoor plazas and terraces. For a bird's eye view of San Diego Harbor, visit the Hyatt Regency, the city's highest waterfront hotel. The city's extensive trolley system is an ideal way to tour the downtown and historic Old Town, and one- to four-day trolley passes can be purchased at The Transit Store, 102 Broadway. Coronado, located across the harbor from downtown, can be reached via the San Diego-Coronado Bridge or by scheduled ferry service.

Shopping & Dining – **Seaport Village**, next to the Convention Center, is a large waterfront complex of shopping, dining and entertainment (and is also a good place to observe the U.S. Navy's Pacific Fleet of cruisers, carriers, destroyers and other large vessels docked across the bay on Coronado). The architecturally acclaimed **Horton Plaza** with its six open-air levels of upscale shops and restaurants, was built in the 1980s and began the downtown's revitalization. Adjacent to the Plaza is the historic **Gaslamp Quarter** where shops, galleries and restaurants are housed in restored, 19th-century buildings.

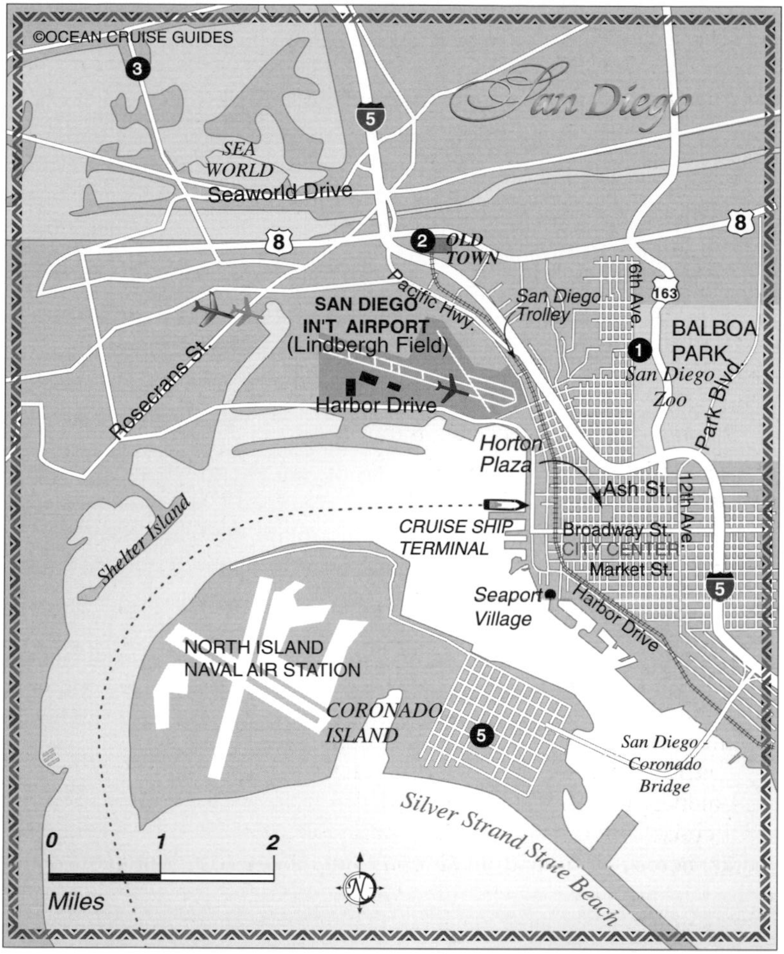

Beaches – The white sand beaches of Coronado are a popular beach destination, as is family-oriented Silver Strand State Beach, situated on the long sandbar joining Coronado with the mainland. More beautiful beaches lie north of downtown San Diego in the beach communities of Pacific Beach, Mission Beach and La Jolla.

Golf – There are numerous municipal courses in the San Diego area, including the oceanside Torrey Pines Golf Course in La Jolla where

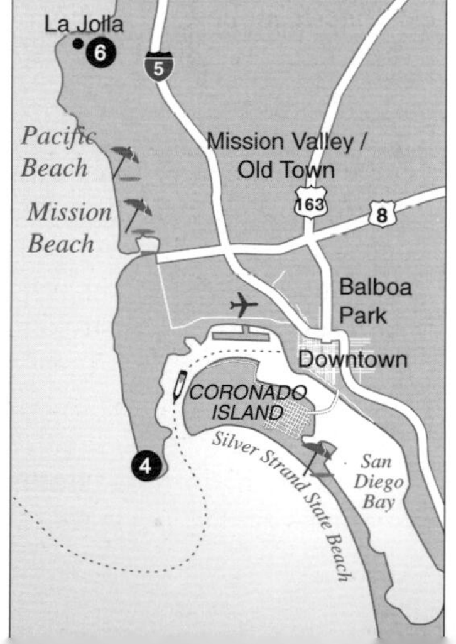

the annual Buick Invitational is played each February. Tee times at public courses can be obtained from the concierge at your hotel.

Local Attractions

(1) Balboa Park – This beautifully landscaped park covers 1,200 acres and is home to the world-famous **San Diego Zoo**, itself designed as a 100-acre tropical garden. The Zoo houses 800 different species, including rare giant pandas on long-term loan from China, and can be toured on foot or by taking a three-mile guided bus tour. Other attractions in Balboa Park are a fine art gallery, the San Diego Aerospace Museum and 14 other museums. Much of the Park's architecture dates from the Panama-California Exposition of 1915 and the California Pacific International Exposition of 1935, and includes the Old Globe Theater, the California Tower with its working 100-bell carillon and the Spiracles Organ Pavilion, which features concerts on Sunday afternoons. The free Balboa Park Tram runs daily.

(2) Old Town – This was the heart of San Diego when Spain, followed by a newly independent Mexico, governed California. Many of the Spanish colonial buildings clustered around the Old Town Square were built between 1820 and 1869, and are now part of a state historical park.

(3) Mission Bay Park – Mission Bay beach community is home to a huge public aquatic park stretching along 17 miles of oceanfront beaches and containing designated areas for various outdoor sports. Mission Bay is also home to **SeaWorld San Diego**, a marine park featuring trained killer whales and dolphins, as well as manatees, penguins, beluga whales and polar bears.

An aerial view of San Diego Bay and San Diego-Coronado Bridge.

San Diego's cruise ship terminal is at the city's doorstep.

(4) Cabrillo National Monument – Situated on Point Loma, this monument marks the site where Spanish conquistadors, led by Juan Rodriguez Cabrillo, landed in 1542. This rocky point, providing a panoramic view of San Diego Bay, is also an ideal spot to watch for migrating gray whales which spend the winter months (December to March) in the waters off Baja California before returning to northern waters for the summer.

(5) Coronado – The centerpiece of this bayside beach community is the illustrious Hotel Del Coronado. Built in 1888, this landmark building of turrets, cupolas and verandahs was featured in Billy Wilder's classic *Some Like It Hot*. A seven-storey tower and poolside complex have been added to the original Victorian structure, and the hotel features shops, restaurants and other resort amenities. There are other hotels and charming cottages in the vicinity, and the village itself features a large central park and the popular Ferry Landing Marketplace.

(6) La Jolla (pronounced le hoi ye) – A 20-minute drive from downtown San Diego, this upscale resort is well known for its beautiful ocean beaches, sea-washed caves and abundance of tidepools. Situated in between the especially beautiful La Jolla Shores and Black's Beach is the Scripps Institution of Oceanography and Birch Aquarium where an outdoor tidepool exhibit introduces visitors to the shore life that can be seen in La Jolla Cove. Just south of La Jolla Cove, along the waterfront, is the Museum of Contemporary Art.

LOS ANGELES

At a California race track in the 1860s, a gifted English eccentric named Eadweard Muybridge set up a row of cameras with shutters tripped by wires and successfully took the first serial photographs of a horse running. This was the beginning of the motion picture industry, which quickly progressed with the development of a camera using celluloid film and a projection device for screening 10-minute films. The first American motion picture studios were located in New York, but when Thomas Edison attempted to gain a monopoly on the industry in 1909 by claiming patents on many of the technical elements involved, a number of independent producers moved their studios to a suburb of southern California where they could flee to Mexico if faced with legal injunctions. In a few short years, Hollywood became the movie capital of America, if not the world.

Today, Los Angeles is home to countless studios in the motion picture, television, radio and recording fields, and the allure of Hollywood endures, the city's landmark buildings and beaches having appeared in countless films and television shows over the years. Los Angeles is the second largest U.S. city in both population and area, and is one of the nation's busiest ports and a leading producer of a huge range of goods, from aerospace equipment to household furniture, but in the public consciousness it is first and foremost the home of Hollywood. Back in the 18th century, America's future entertainment capital was a cattle-ranching center and capital of the Spanish colonial province Alto California. Founded in 1781 as The Town of Our Lady the Queen of the Angels of Porciuncula, the settlement was captured from the Mexicans by U.S. forces in 1846. Los Angeles enjoyed steady growth following the completion of two intercontinental railroads and the discovery of oil in the late 1800s. The opening of the Panama Canal in 1914 spurred the growth of its port, and the city boomed during World War II, when thousands of African-Americans arrived to fill factory jobs. Growth continued after the war, and the expanding city absorbed surrounding communities. The influx of immigrants of various ethnic backgrounds, including Hispanics and Asians, created a cosmopolitan and sprawling metropolis that now encompasses five counties and over 15 million people. The only major U.S. city without a public transportation system, Greater Los Angeles is a land of freeways, cars and traffic congestion. The dense smog this creates, however, has not dulled the glamour and glitz of Tinseltown.

Getting Around – Los Angeles Harbor, situated in San Pedro Bay, is one of the world's greatest manmade harbors, built with breakwaters, channels, piers and wharves. Downtown Los Angeles is 21 miles due north of Los Angeles Harbor, and Hollywood is 7 miles northwest of downtown. The Los Angeles International Airport is about 20 miles from Los Angeles Harbor.

Shopping & Dining – Beverly Hills' three-block stretch of **Rodeo Drive** between Santa Monica and Wilshire Boulevard is L.A.'s most famous shopping strip. In addition to the specialty stores and fashion boutiques on Rodeo Drive and surrounding streets, department stores in the vicinity include Barneys New York, Neiman-Marcus, Robinsons-May and Saks Fifth Avenue, all located on Wilshire Boulevard. Other shopping venues in the L.A. area include the seaside community of Santa Monica where the pedestrian-only 3rd Street Promenade is lined with boutiques and restaurants.

Beaches – The reclusive, and exclusive, resort area of **Malibu** is where many of the show business stars own homes along a beach escarpment overlooking Santa Monica Bay. **Santa Monica**, south of Malibu, has three miles of oceanfront beach. Its famous pier, with its 46-horse carousel, was built in 1906 and has appeared in numerous films, including *The Sting*. The main attraction at **Venice City Beach** is the mile-and-a-half boardwalk, dotted with street entertainers and bustling with cyclists and rollerbladers. Just south of the beach is **Marina Del Rey**, an enormous man-made marina.

LOCAL ATTRACTIONS

Downtown Los Angeles – The city's original Spanish settlement is preserved by **(1) El Pueblo de Los Angeles Historic Park**. On the north side is Olvera Street, a Mexican street market originally called El Paseo de Los Angeles (Walk of the Angels). Facing the park's east side is **Union Station**, built in 1939 in the Spanish-mission style and featured in numerous Hollywood films, including *The Way We Were*. Two blocks south of the park is the **(2) Civic Center,** where **City Hall**, which served as Clark Kent's 'Daily Planet' in TV's old *Superman* series, provides panoramic views from its tower. Also in the vicinity is the **Los Angeles Music Center for the Performing Arts** and the **Dorothy Chandler Pavilion**, a former venue for the Academy Awards, as well as the **Museum of Contemporary Art** at California Plaza which houses a 5,000-piece collection representing art from 1940 to the present. The Victorian-era **Bradbury Building** on Broadway, once the city's main shopping and entertainment street, has appeared in many a movie, including *Chinatown* and *Blade Runner*, and the beaux-arts **Biltmore Hotel** on Grand Avenue, which opened in 1923, hosted the Academy Awards in the 1930s. Another landmark is the postmodern **Westin Bonaventure Hotel** on Figueroa Street, its five shimmering cylinders sheathed in mirrored glass.

Wilshire Boulevard is a main thoroughfare which runs for 16 miles from downtown L.A. to Santa Monica Bay. Major attractions along Wilshire include the renowned **(3) Los Angeles County Museum of Art**, with its huge collection of art from ancient times to present. The Museum is housed in a large complex situated in a park it shares with the prehistoric **La Brea Tar Pits**, where fossils extracted from oil upwellings are displayed in an adjacent museum. A few blocks north, at 3rd Street and Fairfax Avenue, is the open-air **(4) Farmers Market**, a hub for locals and tourists with over 100 stalls and 20 restaurants.

Hollywood & Beverly Hills – The heart of Hollywood is the intersection of **(5) Vine Street and Hollywood Boulevard**, overlooked by the Capitol Records Tower which resembles a stack of 45s. A few blocks west along Hollywood Boulevard is the **Hollywood Walk of Fame**, a mile of sidewalk where the names of legendary entertainers are embossed in brass. Farther west along Hollywood Boulevard is the famous **Mann's Chinese Theatre** (formerly Grauman's) where many a motion picture premiere has been commemorated with the hand, foot and nose prints of stars placed in soft concrete in the foyer.

Nestled in the hills north of Hollywood Boulevard is the **(6)**

(Above, right) Mann's Chinese Theatre and one of many famous hand and foot prints. (Below) Disneyland theme park.

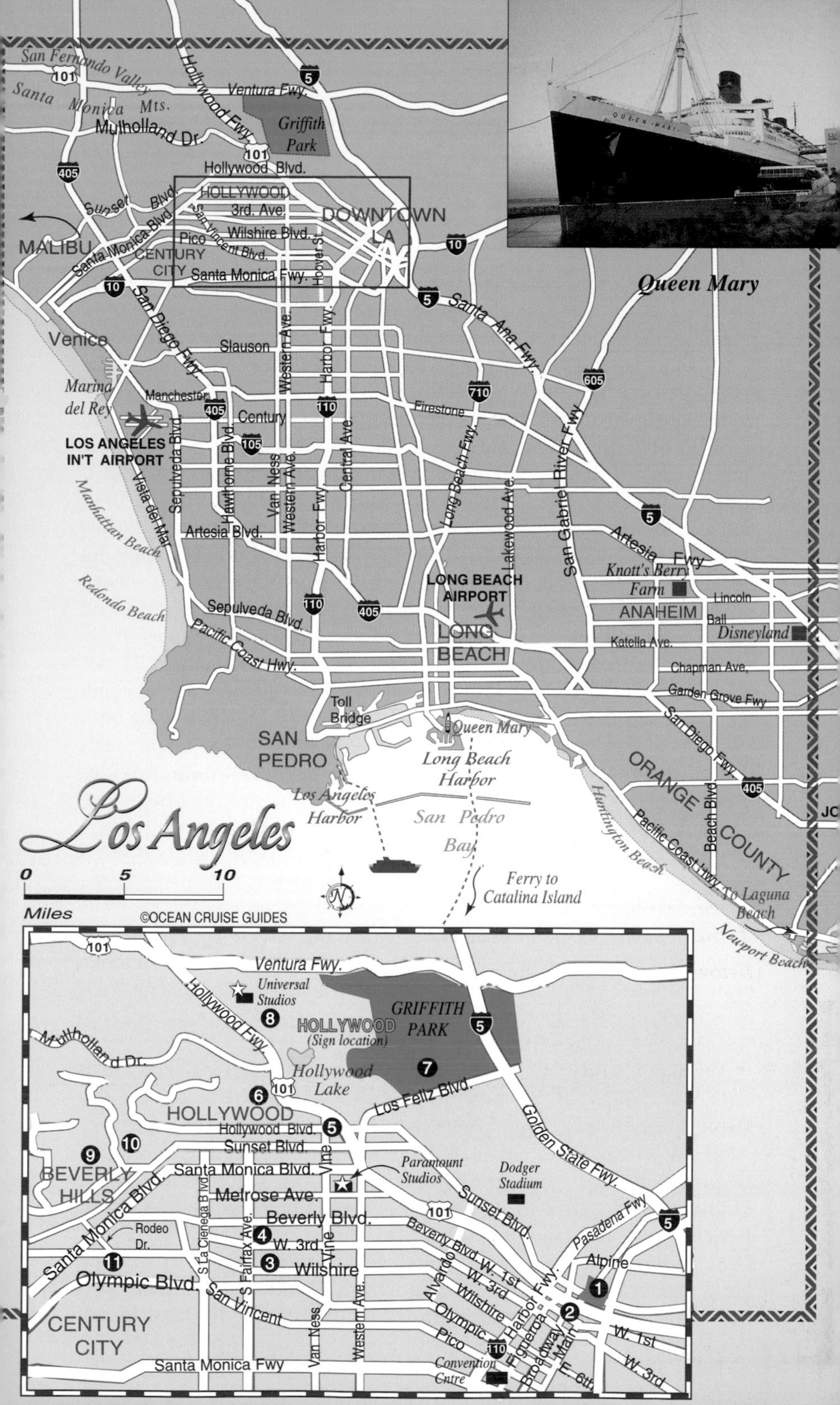

Los Angeles
Queen Mary
San Fernando Valley
Santa Monica Mts.
Mulholland Dr.
Hollywood Fwy.
Ventura Fwy.
Griffith Park
Hollywood Blvd.
HOLLYWOOD
3rd. Ave.
Wilshire Blvd.
DOWNTOWN LA
Sunset Blvd.
Santa Monica Blvd.
MALIBU
Pico
CENTURY CITY
San Vincent Blvd.
Santa Monica Fwy.
Hoover St.
Santa Ana Fwy.
San Diego Fwy
Venice
Slauson
Western Ave.
Harbor Fwy.
Marina del Rey
Manchester
Century
Firestone
LOS ANGELES IN'T AIRPORT
Sepulveda Blvd.
Hawthorne Blvd.
Van Ness
Central Ave.
Long Beach Fwy.
Lakewood Ave.
San Gabriel River Fwy
Manhattan Beach
Vista del Mar
Artesia Blvd.
Artesia Fwy
Knott's Berry Farm
LONG BEACH AIRPORT
Lincoln
ANAHEIM
Ball
Disneyland
Katella Ave.
Redondo Beach
Sepulveda Blvd.
Pacific Coast Hwy.
LONG BEACH
Chapman Ave.
Garden Grove Fwy
Toll Bridge
San Diego Fwy.
SAN PEDRO
Queen Mary
Long Beach Harbor
ORANGE COUNTY
Beach Blvd
Los Angeles Harbor
San Pedro Bay
Huntington Beach
Pacific Coast Hwy
Ferry to Catalina Island
To Laguna Beach
Newport Beach
0 5 10
Miles
©OCEAN CRUISE GUIDES
Ventura Fwy.
Universal Studios
Hollywood Fwy.
GRIFFITH PARK
HOLLYWOOD (Sign location)
Mulholland Dr.
Hollywood Lake
Los Feliz Blvd.
HOLLYWOOD
Golden State Fwy.
Hollywood Blvd.
Sunset Blvd.
BEVERLY HILLS
Santa Monica Blvd.
Vine
Paramount Studios
Dodger Stadium
Melrose Ave.
S La Cienega Blvd
Sunset Blvd.
Beverly Blvd.
Pasadena Fwy
Rodeo Dr.
W. 3rd
Beverly Blvd.
W. 1st
Alpine
Wilshire
W. 3rd
Olympic Blvd.
S Fairfax Ave.
Alvarado
Wilshire
Harbor Fwy.
San Vincent
CENTURY CITY
Olympic
Figueroa
W. 1st
Pico
Van Ness
Western Ave.
Broadway
Main
Santa Monica Fwy
Convention Centre
E. 6th
W. 3rd

Hollywood Bowl, an amphitheatre where summer evening concerts are held. Nearby **(7) Griffith Park**, containing a zoo and planetarium, is one of the largest urban parks in the world, occupying land donated to in 1896 by a mining tycoon. Scenes from the TV series *Bonanza* and the James Dean film *Rebel Without a Cause* were shot here.

Just north of Hollywood, on the edge of the **San Fernando Valley**, is **(8) Universal Studios Hollywood** where visitors to this popular theme park are transported around a 420-acre complex and introduced to the movie art of special effects, including an encounter with King Kong and aliens armed with death rays. The Valley is home to most of the major film and television studios, and tours are available at Warner Bros. Studios and NBC Television Studios.

West of Hollywood is **Beverly Hills**, an exclusive residential area where many of the stars reside in hedge-hidden mansions. The pastel-pink **(9) Beverly Hills Hotel** on Sunset Boulevard was built in 1912 and was, for decades, the place where movie producers would cut deals in the Polo Lounge. The neo-Gothic **(10) Greystone Mansion** on Doheny Road was built by a wealthy oilman in 1927 and is now owned by the city of Beverly Hills, its manicured grounds open to visitors and the setting for scenes in *The Witches of Eastwick.*

Rodeo Drive is perhaps the most famous street in Beverly Hills (see shopping section) and the **(11) Regent Beverly Wilshire**, at the south end of Rodeo Drive, is another landmark hotel, its Wilshire wing built in 1928. Scenes for the hit movie *Pretty Woman* were shot in the presidential suite. Nearby is the **Beverly Hills Trolley**, which provides street tours of local landmarks and the former homes of celebrities.

Long Beach – Located about 5 miles east of Los Angeles Harbor, Long Beach is where the ***Queen Mary*** has been permanently docked since 1967. Daily tours of this 1930s Cunard liner are available to the public, its onboard facilities including several restaurants and shops as well as a hotel. The geodesic dome beside the *Queen Mary*'s dock used to house Howard Hughes's *Spruce Goose* before being converted into a cruise facility by Carnival Corporation, which also constructed an adjacent docking pier for its cruise ships. Ferry service connects Long Beach with **Catalina Island**, lying 22 miles offshore.

Orange County – Tourist attractions include **Knott's Berry Farm** with its replica of an early California Gold Rush Town, and **Disneyland**, the huge amusement park that has been the centerpiece of Anaheim (Orange County's tourist hub) since opening in 1955. Beautiful beaches line the coast of Orange County, including **Huntington Beach** with its broad white-sand beaches, and **Newport Beach** where an island-dotted harbor is home to hundreds of yachts. Other popular beach communities are **Laguna Beach**, its hillside homes popular with artists, and **Dana Point**, one of southern California's top surfing destinations and named for Richard Henry

Dana, author of *Two Years Before the Mast* in which he describes the local harbor as it was more than a century ago. **San Juan Capistrano** is home to a famous Spanish mission, founded by Padre Junipero Serra in 1776 and named after St. John of Capistrano, a Crusader. The stone church was completed in 1806 but only the chapel survived an earthquake in 1812. For decades swallows would arrive at the mission from their winter home in Argentina on or about March 19, the feast day of St. Joseph, but in recent years the number of swallows returning to the mission has dwindled because of scaffolding that surrounds the church and the development boom in the area.

SAN FRANCISCO

The city by the bay began in 1776 as a Spanish mission called San Francisco de Asis, its nearby presidio overlooking Golden Gate at the entrance to San Francisco Bay. This small settlement was called Yerba Buena when claimed by an American naval force in 1846, and it remained a quiet village until gold was discovered two years later at an inland sawmill near Coloma. As gold seekers converged on this sleepy port by steamship, the local population grew from 800 to 25,000 in the space of two years. The waterfront became known as the Barbary Coast for its seedy activities, and a period of lawlessness prevailed until vigilantes were organized to keep the peace.

A century later the former gold rush town had become a major commercial port and financial hub. Then, in the mid-20th century, San Francisco was discovered by the counterculture, attracting the beatniks of the 1950s, the hippie generation of the 1960s and a large gay population. San Francisco's reputation for social tolerance remains part of its appeal and the city is consistently rated as one of the most beautiful in the world. Visitors come to ride those vintage cable cars up and down streets lined with Victorian townhouses, and to gaze from hilltops across San Francisco Bay where fog often obscures all but the uppermost spans of the famous Golden Gate Bridge.

Getting Around – The cruise ships dock at historic Pier 35, within walking distance of several waterfront attractions, the cable car stations and the vintage street cars that run along The Embarcadero and Market Street. The cable cars, which fill up quickly in the summer months, can be caught at the turnaround stations or at various stops along the way. They are hauled by cables that are in constant motion beneath the street and the car's 'gripman' operates a device beneath the car that grabs onto the cable. Union Square, North Beach, Nob Hill, Chinatown and SoMa can all be reached by cable car, while other areas of interest, such as Haight Ashbury, Golden Gate Park and Presidio can be reached by city buses, street cars or taxi. In addition to ship-organized shore excursions, numerous tour operators offer city tours and scenic drives. Alcatraz Island can be accessed by passenger ferry from Pier 41. A

(Left) The Powell-Hyde cable car provides hillside views of San Francisco Bay and Alcatraz Island. (Below) The cruise ships dock at Pier 35 where the city's famous skyline includes Coit Tower and the Transamerica Pyramid.

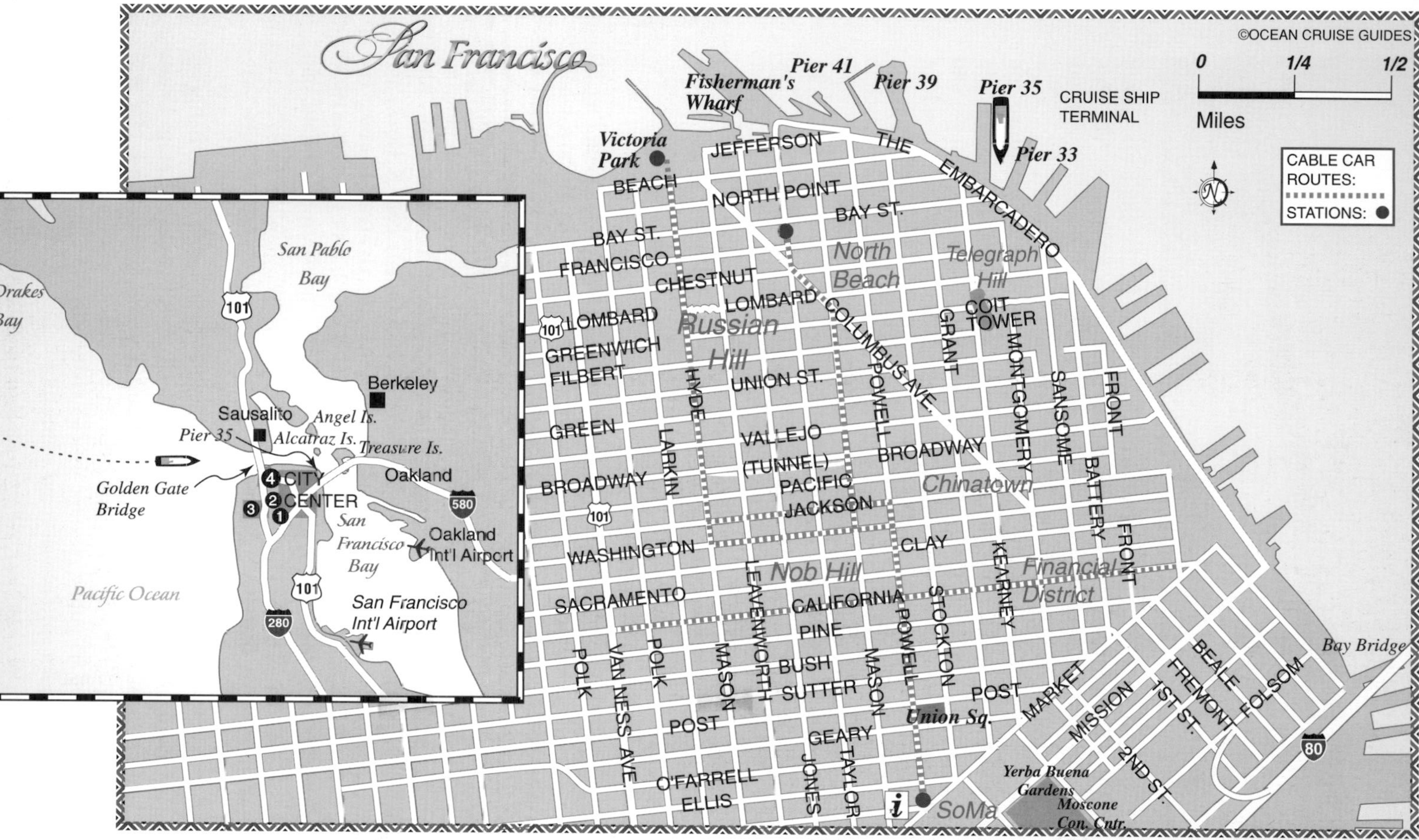
San Francisco
©OCEAN CRUISE GUIDES
0
1/4
1/2
Miles
CABLE CAR ROUTES:
STATIONS:
Pier 41
Pier 39
Pier 35
Pier 33
CRUISE SHIP TERMINAL
Fisherman's Wharf
Victoria Park
THE EMBARCADERO
JEFFERSON
BEACH
NORTH POINT
BAY ST.
FRANCISCO
CHESTNUT
LOMBARD
GREENWICH
FILBERT
UNION ST.
GREEN
VALLEJO
BROADWAY
(TUNNEL)
PACIFIC
JACKSON
WASHINGTON
CLAY
SACRAMENTO
CALIFORNIA
PINE
BUSH
SUTTER
POST
GEARY
O'FARRELL
ELLIS
POLK
VAN NESS AVE.
LARKIN
HYDE
LEAVENWORTH
MASON
JONES
TAYLOR
POWELL
STOCKTON
GRANT
KEARNEY
MONTGOMERY
SANSOME
BATTERY
FRONT
COLUMBUS AVE.
COIT TOWER
North Beach
Telegraph Hill
Russian Hill
Nob Hill
Chinatown
Financial District
Union Sq.
SoMa
Yerba Buena Gardens
Moscone Con. Cntr.
MARKET
MISSION
1ST ST.
2ND ST.
FREMONT
BEALE
FOLSOM
Bay Bridge
101
80
Drakes Bay
San Pablo Bay
Berkeley
Sausalito
Angel Is.
Alcatraz Is.
Treasure Is.
Pier 35
Golden Gate Bridge
CITY CENTER
Oakland
580
San Francisco Bay
Oakland Int'l Airport
Pacific Ocean
San Francisco Int'l Airport
280

Golden Gate – The most famous suspension bridge in the world.

promenade called the Herb Caen Way runs along the city's revitalized waterfront (the Embarcadero) from Fisherman's Wharf to The Bay Bridge. A taxi from the airport to downtown costs about $35, and the minibus shuttle is $11.

Shopping & Dining – The retail area around **Union Square** and **Market Street** is the city's best-known shopping enclave, containing premier department stores such as Saks Fifth Avenue and Macy's, and internationally known fashion houses. Maiden Lane, on the east side of Union Square, is lined with boutiques, and more shops are housed in the San Francisco Shopping Centre. Few cities eclipse San Francisco in terms of eclectic restaurants and fine dining. Superb French cuisine is served at La Folie in Russian Hill, and a cocktail with a view can be enjoyed in the rooftop Crown Room at the Fairmont Hotel. The **Embarcadero**, the city's original working waterfront which had fallen into disrepair, was revitalized following the collapse of the elevated Embarcadero Freeway during the October 17, 1989, earthquake, and is today one of San Francisco's most stylish areas to dine, shop and party.

Local Attractions

Fisherman's Wharf encompasses the waterfront between Pier 39 and the Municipal Pier, and includes adjacent **Victorian Park** where the ship-shaped **National Maritime Museum** is located. A panoply of restaurants, shops, street performers, foodstands and fishboat docks, this waterfront area's most-visited attraction (one of the top three in California) is **Pier 39**, where broad boardwalks dotted with benches create a village-like atmosphere for this colorful complex of specialty shops and restaurants. Sea lions congregate on adjacent K Dock, and boat trips depart every hour from Pier 41 for **Alcatraz Island**. 'The Rock' was once a notorious high-security prison housing the likes of Al Capone, "Machine Gun" Kelly and Robert "The Birdman" Stroud, and is now a tourist attraction drawing over a million visitors annually.

North Beach, an Italian section of excellent eateries and delicatessens, became an enclave for beatniks in the mid-1950s whose famous hangouts included Lawrence Ferlinghetti's City Lights Bookstore at 261 Columbus and the Hungry I, where Lenny Bruce honed his stand-up comedy. The **Coit Tower** on **Telegraph Hill** was built in 1933 with a bequest from an eccentric named Lillie Hitchcock Coit and its public elevator whisks visitors to the top of this 210-foot column for spectacular views of the city.

Russian Hill is home to **Lombard Street**, said to be the most crooked street in the world, while **Nob Hill** is the home of millionaires. **Chinatown** is a 24-block area of residential and commercial streets, its attractions including the dragon-crested gate at Grant Avenue and Bush Street, several temples and dozens of exotic food stalls.

South of Market Street is **SoMa,** where the **San Francisco Museum of Modern Art, Sony's Metreon** family entertainment complex and numerous galleries surround **Yerba Buena Gardens**.

(1) Mission District is named for Mission Dolores, a Spanish mission established in 1782 and originally called San Francisco de Asis. **(2) Haight Ashbury** is where the "flower children" of the 60's hung out, and nearby **(3) Golden Gate Park** contains two natural history museums, an aquarium and a planetarium. **(4) Presidio Park** is the site of the original Spanish fort, built in 1776, now administered by the National Park Service.

OUT-OF-TOWN ATTRACTIONS

South of San Francisco, scenic Highway 1 hugs the coast and connects charming seaside towns on the 2 1/2 hour drive to the Monterey Peninsula known for its world-class golf courses and the famous 17-Mile Drive. The resort town of **Monterey**, an enclave of writers and artists, is one of California's oldest cities, founded in 1770 and the capital of Alta California for much of the Spanish colonial era. California's first newspaper was established in Monterey in 1846, and attractions include the Spanish-built Presidio and historic Cannery Row, of John Steinbeck fame. **Carmel-by-the-Sea** is an upscale village on Carmel Bay, named in 1602 by Carmelite friars on a Spanish expedition. It too is an artists' and writers' community, and the burial place of Father Junipero Serra is at a nearby mission. South of Carmel is **Big Sur**, a rugged stretch of coast where the Santa Lucia Mountains abut the Pacific Ocean.

North of San Francisco, the fertile **Napa Valley** has been growing grapes for wine since the late 1870s, shortly after Napa was incorporated. Today the wineries of Napa Valley, and nearby **Sonoma Valley**, are attracting a growing number of visitors to the region where gently rolling hillsides, cloaked with vineyards, create a Provence-like scene. **Sonoma** was the first to cultivate grape vines and its shaded central plaza of fountains and rose gardens is overlooked by colonial-style adobe buildings. The town developed as a summer resort for San Franciscans, while **Napa** began as an important river port, busy with the comings and goings of coastal ships which, along with the Napa Valley Railroad Company, converged on this bustling commercial center. The historic Napa River Inn and adjoining Hatt Market, where farmers bring their wares and local artists display their works, are now listed on the National Register of Historic Places.

VANCOUVER, CANADA

Considered Canada's most scenic city, its harbor backed by forested mountains and fronted by glistening high-rise buildings, Vancouver is the northernmost port of call on Panama Canal repositioning cruises. The ships dock in the heart of downtown at Canada Place, a landmark complex crowned with white sails, or at Ballantyne Pier, a refurbished heritage facility situated a short taxi ride from the downtown core.

For a panoramic overview of the city, visit **(1) The Lookout!**, downtown Vancouver's highest viewpoint at the top of the Harbour Centre Tower, a few blocks east of Canada Place. Some prominent buildings to look for: **(2) Hotel Vancouver** on Georgia Street (a grand railway hotel that was completed in 1939); **(3) Marine Building** on Burrard Street (Vancouver's finest example of art deco architecture); **(4) Library Square** on Georgia Street (a modern, coliseum-like structure housing Vancouver's main library as well as shops and restaurants); the **(5) Law Courts** at Robson Square (a long, low building with a sloped glass roof and streaming waterfalls designed by Vancouver architect Arthur Erickson) and the **(6) Vancouver Art Gallery** (a former court house designed by Francis Rattenbury in the Beaux Arts style and now housing a permanent collection of works by Emily Carr).

Gastown, an easy walk from Canada Place, was Vancouver's original townsite, founded in 1867 by a smooth-talking saloon keeper named John 'Gassy Jack' Deighton. Gastown's western entrance is marked by **(7) The Landing** – a refurbished heritage complex of shops and restaurants – at the junction of Cordova and Water Streets. Visitors can stroll along Water Street, past the working steam clock, to **(8) Maple Tree Square** where Gassy Jack's saloon once stood.

In the city's West End, attractions include **(9) English Bay Beach**, where waterfront restaurants overlook the beach and bay, and adjacent **(10) Sunset Beach** where a passenger ferry can be boarded for the short trip across False Creek to **(11) Granville Island**, a revitalized industrial area that attracts year-round visitors to its public market, crafts boutiques, restaurants and live theatres. Also in the West End is Vancouver's famous **(12) Stanley Park**, containing 1,000 acres of forest and trails. A pedestrian seawall encircles the park, which can also be toured by vehicle. Among the park's many attractions are a rose garden, totem pole display, aquarium and several good restaurants.

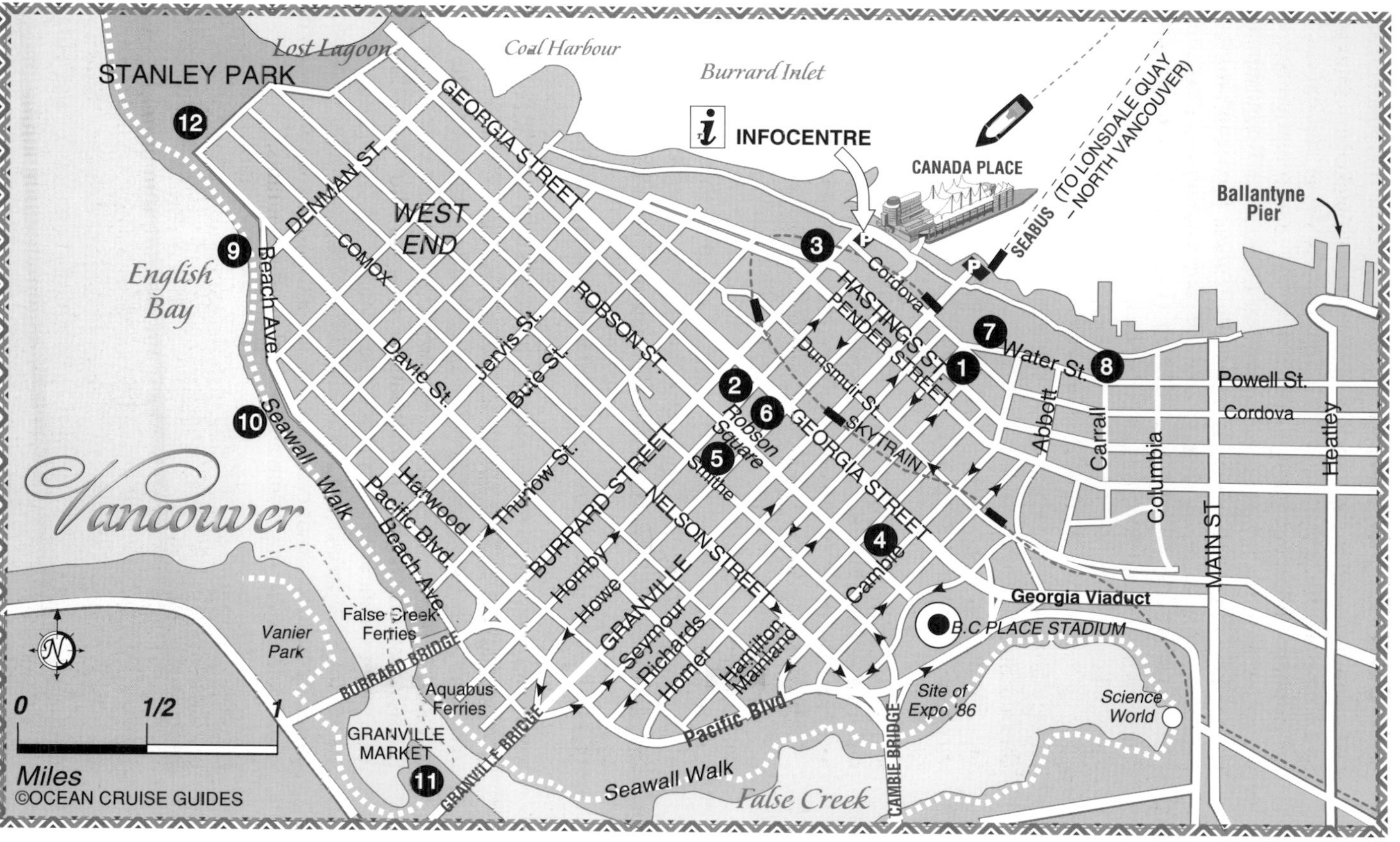
Vancouver
STANLEY PARK
Lost Lagoon
Coal Harbour
Burrard Inlet
English Bay
INFOCENTRE
CANADA PLACE
SEABUS
(TO LONSDALE QUAY – NORTH VANCOUVER)
Ballantyne Pier
Powell St.
Cordova
Heatley
MAIN ST
Columbia
Carrall
Abbott
Water St.
Cordova
HASTINGS ST.
PENDER STREET
Dunsmuir St.
SKYTRAIN
GEORGIA STREET
Cambie
B.C PLACE STADIUM
Georgia Viaduct
Science World
Site of Expo '86
CAMBIE BRIDGE
False Creek
Pacific Blvd
Seawall Walk
Hamilton
Mainland
Homer
Richards
Seymour
GRANVILLE
Howe
Hornby
BURRARD STREET
NELSON STREET
Smithe
Robson Square
ROBSON ST.
Thurlow St.
Bute St.
Jervis St.
Davie St.
Harwood
Pacific Blvd.
Beach Ave.
WEST END
COMOX
DENMAN ST.
GEORGIA STREET
Beach Ave.
Seawall Walk
Aquabus Ferries
GRANVILLE MARKET
GRANVILLE BRIDGE
BURRARD BRIDGE
False Creek Ferries
Vanier Park
0
1/2
1
Miles
©OCEAN CRUISE GUIDES

CARNIVAL CRUISE LINES: The 'Fun Ships' of this mainstream cruise line, founded in the mid-1960s, attract a high number of families and first-time cruisers. The ships boast a theme decor and excellent facilities for children and teens. Carnival offers year-round cruises to the Mexican Riviera. Roundtrip, 3-, 4- and 7-day Mexican Riviera cruises are available from Long Beach (Los Angeles), and 8-day roundtrip cruises are offered out of San Diego. Officers are Italian and service staff are international. Average passenger/space ratio is 35. (Website: carnivalcruises.com)

Carnival Spirit, 2001 – 84,000 tons

CELEBRITY CRUISES: Founded in 1990 by the Greek line Chandris Inc., Celebrity Cruises is now owned by Royal Caribbean International. A premium cruise line, Celebrity is noted for its gourmet cuisine and finely appointed ships that appeal to experienced cruisers. Celebrity offers 14- to 16-day trans-canal cruises between Fort Lauderdale or Miami, and San Diego or Los Angeles, and 11- and 12-night partial transits on roundtrip cruises out of Galveston. Mexican Riviera cruises include a 10-day roundtrip from San Francisco and 7- to 11-day roundtrip cruises from San Diego. Officers are Greek and service staff are international. Average passenger/space ratio is 41. (Website: celebritycruises.com)

Galaxy, 1996 – 77,000 tons

CRUISE WEST: A pioneer of small-ship cruising in Alaska, Cruise West has expanded its itineraries to include Baja California and the Sea of Cortez, Costa Rica and the Panama Canal. The fleet's ships carry from 70 to 114 passengers, all in outside cabins. The onboard atmosphere is informal, with passengers welcome on the bridge, and these cruise vessels can maneuver close to shore. Onboard naturalists provide background to the customized shore excursions which focus on the region's natural beauty and indigenous wildlife. Panama Canal/Costa Rica cruises are 10-day itineraries between San Jose and Colon, Panama. 7- and 8-day Costa Rica cruises are round-trip from San Jose. 8-day Sea of Cortes

Spirit of Alaska – 97 tons

cruises are from Los Cabos. Officers and crew are American. (Website: cruisewest.com)

CRYSTAL CRUISES: Owned by NYK of Japan, this luxury line offers a variety of Panama Canal itineraries which feature tailor-made shore excursions to suit individual preferences. Crystal ships carry about 1,000 passengers and are finely appointed with spacious interiors and all outside cabins. Trans-canal cruises are 11- to 16-day itineraries between Miami or Tampa on the Caribbean side, and Los Angeles or Costa Rica on the Pacific side. Crystal also services the Mexican Riviera with 7- to 15-day round trips from Los Angeles. Officers are Scandinavian and service staff are international. Average passenger space ratio is 52. (Website: crystalcruises.com)

Crystal Symphony, 1995 – 51,000 tons

HOLLAND AMERICA LINE: This company's connection with North America began in 1873 with regular service between New York and Rotterdam. Now based in Seattle, HAL began offering holiday cruises in the 1960s and has established a loyal following for its growing fleet of spacious ships. Classic in design, they cut a fine profile with their distinctive sheer and blue hull. Traditional features include a full-wrap teak promenade deck, and fine art and antiques displayed throughout the public areas. HAL offers a selection of 11- to 22-day trans-canal cruises each spring and fall, between Fort Lauderdale or Tampa on the Caribbean side, and San Diego, Seattle or Vancouver on the Pacific side. Partial transits are offered from October through April on 10-day roundtrip cruises from Fort Lauderdale and these feature a deck party at the entrance to the Canal. HAL also offers 5-, 7- and 10-day roundtrip Mexican Riviera and Sea of Cortez cruises out of San Diego. Officers are Dutch and service staff are Indonesian and Filipino. Average passenger space ratio is 42. (Website: hollandamerica.com)

Volendam, 2000, – 63,000 tons

NORWEGIAN CRUISE LINE: This company is credited as one of the first lines to invent modern cruising with trips from Miami to the Bahamas in the mid-1960s. A mainstream cruise line with excellent entertainment, sports facilities and children's programs, NCL appeals to active couples and families. NCL's spring and fall Panama Canal cruises are 15 to 23 days in length and run between Miami or Houston

Norwegian Dream, 1992 – 50,000 tons

on the Caribbean side, and Los Angeles or San Francisco on the Pacific side. A special 15-day Miami-to-Santiago sailing includes a port call at Lima (Callao), Peru, for an optional tour to the Inca ruins of Machu Picchu. Officers are Norwegian and service staff are international. Passenger/space ratio is 33. (Website: ncl.com)

MSC ITALIAN CRUISES: This Italian line is owned by Mediterranean Shipping Company, one of the world's largest freight container companies. The fleet's passenger liners are mid-sized and traditional in design, appealing to experienced cruisers, and the mix of passengers is international. Partial transits of the Canal are offered out of Fort Lauderdale on 11-night itineraries. Officers and service staff are mostly Italian. (Website: mscitaliancruises.com)

OCEANIA CRUISES INC: This luxury line's mid-sized ships carry 684 passengers in style, offering gourmet cuisine and attentive service in a country-club casual atmosphere. Partial canal transits are available on 14-day itineraries out of Miami, and 16-day trans-canal cruises run betweem Miami and Los Angeles. Officers and service staff are international. (Website: oceaniacruises.com)

Marco Polo, 1966 – 20,000 tons

ORIENT LINES: This premium line has developed a reputation for interesting itineraries around the world which appeal to the seasoned traveler, including an extensive 31-day cruise of South America, Mexican Riviera, Panama Canal and the Caribbean. Officers are European and crew Filipino. Passenger/space ratio is 29. (Website: orientlines.com)

Dawn Princess, 1997 – 77,000 tons

PRINCESS CRUISES: Well known for its role in *The Love Boat* television show in the 1970s, this line is now owned by Carnival Corporation and based near Los Angeles. From the start, when *Princess Italia* first steamed north to Alaska in 1969, Princess Cruises established a reputation for a high standard of service. Since acquiring the Italian Sitmar line in the mid

1980s, Princess Cruises has experienced phenomenal growth and has launched over half a dozen new ships since 1996. These new megaships have all the modern facilities cruise passengers have come to expect, including several swimming pools, health spa, tennis court, computer center and show lounges, as well as traditional favorites such as a full wrap teak promenade deck and an intimate wood panelled pub. A high number of staterooms have a verandah, while the public areas are beautifully appointed with wood panelling and marble flooring. Princess has succeeded in appealing to a wide market, from retired couples to young families, with ships that are well laid out with excellent amenities. Children's facilities are also good with a spacious playroom, teen center and youth counsellors on all of the newer ships. Princess offers 15-day Panama Canal transits between Fort Lauderdale and Los Angeles, and 17-day itineraries between Fort Lauderdale, and Seattle or Vancouver. A partial transit of the canal is available on 10-day roundtrip cruises from Fort Lauderdale. The company also offers 10-day cruises between Acapulco and San Juan, Puerto Rico, as well as a 19-day round trip from Los Angeles which includes a night in the Canal. Mexican Riviera cruises are available out of Los Angeles (7-day roundtrip) and San Francisco (10-day roundtrip). Officers and service staff are international. Average passenger/space ratio is 40. (Website: princess.com)

RADISSON SEVEN SEAS: This luxury line offers small-ship intimacy, spaciousness and fine cuisine. 13- to 17-day cruises are available between Los Angeles or San Francisco, and Fort Lauderdale. Officers are European and service staff are international. Average passenger/space ratio is 54. (Website: rssc.com)

Seven Seas Navigator, 1999 – 30,000 tons

ROYAL CARIBBEAN INTERNATIONAL: Well known for its strong presence in the Caribbean, RCI also operates popular Canal itineraries and cruises from California to the Mexican Riviera. RCI's handsome, modern megaships offer spacious and impressive public areas such as a multi-deck atrium with glass elevators and the company's hallmark Viking Crown Lounge – a glass-wrapped observation lounge located on the highest

Brilliance of the Seas, 2002 – 90,000 tons

deck to provide passengers with a panoramic view of the passing scenery. This is the cruise line that has introduced onboard activities not normally associated with taking a cruise, such as rock climbing up a wall constructed on the back of the ship's funnel. Family suites, a spacious playroom and teen center, and excellent youth staff, make RCI a good choice for families. RCI offers 14-night trans-canal cruises between Fort Lauderdale or Miami on the Caribbean side and San Diego on the Pacific side. 10- or 11-night partial-transit cruises are available throughout the winter from Miami. Spring and fall Canal cruises (12- or 14-night) run between San Diego, and Miami or San Juan, Puerto Rico. RCI also services the Mexican Riviera on 7-night roundtrip sailings from Los Angeles (October through April). Officers are Scandinavian and service staff are international. (Website: royalcaribbean.com)

SEABOURN CRUISE LINE: Widely considered the ultimate in luxury cruising, Seabourn offers nothing but the finest food, all-suite accommodations and white-glove service. The fleet's mega-yachts each carry 208 passengers and winter itineraries include several 14-day cruises between Fort Lauderdale and Puerto Caldera, Costa Rica. Seabourn combines interesting itineraries with unique shore excursions and some excellent pre- and post-cruise tour options. Officers are Norwegian. Passenger/space ratio is 46. (Website: seabourn.com)

Seabourn Spirit, 1989 – 10,000 tons

SILVERSEA: Consistently rated the Number One Small Ship Cruise Line by Conde Nast Traveler, this luxury line offers one or two Canal transits per year. Average space ratio: 60. (Website: silversea.com)

WINDSTAR CRUISES: This is a premium line of high-tech sailing ships, each accommodating 150 passengers (except Wind Surf which carries 312 passengers). Windstar ships appeal to cruisers seeking luxury in a casual setting along with a bit of sailing adventure. A 14-day trans-canal itinerary is offered between Costa Rica's Puerto Caldera, and Bridgetown, Barbados. Officers are British. Average space ratio is 36. (Website: windstarcruises.com)

Wind Spirit, 1988 – 6,000 tons

PHOTO AND ILLUSTRATION CREDITS:

Circa Art,47, 148 (top left), 308 (top & bottom insets)
Colon 2000 (Aventuras 2000), 20 (bottom right), 85, 208 top and bottom, 209, 237 (top), 239
CORBIS, 63, 65
Bettmann Archives, 79
Underwood & Underwood, 82, 92 (top & bottom), 103, 234 (top), 312
DeFreitas, Michael, 91, 93 (top & bottom), 96 (inset), 97 (full page, two insets), 99, 100, 101, 129 (top & bottom left), 131 (bottom), 132 (top), 133 (top), 136 (top), 137 (top & bottom), 156 (bottom), 157 (top), 167, 171, 173, 189 (top & bottom), 192 (bottom right), 270, 309, 316 (all), 317 (inset)
DeJong, Brenda, 266 (top)
Gerretsen, Martin, 2, 23 (bottom), 276
Hamming Publishing Co., 4
Holland America Line, 8, 169, 224, 229 (top)
John Huston Museum, 295 (top)
Kaehler, Wolfgang / CORBIS, 241
Lees, Judi, 21 (middle, bottom), 29 (bottom), 31 (right), 244 (top & bottom), 245, 256 (top & bottom), 257 (top & bottom), 259, 261, 262, 263, 277 (all)
Library of Congress, 51, 58, 63, 65, 72, 74, 76, 77, 210, 212, 213, 215 (top), 218, 221, 231, 234 (bottom), 235
Mays, Buddy / Corbis, 92 top
Mary Evans Picture Library, 50 a & 50b
Nakano, Alan, 102
Naval Musuem, Madrid, 269 (bottom)
NASA, 46
Norris-Jones, Raymond, 156 (top)
Norwegian Cruise Line, 112
Otis, F.N. 54 (from The Illustrated History of the Panama Railroad)
Panama Canal Authority,3, 20 (bottom, right), 55, 57, 70, 75, 76, 77, 80, 81, 84, 215 (bottom), 217, 219 (top), 222 (bottom), 229 (middle), 232, 236 (middle), 237 (bottom two)
Persson, Gordon, 39 (bottom), 157 (bottom), 168, 181 (top)
Princess Cruises, 38, 124, 165, 228 (lower left), 233 (bottom)
Puerto Rico Tourism Company, 126, 133
Rhodes, George, 104
Royal Caribbean International, 37
San Diego, Port of / Dale Frost 313
Schafer Kevin / CORBIS, 92 bottom
Vancouver, Port of, 324
All other photos by Anne Vipond.